KINA

COMPUTATIONAL LINGUISTICS

International Series in
MODERN APPLIED MATHEMATICS AND COMPUTER SCIENCE
General Editor E. Y. RODIN
Volume 5

RELATED PERGAMON TITLES:
Earlier Volumes in the Series
L. COOPER and M. W. COOPER
Introduction to Dynamic Programming

T. L. SAATY and J. M. ALEXANDER
Thinking with Models

R. SURI
Resource Management Concepts for Large Systems

R. BELLMAN *et al.*
Mathematical Aspects of Scheduling and Applications

Also of interest

G. E. LASKER
Applied Systems and Cybernetics

Pergamon Journals
Computers and Graphics
Computers and Mathematics with Applications
Computer Languages
Computer State of the Art Reports
Mathematical Modelling

Full details of all Pergamon publications/free specimen copy of any Pergamon journal available on request from your nearest Pergamon office.

COMPUTATIONAL LINGUISTICS

Edited by

NICK CERCONE

*Computing Science Department, Simon Fraser University, Burnaby,
British Columbia, Canada V5A 1S6*

PERGAMON PRESS

OXFORD · NEW YORK · TORONTO · SYDNEY · PARIS · FRANKFURT

U.K.	Pergamon Press Ltd., Headington Hill Hall, Oxford OX3 0BW, England
U.S.A.	Pergamon Press Inc., Maxwell House, Fairview Park, Elmsford, New York 10523, U.S.A.
CANADA	Pergamon Press Canada Ltd., Suite 104, 150 Consumers Road, Willowdale, Ontario M2J 1P9, Canada
AUSTRALIA	Pergamon Press (Aust.) Pty. Ltd., P.O. Box 544, Potts Point, N.S.W. 2011, Australia
FRANCE	Pergamon Press SARL, 24 rue des Ecoles, 75240 Paris, Cedex 05, France
FEDERAL REPUBLIC OF GERMANY	Pergamon Press GmbH, Hammerweg 6, D-6242 Kronberg-Taunus, Federal Republic of Germany

Copyright © 1983 Pergamon Press Ltd.

First edition 1983

Library of Congress Cataloging in Publication Data

Main entry under title:
Computational linguistics.
(International series in modern applied mathematics
and computer science; v. 5)
"First published in Computers and Mathematics with
Applications, volume 9, number 1"—Verso of t.p.
1. Linguistics—Data processing—Addresses, essays,
lectures. I. Cercone, Nick J. II. Series.
P98.C612 1983   410'.28'54   83-8039

British Library Cataloguing in Publication Data

Computational linguistics.—(International series in
modern applied mathematics and computer science;
v5)
1. Linguistics—Data processing
I. Cercone, Nick J. II. Series
410'.28'54 P98

ISBN 0-08-030253-X

Published as a special issue of the journal *Computers and Mathematics with Applications,* Volume 9, Number 1 and supplied to subscribers as part of their normal subscription. Also available to non-subscribers.

Printed in Great Britain by A. Wheaton & Co. Ltd., Exeter

PREFACE

This special collection of papers represents a relatively comprehensive overview of the variety of important research in computational linguistics currently taking place in North America. The primary contributors to this edition include computing scientists, philosophers, psychologists and linguists; their professions are indicative of the disparate approaches which each has brought to further research in computational linguistics.

Twenty active and well-known researchers in computational linguistics were invited to contribute to this volume, but unfortunately not all were able to do so; the contents of this volume are not as complete as it might otherwise be. The fifteen papers representing nineteen authors' contributions cover a breadth of computational linguistics consisting of:

(1) Theoretical foundations: the logical foundations of knowledge representation; semantic analyses; and model-theoretical semantics.
(2) Parsing: parsing strategies for natural language; computational aspects of parsing; perspectives on parsing issues.
(3) Discourse processing: psychological and linguistic modelling; discourse analysis.
(4) Text analysis: text and content analysis; text generation.
(5) Natural language understanding and knowledge organisation: memory models; learning; inference techniques.
(6) Programming systems for computational linguistics: knowledge representation languages; special purpose languages.
(7) Programming environments: programming considerations for computational linguistics.
(8) Interactive applications: natural language front-end processors to database systems; the human factors interface.

The narrow approaches to machine translation of the early 1960s pale when compared to the considerable assortment of methodologies available to the modern computational linguist. The growth in the number of publications devoted to computational linguistics parallels a similar increase in computing science literature and is indicative of its rapid development. This impressive maturation has been accompanied by an equally exciting change in the nature of experiments, systems and theoretical speculation. Only a decade or so ago researchers were content to speculate about the results of a program demonstrating limited comprehension in a "micro-world". Contemporary results indicate a broader framework for investigations into the theory and applications of research in computational linguistics.

The challenges of integrating the various approaches to problems faced by computational linguistics were difficult and, at times, frustrating. I owe each contributor a debt of gratitude, first for writing a new and totally original article for this collection and also for rewriting, editing, and reviewing. Each author constructively and patiently reviewed three other authors' submissions which has helped to improve the contents, coherence, and style of the entire issue. I am immeasurably indebted to Ms. Josie Backhouse for her extraordinary organisational efforts and her attention to every aspect concerned with this special collection. The entire volume represents over a year of hard work which significantly extended my original plans for publication. Hopefully, the extra time was well-spent and will make this issue a classic reference for the future.

CONTENTS

Introduction   ix

Interpreting network formalisms   1
DAVID J. ISRAEL

Some representational issues in default reasoning   15
RAYMOND REITER and GIOVANNI CRISCUOLO:

Generating language from conceptual graphs   29
JOHN F. SOWA

Semantic processing of texts in restricted sublanguages   45
RICHARD I. KITTREDGE

The control of inferencing in natural language understanding   59
ABE LOCKMAN and DAVID KLAPPHOLZ

What the speaker means: the recognition of speakers' plans in discourse   71
CANDACE L. SIDNER

Formal semantic and computer text processing, 1982   83
J. G. MEUNIER and F. LEPAGE

ARGOT: a system overview   97
JAMES F. ALLEN

Description directed control: its implications for natural language generation 111
DAVID D. MCDONALD

Understanding novel language   131
GERALD F. DEJONG and DAVID L. WALTZ

A computational approach to fuzzy quantifiers in natural languages   149
LOTFI A. ZADEH

Recognition mechanisms for schema-based knowledge representations   185
WILLIAM S. HAVENS

An approach to the organization of knowledge and its use in natural language
recall tasks   201
GORDON I. MCCALLA

Minimal and almost minimal perfect hash function search with application to natural
language lexicon design   215
NICK CERCONE, MAX KRAUSE and JOHN BOATES

Extended natural language data base interactions   233
BONNIE WEBBER, ARAVIND JOSHI, ERIC MAYS and KATHLEEN MCKEOWN

Index   245

INTRODUCTION

COMPUTATIONAL LINGUISTICS research should develop a general theory of natural language understanding as a foundation for computer programs which understand natural language. Any theory of natural language understanding must account for the representation, organisation and subsequent utilisation of knowledge (e.g. for making plausible inferences, associating meaningful pieces of discourse, etc.).

Active and well-known researchers in computational linguistics were invited to contribute such that each of the following topics would be given at least two, often disparate, viewpoints: (1) theoretical foundations for computational linguistics; (2) parsing strategies for natural language; (3) modelling of discourse processes; (4) text analysis and generation; (5) natural language understanding systems and knowledge organisation; (6) programming systems for computational linguistics; (7) programming environments and considerations for computational linguists; and (8) interactive applications such as natural language front-ends to database systems. The papers as finalised represent a great diversity of topics, methods, and approaches. Philosophers, linguists, engineers, and computing scientists contributed to this volume divided roughly evenly between Canadian and American institutions.

Theoretically oriented papers include those discussing the adequacy of representational formalisms and their interpretation in natural language understanding computer programs. Most pragmatically oriented papers apply novel techniques to existing systems to enhance their "naturalness".

David Israel postulates that the underlying argument between the logical formulae and the semantic network formalism proponents is not merely one of their precision and computer-interpretable properties as a mathematical notation but of a much wider context. Dr. Israel sketches semantic accounts for at least two kinds of semantic network formalisms. The first account is based on the notion of inheritance, the other is not. Dr. Israel maintains that a critical condition of [representational] adequacy is fidelity to some of the intuitions of the creators of the formalisms.

In an earlier paper Ray Reiter proposed a logic for default reasoning to provide a representation for common sense facts (among other things). In this paper Dr. Reiter and his collaborator Giovanni Criscuolo address some of the representational issues in default reasoning, particularly when anomalous default assumptions are derived. The non-normal default rules required to deal with default interactions lead to a new concept of integrity, distinct from the conventional integrity issues of first order data bases.

John Sowa describes how to generate language from conceptual graphs, a semantic representation that has a direct mapping to natural language. He presents a universal algorithm for scanning the graphs, together with a version of augmented phrase structure grammar for specifying the syntax of particular languages. Since the graphs may allow the generation of multiple surface structures, Dr. Sowa combines them with phrase structure rules to enforce context-sensitive conditions.

Practical results in information retrieval and automatic translation have recently been achieved for naturally-occurring texts in certain narrow technical areas. Richard Kittredge discusses the semantic processing of texts in restricted sublanguages. By way of illustration he outlines a procedure for processing stock market reports into a predicate-argument representation of their content and discusses potential applications of the procedure beyond information retrieval.

Professors Lockman and Klappholz discuss the problems of resolving ambiguities when understanding natural languages. To satisfy this requirement complex inferencing from a large database of world knowledge must take place. Critical to this task, and one for which humans adapt quite readily, is the control of such inferences. Their paper discusses the problems involved in such control of inferencing and an approach to their solution is presented based on determining where each successive sentence "fits" into the text as a whole.

Human conversational participants depend upon the ability of their partners to recognise their intentions, so that their partners may respond appropriately. In such interactions, the speaker encodes his intentions about the hearer's response in a variety of sentence types. Instead of telling the hearer what to do, the speaker may just state his goals, and expect a response that meets these goals at least part way. Candace Sidner presents a new model for recognising the speaker's intended meaning in determining a response. The model shows that this recognition makes use of the speaker's plan, his beliefs about the domain and about the hearer's relevant capacities.

J. G. Meunier and F. Lepage explore new paths for formal semantic and computer text processing of large non-preedited natural language texts. They describe the traditional approaches to this problem, then discuss certain semantic aspects in computer text processing. They use a model theoretic approach embedded in an algebraic language and follow the hypothesis: discourse in a text constitutes a semantic space built of an ordered set of sentences which are of different logical types and which present a specific pattern of coherence expressible in a syntactic manner.

James Allen gives a system overview of ARGOT, a long-term research project that has the ultimate aim of describing a mechanism that can partake in an extended English dialogue on some reasonably well specified range of topics. Dr. Allen describes progress made towards this goal and outlines the current research in which the project is focussed. The underlying current theory and system built according to that theory is outlined and deficiencies in the system presented. The new system, ARGOT, under development is then described.

The implications for natural language generation of description directed control are examined by David McDonald. In description directed control the controlling data structure is the surface-level linguistic description of the very text being generated. This constituent structure tree is itself generated depth-first by the incremental realisation of a hierarchical description of the speaker's communicative goals organised according to the scope and importance of its components. The process of traversing the surface structure gates and constrains the realisation process; all realisations are thus subject to the grammatical constraints that accrue to the surface structure at which they occur, as defined by the grammatical annotation of the surface structure tree.

Gerald DeJong and David Waltz outline concerns which must be addressed if a machine is to cope with understanding novel languages. They state that systems which operate primarily by pattern matching are less interesting than systems which have general rules which can be used to generate a meaning representation for unanticipated inputs. They discuss a wide variety of types of unanticipated input and give many examples of these types.

The computational approach to fuzzy quantifiers which Professor Zadeh describes in his paper may be viewed as a derivative of fuzzy logic and test-score semantics. In this semantics, the meaning of a semantic entity is represented as a procedure which tests, scores and aggregates the elastic constraints which are induced by the entity in question.

William Havens is concerned with generalising formal recognition methods from parsing theory to schemata knowledge representations. The notion of a schemata as a suitable representation for a variety of artificial intelligence tasks is discussed and a number of contemporary problems with current schemata based recognition systems are presented. Professor Havens shows how to integrate top-down and bottom-up search in schemata representations.

The viewpoint espoused by Gordon McCalla in his paper is that natural language understanding and production is the action of a highly integrated domain-specific specialist. He first describes an object-oriented representation scheme which allows these specialists to be built and then the organisation of these specialists into a four-level goal hierarchy that enables the modelling of natural language conversion. Six specific kinds of recall tasks are outlined in terms of these structures and several dialogues examined.

Nick Cercone, Max Krause and John Boates present a set of tools for the computer lexicographer. They have devised three alternative algorithms which produce minimal and almost minimal perfect hash functions for table sizes suitable for functional computer lexicons. A semi-interactive system has been built based on one algorithm and it has been used to construct natural language lexicons whose size is over 60,000 words.

A natural language interface which gives extended natural language database interactions is presented by Bonnie Webber, Aravind Joshi, Eric Mays and Kathleen McKeown. They discuss two complementary directions for extending natural language interfaces to databases: (1) broadening the range of query types that can be handled; and (2) extending the range of responses that can be provided.

It is my fervent hope that this collection of fifteen papers will both advance knowledge and broaden the experience of present-day practitioners of computational linguistics. For those researchers with only a passing interest in computational linguistics and artificial intelligence this collection should serve as an introduction to the diversity and depth of work in the field.

Vancouver, BC. April, 1983   Nick Cercone

Comp. & Maths. with Appls. Vol. 9, No. 1, pp. 1–13, 1983
Printed in Great Britain.

0097–4943/83/010001–13$03.00/0
Pergamon Press Ltd.

INTERPRETING NETWORK FORMALISMS†

DAVID J. ISRAEL

Bolt Beranek and Newman Inc., Cambridge, MA 02238, U.S.A.

Abstract—In a recent paper, Reiter and Criscuolo[3] remark "that (semantic) networks are notational variants of logical formulae is by now a truism in Artificial Intelligence circles". Shamelessly exploiting the foregoing quote as a pretext, I attempt to sketch adequate semantic accounts for at least two (kinds of) semantic network formalisms; one, based on the notion of inheritance, one, not. A crucial condition of adequacy to be satisfied is fidelity to some of the intuitions of the creators of the formalisms.

1. IMPRIMATUR

Whatever else we decide to include under A.I., I would like to join those who claim for it the task of developing, maintaining, and using computer-interpretable formalisms for represesenting knowledge.... One might view some of the representational formalisms being studied in A.I. as attempts to create languages that possess the precision and computer-interpretable properties of a mathematical notation, but do so for a much wider range of concepts than those dealt with by classical mathematics[1].

2. DOCTRINAL PREAMBLE

One often hears that modal (or some other) logic is pointless because it can be translated into some simpler language in a first-order way. Take no notice of such arguments. There is no weight to the claim that the original system must therefore be replaced by the new one. What is essential is to single out important concepts and to investigate their properties. The fact that the real numbers can be defined in terms of sets is no argument for being interested in *arbitrary* sets. One must look among the sets for the significant ones and cannot be censured if one finds the intrinsic properties of the reals more interesting than any of their formulations in set theory. Of course if we can argue that set theory provides other significant concepts, then we may find some reason for going beyond the real numbers (and it is not hard to find the reasons!). But clearly this discussion cannot proceed on purely formal grounds alone[2].

AMEN!

3. INTRODUCTION

In a recent paper, Reiter and Criscuolo remark that "the fact that networks are notational variants of logical formulae is by now a truism in Artificial Intelligence circles"[3]. Let us put aside the empirical, sociological claim—about which I am more than willing to defer to Messrs. Reiter and Criscuolo. Let us look rather at the content of the truism itself.

When we do so, we notice a certain ambiguity. Perhaps, Reiter and Criscuolo are supposing that there is at least one logical language for whose formulae the "sentential analogues" of each and every semantic network formalism are notational variants. Or, switching the quantifiers, perhaps the claim is that for every semantic network formalism there is at least one logical language of which it is a notational variant. Now these are two very different claims. (One could easily imagine a third, stronger claim, being presupposed, viz. that all semantic network schemes are notational variants of, in particular, the language and logic of classical, first-order quantification theory. I will, in what follows, address myself to this strongest, most specific, view as well.)

I am not going to speculate on which of the three views Reiter and Criscuolo really had in mind. Indeed, the quote from Reiter and Criscuolo is the merest pretext for the present paper. I intend to sketch quite different semantic accounts for two different (kinds of) semantic network formalisms, one organized around the notion of inheritance, the other, not; the latter, keyed to a certain family of intensional contexts, the former, not. Most important, *the semantic accounts will differ* and, with luck, *the differences will reflect differences in the central intuitions of the*

†This research was supported by the Office of Navy Research under Contract No. N00014-77-C-0371.

semantic net theorists concerned. The aim is, simply, to try to take semantic net theorists at their word; and to show that, in doing so, one must range fairly far and wide beyond the confines of standard first-order logic. I am not going to argue for adopting any particular semantic net formalism; nor am I going to examine any of the intuitions motivating the work to be discussed.

To make clear my intentions, let me note two ways in which one might fail to take the "semantic(s)" in "semantic network" seriously. The first is embodied in the work of Quillian, Collins *et al.*, work which originated the semantic network tradition. By my lights, the structures described in this work are not intended to be languages; rather they are part of a theory or model of a certain range of memory-related psychological phenomena. The nodes in the network might be words, or even sets of sentences, but the accounts of the network are not semantic accounts; they do not constitute a semantic theory. There is no attempt to account for the meaningfulness, or describe the meaning, of the nodes. This, of course, is no criticism of the work; nor am I suggesting that the researchers in question were confused about the present point. So much for the first way of not taking the "semantics" of semantic network formalisms seriously.

As a second way of not taking the semantics of semantic net formalisms seriously, I have in mind the following doctrine: the only way to interpret semantic network formalisms semantic-ally, *no matter what the semantic network theorists may say,* is to treat them as notational variants of standard first-order languages, with their standard "Tarski-style" semantics. This might best be described as a way of not taking semantic network *theorists* seriously. It is against this view, in particular, that I mean to deploy the quotation from Dana Scott with which I started. Of course, for all I know, no one holds this view; in which case, I am arguing only against phantoms of my own fevered imagination. So much the better. I, at any rate, want to try to take some semantic net theorists at their very word. Let the appropriate semantic account fall out however it may.

4. SNePS

I want first to discuss a system in which the notion of inheritance plays no (special) role. It would also be nice to have a case in which the theorists are both explicit about their motivating intuitions and diligent in presenting sufficient detail on which to hang semantic speculation. Sad to say, this narrows the field down quite a bit. Still, there are at least two choices; the (atypically nameless) system of Schubert, Cercone and Goebel[4] and Shapiro's SNePS[5, 6]. I have decided to examine the latter; and this, for two reasons. First, Shapiro (and Shapiro and Maida[7, 8]) presents a fairly explicit "philosophy of semantic networks", as well as an enormous body of detailed description of the workings of the system. I think the philosophy is widely shared and trying to account for the considerations operative in its formulation raises interesting problems. Second, Schubert *et al.* are too explicit for my purposes. It is quite clear that they view their formalism as a Montague-style type-theoretic, intensional system. It would, I think, be illuminating to work out in detail a semantic account for the system described in [4]; but there can anyway be no doubt about the "logical space" within which we would find ourselves. This is not the case, or so I shall claim, for SNePS. A semantic account appropriate to *it* will force us to wander into largely, though not completely unexplored, territory. (And this, I also claim, is no argument against SNePS. Remember the wisdom of the great Scott.)

Shapiro has argued that we should impose the following conditions on semantic networks:

(1) Each node represents a unique concept.

(2) Each concept represented in the network is represented by a node.

(3) Each concept represented in the network is represented by a unique node (the Uniqueness Principle).

(4) Arcs represent non-conceptual (logical?—*D.I.*) binary relations between nodes[7, 8].

In what follows I shall take Shapiro to be simply describing SNePS, thus ignoring his arguments for imposing these conditions on *all* semantic networks. I shall also (largely) ignore the fourth condition and, for that matter, a fifth: "the knowledge represented about each concept is represented by the structure of the entire network connected to the node representing that concept."

On the basis of these conditions, Shapiro (and Shapiro and Maida) contend that "all nodes of a semantic network represent only intentions"[7]. Again, I shall take this as describing SNePS, not as prescribing for all semantic networks.

Now what are we to make of this? Raising the question this way raised the issue as to whether my intensions toward SNePS are honorable. I hope they are. Appearances to the contrary notwithstanding, I am not singling out a few lines, ripped out of context, for malicious attention. First, no malice is intended and I trust no harm is done. Second, and more important, my reconstruction of SNePS *attempts* to embrace a large number of the claims and arguments in the texts. I will not attempt to support my claim in this respect by citation. I hope that any one who has read the papers will agree that I have presented at least *one* way of construing them—not the only way, and perhaps not the way favored by the authors. As for those who have not read the material, I fear they shall have to take me at *my* (immediately preceding) word.

Let's remind ourselves of the project. We are to find *a* language-cum-semantics which can reasonably be taken to be that formal system, formulae of which correspond to the sentential pieces of SNePS. What, for instance, does the logical vocabulary of our target language consist of? Here we get help for [6, 9]. For our purposes, what's crucial is that the logical constants mentioned are generalizations of the familiar truth-functional connectives and quantifiers. But what of the quantifiers; over what do the bound variables range; what kinds of things are assigned to the variables?

We might as well start at the beginning and specify how atomic predicational formulae are to be understood. The standard way of handling intensions in contemporary logic is to treat them as functions from an index set of contexts or possible worlds into some set-theoretic construct on the domain of the model structure. So, to take an important instance, properties—the intensions associated with monadic predicates—are explicated as functions from the index set into subsets of the domain of possible individuals. We might, then, try imagining a model structure consisting of a domain D of possible† entities, a non-empty set I (the index set or the set of possible worlds), and (optionally) a distinguished element w of I to represent the real world. Now define an *individual concept* in such a model structure as a function ic from I into D. (Total or partial? The traditional answer has always been total; but it is not clear what answer is appropriate to SNePS.)‡

What, then, can we say about individual terms, about individual variables, individual constants, and definite descriptions of individuals? Given what Shapiro says, it is hard to see how there is any alternative to a uniform intensional treatment. In specifying models for SNePS, all such terms (including, nota bene, individual variables) get interpreted by being associated with individual concepts (not individuals, not members of D). A model for SNePS will associate with each individual constant an individual concept (a member of the set of functions from I into D) and assignments relative to such a model will do the same for individual variables. This means that the modal language-cum-logic is not of the standard variety. I said that I would be assuming the general framework of Kripke–Montague style model-theoretic accounts; however, neither Kripke nor Montague propose semantic accounts in which the individual variables get assigned individual concepts. Dana Scott's advice that one opt for just such a uniform treatment of all individual terms [2], which, as it happens Shapiro seems to be following, has been followed by just about no one else except Aldo Bressan in "A General Interpreted Modal Calculus"[13].

Enough about individual terms; how shall we handle predicate letters? Remember: all nodes are intensional. Individual terms are associated with individual concepts, not with possible individuals; so we can not, in good conscience, assign (e.g.) to one-place predicate letters functions from I to subsets of D. That is, we can't assign to one-place predicate letters sets of possible individuals. The obvious move *might seem to be* to associate sets of individual concepts with monadic predicate letters; but this does not render "predicate-nodes" truly intensional. The extension of a predicate at a world is no doubt a set of individual concepts; but

---

†Or to be faithful to Shapiro; conceivable.

‡As we shall see, there are reasons for thinking this effort to reconstruct SNePS-style intentions in terms of Kripke–Montague model-theoretic treatments of intensional contexts slightly misguided. I shall suppress them till the end of my discussion of SNePS. As for such model-theoretic treatments themselves, the classic sources are [10–12].

what is its intension? Surely, it is (as both Bressan and Scott insist) a function from I into the power set of the set of individual concepts. Or what comes to the same thing, a function from individual concepts into propositions, where these are functions from I into $\{T, F\}$. (Shapiro is explicitly committed to "propositional nodes"—nodes for "concepts of the TRUE" and "concepts of the FALSE" [7, 8].) So, predication is an intensional functor.

By the way, this does make it a little hard to understand what Shapiro says about MEMBER and CLASS arcs, and the relation between these and ISA arcs [6]. Arcs represent "structural relations", which, given the examples, must mean binary logical functors. So ISA links represent the predication functor; but this functor must be intensional, i.e. at each world i, the truth value of "Fx" (x is an F) is not a function solely of the extension of "x" in i. In general, the relation between "Fx" and "x is a member of the set $\{y: Fy\}$" is complicated. In particular, it is relatively straightforward only for extensional predicates, predicates which informally meet the following condition: they apply to a given ic x (at i) iff they apply to any d such that $d = x(i)$. The truth value at a world of a sentence predicating an extensional predicate to an ic does depend only on the extension of that ic at that world.†

Skipping lots of nasty details, we are now in a position to wave our hands, with some confidence, over the first order quantifiers. But note the "first-order" in the foregoing. Shapiro explicitly mentions the availability of higher-order constructs in SNePS. Thus, he says we can have nodes representing the second-order concepts of a property being extensional and of a property being intensional [7]. It's not clear how high we can go in this vein, and for reasons of space I herewith demur.‡

Finally, there is the problem of propositional concepts. There are problems, in particular, about sentences embedded in intensional functors, such as "Necessarily . . . " or "S believes that . . ." About the first, Shapiro doesn't have much to say. Later, I shall suggest that the reason why he doesn't, throws light on the fact that many of the choices we've made in giving a semantic account of SNePS seem ill-motivated by the texts.

The only intensional contexts Shapiro (and Shapiro and Maida) discusses are propositional attitude contexts, those involving verbs such as "know", "believe", etc. These contexts are treated, moreover, as relational; i.e., "know", "believe" (taken in their sentential complement mode) are treated, not as intensional operators, but as two-place predicates whose relata are individual concepts of subjects and either propositions or propositional concepts.§ None of this tells us very much about how they would treat the standard modalities. Why no mention of these modalities, the hard-core intensional operators?

The answer to the mystery of the missing modalities is to be found, I think, in the intuitions behind the Principle of Uniqueness. The crucial motivation is the view that the "nodes [of a semantic network] represent the concepts and beliefs of a thinking, reasoning, language using being (e.g. a human)" [7]. Hence the centrality of the propositional attitudes. But these generate contexts which are arguably not just intensional but hyperintensional (and perhaps to the nth degree). (The slightly garish term is due to Cresswell [14].) Hyperintensional contexts are those in which substitution of logically equivalent sentences or strictly identical terms is not guaranteed to preserve truth. Thus, to take a particularly startling case, it is arguable that from the fact that S believes that P and Q it does not follow that S believes that Q and P. Again, from that the fact that S believes that 4 is even, it does not follow that S believes that the square of 2 is even. (Or that 4 is not odd.) Now Shapiro and Maida certainly seem to view belief contexts as hyperintensional and it is this which gives sense to the Principle of Uniqueness: no two distinct nodes (represent expressions which) are intersubstitutable *salve veritate* in all the contexts the language can generate. That is, every distinction between nodes made purely syntactically by the language is a semantically significant distinction—there is some context which semantically "separates" any two distinct expressions. Thus Shapiro: "No two distinct nodes represent truly equal

---

†Needless to say, identity between elements of D is world-relative; the primitive notion is strict identity between ic's, i.e. co-extensiveness at all i. For simplicity, we assume totality.

‡I should note, though, that Bressan's is an omega-type intentional system, as are some of the Montague logics.

§As a reminder, a proposition—the intension of a sentence—is a function from I into $\{T, F\}$. A propositional concept would be an individual concept whose extension at a world is a proposition; it is a function from I into functions from I into $\{T, F\}$.

concepts"[7].† Given this, it is clear enough why they would want to treat belief-contexts relationally; for there can be no question of a "logic of belief"—there are no laws to govern the behavior of a logical functor for belief.‡ And, given the very same, it is clear enough why so little is said about the standard modalities, which are merely (not hyper-) intensional.

There is no very happy account of hyperintensionality from within the model-theoretic framework (or elsewhere); although there are attempts. A move first proposed by Carnap in [17] is to specify a finer-grained notion than logical equivalence, to that of *intensional isomorphism*, in terms of the construction trees of complex expressions and the intensions assigned the constituent expressions. For example, take two sentences which are purely truth-functional tautologies, hence which are true in the same (namely, all) possible worlds. They might, however, be formed out of different constituents and these might have different intensions, etc. This move might or might not handle the case of sentential conjunction raised above; and, of course, one most certainly has the option of stipulating that if someone believes that P & Q, s/he believes that Q & P.§

To return to the central point: if one is focussing on propositional attitude, allegedly hyperintensional contexts, it can seem like a waste of time to introduce model-theoretic accounts of intensionality at all. Thus the air of desperation about the foregoing attempt to use such an account (albeit a non-standard one) to explicate a semantic net formalism that is focussed on the propositional attitudes.

(More than) enough has been said, I hope, to support my claim that in taking SNePS seriously, in particular in attempting to present a semantic account which honors some of the intuitions of its creator(s), one is led into rather interesting, if slightly forbidding, logical terrain. Of course, enough has also been said to prove beyond a shadow of a doubt that there are significant open problems to be solved before a fully adequate account can be given; the major one being that of providing a model-theoretic account of propositional attitude contexts which is both formally impeccable and at least a little plausible.¶

5. INHERITANCE

I want now to take a look at those semantic network formalisms in which the notion of inheritance is central. Here, too, the work is motivated by a certain "family" of intuitions. I would not want to try to ascribe these intuitions to any one in particular and perhaps no one believes all of them. I will state them baldly and without comment. (If you'd like, you may imagine me to be making up a position out of whole cloth and then, perversely, imposing upon myself the duty of making formal sense out of it.)

(1) The graph-theoretic nature of semantic networks counts for something above and beyond "ease" of formulating and implementing access and retrieval algorithms.

(2) There is something in principle wrong about the way in which standard semantic accounts separate the language from "theories" expressed in the language—not enough is fixed by the specification of the language itself. In some sense, different languages implicate different theories.

(3) Somehow the central role in thought (and language) of kind terms, in particular of natural kind terms, must be captured—and to do this, one must take seriously the fact that natural kinds come in families on which hierarchical, taxonomic relations are defined.

These three "intuitions" coalesce to form a certain perspective on semantic nets.‖ This

†Note: it is one thing to require that no two primitive terms are co-intensional; it is quite another to argue that no two terms—primitive or not—are such. This latter, though, seems to be the Shapiro-Maida position.

‡It is not necessary to hold this view of the hyperintensionality of propositional attitude contexts to dissuade one from the logical operator position; see Montague[15, 16]. But it sure as heck is sufficient.

§Doubts have been raised about the efficacy of such a move, especially with respect to the iteration of propositional attitudes over different subjects. In particular, try Mates's matrix: Let D and D' be two intensionally isomorphic sentences. Then the following are also intensionally isomorphic: (a) Whoever believes (that) D, believes (that) D. (b) Whoever believes (that) D believes (that) D'. But nobody wonders whether anybody doubts that whoever believes D believes D; but some philosopher may well wonder whether anybody doubts that whoever believes D believes D'[18].

¶There have, of course, been significant attempts in this direction; in the A.I. literature the outstanding candidates are [19] and [20]. Needless to say, there is much, much more that needs to be said; sad to say, it will here go unsaid.

‖Actually, I do not in this paper take natural kinds as seriously as one might; in particular, not as seriously as I do in [21].

perspective often carries along with it a commitment to some theory or other of prototypes and this commitment is often understood, mistakenly, as constituting an essential constraint on any semantic account of such a semantic net formalism. (For more on this, see [22].) In what follows, I shall completely ignore all issues about prototypes.†

Some preliminary comment on (2) is called for. I have often thought that there was a systematic confusion of language and theory evident in the work on semantic networks. One was never given a specification of the "language" neat; rather, what one got were notations for particular sentences and one was supposed to be able to go on from there. But how is one to know how to go on, unless one knows, at the very least, what is fixed and structural, as against what is subject to variation by way (e.g.) of varying meaning assignments?‡ Despite (or because of) my worries about this confusion, I think it worthwhile to attempt a rational reconstruction of the intuition that a partial theory of the world is "directly" embedded in the languages we use in thinking and speaking about that world.

The best way to shed a little light on the second of our central intuitions is by contrast. The standard mode of specifying a quantification language (or language scheme) includes the specification of a typically infinite set of typically infinite sets of predicate letters of all possible arities. To interpret such a language in the classical model-theoretic way, one assigns a set as the domain for the variables and an extension to each predicate letter. In the standard vein, these assignments are to subsets of the n-place Cartesian product of the domain of the variables (for n-place predicates).§

The predicates, individually, are syntactically unstructured and, collectively, are no more than members of various unordered sets. That is to say, from a semantic point of view, there are no constraints on the interpretations assigned to the members of any set of predicate letters beyond that imposed by the arity of the individual predicates. (So, e.g. two-place predicates must be assigned subsets of the set of all ordered pairs of members of the domain, etc.) In fact, though, there is a kind of constraint: there are to be no semantic interdependencies among the extensions of the predicates. That the assignments to predicate letters be independent of one another mandates that the specification of the language cannot impose any relationships among the extensions of the predicates. Hence, the standard scheme imposes a requirement of logical independence among atomic sentences.

For instance, if one has two one-place predicate letters, "P" and "Q", one would not (indeed, on many accounts, should not) assign to "Q" the complement of the set assigned to "P"; that's a job for the negation operator. One can, of course, specify a theory in the language which has "$(x)(Qx < - > - Px)$" as a theorem; but one can also formulate in the same language a theory according to which "Q" and "P" are coextensive.¶

The picture sketched above should be familiar, but it does not seem to fit very well that body of work by researchers in Artificial Intelligence which focuses on the related notions of taxonomic structures and inheritance. I shall now present a mildly non-standard account in which those notions are indeed central.

6. THE SEMANTICS OF INHERITANCE

You may think of the sentences of the language as looking a lot like the sentences of a standard first-order language, with a few wrinkles, of course. There will be a finite number of

---

†As an aside, the semantic net formalism I have most clearly and fully in mind is KL-ONE, which likewise eschews prototypes (see [23, 24]).

‡Let me remind you of the quotation from [7]: "A semantic network models the knowledge structure of a thinking, reasoning, language using being. In this case, nodes represent the concepts and beliefs such a being would have." This certainly sounds like an identification of a given network with a particular creature's view of its world.

§A point of terminology: logician-types divide on usage here. I tend to speak of one and the same language being susceptible to many different meaning assignments (interpretations). Others speak, rather, of different—applied—languages as instances of the same language scheme. Anything said in one mode can be translated into the other. I leave it to the reader to make the requisite transformations.

¶We couldn't, in the foregoing, talk of the co-extensiveness of "Q" and "not-P"; at least not if we were restricting ourselves to the resources available in standard first-order languages. For complex predicates are not among those resources; so, in *strictu sensu*, there is no predicate available to play the role—solely in virtue of its structure or solely in virtue of the specification of the language and the standard semantic account—of the complement of another predicate. Rather, we must make do with (complex) open sentences.

primitive predicates of not all possible degrees.† The crucial feature of the account resides in the requirement that integral to specifying the semantics of the language is the specification of an algebraic structure of properties (concepts, intensions) by which the assignment of extensions to the predicates is constrained.

One more preliminary point: the elements of the algebraic structures are to be understood as properties. The "linguistic" representatives of these are, in the first instance, lambda-abstracts interpreted as singular terms denoting properties. These are then associated with monadic predicate letters of the language. When we get around to exploiting lambda-abstraction as a complex predicate-forming operator, predicates of the language will look a lot like the singular terms for properties with which they are correlated. This is unfortunate and *could* easily be remedied by choosing a different notation for the complex predicate forming operator. (But it won't be so remedied.) Occasional reminders of the distinction between singular terms for properties, on the one hand, and predicates, on the other, will be sprinkled about.

In the first instance, we shall limit ourselves to properties, properly so-called; i.e. syntactically speaking, to monadic predicates. Even here choices arise. First, is there one most general, all inclusive property? From the graph-theoretic point of view, is the structure a tree, or is it rather a forest (an unrooted or multi-rooted tree)? Second, are there cases in which a primitive property is immediately included in more than one primitive property—has more than one immediate ancestor in the structure? (Are there cases of multiple inheritance among the primitive properties?) This is the question, from a graph-theoretic point of view, as to whether the structure is a tree (rooted or not) or an upper semi-lattice (perhaps rootless).

I need not make a decision on these points; such a choice is up to a user of the scheme I am describing, and his/her decision, in turn, depends on the structure of the domain of application and/or his/her conceptualization of that domain. I should, however, be able to show how an account would be given in each case. So I shall begin with the simplest case, that in which the structure is an honest-to-goodness tree.

The ordering relation which generates the algebraic structure is property inclusion (or porperty entailment), taken as primitive. There is another significant semantic relation: the relation among the immediate descendants of a given node, that is, among siblings. Such properties are taken to mutually exclude one another. (One can then define property independence in terms of inclusion and exclusion.) The intuition, here, is as follows: imagine a portion of the structure which begins with a node for the property of being a mammal. This has, say, 10 immediate descendants marked as mutually exclusive, among which are, e.g. the property of being a cat, the property of being a pig, etc. Each includes the property of being a mammal, and each excludes all the others. Crucially, there is no requirement that the sequence of mutually exclusive immediate descendants exhausts the immediately superior property. So also, in the case at hand, there is no assumption that the language has primitive predicates for each of the mammalian species. Rather, we want to allow for the discovery of new primitive properties (new species), and their introduction into the language, though not perhaps without limit. I shall return to this point in a moment.‡

Given the above, it's fairly easy to see how the structure of properties should constrain the assignments of extensions to the primitive predicates, those predicates which are associated with nodes in the structure. Such predicates are interpreted, first, by assigning them intensions, properties. The structure among these properties, then, generates the relations among the extensions (sets) associated with the predicates. Specifying a model for such a system would go

---

†We will be able to generate non-primitive predicates of any arity by way of composition, e.g. by forming relational products. But we assume that there are only finitely many primitive properties within the ken of the language, at least to begin with.

‡As should by now have been made clear, and in case it hasn't: "primitive" does not mean "simple". The guiding intuition is that the relation between genus and species is like that between determinables, such as the property of being colored, and determinates, such as the property of being red. The latter includes the former; but the property of being red is not to be analyzed as *consisting* of the property of being colored together with some other property (unless that other property is that of being red). Nor is the property of being colored to be analyzed as an infinite disjunction of its determinates; indeed, it does not *include* any of them; though, to repeat, each of them includes it. In general, more general primitives (determinables) are simpler than the less general primitives (determinates). For a related, but different view, see [25, 26].

as follows: first, the entire domain is assigned to the topmost primitive.† The extension assigned to a node D which is an immediate descendant of node A must be a subset of the extension assigned to A. Moreover, given that D belongs to an n-tuple of immediate descendants of A marked as mutually exclusive, the sets assigned to the members of the n-tuple must be disjoint subsets of the set assigned to A. In general, however, this family of sets will not exhaust the set assigned A. (This, of course, is the extensional reflection of the point made above with respect to the intensional structure.)

Suppose, for example, that there are 10 immediate descendants of MAMMAL, marked as mutually exclusive. There will be admissible models in which the extension assigned MAMMAL is not simply the union of the extensions assigned its immediate descendants. The primary fact, however, is that the property of being a mammal is not the "logical (conceptual) sum" of its immediate subordinates. It is not, that is, definable in terms of them; it is not—*ex hypothesi*—definable at all.‡

To accommodate multiple inheritance—to allow our structure to be an (upper) semilattice—we need enter only one amendment. Where D is immediately subordinate to $A1, \dots An$, the extension assigned to D is, in general, a proper subset of the intersection of the extensions assigned to its immediate ancestors. Again, there can be models in which the extension assigned to D is the intersection of the sets assigned to $A1, \dots An$; but we are assuming that D is a primitive and thus that it is not definable in terms of the other primitives.§

Finally, we shall take a quick look at the unrooted (or multi-rooted) option. Should the assignments to the n topmost nodes be independent, identical, or should they rather be mutually exclusive? The first of these options best fits the natural treatment of assignments to parallel and independent nodes. The question to be asked, of course, is what intuitions motivate the move to a forest? My own perusal of the relevant literature convinces me that there is one kernel intuition, which yields, at the very least, a forest with two topmost nodes. The kernel intuition is our old friend, intuition (3), in disguise. There is to be one tree for kinds of things and another for qualities of things. Kinds must be distinguished from qualities; being a cat must be distinguished (in kind, no doubt) from being red.

If this is the operative intuition, I would assume that the assignments would go as follows: the whole domain is assigned to the topmost node in "thing-hierarchy". Within that hierarchy things go as before. But now what to do with the quality sub-tree? If one buys the third intuition in a strong form, qualities don't belong to particular things; but only to particular F's or G's, where "F" and "G" are schematic placeholders for common nouns. To buy this intuition, then, is to hold that all predications (attributions) of a quality to an individual are really attributions of the quality to a particular instance of some kind. Put another way: this intuition leads one to deny that kinds of things and qualities of things should be treated as on a par—as both independently determining extensions. (There is such an entity as the set of cats: a set of things which are cats; but there is no such set as the set of things which are red. Still, there is a set of cats which are red.) So, the appropriate move would be to treat the hierarchy of qualities in a quite different way than the taxonomy of kinds: the predicates correlated with these nodes do not get assigned extensions. Such predicates are treated as belonging to a different logical type than the predicates correlated with kind-properties. A plausible line is to treat qualities as functions from kinds to kinds, and in the first instance, as functions from primitive kinds to defined kinds.¶

---

†I'm assuming, for the sake of simplicity and familarity, a standard first-order model structure. In earlier versions of this paper, I had not attempted to satisfy the seemingly deep-seated psychological need for specifying such a structure for the language. One alternative was to eschew sets as extensions of predicates altogether and stick with properties; another, a variant of suggestions due to van Fraassen[25, 26], was set-theoretic with a vengence. That I treat the relationship between the intensional structure and the class of admissible models in the way I do here is due almost entirely to the philosopher and logician George Smith. For more on this, see the acknowledgement at the end of the paper.

‡Note this has the consequence that there can be models in which there are individuals which are assigned to no other predicate than the one correlated with the highest node(s), and so on down for intermediate predicates, e.g. individuals that are—in a given model—mammals, without belonging to any specified species of mammal. For a like-minded view, see [27].

§We can, of course, introduce a term for the non-primitive property in question—$(\text{LAMBDA}(x)\,(A1(x)\,\&\dots\&\,An(x)))$; just as in the case discussed above, we could have $(\text{LAMBDA}\,(x)(A1(x)v\dots vAn(x)))$. Reminder: these lambda expressions are property-designators; they are not to be confused with the complex predicates with which they are correlated. More on complex properties and complex predicates below.

¶Syntactically, then, "adjectives", quality-predicates, are of the category CN/CN; this, of course, is the treatment they receive in Montague style grammars for natural languages.

This last discussion raises the possibility of yet another deviation in syntax from standard first order languages in the direction of sortal quantifiers. We might require that all quantification, indeed all variable binding, including lambda-abstraction, be kind-restricted. Here there are options: one has been explored by Barwise and Cooper[28]; another, closer on the surface to standard first-order notation has been advanced by Gupta[29]. Distinguish between predicates, properly so called, and common nouns, and stipulate that if and only if C is a common noun, x a variable and F a formula, then $(Vx, C)F$ is a formula. Also, iff as above, then (LAMBDA $(x, C)F$) is a complex, defined predicate—correlated with the defined property of being a C which is F. The crucial point is that variable binding requires a sortal. No predication without classification; no quantification without classification either.†

Two last points. First, I have said nothing about whether the formation of complex properties by qualification of simple kinds is unrestricted. For instance, I have said nothing to rule in or out such properties as being a number which is red or being an idea which is green.‡ This point is connected with the second one. Once we have split up our tree into a forest, why not split up our sub-trees. So, for instance, why assume a single topmost node in the kind hierarchy, a node, presumably, for the property of being a thing? Surely, we can split here as well, separating off a tree of physical things from a three of abstract entities, etc. We can, then, do the same for qualities and somehow express selection restrictions blocking the anomalous "kinds" instanced above. All these things are possible, and some of them may even be desirable. Here, too, I shall beg off pursuing the details of the various options open to us.

I won't now go into any details of the ways of extending our structures to handle the correlates of many-placed predicates. I do, however, assume that there are only finitely many primitives, so for some n, there will be no primitive relations of degree n or greater. Relations of such degrees there will be generated (e.g.) by taking relational products of relations of lesser degree. There are, of course, a number of questions to be answered and a number of options to be explored. E.g. shall we allow inclusion relations between relations of different degree; and if so, how shall we handle such cases? How shall we mark, e.g. the fact that for a given ordered pair $\langle x, y \rangle$ to be in the extension associated with a certain two-place predicate, the first element must have a certain property or belong to some specified kind? I will simply note here that there are no significant obstacles to the extension to polyadic relations, whichever of the options available to us in the monadic case we decide to extend to the polyadic.

Finally, a brief mention of complex, defined properties and their associated complex predicates. From what was said above, it should be clear that there are options as well with respect to the kinds of complex concept forming operators we allow. For instance, if one opts for the single rooted structure, one may opt for standard, unrestricted Boolean compounds. So, one would expect a node for the defined property of being a red cat: (LAMBDA (x) (cat (x) & red (x))) which in every admissible model will be assigned the intersection of the sets assigned to its two constituent primitives. If, on the other hand, one is attracted to the picture suggested by intuition (3), the relevant complex concept-forming functor will be of the CN/CN variety, i.e. the compound will really be a result of function application. Moreover, one might want to

---

†A few remarks are in order here. It would be misleading to suggest that the only deviations to be encountered here were syntactic. Roughly in order of increasing distance from the familiar: We can opt for sortal quantification, but allow both those predicates associated with sorts or kinds and those associated with qualities to determine sets as extensions. Needless to say, not all qualities are created equal; compare "male criminals" with "alleged criminals" with "tall criminals". Arguably, only the first could plausibly be treated in terms of set-theoretic intersection anyway. For more on this, see [30]. To remain as close as possible to standard first-order model structures, we would then simply posit that the intensions associated with the first kind of monadic predicate were a special kind of property, viz. that of belonging to a particular natural kind, leaving this last notion primitive so far as the specification of the semantic account is concerned. This is what we have done with the notion of a property; we have most emphatically not explicated this notion in the standard modal model-theoretic way as a function from possible worlds to sets of (possible) individuals. Just as in standard model-theoretic treatments of modality the notion of possible world is unexplicated. The next option should now be obvious; we can move to a modal model structure and assign different semantic types to predicates for kinds and predicates for qualities. For a version of this move, less radically deviant than Bressan's, see Gupta's "The Logic of Common Nouns". More radical still is the analysis in terms of function application. One alternative would be a variant of the account given by Barwise and Cooper; this has the attractive feature of not going unnecessarily modal. Here, too, we would take the notion of natural kinds as primitive from the point of view of semantic theory.

‡From a syntactic point of view: I have not discussed restrictions on that mode of complex "predicate" forming which consists of applying an adjectival modifier to a kind term. Semantically speaking, I'm avoiding giving a semantical account of sortal incorrectness or anomaly. For one such account, see [31].

block Boolean compounds of (primitive) kind terms (e.g. both (LAMBDA (x) (cat (x) & dog (x))) and (LAMBDA (x) (flower (x) v mouse (x))). Surely, one will want to allow some such combinations of qualities, even if only sortally restricted combinations; e.g. (LAMBDA (x, cat) (white (x) v black (x))). But, then what of (LAMBDA (x, cat) (white (x) & black (x))— assuming WHITE and BLACK are marked as mutually exclusive under COLORED? Once all these decisions are made, one can specify the nature of the resulting structure of all possible properties—primitive and defined. Once again, I forego the messy details.

Enough has been said, I hope, to make fruitful an attempt to answer the question that will naturally arise in the mind of anyone used to a more orthodox account. Why not capture all these intuitions about semantic interdependencies among primitives by way of meaning postulates? This last is the traditional alternative mode of capturing the intuition that items in the extralogical vocabulary can partially determine the implication relations among sentences.†

There are, I think, reasons for preferring the semantic network picture. First, the meaning postulate account denies (or does not account for) the distinction between analytic sentences, whose necessity is grounded in the internal structure of their non-logical vocabulary, and either logical truths or non-logical necessary truths. So for instance, the account takes no official cognizance of the distinction between sentences such as "Every even number is the sum of two primes", and "All cats are mammals". The first, if true, is a necessary truth about the natural numbers; it is not a logical truth. The second, according to a particular instance of the account I have sketched, is rendered true solely by the full specification of the language to which that sentence belongs; yet it too is not, in the standard sense, a truth of logic. Nor does the traditional account distinguish either of the above two sentences from "All squares are rectangles" or "All squares are either squares or red".‡

To return for a moment to pure description. If someone wanted to specify as part of the determination of his/her language that the predicate associated with the property of being a mammal was analytically entailed by that associated with the property of being a cat, one could do so by arranging the intensional structure associated with the language in the right way. And this dependency between the two primitive predicates would be something over and above the necessity of the associated universalized conditional sentence.§

The first reason for preferring a semantic network account to one in terms of meaning postulates introduces a second. One major difference between the non-standard account sketched and the traditional alternative is that meaning postulates are simply sentences of the language picked out from their siblings in just the same way that axioms are picked out in standard axiomatizations—namely, by being stuck in a list with the metalinguistic heading "AXIOM" ("MEANING POSTULATE") prefixed to it. The crucial point here is that, in the standard accounts, one uses the meaning postulates precisely *as axioms*. The set of "analytic" sentences is identified with the set of (standard) logical consequences of the postulates; for the finicky, the purely logical truths are often subtracted. Thus the meaning postulates enter into the explication of analyticity solely in virtue of their logical form plus their tag. The interpretations of the syntactic primitives covered by the postulates are not incorporated into the specification of the language. In the nonstandard account, on the other hand, the primary necessities are not *formal*; the relation of "predicate inclusion" that holds between (e.g.) "cat" and "mammal" is not a function of their logical forms; they are both syntactically simple

---

†The idea is due to Carnap and has been extensively exploited by Montague and his followers (see [16, 17]). Ron Brachman and myself raised this possibility in [22] (see also [27]).

‡The differences alluded to above are tricky matters. Why not claim that the necessary truth of the second sentence is grounded in facts about the world of living things and their essences? This is Kripke's view in [32]. I am sympathetic to this rejoinder; still, a few points can be made. First, I am simply presenting for your delectation and delight a view according to which *there is* a distinction between sentences whose necessity is grounded in extra-linguistic matters of fact and those (perhaps *also*) grounded in the very structure of the language itself; though not in the way the truths of logic are so grounded. According to the present proposal, one can accommodate these distinctions. So much by way of "argumentation".

§The arcs in the conceptual structure between super- and subordinate nodes do not realize the complex syntactic operation of forming the universalized conditional sentence in whose matrix the open sentence whose predicate is that correlated with the subordinate node is the antecedent and whose consequent is the open sentence associated with the superordinate node. Nodes and links are one thing; sentences another. Of course, the abstract syntax of the language could be realized by a set of graph-type structures and operations thereon, rather than the usual linear, one-dimensional structures. To take this last point as important is to trivialize the first of our three guiding intuitions.

predicates and hence are devoid of significant logical form.† In this respect, compare "(x) (Crow $(x) - \rangle$ Bird (x)))" and "(x) (Crow $(x) - \rangle$ Black (x)))". These sentences are of exactly the same syntactic type; but, again on at least one plausible instance of the scheme sketched, the truth of the first is grounded in property inclusion and, thereby, in the language itself; not so that of the second.

This second point leads us to the third and penultimate point. The relations of inclusion or entailment between primitive predicates are not, we have noted, a matter of logic at all. Rather, they are determined solely by the structure of primitives; and, in principal, all such relations can be "read right off" from the structure. Indeed, a central feature of the account given here is that it allows us to make a sharp distinction between matters of logic and matters of language. Matters of logic are matters of logical form; there is no room for such concerns to intrude on the inclusion relations among the primitive predicates. Computationally, matters of logic relate to inferential operations; more concretely, to the application of rules of transformation. These last are aptly named. Where there is deduction, there are steps, steps which involve the manipulation and generation (broadly speaking, the transformation) of terms or of formulae. There are no such steps involved with respect to determining the crucial semantic relationships among primitive predicates; there is nothing beyond lookup. That is, we stipulate that the algebraic structure of primitives must be specified completely in advance. That specification can be seen as being realized in a number of ways; but in the abstract it is as if attached to each node was a specification of the paths on which it is located, and of course, its relative location on that path. There is no computation to be done beyond seeing whether a given other predicate does or does not appear on such a path (and where). If this latter does, in a particular implementation, require computation, that is solely a function of the implementation. To put the point in yet another, and clearer, way: the computational steps involved in actually traversing the tree and establishing relative locations among a given set of nodes are not to be identified with the computational steps involved in implementing a proof procedure which is sensitive to the logical forms of the expressions over which its operations are defined.

Finally, one minor point about the alternative account using meaning postulates. Let's look at an extremely simple case in which there is one node, A, which immediately dominates two others, $A1$ and $A2$, respectively. We assume that these two subordinate nodes are marked as mutually exclusive. What would the set of meaning postulates be? At first, things are simple: "(x) ($A1(x) - \rangle$ $A(x)$))", "(x) ($A2(x) - \rangle$ $A(x)$))", "(x) ($A1(x)$ $- \rangle -$ $A2(x)$))". Now, how about "$-(x)$ ($A(x) - \rangle$ ($A1(x)$ v $A2(x)$))"? By itself, this won't do. Though it's crucial that "A"'s extension not be determined in all models to be simply the union of the extensions assigned to "$A1$" and "$A2$", we don't want to rule out that the set of A's actually is, as it happens, just that union. Another option is to take advantage of the resources of set theory. In every case like the one at hand, we can simply introduce a predicate, "$A3$"—which will, of course, be a syntactically simple predicate, for in the standard story, there are no others—and assign to it the following set: $\{x| Ax \& - A1x \& - A2x\}$. The set assigned to "$A3$" can be empty or not. This assignment goes somewhat against the grain of the standard story, since it is completely a function of the assignments to the other predicates, and because now the same is true of the assignment to "A".

Moreover, note the following: if we stipulate that predicates are, in the first place, correlated with properties, and if we take seriously the distinction between primitive and defined properties, then there is no reason to assume that there is a primitive predicate (one correlated with a primitive property) whose associated extension just is the logical difference between "A"'s extension and the union of the extensions of "$A1$" and "$A2$". Indeed, the only way we might have of representing the extension of "$A3$" is by way of a set abstract in which the subsuming predicate ("A") makes an essential appearance. (Surely we can assume that we can't always present the relevant sets by lists of their members.)‡

There are other options, of course. One is to go modal. First, we prefix all of the foregoing (except the denial of exhaustion of A's) with a necessity operator. Then, what we want is that

---

†I trust the reader will pardon the sloppiness involved in talk of "predicate" as opposed to "property" inclusion.

‡I have presumed that it is a condition of adequacy that the primitive character of the properties be captured by the postulates. This requirement, of course, might be challenged.

there can be A's which are neither $A1$'s nor $A2$'s. I.e. "It is not necessary that (x) $(A(x)$ $-)$ $(A1(x)$ v $A2(x))$". (Or: "It is possible that there be an A which is neither an $A1$ nor an $A2$".) The modal move is not unnatural; but it strikes me as better not to introduce modalities until one has to, to handle explicit modal operators for example. Let's not muck about with other worlds until we've done what we can with the resources available to us in this one.

I shall refrain from going on at any length at all about the most appropriate account of the logical connectives in the kind of scheme I've sketched. In a sense, what I've said about the non-logical vocabulary *can* be seen as imposing no constraints on a semantic account of the logical vocabulary, especially if we confine our attention to logical operations on sentences, and ignore the use of logical operators in forming complex, defined predicates.†

Acknowledgements—Work on this paper was inspired by discussions, over 3 yrs, with Rusty Bobrow, Ron Brachman, Hector Levesque, Jim Schmolze, Brian Smith, Bill Woods and (other) members of what might be called the KL-ONE WORKING GROUP. It is from them that I learned whatever I know about semantic networks. Thanks also to John Mylopoulos and other members of the Computer Science Department at the University of Toronto who were subjected to this material in not yet digested form and let me live to tell about it; and to Bob Moore for a stimulating correspondence on the material.

With respect to the section on inheritance, a special acknowledgement is due to George Smith, of the Tufts University Philosophy Department. It was he who convinced me of the utility of connecting up the account in terms of property inclusion with an account of the constraints on admissible models of the standard first-order variety. (Indeed the account of the simplest case, that of the honest-to-goodness tree, a case I had ignored, is his.) It was, as well, he who convinced me that the connection between property-inclusion and analytic entailments *a la* Anderson-Belnap really could be given a natural and plausible theoretical grounding for the case of natural languages. The present work (which, as noted, touches neither on purely logical matters nor on issues in the semantics of natural languages) would have been even more deviant in conception than it is, if he hadn't shared with me his current work (in the form of chapters of a manuscript written in collaboration with Jerrold Katz) on the semantics of natural languages[34].

Notwithstanding the foregoing, the above are individually, and collectively, innocent. The buck (and the paper) stops here.

REFERENCES

1. N. Nilsson, Artificial intelligence: engineering, science, or slogan?" *AI Magazine* **3**(1), 2–8 (1982).
2. D. Scott, Advice on modal logic. In *Philosophical Problems in Logic* (Edited by K. Lambert), pp. 143–172. D. Reidel, Dordrecht (1970).
3. R. Reiter and G. Criscuolo, Some representational issues in default reasoning. *Tech. Report* 80-7, Dept. of Computer Science, The University of British Columbia, August 1980.
4. L. K. Schubert, R. G. Goebel and N. J. Cerone, The structure and organization of a semantic net for comprehension and inference. In *Associative Networks: Representation and Use of Knowledge by Computers* (Edited by N. V. Findler), pp. 121–175. Academic Press, New York (1979).
5. S. C. Shapiro, A net structure for semantic information storage, deduction, and retrieval. *Proc. 2nd Int. Joint Conf. Artificial Intelligence*, IJCAI, London, England, pp. 512–523 (1971).
6. S. C. Shapiro, The SNePS semantic network processing system. In *Associative Networks: Representation and Use of Knowledge by Computers* (Edited by N. V. Findler), pp. 179–203. Academic Press, New York (1979).
7. S. C. Shapiro, What do semantic network nodes represent? *Tech. Rep.* 7, Dept. of Computer Science, State University of New York at Buffalo (July 1981).
8. S. C. Shapiro and A. S. Maida, Intentional concepts in propositional semantic networks. *Tech. Rep.* 171, Dept. of Computer Science, State University of New York at Buffalo (Feb. 1981).
9. S. C. Shapiro, Using non-standard connectives and quantifiers for representing deduction rules in a semantic network. Presented at *Current Aspects of AI Research*, a seminar held at the Electrotechnical Laboratory, Tokyo.
10. S. Kripke, A completeness theorem in modal logic. *J. Symbolic Logic* **24**, 1–14 (1959).
11. S. Kripke, Semantical analysis of modal logic I. *Zeitschrift fur Mathematische Logik und Grundlagen der Mathematik* **9**, 67–96 (1963).
12. R. Montague, Logical necessity, physical necessity, ethics, and quantifiers. In *Formal Philosophy* (Edited by R. Thomason), pp. 71–83, Yale University Press, New Haven (1974).
13. A. Bressan, *A General Interpreted Modal Calculus.* Yale University Press, New Haven (1972).
14. M. Cresswell, Hyperintentional logic. *Studia Logica* **34**(1), 25–38 (1975).
15. R. Montague, Pragmatics and intentional logic. In *Formal Philosophy* (Edited by R. Thomason), pp. 119–147. Yale University Press, New Haven (1974).
16. R. Montague, The proper treatment of quantification in ordinary English. In *Formal Philosophy* (Edited by R. Thomason), pp. 247–270. Yale University Press, New Haven (1974).
17. R. Carnap, *Meaning and Necessity*, 2nd Edn. University of Chicago Press, Chicago (1955).
18. B. Mates, Synonymity. In *Semantics and the Philosophy of Language* (Edited by L. Linsky), pp. 111–136. University of Illinois Press, Urbana (1952).
19. J. McCarthy, First order theories of individual concepts and propositions. In *Machine Intelligence* 9 (Edited by J. Hayes, D. Michie and L. Mikulich), pp. 129–147. Halsted Press, New York (1979).
20. R. C. Moore, Reasoning about knowledge and action. *Tech. Rep.* 191, Artificial Intelligence Center, SRI International (Oct. 1980).

†I must 'fess up, though; I think there may well be more or less appropriate accounts of the connectives in this regard. In particular, if one wants to take the inclusion metaphor seriously, a natural family of logics to look into are the Relevance Logics of the Pittsburgh School of Logic (see [33, 25]).

21. D. Israel, On the semantics of taxonomy-based networks. Technical note to be published as a BBN Technical Report.
22. D. Israei and R. Brachman, Distinctions and confusions: a catalogue raissone. *Proc. 7th Int. Joint Conf. Artificial Intelligence*, IJCAI, Vancouver, pp. 452–458 1981.
23. R. J. Brachman, A structural paradigm for representing knowledge. *Tech. Rep.* 3605. Bolt, Beranek & Newman Inc. (May 1978).
24. R. J. Brachman, An introduction to KL-ONE. In *Research in Natural Language Understanding, Annual Report* (1 Sept. 1978–31 Aug. 1979) Edited by R. J. Brachman *et al.*), pp. 13–46. Bolt, Beranek & Newman, Cambridge (1980).
25. B. van Fraassen, Facts and tautological entailments. *J. Philosophy* 66, 477–487 (1969).
26. B. van Fraassen, Extension, intention, and comprehension. In *Logic and Ontology* (Edited by M. K. Munitz), pp. 101–131. New York University Press, New York (1973).
27. P. Kay, A model-theoretic approach to folk taxonomy. *Social Sci. Inform.* 14(5), 151–166 (1975).
28. J. Barwise and R. Cooper, Generalized quantifiers and natural languages. Unpublished manuscript (1980).
29. A. Gupta, *The Logic of Common Nouns.* Yale University Press, New Haven (1980).
30. J. A. W. Kamp, Two theories about adjectives. In *Formal Semantics of Natural Language* (Edited by E. L. Keenan), pp. 123–155. Cambridge University Press, Cambridge (1975).
31. R. Thomason, A semantic theory of sortal incorrectness. *J. Philosophical Logic* 1, 209–258 (1972).
32. S. Kripke, Naming and necessity. In *Semantics of Natural Language* (Edited by D. Davidson and G. Harman), pp. 253–355. D. Reidel, Dordrecht-Holland.
33. A. Anderson and N. Belnap, *Entailment.* Princeton University Press, Princeton (1975).
34. G. E. Smith and J. J. Katz, Intentionally admissible models: the extensional interpretation of intensional semantics. Manuscript in preparation.

Comp. & Maths. with Appls. Vol. 9, No. 1, pp. 15–27, 1983
Printed in Great Britain.

0097–4943/83/010015–13$03.00/0
Pergamon Press Ltd.

SOME REPRESENTATIONAL ISSUES IN DEFAULT REASONING

RAYMOND REITER

Department of Computer Science, Rutgers University, New Brunswick, NJ 08901, U.S.A.

and

GIOVANNI CRISCUOLO

Istituto di Fisica Teorica, University of Naples, Naples, Italy

Abstract—Although most commonly occurring default rules are normal when viewed in isolation, they can interact with each other in ways that lead to the derivation of anomalous default assumptions. In order to deal with such anomalies it is necessary to re-represent these rules, in some cases by introducing non-normal defaults. The need to consider such potential interactions leads to a new concept of integrity, distinct from the conventional integrity issues of first order data bases.

The non-normal default rules required to deal with default interactions all have a common pattern. Default theories conforming to this pattern are considerably more complex than normal default theories. For example, they need not have extensions, and they lack the property of semi-monotonicity.

Current semantic network representations fail to reason correctly with defaults. However, when viewed as indexing schemes on logical formulae, networks can be seen to provide computationally feasible heuristics for the consistency checks required by default reasoning.

1. INTRODUCTION

In an earlier paper[1] one of us proposed a logic for default reasoning. The objective there was to provide a representation for, among other things, common sense facts of the form "Most A's are B's", and to articulate an appropriate logic to characterize correct reasoning using such facts.† One such form of reasoning is the derivation of default assumptions: given an individual which is an A, conclude that "This particular A is a B". Because some A's are not B's this conclusion must be treated as a default assumption or belief about the world, since subsequent observations in the world may yield that "This particular A is not a B". The derivation of the belief that "This particular A is a B" is a form of plausible reasoning which is typically required whenever conclusions must be drawn from incomplete information.

It is important to note that not all senses of the word "most" lead to default assumptions. One can distinguish two such senses:

(1) A purely statistical connotation, as in "Most voters prefer Carter." Here, "most" is being used exclusively in the sense of "the majority of". This setting does not lead to default assumptions: given that Maureen is a voter one would not want to assume that Maureen prefers Carter. Default logic makes no attempt to represent or reason with such statistical facts.

(2) A prototypical sense, as in "Most birds fly." True, there is a statistical connotation here—the majority of birds do fly—but in addition a characteristic of a prototypical or normal bird is being described in the following sense: given a bird Polly, one is prepared to assume that it flies unless one has reasons to the contrary.‡ It is towards such prototypical settings that default logic is addressed.

The concept of a prototypical situation is central to the frames proposal of [5] and is realized in such frame inspired knowledge representation languages as KRL[6] and FRL[7]. That these are alternative representations for some underlying logic has been convincingly argued in [8]. Default logic presumes to provide a formalization of this underlying logic.

The approach taken by default logic is to distinguish between prototypical facts, such as "Typically dogs bark", and "hard" facts about the world such as "All dogs are mammals" or

---

†Other closely related work with much the same motivation is described in [2–4].

‡One way of distinguishing between these two senses of "most" is by replacing its setting using the word "typically". Thus, "Typically voters prefer Carter" sounds inappropriate, whereas "Typically birds fly" feels correct. In the rest of this paper we shall use "typically" whenever we are referring to a prototypical situation.

"Scott wrote Waverly". The former are viewed as rules of inference, called *default rules*, which apply to the "hard" facts. The point of view is that the set of all "hard" facts will fail to completely specify the world—there will be gaps in our knowledge—and that the default rules serve to help fill in those gaps with plausible but not infallible conclusions. A *default theory* then is a pair (D, W) where D is a set of default rules applying to some world being modelled, and W is a set of "hard" facts about that world. Formally, W is a set of a first order formulae while a typical default rule of D is denoted

$$\frac{\alpha(\mathbf{x}): M\beta_1(\mathbf{x}), \ldots M\beta_n(\mathbf{x})}{w(\mathbf{x})}$$

where $\alpha(\mathbf{x}), \beta_1(\mathbf{x}), \ldots \beta_n(\mathbf{x}), w(\mathbf{x})$ are all first order formulae whose free variables are among those of $\mathbf{x} = x_1, \ldots x_m$. Intuitively, this default rule is interpreted as saying "For all individuals $x_1, \ldots x_m$, if $\alpha(\mathbf{x})$ is believed and if each of $\beta_1(\mathbf{x}), \ldots \beta_n(\mathbf{x})$ is consistent with our beliefs, then $w(\mathbf{x})$ may be believed." The set(s) of beliefs sanctioned by a default theory is precisely defined by a fixed point construction in [1]. Any such set is called an *extension* for the default theory in question, and is interpreted as an acceptable set of beliefs that one may entertain about the world being represented.

It turns out that the general class of default theories is mathematically intractable. Accordingly, many of the results in [1] (e.g. that extensions always exist, a proof theory, conditions for belief revision) were obtained only for the class of so-called *normal* default theories, namely theories all of whose defaults have the form

$$\frac{\alpha(\mathbf{x}): Mw(\mathbf{x})}{w(\mathbf{x})}.$$

Such defaults are extremely common; for example "typically dogs bark.":

$$\frac{\text{DOG}(x): M \text{ BARK}(x)}{\text{BARK}(x)}.$$

"Typically American adults own a car.":

$$\frac{\text{AMERICAN}(x) \wedge \text{ADULT}(x): M((Ey) \cdot \text{CAR}(y) \wedge \text{OWNS}(x, y))}{(Ey) \cdot \text{CAR}(y) \wedge \text{OWNS}(x, y)}.$$

Many more examples of such normal defaults are described in [1]. Indeed, the claim was made there that all naturally occurring defaults are normal. Alas, this claim appears to be true only when interactions involving default rules are ignored. For normal default theories such interactions can lead to anomalous conclusions.

It is the purpose of this paper to describe a variety of settings in which interactions involving defaults are important, and to uniformly generalize the notion of a normal default theory so as to correctly treat these interactions. The resulting *semi-normal* default theories will then be seen to have some interesting properties: for example they need not have extensions, and they lack the semi-monotonicity property which all normal theories enjoy. We shall also see that the interactions introduced by default rules lead to a new concept of data base integrity, distinct from the integrity issues arising in first order data bases. A final objective of this paper is to analyze current network representations with respect to their ability to correctly reason with defaults. On this count such representations will be found deficient. However, when viewed as indexing schemes on logical formulae, networks will be seen to redeem themselves; they can provide computationally feasible heuristics for the consistency checks required by default reasoning.

2. INTERACTING NORMAL DEFAULTS

In this section we present a number of examples of default rules which, in isolation, are most naturally represented as normal defaults but whose interaction with other defaults or first order formulae leads to counterintuitive results. In each case we show how to "patch" the representation in order to restore the intended interpretation. The resulting "patches" all have a uniform character, which will lead us in Section 4.2 to introduce the notion of a semi-normal default theory.

2.1 "Typically" is not necessarily transitive
Consider:

"Typically A's are B's:

$$\frac{A(x):MB(x)}{B(x)} \tag{2.1}$$

"Typically B's are C's:

$$\frac{B(x):MC(x)}{C(x)}. \tag{2.2}$$

These are both normal defaults. Default logic then admits the conclusion that "Typically A's are C's" in the following sense: if a is an individual for which $A(a)$ is known or believed, and if $\sim B(a)$ and $\sim C(a)$ are *not* known or believed, than $C(a)$ may be derived. In other words, normal default theories impose transitivity of typicality judgments. But these need not be transitive, for example:

"Typically high school dropouts are adults."⎫
"Typically adults are employed."   ⎬ (2.3)
                                         ⎭

From these one would not want to conclude that "Typically high school dropouts are employed."† Transitivity must be blocked. This can be done in general by replacing the normal default (2.2) by the non-normal default

$$\frac{B(x):M(\sim A(x) \wedge C(x))}{C(x)}. \tag{2.4}$$

To see why this works, consider a prototypical individual a which is an A, i.e. $A(a)$ is given. By (2.1) $B(a)$ can be derived. But $B(a)$ cannot be used in conjunction with (2.4) to derive $C(a)$ since the consistency condition $\sim A(a) \wedge C(a)$ of (2.4) is violated by the given $A(a)$. On the other hand, for a prototypical individual b which is a B (i.e. $B(b)$ is given) (2.4) can be used to derive $C(b)$ since we do not know that $A(b)$—so that the consistency condition of (2.4) is satisfied.

The introduction of non-normal defaults like (2.4) is a particularly unpleasant solution to the transitivity problem, for as we shall see in Section 4.2, the resulting non-normal default theories lack most of the desirable properties that normal theories enjoy. For example, they sometimes fail to have an extension, they lack semi-monotonicity, and their proof theory appears to be considerably more complex than that for normal theories. Accordingly, to the extent that it can be done, we would prefer to keep our representations "as normal as possible". Fortunately transitivity can be blocked using normal defaults whenever it is the case that in addition to (2.1) and (2.2) we have "Typically B's are not A's." This is the case for example (2.3): "Typically adults are not high school dropouts." Under this circumstance, the following normal representation blocks transitivity:

$$\frac{A(x):MB(x)}{B(x)} \tag{2.5}$$

$$\frac{B(x):M \sim A(x)}{\sim A(x)} \tag{2.6}$$

$$\frac{B(x) \wedge \sim A(x):MC(x)}{C(x)}. \tag{2.7}$$

†Nor would we want to conclude that "Typically high school dropouts are not employed." Rather we would remain agnostic about the employment status of a typical high school dropout.

Notice how, when given that $B(a)$, a simple back-chaining interpreter would establish the goal $C(a)$. Back-chaining into (2.7) yields the subgoal $B(a) \land \sim A(a)$. This splits into the subgoal $B(a)$, which is given and hence solved, and the subgoal $\sim A(a)$. This latter back-chains into (2.6) yielding the subgoal $B(a)$ which is solved. There remains only to verify the consistency requirements associated with the defaults (2.6) and (2.7) entering into the proof, i.e. to verify that $\{C(a), \sim A(a)\}$ is consistent with all of the first order formulae in force. Such a back-chaining default reasoner is an incomplete realization of the complete proof procedure of [1]. The reader might find it instructive to simulate this back-chaining interpreter for the case that $A(a)$ is given, in order to see how a derivation of $C(a)$ is prevented.

Notice also that the representation (2.5)–(2.7) yields a very interesting prediction. Given an individual a which is simultaneously an instance of A and B, we cannot conclude $C(a)$. This prediction is confirmed with respect to example (2.3): Given that John is both a high school dropout and an adult, we do not want to assume that John is employed. Notice that the non-normal representation (2.1) and (2.4) yields the same prediction. We shall have more to say about defaults with common instances of their prerequisites in Section 2.3.†

A somewhat different need for blocking transitivity arises when it is the case that "Typically A's are not C's", i.e. in addition to (2.1) and (2.2) we have

$$\frac{A(x) : M \sim C(x)}{\sim C(x)}. \qquad (2.8)$$

For example,

$$\left.\begin{array}{l} \text{"Typically university students are adults."} \\ \text{"Typically adults are employed."} \\ \text{"Typically university students are not employed."} \end{array}\right\} \qquad (2.9)$$

Under these circumstances, consider a prototypical instance a of A. By (2.1) and (2.2) $C(a)$ can be derived. But by (2.8) $\sim C(a)$ can be derived. This means that the individual a gives rise to two different extensions for the fragment default theory (2.1), (2.2) and (2.8). One of these extensions—the one containing $C(a)$—is intuitively unacceptable; only the other extension—the one containing $\sim C(a)$—is admissible. But a fundamental premise of default logic is that *any* extension provides an acceptable set of beliefs about a world. The problem then is to eliminate the extension containing $C(a)$. This can be done by replacing the normal default (2.2) by the non-normal (2.4), exactly as we did earlier in order to block the transitivity of "typically". Now, given $A(a)$, $B(a)$ can be derived from (2.1), and $\sim C(a)$ from (2.8). $C(a)$ cannot be derived using (2.4) since its consistency requirement is violated. On the other hand, given a prototypical instance b of B, $C(b)$ can be derived using (2.4).

Once again a non-normal default has been introduced, something we would prefer to avoid. As before, a normal representation can be found whenever it is the case that "Typically B's are not A's." This is the case for example (2.9): "Typically B's are not A's." This is the case for example (2.9): "Typically adults are not university students." Under this circumstance the following normal representation will do:

$$\frac{A(x) : MB(x)}{B(x)}$$

$$\frac{B(x) : M \sim A(x)}{\sim A(x)}$$

$$\frac{B(x) \land \sim A(x) : MC(x)}{C(x)}$$

$$\frac{A(x) : M \sim C(x)}{\sim C(x)}.$$

†If

$$\frac{\alpha(\mathbf{x}) : M\beta_1(\mathbf{x}), \dots M\beta_n(\mathbf{x})}{w(\mathbf{x})}$$

is a default rule then $\alpha(\mathbf{x})$ is its *prerequisite*.

Typically A's are B's. / Typically B's are C's.	Default Representation
No A is a C.	$(x) . A(x) \supset \sim C(x)$ $\dfrac{A(x) : MB(x)}{B(x)}$ $\dfrac{B(x) : MC(x)}{C(x)}$
All A's are C's.	$(x) . A(x) \supset C(x)$ $\dfrac{A(x) : MB(x)}{B(x)}$ $\dfrac{B(x) : MC(x)}{C(x)}$
Typically A's are C's.	$\dfrac{A(x) : MB(x)}{B(x)}$ $\dfrac{B(x) : MC(x)}{C(x)}$
It is not the case that A's are typically C's. Transitivity must be blocked.	$\dfrac{A(x) : MB(x)}{B(x)}$ $\dfrac{B(x) : M(\sim A(x) \wedge C(x))}{C(x)}$
Typically B's are not A's. It is not the case that A's are typically C's. Transitivity must be blocked.	$\dfrac{A(x) : MB(x)}{B(x)}$ $\dfrac{B(x) : M \sim A(x)}{\sim A(x)}$ $\dfrac{B(x) \wedge \sim A(x) : MC(x)}{C(x)}$
Typically A's are not C's.	$\dfrac{A(x) : MB(x)}{B(x)}$ $\dfrac{B(x) : M(\sim A(x) \wedge C(x))}{C(x)}$ $\dfrac{A(x) : M \sim C(x)}{\sim C(x)}$
Typically B's are not A's. Typically A's are not C's.	$\dfrac{A(x) : MB(x)}{B(x)}$ $\dfrac{B(x) : M \sim A(x)}{\sim A(x)}$ $\dfrac{B(x) \wedge \sim A(x) : MC(x)}{C(x)}$ $\dfrac{A(x) : M \sim C(x)}{\sim C(x)}$

Fig. 1.

Notice that this representation predicts that any individual which is simultaneously an instance of A and B will be an instance of not C, rather than an instance of C. This is the case for example (2.9): given that Maureen is both a university student and an adult one wants to assume that Maureen is not employed.

Figure 1 summarizes and extends the various cases discussed in this section. The first three entries of this table are unproblematic cases which were not discussed, and are included only for completeness.

2.2 Interactions between "all" and "typically"

Phenomena closely related to those stemming from the non-transitivity of "typically" arise from interactions between normal defaults and certain universally quantified first order formulae. Consider

"All A's are B's." $(x).A(x) \supset B(x)$ (2.10)

"Typically B's are C's." $\dfrac{B(x) : MC(x)}{C(x)}.$ (2.11)

Default logic forces the conclusion that "Typically A's are C's" in the sense that if a is a prototypical A then it will also be a C. But this conclusion is not always warranted, for example:

$$\left.\begin{array}{l} \text{"All 21-yr-olds are adults."} \\ \text{"Typically adults are married."} \end{array}\right\} \tag{2.12}$$

Given that John is a 21-yr-old, we would not want to conclude that he is married. To block the unwarranted derivation, replace (2.11) by

$$\frac{B(x):M(\sim A(x) \wedge C(x))}{C(x)}. \tag{2.13}$$

As was the case in Section 2.1 the introduction of this non-normal default can be avoided whenever it is the case that "Typically B's are not A's"† by means of the representation (2.10) together with

$$\left.\begin{array}{c} \dfrac{B(x):M \sim A(x)}{\sim A(x)} \\[2em] \dfrac{B(x) \wedge \sim A(x):MC(x)}{C(x)} \end{array}\right\} \tag{2.14}$$

Notice that this representation, as well as the representation (2.10) and (2.13) predicts that no conclusion is warranted about the C-ness of any given common instance of A and B.

A related problem arises when it is the case that "Typically A's are not C's" so that, in addition to (2.10) and (2.11) we have

$$\frac{A(x):M \sim C(x)}{\sim C(x)}. \tag{2.15}$$

For example:
"All Québecois are Canadians."
"Typically Canadians are native English speakers."
"Typically Québecois are not native English speakers."

As in Section 2.1, a prototypical instance a of A will give rise to two extensions for the theory (2.10), (2.11) and (2.15), one containing $C(a)$; the other containing $\sim C(a)$. To eliminate the extension containing $C(a)$, replace (2.11) by (2.13).

As before, the introduction of the non-normal default (2.13) can be avoided whenever it is the case that "Typically B's are not A's", by means of the representation (2.10), (2.14) and (2.15).

Figure 2 summarizes the cases discussed in this section. The first three entries of this table are unproblematic cases which were not discussed, and are included only for completeness.

2.3 *Conflicting default assumptions: prerequisites with common instances*

In this section we discuss the following pattern, in which a pair of defaults have contradictory consequents but whose prerequisites may share common instances:‡

$$\left.\begin{array}{c} \dfrac{A(x):M \sim C(x)}{\sim C(x)} \\[2em] \dfrac{B(x):MC(x)}{C(x)}. \end{array}\right\} \tag{2.16}$$

---

†Note that example (2.12) seems not to have this character. One is unlikely to include that "Typically adults are not 21 years old" in any representation of a world.

‡If

$$\frac{\alpha(\mathbf{x}):M\beta_1(\mathbf{x}), \dots M\beta_n(\mathbf{x})}{w(\mathbf{x})}$$

is a default rule, then $\alpha(\mathbf{x})$ is its *prerequisite* and $w(\mathbf{x})$ its *consequent*.

All A's are B's. Typically B's are C's.	Default Representation
No A is a C.	$(x) \cdot A(x) \supset \sim C(x)$ $(x) \cdot A(x) \supset B(x)$ $\dfrac{B(x) \; : \; MC(x)}{C(x)}$
All A's are C's.	$(x) \cdot A(x) \supset C(x)$ $(x) \cdot A(x) \supset B(x)$ $\dfrac{B(x) \; : \; MC(x)}{C(x)}$
Typically A's are C's.	$(x) \cdot A(x) \supset B(x)$ $\dfrac{B(x) \; : \; MC(x)}{C(x)}$
It is not the case that A's are typically C's Transitivity must be blocked.	$(x) \cdot A(x) \supset B(x)$ $\dfrac{B(x) \; : \; M(\sim A(x) \wedge C(x))}{C(x)}$
Typically B's are not A's. It is not the case that A's are typically C's. Transitivity must be blocked.	$(x) \cdot A(x) \supset B(x)$ $\dfrac{B(x) \; : \; M \sim A(x)}{\sim A(x)}$ $\dfrac{B(x) \wedge \sim A(x) \; : \; MC(x)}{C(x)}$
Typically A's are not C's.	$(x) \cdot A(x) \supset B(x)$ $\dfrac{B(x) \; : \; M(\sim A(x) \wedge C(x))}{C(x)}$ $\dfrac{A(x) \; : \; M \sim C(x)}{\sim C(x)}$
Typically B's are not A's. Typically A's are not C's.	$(x) \cdot A(x) \supset B(x)$ $\dfrac{B(x) \; : \; M \sim A(x)}{\sim A(x)}$ $\dfrac{B(x) \wedge \sim A(x) \; : \; MC(x)}{C(x)}$ $\dfrac{A(x) \; : \; M \sim C(x)}{\sim C(x)}$

Fig. 2.

The problem here is which default assumption (if any) should be made when given an instance a of both A and B, i.e. should $C(a)$ be assumed, or $\sim C(a)$ or neither? Two cases have already been considered:

(1) If it is the case that all A's are B's, then row 6 and possibly row 7 of Fig. 2 provide representations; in both $\sim C(a)$ is derivable whenever $A(a)$ and $B(a)$ are simultaneously given.

(2) If it is the case that "Typically A's are B's" then row 6 and possibly row 7 of Fig. 2 provide representations in both of which $\sim C(a)$ is derivable given $A(a)$ and $B(a)$.

The problematic setting is when there is no entailment relationship between A and B. For example:

$$\left.\begin{array}{l}\text{``Typically Republicans are not pacifists.''}\\ \text{``Typically Quakers are pacifists.''}\end{array}\right\} \qquad (2.17)$$

Now, given that John is both a Quaker and a Republican, we intuitively want to make no assumptions about his warlike nature. This can be done in the general case by replacing the representation (2.16) by the non-normal defaults

$$\left.\begin{array}{c}\dfrac{A(x) : M(\sim B(x) \wedge \sim C(x))}{\sim C(x)} \\[2em] \dfrac{B(x) : M(\sim A(x) \wedge C(x))}{C(x)} \, . \end{array}\right\} \qquad (2.18)$$

This representation admits that a typical A is not a C, a typical B is a C, but a typical A which is also a B leads to no conclusion.

When it is the case that "Typically A's are not B's" and "Typically B's are not A's" the non-normal defaults (2.18) can be replaced by the following normal ones:

$$\frac{A(x): M \sim B(x)}{\sim B(x)}$$

$$\frac{B(x): M \sim A(x)}{\sim A(x)}$$

$$\frac{A(x) \wedge \sim B(x): M \sim C(x)}{\sim C(x)}$$

$$\frac{B(x) \wedge \sim A(x): MC(x)}{C(x)}.$$

This appears to be the case for example (2.17):

"Typically, Republicans are not Quakers."

"Typically, Quakers are not Republicans."

It is not always the case that the pattern (2.16) should lead to no default assumptions for common instances of A and B. Consider:

"Typically full time students are not employed."

"Typically adults are employed."

Suppose that John is an adult full time student. One would want to assume that he is not employed. So in general, given the setting (2.16) for which the default assumption $\sim C$ is preferred for common instances of A and B, use the following non-normal representation:

$$\frac{A(x): M \sim C(x)}{\sim C(x)}$$

$$\frac{B(x): M(\sim A(x) \wedge C(x))}{C(x)}.$$

Whenever, in addition, it is the case that "Typically B's are not A's," use the following normal representation:

$$\frac{A(x): M \sim C(x)}{\sim C(x)}$$

$$\frac{B(x): M \sim A(x)}{\sim A(x)}$$

$$\frac{B(x) \wedge \sim A(x): MC(x)}{C(x)}.$$

3. DEFAULT INHERITANCE IN HIERARCHIES: NETWORK REPRESENTATIONS

We have focused, in Section 2, on certain fairly simple patterns of default rules. Our choice of these patterns was conditioned by their frequent occurrence in common sense reasoning, and by the fact that they are typical of the kinds of default knowledge which various "semantic" network schemes presume to represent and reason with. Most such networks are designed to exploit the natural hierarchical organization of much of our knowledge about the world and rely heavily for their inferential power upon the inheritance of properties associated with a general class "down the hierarchy" to more restricted classes. Networks usually provide for defaults and their inheritance, although they do not all distinguish in their graphical notation between default rules and exception-free statements about the world.†‡ In any event those systems which

---

†So that the representations often appear to be inconsistent. See [9]. Of course, once a proper semantics is defined for the network[10, 11] the apparent inconsistency evaporates. Advocates of the need to reason from inconsistent information are, in part, confusing default rules with first order facts about a world.

‡The SNePS system[12] does make this distinction through the introduction of an "almost-all" "quantifier".

deal with defaults appear to rely exclusively on a shortest path heuristic, embedded in the network interpreter, for computing default inheritances in hierarchies [9, 13].

To see what this device is and why it is deemed necessary, consider:

"Typically, students are full time."

$$\frac{STUDENT(x) : M \ FULL\text{-}TIME(x)}{FULL\text{-}TIME(x)}$$

"Typically, night students are not full time."

$$\frac{NIGHT\text{-}STUDENT(x) : M \sim FULL\text{-}TIME(x)}{\sim FULL\text{-}TIME(x)}.$$

"All night students are students."

$$(x). \ NIGHT\text{-}STUDENT(x) \supset STUDENT(x).$$

A network representation for these facts might look something like that of Fig. 3. (We have slightly modified the notation of [13].) Now suppose that John is a night student. We want to conclude that he is not full time, not that he is full time. But what is to prevent a network interpreter from traversing the MEMBER and ISA link from John to NIGHT-STUDENT to STUDENT and thence via the default PROP link to FULL-TIME? Enter the shortest path heuristic. Basically this says that an individual, e.g. John, will inherit a property P provided there is a path from the node "John" to the node "P" and there is no shorter or equal length path from John to "not P". This is a slightly more precise statement of that in [14]:

"Any property true of a concept in the hierarchy is implicitly true of anything linked below it, unless explicitly contradicted at the lower level."

It is easy to see that this principle, as applied to Fig. 3, will prevent the unwarranted assumption that John is full time.

Unfortunately, except in the simplest of cases, the shortest path heuristic is wrong. For example, consider a slightly embellished version of the Quaker–Republican defaults:

"Typically, Quakers are pacifists."
"Typically, Republicans are hawks."
"No hawk is a pacifist."

Suppose that John is a Quaker Republican. Then there is a path from "John" to "PACIFIST" as well as one from "John" to "~PACIFIST" and the former path is shorter than the latter. The shortest path heuristic would thus predict that John is a pacifist whereas intuitively no default assumption is warranted.

Despite our criticism of the shortest path heuristic, we nevertheless feel that there is a

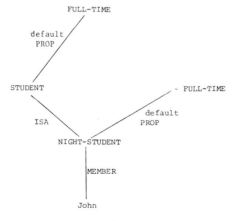

Fig. 3.

profound *implementation* principle lurking here. One of the most serious computational difficulties afflicting default logic is the requirement that one test for the consistency of all of the default assumptions entering into a derivation. For example:

"Typically birds fly except for penguins, ostriches, oil covered birds, dead birds, etc."

$$\frac{BIRD(x): MFLY(x)}{FLY(x)}$$

$$(x).PENGUIN(x) \supset \sim FLY(x)$$

$$(x).OSTRICH(x) \supset \sim FLY(x)$$

etc.

Now suppose given BIRD (tweety), and nothing else about tweety. Then FLY (tweety) can be derived provided that FLY (tweety) *is consistent with all of the first order facts in the data base.* One way of establishing consistency is by failing to derive a contradiction from all of the consequences of the formula FLY (tweety). Of course, it is undecidable in general whether or not a set of formulae is consistent, but let's try anyway. From FLY (tweety) one can derive ~PENGUIN (tweety), ~OSTRICH (tweety), ~DEAD-BIRD (tweety), etc. So with this method of performing the consistency check, one must consider *all of the possible exceptions* to the default rule about flying birds! Since the exceptions to flight are legion we are faced with a potentially overwhelming computation. Ideally, we do not want even to entertain the possibility of an exception unless the given facts naturally compel us to do so. The only way of testing consistency which avoids "conscious" consideration of all of the exceptions to flight is to begin with the given fact BIRD (tweety), and using only the first order facts in the data base derive all consequences of this; if ~FLY (tweety) is not one of these consequences then consistency is guaranteed.

Now consider Fig. 4 which is a network representation of this same setting. We can tell at a glance that FLY (tweety) is consistent with our knowledge: ~FLY (tweety) is not derivable because there is no directed path from "tweety" to "~FLY". *Potential derivation chains in the logical representation are explicit as directed paths in the network representation.* Now the consistency check which began with BIRD (tweety) and derived all consequences of this corresponds in the network to an exploration of all paths from "tweety". If there is no such path to "~FLY" then the consistency of FLY (tweety) is assured. Now computationally the exploration of all directed paths beginning at node "tweety" might not appear very promising since the search will get mired in all of the links in that part of the hierarchy lying above the node "BIRD". But recall that we are testing consistency only with respect to all of the first order facts about the world, *not the default rules. Hence no path containing a default PROP link need be considered,* and most network links are of this kind. Moreover, hierarchies tend to be shallower than they are broad. Hence the search for a path from "tweety" to "~FLY" in the hierarchy above "BIRD" appears feasible. It follows that a good strategy is to perform a unidirectional search from "tweety"; if "~FLY" is not encountered, then the default assumption FLY (tweety) is acceptable. This strategy has the computationally important consequence that the myriad possible exceptions to flight are never "consciously" entertained.

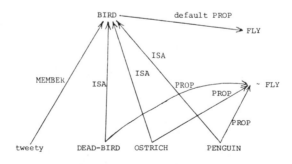

Fig. 4.

Now what is really going on here? The answer is apparent from the observation that *a semantic network reflects a particular choice of an indexing scheme on formulae.*† The indexing scheme is such that whenever an entailment relation logically holds between two nodes, then those nodes are connected by a directed path; network paths correspond to derivation chains in the underlying logical representation. The nonexistence of a path in Fig. 4 from "tweety" to " ~ FLY" guarantees that ~FLY (tweety) cannot be derived, i.e. that FLY (tweety) is consistent with the first order formulae of the data base.

Now there exist far more sophisticated indexing schemes on formulae than any provided in the literature on semantic networks (see, for example, [16], or the indexing on clauses in PROLOG [17]).

Normally such schemes are used to improve the efficiency of theorem provers although they can be used for the construction of plans in deductive search[18]. The discussion of paths in networks and their relationship to consistency suggests another use of indices on formulae: the path structure of the index scheme can provide a powerful and computationally feasible heuristic for the consistency checks required in default reasoning. An example of such an heuristic is the following, with reference to our bird example:

If node "~FLY" cannot be found within a sufficiently large radius r of the node "tweety" (i.e. if no directed path of length r or less from "tweety" to "~FLY" exists in the index structure) then it is likely that FLY (tweety) is consistent with the given first order data base.

It seems to us that an heuristic of this kind is precisely the sort of resource limited computation required for common sense reasoning[9]. Moreover, there is a very good theoretical justification for appealing to a resource limitation in this setting; consistency is not even a semi-decidable property of first order theories‡ so that some sort of heuristic must be applied. What is interesting about this formal analysis is that the nature of, and reasons for, at least one form of resource limited computation can be theoretically articulated.

Notice also that this consistency heuristic is simply a path finding procedure for directed graphs. *No deductions are performed.* Rather, the non existence of a sufficiently long path of a certain form strongly suggests the consistency of some set of formulae.

4. DISCUSSION

In this section we discuss some issues raised by the results of the previous sections. Specifically, we address the question of data base integrity arising from default interactions, as well as some of the formal problems associated with the non-normal default rules introduced to correctly represent these interactions.

4.1 *Integrity of default theories*

As we have seen, default rules can interact with one another in highly complex ways. The addition of a new default rule to a representation may create interactions leading to unwarranted conclusions, even though in isolation this rule may appear perfectly correct.

This observation leads to a new concept of data base integrity, one with quite a different character than the integrity issues arising in data base management systems[19] or in first order data bases[20, 21]. For such systems an integrity constraint specifies some invariant property which every state of the data base must satisfy. For example, a typical integrity constraint might specify that an employee's age must lie in the range 16–99 yr. Any attempt to update the data base with an employee age of 100 would violate this constraint. Formally one can say that a data base satisfies some set of integrity constraints if the data base is logically consistent with the constraints. The rôle of integrity constraints is to restrict the class of models of a data base to include as a model the particular world being represented. Now the objective of the default representations of Section 2 had precisely this character; we sought representations which would rule out unwarranted default assumptions so as to guarantee a faithful representation of real world common sense reasoning. But notice that there was no notion of an integrity constraint with which the representation was to be consistent. Indeed, consistency of the representation cannot be an issue at all since *any* default theory will be consistent provided its

†The fact that networks are notational variants of logical formulae is by now a truism in Artificial Intelligence circles (see [10, 15]).

‡I.e. the consistent first order theories are not recursively enumerable.

first order facts are[1, Corollary 2.2]. It follows that, while there is an integrity issue lurking here, it has a different nature than that of classical data base theory.

We are thus led to the need for some form of integrity maintenance mechanism as an aid in the design of large default data bases. The natural initial data base design would involve representing all default rules as normal defaults, thereby ignoring those potential interactions of the kind analyzed in Section 2. An integrity maintenance system would then seek out possible sources of integrity violations and query the user as to the appropriate default assumptions to be made in this setting. Once the correct interpretation has been determined, the system would appropriately re-represent the offending normal default rules. For example, when confronted with a pair of default rules of the form (2.16), the system would first attempt to prove that A and B can have no common instance, i.e. that $W \cup \{(Ex).A(x) \wedge B(x)\}$ is inconsistent, where W is the set of first order facts. If so, this pair of defaults can lead to no integrity violation. Otherwise the system would ask whether a common instance of A and B is typically a C, a $\sim C$, or neither, and depending on the response would suitably re-represent the pair (2.16), if necessary by non-normal default rules.

4.2 Semi-normal default theories

In Section 2 we had occasion to introduce certain non-normal default rules in order, for example, to block the transitivity of "typically". Inspection of the representations of that section will reveal that all such non-normal default rules share a common pattern; they all have the form

$$\frac{A(x):M(\sim B(x) \wedge C(x))}{C(x)}.$$

Accordingly, it is natural to define a default rule to be *semi-normal* iff it has the form

$$\frac{\alpha(\mathbf{x}):M(\beta(\mathbf{x}) \wedge w(\mathbf{x}))}{w(\mathbf{x})}$$

where α, β and w are formulae of first order logic with free variables among $\mathbf{x} = x_1, \ldots x_m$. A default theory is *semi-normal* iff all of its default rules are semi-normal. Normal default rules are a special case of semi-normal, in which $\beta(\mathbf{x})$ is the identically true proposition.

[1] investigates the properties of normal default theories. Among the results obtained there are the following:

(1) Every normal theory has an extension.

(2) Normal theories are *semi-monotonic*, i.e. if D_1 and D_2 are sets of normal default rules and if E_1 is an extension for the theory (D_1, W), then the theory $(D_1 \cup D_2, W)$ has an extension E_2 such that $E_1 \subseteq E_2$.

One consequence of semi-monotonicity is that one can continue to maintain one's old beliefs whenever a normal theory is updated with new normal defaults. Another is a reasonably clean proof theory.

Unfortunately, semi-normal default theories enjoy none of these nice properties. For example, the following theory has no extension:

$$\frac{:M(A \wedge \sim B)}{A} \qquad \frac{:M(B \wedge \sim C)}{B} \qquad \frac{:M(C \wedge \sim A)}{C}.$$

To see that semi-monotonicity may fail to hold for semi-normal theories consider the theory

$$\frac{:M(A \wedge B)}{B}.$$

This has unique extension $Th(\{B\})$ where, in general, $Th(S)$ is the closure of the set of formulae S under first order theoremhood. If the new default rule $(: M \sim A/\sim A)$ is added to this theory a new theory is obtained with unique extension $Th(\{\sim A\})$ and this does not contain $Th(\{B\})$.

Most of the formal properties of semi-normal default theories remain unexplored. Two problems in particular require solutions: Under what conditions are extensions guaranteed to exist, and what is an appropriate proof theory?

5. CONCLUSIONS

Default theories are complicated. Unlike theories represented in first order logic, default theories lack extensibility. Whenever a new default rule is to be added to a representation its potential interactions with the other default rules must be analyzed. This can lead to a re-representation of some of these defaults in order to block certain unwarranted derivations. All of which leads to a new concept of data base integrity, distinct from the integrity issues arising in first order data bases. These observations also suggest the need for a default integrity maintenance system as a tool for aiding in the design of large default data bases. Such a system would seek out potentially interacting defaults during the data base design phase and query the designer about the consequences of these interactions.

Default theories are computationally intractable in principle because of the consistency checks required by their proof methods. Semantic networks provide an indexing scheme on first order formulae, but many other schemes are possible. An important role of indexing is the provision of an efficient heuristic for consistency checking without the need to perform deductions. Such consistency checks are prime examples of the kind of resource limited computations required in common sense reasoning.

Semi-normal default theories are complicated. They have none of the nice properties that make normal theories so appealing. Most of their formal properties are totally unexplored. At the very least a proof theory is needed, as well as conditions under which extensions are guaranteed to exist.

Acknowledgements—Many of the results and examples of this paper were inspired by a conversation that one of us (R.R.) had with N. Sridharan one afternoon in Vancouver. It was he who first pointed out to us the need for non normal defaults in common sense reasoning. We are also indebted to David Israel for his valuable comments on an earlier draft of this paper.

This work was done with the financial assistance of the National Science and Engineering Research Council of Canada Grant A7642. G. Criscuolo was sponsored by the Council for a 6-month research position with the Department of Computer Science at the University of British Columbia.

REFERENCES

1. R. Reiter, A logic for default reasoning. *Artificial Intell.* **13**, 81–132 (1980).
2. J. McCarthy, Circumscription—a form of non-monotonic reasoning. *Artificial Intell.* **13**, 27–39 (1980).
3. D. McDermott, Nonmonotonic logic II: nonmonotonic modal theories. *J. ACM* **29**(1), 33–57 (1982).
4. D. McDermott and J. Doyle, Non-monotonic logic I. *Artificial Intell.* **13**, 41–72 (1980).
5. M. Minsky, A framework for representing knowledge. In *The Psychology of Computer Vision* (Edited by P. Winston). McGraw-Hill, New York (1975).
6. D. G. Bobrow and T. Winograd, An overview of KRL, a knowledge representation language. *Cognitive Sci.* **1**(1), 3–46 (1977).
7. R. B. Roberts and I. Goldstein, The FRL Manual. *A.I. Memo No.* 409, MIT, Cambridge, Mass (1977).
8. P. J. Hayes, The logic of frames. *Tech. Rep.*, Dept of Computer Science, University of Essex, Colchester, U.K. (1977).
9. T. Winograd, Extended inference modes in reasoning by computer systems. *Artificial Intell.* **13**, 5–26 (1980).
10. L. K. Schubert, Extending the expressive power of semantic networks. *Artificial Intell.* **7**(2), 163–198 (1976).
11. W. A. Woods, What's in a link? In: *Representation and Understanding* (Edited by D. G. Bobrow and A. Collins), pp. 35–82. Academic Press, New York (1975).
12. R. Bechtel and S. C. Shapiro, A logic for semantic networks. Dept. of Computer Science, Indiana University, *Tech. Rep. No.* 47 (1976).
13. S. C. Shapiro, Path-based and node-based inference in semantic networks, *PROC. TINLAP II*, Urbana, Ill., pp. 219–225, July 1978.
14. T. Winograd, Frame representations and the declarative/procedural controversy. In *Representation and Understanding* (Edited by D. G. Bobrow and A. Collins), pp. 185–210. Academic Press, New York (1975).
15. P. J. Hayes, In defence of logic. *Proc. IJCAI-77*, pp. 559–565, MIT, Cambridge, Mass., 22–25 August 1977.
16. R. A. Kowalski, A proof procedure using connection graphs. *J. ACM* **22**, 572–595 (1974).
17. K. L. Clark and F. G. McCabe, IC-PROLOG reference manual. *CCD Rep.* 79/7, Imperial College, London (1979).
18. C. Kellog, P. Klahr and L. Travis, Deductive planning and pathfinding for relational data bases. In *Logic and Data Bases* (Edited by H. Gallaire and J. Minker), pp. 179–200. Plenum Press, New York (1978).
19. M. M. Hammer and D. J. McLeod, Semantic integrity in a relational data base system. *PROC. Int. Conf. on Very Large Data Bases*, Framington, Mass., 25–47 Sept. 1975.
20. J. M. Nicolas and K. Yazdanian, Integrity checking in deductive data bases. In *Logic and Data Bases* (Edited by H. Gallaire and J. Minker), pp. 325–344. Plenum Press, New York (1978).
21. R. Reiter, Data bases: a logical perspective, ACM SIGART, SIGMOD, SIGPLAN. *Proc. Workshop on Data Abstraction, Data Bases and Conceptual Modelling*, Pingree Park, Colorado, pp. 174–176, 23–26 June 1980.

Comp. & Maths. with Appls. Vol. 9, No. 1, pp. 29–43, 1983
Printed in Great Britain.

0097–4943/83/010029–15$03.00/0
Pergamon Press Ltd.

GENERATING LANGUAGE FROM CONCEPTUAL GRAPHS

JOHN F. SOWA

IBM Systems Research Institute, 205 East 42nd Street, New York, NY 10017, U.S.A.

Abstract—Conceptual graphs are a semantic representation that has a direct mapping to natural language. This article presents a universal algorithm for scanning the graphs, together with a version of augmented phrase-structure grammar for specifying the syntax of particular languages. When combined with a specific grammar, the universal algorithm determines a mapping from graphs to language with several important properties: multiple surface structures may be generated from a common underlying structure, constraints on the mapping result from the connectivity of the graphs rather than *ad hoc* assumptions, and the graphs combined with phrase-structure rules enforce context-sensitive conditions.

1. CONCEPTUAL GRAPHS

Conceptual graphs evolved as a semantic representation for natural language. The earliest forms, called *existential graphs*, were invented by the philosopher Charles Sanders Peirce[1] as a replacement for the linear notations of symbolic logic: Peirce was impressed by the diagrams of molecules in organic chemistry and believed that a graphical notation for logic could simplify the rules of inference. In linguistics, Tesnière[2] used similar notations for his *dependency grammar*. The earliest forms implemented on a computer were the *correlational nets* by Ceccato[3] and the *semantic nets* by Masterman[4]. Under various names, such as *conceptual dependency graphs*[5], *partitioned nets*[6], and *structured inheritance nets*[7], graph notations have become a popular form for representing knowledge. Although every author uses a different notation and terminology, certain themes are common to most versions:

• Concepts: Nodes of the graphs represent concepts of entities, attributes, events and states.

• Instances: Different nodes of the same concept type refer to different instances of that type, unless they are marked with a *name* or other symbol to indicate the same instance.

• Conceptual relations: Arcs of the graphs represent relationships that hold between the instances of the concepts they are linked to. Labels on the arcs indicate case relations as well as causal and logical links between propositions.

• Type hierarchy: Concepts are ordered according to levels of generality, such as COLLIE, DOG, ANIMAL, LIVING-THING, ENTITY. In various theories, the hierarchy may be a tree, a lattice, or a general acyclic graph.

Schemata: A commonly occurring pattern is represented by a stereotyped conceptual graph called a *schema*. Other terms for such patterns are *frames*, *scripts*, *MOPs* and *scenarios*.

• Inheritance: Schemata that represent properties of some type of concept are inherited by all subtypes of that concept.

Figure 1 shows a conceptual graph in the notation developed by Sowa[8]. The boxes represent concepts of entities (monkey, walnut, spoon, shell) and a concept of an action (an instance of eating). The circles represent conceptual relations: a monkey is the agent of eating, the object eaten is a walnut, the instrument of eating is a spoon, and the material of the spoon is a shell, which is a part of the same walnut that is being eaten. Although the graph notation is readable, it is difficult to type at a computer terminal; for ease of typing, the equivalent linear notation uses square brackets for concepts like [MONKEY] or [EAT] and rounded parentheses for conceptual relations like (AGNT) or (OBJ). Following is a linear representation of Fig. 1:

```
[EAT]-
    (AGNT)→[MONKEY]
    (OBJ)→[WALNUT:*x]
    (INST)→[SPOON]→(MATR)→[SHELL]←(PART)←[WALNUT:*x].
```

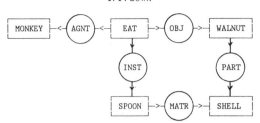

Fig. 1. A conceptual graph.

The hyphen "-" after the concept [EAT] indicates that the relations connected to [EAT] are continued on subsequent lines. If the graph has the form of a chain, it can be drawn on a single line; if it is a tree, it may be drawn on multiple lines with indentation and punctuation to show the tree structure; but if it contains a cycle, some concept node on the cycle must be repeated, and a variable symbol must be used to show cross references. In this case, the concept [WALNUT] was repeated, and the variable *x shows that both occurrences of [WALNUT] refer to the same entity.

The character strings written inside the boxes and circles of a conceptual graph are called *type labels*. Although some notations draw explicit arcs to show types and subtypes, such notations tend to look cluttered. Since the types are so pervasive, they are shown by labels inside the nodes instead of explicit arcs connecting box and circle nodes to definition nodes. A concept that has nothing but a type label (or a variable like *x) inside the box is called a *generic concept*; it refers to an unspecified individual of that type. An *individual concept* contains a serial number like #3829 or a name like Jocko after the type label; the name or serial number identifies a particular individual called the *referent* of the concept. Other kinds of referents that can occur inside concept boxes include sets, generic sets, partially specified sets and contexts containing one or more nested conceptual graphs. Following are examples of concepts with such referents and their readings in English phrases:

Kind of referent	*Notation*	*English reading*
Generic	[MONKEY]	a monkey
Individual	[MONKEY: #3829]	the monkey
Generic set	[MONKEY: {*}]	monkeys
Named individual	[MONKEY: Jocko]	Jocko
Set of individuals	[MONKEY: {Jocko, Mimi}]	Jocko and Mimi
Partially specified set	[MONKEY: {Jocko,*}]	Jocko and others

These English readings are simplified examples of the way a concept node can be mapped into an English word or phrase; the actual choice of articles, pronouns, names and modifiers depends on the entire context, including the speaker's implicit knowledge about the listener's expectations. The above table did not show a nested context as referent, since it would not fit in the available space. As an example, the next graph represents the sentence, *Sam thinks that Jocko loves Mimi*:

[PERSON: Sam]←(AGNT)←[THINK]→(OBJ)→[PROPOSITION:
    [MONKEY: Jocko]←(AGNT)←[LOVE]→(OBJ)→[MONKEY : Mimi]].

Nested contexts are used for embedded clauses, as in this example. They have also been used for logical operations, both in Peirce's existential graphs and in Hendrix's partitioned nets. Logic and model-theoretic denotations are discussed in [8]; this article concentrates on syntactic rules for mapping the graphs into natural language.

2. THE UTTERENCE PATH

The sequence of nodes and arcs that are traversed in mapping a graph to a sentence is called the *utterance path*. If conceptual graphs were always linear chains, the path could start at either end of the chain, visit each node in sequence, and utter the word that corresponds to each concept node. Since conceptual graphs are normally more complex than chains, the path would either have to skip some of the branches, or it would have to take a more circuitous walk that visits some nodes more than once. In a program for generating English, Quillian[9] chose the simple option of tracing a linear path through the graph and ignoring all side branches. McNeill[10], however, developed a psychologically motivated theory of the utterance path that permits more complex traversals. His primary motivation was to develop a theory of performance that could account not only for grammatical utterances, but also for false starts and errors.

The notion of an utterance path for scanning conceptual graphs has a great deal of explanatory power: it unifies observations about language typology and imposes strong, but well-motivated constraints on possible transformations. For complex graphs, the utterance path may visit a given concept node more than once. Various languages of the world are characterized by their preference for uttering the word at the first visit to a node, the last visit, or some intermediate visit:

● *Preorder languages* utter a word at the first visit to the corresponding concept node. Biblical Hebrew, which puts the verb first and puts nouns before the adjectives, is a preorder language.

● *Postorder languages* utter a word at the last visit to the concept node. An example is Japanese, which puts the verb last, puts nouns after the adjectives, and puts postpositions after the nouns.

● *Endorder languages* utter a word at an intermediate visit to the concept node. English and French, which put verbs in the middle, are approximately endorder languages. English, however, has a postorder tendency to put nouns after the adjectives, and French has a preorder tendency to put nouns in front of the adjectives, French is a closer approximation to an endorder language, since it puts some adjectives in front of the nouns and some after them, as in *un joli chapeau rouge* instead of the English form *a pretty red hat.*

The terms *preorder, postorder,* and *endorder* are the common names of different options for scanning trees and graphs. Since preorder languages put the verb first, subject next, and object last, they are also called *VSO languages.* Postorder languages are *SOV languages,* and endorder languages are *SVO languages.* Surveys of languages around the world have found that the three patterns, VSO, SOV and SVO are common, the pattern VOS is rare, and the patterns OSV and OVS do not occur as the default patterns in any known languages[11, 12]. For emphasis, however, most languages permit optional inversions, such as the following English sentence in OSV form:

His new-found friend he took with him to the park.

Such forms, which break the normal pattern of the language, are *marked forms* as opposed to the normal, unemphatic, *unmarked forms.*

A graph with multiple branches, such as Fig. 2, illustrates the possible options for mapping a conceptual graph into a sentence. The first step is to determine a cyclic walk that starts at the main predicate [DRINK] and visits every node at least once. A sequence of concept nodes visited in such a walk would be [DRINK], [BABY], [BLITHE], [BABY], [BELLY], [FAT], [BELLY], [BABY], [DRINK], [MILK], [FRESH], [MILK], [BOTTLE], [NEW], [BOTTLE], [MILK], [DRINK]. The concepts at the ends of the branches, [BLITHE], [FAT], [FRESH] and [NEW], are only visited once; for those concepts, the corresponding word must be uttered at the moment that the walk visits the node. The other concepts are visited several times, and the words could be uttered at any visit. The following four sentences show the order of uttering the words in an endorder language such as English (1), an endorder language such as French (2), a predorder language such as Hebrew (3), and a postorder language such as Japanese (4):

(1) Blithe babies with fat bellies drink fresh milk in new bottles.
(2) Babies blithe with bellies fat drink milk fresh in bottles new.
(3) Drink babies blithe with bellies fat milk fresh in bottles new.
(4) Fat bellies with blithe babies new bottles in fresh milk drink.

The *transformations* of transformational grammar[13] result from different options in scanning the graphs. In English, the passive transformation results from following the arc to (OBJ) before the arc to (AGNT). To show that a nonstandard scan is being made, English grammar rules insert function words and inflections: *are* before the main verb, *by* before the agent, and the past participle *drunk* instead of *drink*. When the passive rules are applied in scanning Fig. 2, the following sentence is generated:

>   Fresh milk in new bottles is drunk by blithe babies with fat bellies.

Any of the eight relations in Fig. 2 could have been chosen as the start of an utterance path. If the relation (PART) between [BABY:{*}] and [BELLY: {*}] had been chosen as the main link, the resulting sentence would be,

>   Blithe babies that drink fresh milk in new bottles have fat bellies.

In English sentences generated from conceptual graphs, the verbs *be* and *have* usually correspond to relations rather than concept nodes. Those verbs occur when the main predicate is not an action, but an attribute like *new* or a noun like *belly*. In such cases, a language like Russian does not require a verb and permits forms like *Bottles new* or *At blithe babies fat bellies*. English also uses the verb *do* as a place holder: if the concept [DRINK] is expressed as the subject rather than the verb, some verb form is needed by the grammar rules; since the concept [DRINK] has already been uttered, the rules insert the verb *do* at the point where the utterance path returns to the concept [DRINK]:

>   Drinking fresh milk in new bottles is done by blithe babies with fat bellies.

As these examples illustrate, the same graph can be expressed in many different sentences, depending on the starting point and direction of the utterance path. Yet not all word orders are possible: the utterance path visits each node a limited number of times, and a concept can be uttered as a word only at one of those visits.

These observations can be embodied in a universal algorithm for generating sentences from conceptual graphs: start at the conceptual relation linking the subject to the main predicate, traverse every arc of every conceptual relation, and utter the word corresponding to a concept at one of the visits to its node. Each language must specify further conditions for determining which visit to a concept is the one when its word is uttered. The following six rules for translating a conceptual graph into a sentence are adapted from Sowa[14]:

(1) The utterance path must visit each concept and relation node at least once. Associated

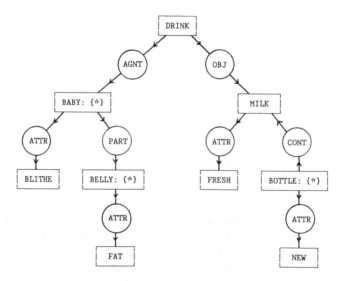

Fig. 2. A conceptual graph.

with each concept is an *utterance mark* that indicates whether the concept was uttered as a word, and with each conceptual relation a *traversal mark* that indicates whether the utterance path has traversed the arcs of that relation.

 • The conceptual relation that links the subject of the sentence to the main predicate is the starting point of the path. For simple active sentences, it is a relation of type AGNT; for passive sentences, it is a relation of type OBJ or RCPT; but in general, it may be a relation of any type.

 • From a concept node *c*, the path does not return to the concept from which *c* was reached until all relations linked to *c* have been traversed at least once.

 • For relations that have not yet been traversed, the syntactic and stylistic rules determine which arc to follow (e.g. in English, the path must visit adverbs of manner before adverbs of time).

(2) Since the path may visit a concept several times, syntactic rules determine when the concept is uttered as a word of the sentence. Some concept types may be expressed in some languages as two words (e.g. verb-particle combinations such as *take off* or *carry out*), which may be uttered at either the same or separate visits to the concept node.

(3) Adjacent concepts in the graph should be expressed consecutively when possible. When Rule 1 requires the utterance path to take a branch or when Rule 2 skips a concept, the utterance must clarify the order of connections with markers such as intonation, inflection, function words, or conventionalized word order.

(4) For graphs nested inside the type or referent field of a concept, the utterance path enters the nested graph when the syntactic rules determine that the containing node is to be expressed. Normally, the entire nested graph is expressed at a single visit to the node, but some syntax rules (such as the *raising rules* of transformational grammer) may permit the utterance path to exit from the nested graph, visit one or more nodes in the outer graph, and then return to finish expressing the nested graph.

(5) If the graph has cycles, a concept that is reachable by two or more different paths will only be uttered once with all of its qualifiers. If syntactic rules would also express the concept at a visit reached by a different path, they must instead generate an *anaphoric expression—* either a pronoun or a short noun phrase that has the minimum number of qualifiers needed for a unique reference in the current context.

(6) The utterance path is a cyclic walk that visits every node of the graph and returns to the concept that represents the main predicate. It a graph is complicated, rules of inference may break it into multiple simpler graphs before expressing it in a sentence.

These six rules allow considerable variation of word order, but they do not permit arbitrary movement of sentence constituents. If conceptual graphs are assumed to be universal deep structures and if all languages obey the same general rules for mapping graphs to sentences, then all languages must show certain regularities in their surface structures. Following are some of the implications:

 • A concept may only be expressed when the utterance path visits its node. Therefore, transformations can move a given constituent only to a limited number of positions in a sentence. Unlike transformational grammar, which requires special assumptions to rule out the unnatural transformations, the rules for scanning conceptual graphs have the correct restrictions built into them.

 • Rules 1 and 6 limit the number of times a node may be visited. In particular, when the path follows a branch of modifiers, all concepts on that branch must be expressed before the walk returns to the main concept.

 • Rule 3 prevents deeply embedded clauses like "The mailman that the dog that the girl that the boy loves owns bit is in the park." Such a sentence skips every other concept in a chain as the walk passes in one direction; on the way back, it skips the ones that were expressed in the first direction. Since the single function word *that* is not sufficient to show which concepts were skipped, that sentence violates the rule. Preferred versions utter adjacent concepts in adjacent content words—either in the active form "The boy loves the girl that owns the dog that bit the mailman that is in the park" or the passive form "In the park is the mailman that was bitten by the dog that is owned by the girl that is loved by the boy."

 • Rule 4 for nested graphs has the same effect as the *cyclic convention* for applying transformations: all the transformations that apply to embedded clauses are performed before those that apply to higher clauses. But it slso permits *raising* [15], where constituents of a nested graph are expressed at different visits to the containing node. Consider the following graph:

$$[\text{BELIEVE}] \rightarrow (\text{OBJ}) \rightarrow [\text{PROPOSITION: } [\text{PERSON: Ivan}] \leftarrow (\text{CONT}) \leftarrow [\text{KITCHEN}]].$$

Since this graph does not include any concept that could be used as a subject for the verb *believe*, the default in English is to use an empty word like *it*:

It is believed that Ivan is in the kitchen.

But another rule of English grammar allows Ivan to be raised to the subject position of the main clause:

Ivan is believed to be in the kitchen.

In generating this sentence, the utterance path enters the nested graph to utter *Ivan*, exists from it to utter the concept [BELIEVE], and then returns to the nested graph to finish the sentence.

3. AUGMENTED PHRASE STUCTURE GRAMMAR

Since the universal rules for translating graphs to sentences allow many options, they must be supplemented with particular rules for any specific language. The specific grammar determines which arc to select first when more than one arc attached to the current node remains to be traversed. It must also specify additional markers such as word inflections and function words. The most general and flexible notation for stating the particular rules is *augmented phrase structure grammar* (APSG), which Heidorn[16, 17] developed for his NLP system. APSG rules have an underlying skeleton of phrase-structure grammar, but they are *augmented* with conditions to be tested and actions to be performed. Heidorn's NLP supports two types of APSG rules: *encoding rules* generate linear text from graphs, and *decoding rules* generate a graph representation of the meaning of a text when parsing.

A common way to write an APSG rule is to start with a standard context-free grammar rule. Then conditions for applying the rule are added on the left of the arrow, and actions are added for each nonterminal symbol on the right of the arrow. As an example, consider the rule that defines a sentence S as a noun phrase NP followed by a verb phrase VP:

$$S \rightarrow NP \; VP.$$

This rule does not show how the NP and VP are derived from a conceptual graph, nor does it show how the person and number from the NP can affect the form of the VP. In an APSG rule, each occurrence of a nonterminal symbol like NP or VP represents a record of *attributes* that may be set of tested. The symbol on the left of the arrow represents the current goal, such as generate a sentence. That symbol is followed by *conditions* that must be true before the rule is invoked. On the right of the arrow, each symbol is followed by a list of *actions* for setting attributes or advancing the current concept node to the next node of the utterance path.Following is the general form of an APSG rule, but with English comments instead of formal symbols:

S (conditions for applying this rule)→
NP (actions for moving the current concept node to the subject and getting the person and number from the current concept)
VP (actions for moving the current concept node to the main ACT, for copying person and number from the NP record, and for copying mode and tense from the S record).

Heidorn's encoding rules have this general form, but with a more succinct, formal notation inside the parentheses. The remainder of this section develops a notation that is based on Heidoin's APSG, but with symbols and terminology adapted to conceptual graphs. The technique of associating attributes with the nonterminal symbols is closely related to *attribute grammars* [18].

APSG rules are a kind of *production rules* that are common in A.I. systems: the l.h.s. of each rule states the conditions for invoking it, and the r.h.s. states some actions to be taken, which typically cause other rules to be invoked later. The conditions and actions operate on *records* that are associated with each of the nonterminal symbols in the rules. The symbol on the left of the rule (S in the above example) is the goal to be satisfied; the symbols on the right (NP and VP in the example) are subgoals to be achieved. There is a special symbol, called the *start symbol*, whose record is created by some high-level process. That symbol (S in this example) triggers the first production rule. That rule then creates new records for NP and VP, which then trigger other rules. The process continues until terminal symbols are reached that generate the actual words of the sentence. In general, the conceptual graph contains semantic information for generating sentences, and the attributes in the records contain syntactic information as well as certain semantic information like mode and tense attributes that are passed from one record to another.

Conditions in APSG rules may test several things: attributes in the current record, the current concept or relation node of the conceptual graph, concepts and relations linked to the current node, or the utterance marks on concepts and traversal marks on conceptual relations. The conditions have the following form:

> attribute "is" ["not"] test;

A rule may have zero or more of these conditions. If there are no conditions, the parentheses after the nonterminal symbol are omitted; if there are two or more conditions, they are separated by semicolons. Following are some examples of typical conditions:

> type (○) is AGNT;
> *referent* (□) is not proper name;
> number is PLURAL;
> tense is not present;
> □→ATTR is not traversed;

In the conditions and actions, □ refers to the current concept node of the conceptual graph, and ○ refers to the current conceptual relation. The functions *type* and *referent* may be applied to one of the nodes: *type*(□) or *type*(○) retrieves the type label from the current node, and *referent*(□) retrieves the referent of the current concept. If the attribute is just a single word like *number* or *tense*, it refers to the record associated with the current nonterminal symbol; the third condition above tests whether the current record has a plural number, and the fourth one tests whether the tense attribute is missing. The symbol □→ATTR refers to the subgraph consisting of the current concept node □ linked by an arc pointing to a conceptual relation of type ATTR.

On the right side of the arrow, three kinds of actions may occur: assignment, move and mark. The assignment assigns values to the attributes in a record, move specifies the direction of movement along the utterance path, and mark indicates which nodes had already been visited.

● When an APSG rule is invoked, none of the records for the symbols on the right of the arrow have any associated attributes. An assignment action causes a new attribute to be created for a record and assigns it a value:

> voice := ACTIVE;
> number := number of *referent*(□);
> tense := tense of VP;

The first assignment simply causes the voice attribute of the current record to have the value ACTIVE. The second one copies the number of the referent of the current concept to the number attribute of the current record. The third one copies the tense of a VP record to the tense of the current record; such copies may only be made from a record of a nonterminal symbol in the current rule that occurs *before* the symbol to which the copy is being made.

 • Move causes the symbol □ or ○ to advance to the next node of the utterance path. All records in a rule start with the node □ at the same point; a move action for a given record affects only that record and not any other record in the rule.

move AGNT→□;

move OBJ←□;

The first move causes the current concept node to become the one linked to the arc pointing *away* from the relation of type AGNT. The second one causes the current concept to be the one linked to the arc pointing *towards* the relation of type AGNT.

 • Mark sets the utterance mark on a concept or the traversal mark on a conceptual relation:

mark □→ATTR traversed;

mark □ uttered;

The first one sets the traversal mark on the relation of type ATTR that is linked to the current concept node, and the second sets the utterance mark on the current concept node.

The symbol □ is the equivalent of a *cursor* that advances from left to right when a linear language is being parsed. Since conceptual graphs are not linear, □ is not automatically advanced, and the rules must include explicit move actions to advance □ and mark actions to keep it from returning to previously visited nodes.

With this notation for conditions and actions, the APSG rule that defines S may be stated. The condition for invoking the S rule is that the current relation node ○ must be of type AGNT:

```
S(type(○) is AGNT)→
    NP (move AGNT→□; mark AGNT→□ traversed;
      case := NOMINATIVE
      person := person of referent(□);
      number := number of referent(□))
    VP (move AGNT←□; voice :=ACTIVE;
      tense := tense of S; mode := mode of S;
      person := person of NP; number := number of NP).
```

On the right of the arrow, the actions for the NP record move the current concept node □ to the concept attached to the arc pointing away from the node ○, mark ○ traversed so that no other rule will traverse it again, set the case attribute NOMINATIVE (needed for pronouns, but not for nouns in English), and finally get the person and number attributes from □. The actions for VP move the node □ to the concept attached to the arc pointing towards ○, set the voice attribute ACTIVE, copy the tense and mode attributes from the original S node, and copy the person and number attributes from the record for the preceding NP node.

If sentence generation had started at a relation of type other than AGNT, the preceding rule would not apply. In that case, the system would search for another rule. If the starting relation had been of type OBJ, it would generate a sentence in passive voice:

```
S(type(○) is OBJ)→
    NP (move OBJ→□; mark OBJ→□ traversed;
      case := NOMINATIVE;
      person := person of referent(□);
      number := number of referent(□);
    VP (move OBJ←□; voice := PASSIVE;
```

tense := tense of S; mode := mode of S;
person := person of NP; number := number of NP).

The form of this rule is identical to the previous one, but the voice attribute of the VP record is now set to PASSIVE, and the NP node is generated from the object of the action instead of the agent. Other rules that apply to a VP record in passive voice will generate a form of the verb *be* and the preposition *by* for the agent (if it is present in the graph).

Unlike transformational grammar, APSG rules need no global movement operations that transpose subject and object. When sentence generation is started at OBJ instead of AGNT, the rules methodically move from node to node in the conceptual graph and end up with a globally well-formed passive sentence. At no time do the rules ever consider anything but local information in nearby nodes of a conceptual graph or records in the current APSG rule. The following rule expands a VP in passive voice in order to generate a form of the verb *be* followed by the main verb as a past participle:

VP (voice is PASSIVE)→
    VERB (type := BE; tense := tense of VP; mode := mode of VP;
        person := person of VP; number := number of VP)
    VP (form := PASTPART).

The VERB record has the verb type set to BE; the tense, mode, person, and number are copied from the original VP record on the left. The only attribute for the new VP record on the right of the arrow is the form attribute set to PASTPART. The new VP no longer has any information about tense, mode, person, or number. The type of the main verb is not stated in the record; the type will be copied from the current node of the conceptual graph when it is needed.

Passive verb phrases can be generated either for main verbs in passive voice or for participial phrases modifying nouns, as in the following sentences:

The books were distributed by the teacher.
Norma ordered books distributed by the teacher.

In both sentences, the phrase, *distributed by the teacher*, has exactly the same form and, for economy, should be generated by exactly the same grammar rules. Following is an APSG rule for noun phrases modified by past participial phrases:

NP (□←OBJ is not traversed)→
    NP (mark OBJ traversed; case := case of NP)
    VP (move OBJ←□; form := PASTPART).

Transformational grammar generates participial phrases by deletions from relative clauses. Yet clauses are more cumbersome, complex constructions than participial phrases. With APSG rules, participial phrases and infinitives can be generated directly by the simpler rules, and clauses are generated as special options for greater emphasis.

The AGNT relation is expressed by the preposition *by* in passive verb phrases, but it is not expressed by any special morpheme in a simple active sentence. The following rule generates a prepositional phase for the agent in passive form:

VP (form is PASTPART; □→AGNT is not traversed)→
    VP (form := PASTPART; mark AGNT traversed)
    PP (type := BY; move AGNT→□).

The concept [BOOK: {*}], which is uttered as *books*, is the object of both [ORDER] and [DISTRIBUTE] in the following graph:

[PEARSON: Normal]→(AGNT)→[ORDER]-
    (OBJ)→[BOOK: {*}]←(OBJ)←(DISTRIBUTE]←(AGNT)←[TEACHER: #8197].

If the utterance path starts at the AGNT relation attached to [ORDER], APSG rules generate the sentence,

       Norma ordered books distributed by the teacher.

If the path had started at the AGNT relation linked to [DISTRIBUTE], the same rules would generate the sentence,

       The teacher distributed books ordered by Norma.

Verb phrases may also include adverbs, direct objects, indirect objects and prepositional phrases. Following is a rule that generates adverbs:

       VP (□→MANR is not traversed)→
          ADV (move MANR→□; mark MANR traversed)
          VP (vform := vform of VP).

To simplify the amount of copying that must be done, attributes may be grouped: vform is the collection of tense, mode, person and number that may be copied with a single assignment. The next rule generates direct objects:

       VP (□→OBJ is not traversed)→
       VP (vform := vform of VP)
       NP (move OBJ→□; mark OBJ traversed;
          case := OBJECTIVE).

After all of the conceptual relations attached to the concept node corresponding to the main verb have been processed, the following rule generates the verb itself:

       VP→VERB(type := *type*(□); vform := vform of VP).

In determining which rule to execute next, the system performs the first rule for the current nonterminal symbol for which the conditions are true. The simple rule that defines VP as just a VERB should therefore be the last one in the list for VP; since it has no conditions, it will always succeed, and no subsequent VP rule would ever be performed.

    To generate noun phrases, the next rule defines NP as a sequence of determiner, adjective, and noun:

       NP (*referent*(□) not proper name; □→ATTR not traversed)→
       DET (get referent from □)
       ADJ (move ATTR→□; mark ATTR traversed)
       NOUN (get type, number from □).

This rule would only apply if the referent of the current node □ was not a proper name and if the node □ was linked to a relation of type ATTR. The action associated with DET extracts information from the referent of □, the action for ADJ moves along the utterance path to the node on the other side of the ATTR relation, and the action for NOUN extracts the type and the number of the referent from the node □.

    After the phrase-structure rules have been applied, lower-level, *lexical rules* must be used to generate the actual words of the language. The lexical rules take into account the concept type, the syntactic category, and other attributes of the nonterminal symbol. What they generate is a character string (or in the case of spoken language, a phonemic representation):

       NOUN (type is BABY; number is PLURAL)→"babies".
       NOUN (type is BABY; number is SINGULAR)→"baby".
       VERB (type is DRINK; tense is PAST)→"drank".

The same concept type may be mapped into different word forms for different syntactic categories:

> NOUN (type is DISTRIBUTE; number is SINGULAR)→"distribution".
> VERB (type is DISTRIBUTE; number is PLURAL; tense is PRESENT)→
> "distribute".

In principle, a separate lexical rule may be stated for every word form. In practice, however, a unified morphological stage would look up each concept type in a dictionary and generate the appropriate word for it. The morphological stage could take account of regular rules like $-s$ for most plural nouns and would only need special rules for exceptions. It could be a much simpler routine than the APSG processor since it would only have to consider adjacent words in order to generate the article *a* before a consonant or *an* before a vowel.

Generating correct articles in English is difficult because the words *the* and *a* have many different uses. At the first mention of an object, the indefinite article *a* introduces it, but subsequent references use the definite article *the* to refer back to it. Often, however, *the* is used to refer to an object that is implicitly introduced into the context:

> Do you have a 1982 penny? I want to check the weight.

Although the weight of the coin was not explicitly mentioned, all of the usual attributes of an object may be assumed as part of the current context whenever the object itself is introduced. Besides the use of articles for individuals, both *the* and *a* may be used in a generic sense:

> The horse is a noble animal.

> A dog is an animal.

A complete study of English articles would require a major treatise. As illustrations, the following three APSG rules generate *the* if the concept is individual, generate *a* if it is generic, and generate the empty string ϵ if it is a generic set (plural):

> DET (*referent*(□) is individual)→"the".
> DET (*referent*(□) is generic)→"a".
> DET (*referent*(□) is {*})→ϵ.

The conditions inside the parentheses could be elaborated to handle other versions of English grammar that make finer distinctions.

Prepositions are usually generated from conceptual relations rather than concept nodes. They are especially sensitive to the direction of the utterance path. Consider the following subgraph of Fig. 2:

> [BABY: {*}]→(PART)→[BELLY: {*}].

If the utterance path is moving from [BABY] to [BELLY], the resulting phrase would be *babies with bellies*. But if it is moving from [BELLY] to [BABY], the result would be *bellies of babies*. Unlike lexical rules for nouns and verbs, the rules for generating prepositions depend on the direction of the utterance path. Following is a rule for generating prepositional phrases:

> PP→
> PREP (copy type, direction from PP)
> NP (set case OBJECTIVE).

Since there are no conditions on the left, this rule applies whenever any prepositional phrase is being generated. Since there is no move stated in the action lists, both PREP and NP have the same □ node as PP. The type and direction are copied from the PP record to the PREP record.

and the NP record has the case attribute set to OBJECTIVE. In English, the case is needed for pronouns, but it is ignored for nouns; other languages would set different case attributes for NP depending on the relation type. The lexical rules for prepositions come in pairs depending on the direction of the utterance path. Following are the rules for the PART and CONT (content) relations:

PREP (type is PART; direction is→)→"of".
PREP (type is PART; direction is ←)→"with".
PREP (type is CONT; direction is →)→ "with".
PREP (type is CONT; direction is ←)→"in".

Note that there is no one-to-one mapping between relations and prepositions: the preposition *with* could have been generated for the types PART and CONT in these rules as well as for INST (instrument) and ACCM (accompaniment).

One of Fillmore's principles of case grammar[19] is that the agent if present becomes the subject; if the agent is missing, then the next choice for subject is the instrument. In APSG rules, that principle would be implemented with a rule like the following:

S(type(O) is INST)→
    NP (move INST→□; mark INST traversed; get person and number from □)
    VP (move INST←□; set voice ACTIVE; copy person and number from NP).

If the earlier rule for S failed, then this would be the next one tried. If these conditions also failed, then the system would continue to scan the list of rules for S until it found one whose conditions were satisfied. At the end of the list, there could be a default rule like the following that would print an error message:

S→ "Sorry, I don't know how to say what I mean."

Since this rule has no conditions, it will always succeed if invoked. But since it isn't very helpful, it is a last resort.

To generate a sentence in Japanese, the following rule could be used to generate the SOV word order. The rule also sets attributes of the noun phrases to generate the postpositions *ga* and *o*, which indicate subject and object in Japanese:

S (AGNT and OBJ links present & not yet traversed)→
    NP (select node linked to AGNT, set postposition GA)
    NP (select node linked to OBJ, set postposition O)
    VERB (mark AGNT an OBJ links traversed).

Appropriate changes in the rules could generate the word orders for any of the other languages, such as Hebrew or French. Type labels like BIRD and BABY happen to look like English words, but they represent abstract concepts. For generating French, lexical rules like the following could be used:

NOUN (type is BIRD; number is SINGULAR)→"oiseau".
NOUN (type is BIRD; number is PLURAL)→"oiseaux".

Although the APSG rules described in this section have never been implemented in exactly the form described here, they are adapted from the encoding rules in Heidorn's NLP system and could be mapped into those rules on a one-for-one basis. The primary difference is that these APSG rules have been specialized to the notation for conceptual graphs, but NLP rules can process other kinds of graphs as well. The following passage was generated by Heidorn's NLPQ system[16] using APSG rules similar to the ones described in this paper:

The vehicles arrive at the station. The time between arrivals of the vehicles at the station is normally distributed, with a mean of 8 min and a standard deviation of 2 min. Seventy-five percent of the vehicles are cars, and the rest are trucks. After arriving at the station, if the length of the line at the pump in the station is less than 2, the vehicles will be serviced at the pump in the station. Otherwise, the vehicles will leave the station. The time for the vehicles to be serviced at the pump in the station is exponentially distributed, with a mean of 5 min for the cars, and 9 min for the trucks. After being serviced at the pump in the station, the vehicles leave the station. (p. 5).

The same graph structure that was mapped into this English passage could also be mapped into other languages—computer languages as well as natural languages. For NLPQ, Heidorn wrote two sets of encoding rules. One set produced the English paragraph above, and the other set mapped the graphs into a program in the GPSS simulation language.

4. MAPPING GRAMMAR, RATHER THAN GENERATIVE GRAMMAR

Speaking involves three stages: determining what to say, how to relate it to the listener, and how to map it into a string of words. In terms of conceptual graphs, the first stage is the selection of some graph or collection of graphs to be expressed. The second stage uses pragmatic concerns to select the starting point and direction of the utterance path, which determines which concept will be the subject and which will be the main predicate. The third stage scans the graph and maps concepts into words. Determining what to say and how to relate it to the listener involves issues of inference and pragmatics that are treated in Sowa[8]; this article has presented the third stage of using APSG rules to map a graph to a sentence.

In generating sentences, APSG rules are invoked in a top-down, goal-directed fashion. The algorithm starts with a single goal—generate sentence, generate paragraph, or even generate story. The initial goal contains a pointer to some node of a conceptual graph: if the goal is to generate a sentence, the pointer would usually select a concept corresponding to the main verb; if the goal is to generate a paragraph or story, the pointer might select a time-ordered sequence of actions, each of which represents a single sentence. The rule invoked for the initial goal makes some tests on the conceptual graph and generates other subgoals —generate noun phrase or generate verb phrase—each of which makes its own tests and generates further subgoals down to the lowest level goals like generating a present tense, third-person, singular form to *be*. As each rule invokes other rules as subgoals, the APSG processor makes a cyclic walk of the conceptual graph: the goal of generating a sentence starts at the relation between subject and main predicate, that goal generates a subgoal that follows the AGNT link to the subject, which may in turn generate further subgoals that follow links for adjectives and other modifiers. When each subgoal is finished, the walk returns to the node that invoked it. At the end, the highest-level subgoal returns to the topmost goal, which corresponds to the starting node of the conceptual graph.

Unlike parsing programs, which use many different techniques, most language generators are based on top-down algorithms, but with different notations and terminology. Simmons and Slocum[20] and Wong[21] use *augmented transition nets*, which are also executed in a top-down fashion. Wong took care to generate correct anaphoric expressions: when introducing an event, his program would say, for example, *A boy broke a window*; but when referring back to the boy, it would say *he, the boy*, or *the boy who broke the window*, depending on the amount of detail needed to specify the referent uniquely. Goldman's BABEL[22] is a top-down program for mapping Schank's conceptual dependency graphs into English. One of Goldman's innovations was to make word choices based on *word-sense discrimination nets*. Since Schank's theory now permits high-level concept types like ADMIT and THREATEN, the major discriminations could be made by an earlier inference stage. BABEL, however, had to make all the word choices itself since its input graphs contained only low-level primitives. Although these authors do not use the term *utterance path* and they do not use the APSG notation, at an abstract level, their algorithms are similar: they execute rules in a top-down order, the graph serves as a control for determining which rules to select, and the order of processing nodes may be described as an utterance path.

Although APSG rules have an underlying skeleton that resembles Chomsky's phrase-structure rules, it is more accurate to call them a mapping grammar, rather than a generative grammar. The theory presented in this article meets Chomsky's original goals of relating multiple surface structures to a common deep structure, but with some major advantages:

● Psychological naturalness: Generation is done by rules of inference and pragmatics, which deal with meaning, rather than rules of syntax that only deal with the forms of expression.

● Computational efficiency: Unlike transformational rules that move large constituents during the generation stage, APSG rules obtain the effects of transformations by changing the direction of the utterance path rather than by moving words and phrases. Since the rules generate words one at a time as they are uttered, they reduce the demands either on human short-term memory or on computer storage.

● Theoretical simplicity: Constraints on transformations arise from the connectivity of the graphs and the possible ways of scanning them. No special assumptions are needed to block transformations that never occur in natural languages because those transformations violate the universal rules that govern the utterance path.

To give a detailed comparison of the conceptual graph theory with transformational grammar is beyond the scope of this article. But the notion of *traces* [23] illustrates the difference between the two approaches: a trace is a residue of a noun phrase that has been moved by a transformation; it has no sound itself, but it changes the intonation pattern of the sentence and blocks certain kinds of contractions. The following example shows the trace *t* that is left when *what* is moved to the front of a sentence by the question transformation:

> Ruby gave what to Clara?
> What did Ruby give *t* to Clara?

In terms of Chomsky's approach, a trace is like a "silent pronoun" that is left behind when a noun phrase is moved from one position in a sentence to another. In terms of conceptual graphs, such fictitious pronouns are not needed: the point at which a trace occurs is a point where the utterance path visits a concept whose utterance mark is set on. The blocking of contractions is caused by a break in normal processing when the utterance path stops at a node and bypasses it. As this example illustrates, conceptual graphs can explain the same kinds of phenomena as transformational grammar, but with fewer *ad hoc* assumptions and a less cumbersome formalism.

Acknowledgements—I would like to thank George Heidorn and Karen Jensen for a number of comments and suggestions that have helped to improve the content and presentation of this paper.

REFERENCES

1. C. S. Peirce, Unpublished manuscripts summarized in D. D. Roberts, *The Existential Graphs of Charles S. Peirce.* Mouton, The Hague (1973).
2. L. Tesnière, *Elements de Syntaxe Structurale*, 2nd Edn. Librairie C. Klincksieck, Paris (1965).
3. S. Ceccato, *Linguistic Analysis and Programming for Mechanical Translation.* Gordon & Breach, New York (1961).
4. M. Masterman, Semantic message detection for machine translation, using an interlingua. *Proc. 1961 Int. Conf. on Machine Translation*, pp. 438–475 (1961).
5. R. C. Schank and G. Tesler, A conceptual parser for natural language. *Proc. IJCAI-69*, pp. 569–578 (1969).
6. G. G. Hendrix, Expanding the utility of semantic networks through partitioning. In *Proc. IJCAI-75*, pp. 115–121 (1975).
7. R. J. Brachman, On the epistemological status of semantic networks. In *Associative Networks: Representation and Use of Knowledge by Computers* (Edited by N. V. Findler), pp. 3–50. Academic Press, New York (1979).
8. J. F. Sowa, *Conceptual Structures: Information Processing in Mind and Machine.* Addison-Wesley, Reading, Mass. (1983).
9. M. R. Quillian, Semantic memory. *Rep. AD-641671*, Clearinghouse for Federal Scientific and Technical Information.
10. D. McNeill, *The Conceptual Basis of Language.* Lawrence Erlbaum, Hillsdale, New Jersey (1979).
11. J. H. Greenberg, Some universals of grammar with particular reference to the order of meaningful elements. In *Universals of Language* (Edited by J. H. Greenberg), pp. 58–90. MIT Press, Cambridge, Mass (1963).
12. S. Steele, Word order variation: a typological study. In *Universals of Human Language* (Edited by J. H. Greenbrg), 4 vols., pp. 585–623. Stanford University Press, Stanford, Calif. (1978).
13. N. Chomsky, *Syntactic Structures.* Mouton & Co., The Hague (1957).
14. J. F. Sowa, Conceptual structures: A model for language. Unpublished manuscript (1968).
15. P. M. Postal, *On Raising.* MIT Press, Cambridge, Mass. (1974).
16. G. E. Heidorn, Natural language inputs to a simulation programming system. *Rep. NPS-55HD72101A*, Naval Postgraduate School, Monterey (1972).

17. G. E. Heidorn, Augmented phrase structure grammar. In *Theoretical Issues in Natural Language Processing* (Edited by R. Schank and B. L. Nash-Webber) pp. 1–5.
18. D. E. Knuth, Semantics of context-free languages. *Math. Systems Theory* **2**, 127–145.
19. C. J. Fillmore, The case for case. In *Universals in Linguistic Theory* (Edited by E. Bach and R. T. Harms), pp. 1–88. Holt, Rinehart & Winston, New York (1968).
20. R. F. Simmons and J. Slocum, Generating English discourse from semantic networks. *Commun. ACM* **15**, 891–905 (1972).
21. H. K. T. Wong, Generating English Sentences from Semantic Structures. *Tech. Rep.* 84, Dept of Computer Science, University of Toronto (1975).
22. N. M. Goldman, Conceptual generation. In *Conceptual Information Processing* (Edited by R. C. Schank) pp. 289–371. North-Holland, Amsterdam (1975).
23. N. Chomsky, Conditions on rules of grammar. In *Current Issues in Linguistic Theory* (Edited by R. W. Cole), pp. 3–50. Indiana University Press, Bloomington (1977).

Comp. & Maths. with Appls. Vol. 9, No. 1, pp. 45–58, 1983
Printed in Great Britain.

0097–4943/83/010045–14$03.00/0
Pergamon Press Ltd.

SEMANTIC PROCESSING OF TEXTS IN RESTRICTED SUBLANGUAGES

RICHARD I. KITTREDGE

University of Montreal, Montreal, Canada H3C 3J7

Abstract—Practical results in information retrieval and automatic translation have recently been achieved for naturally-occurring texts in certain narrow technical areas. For each application, the processing system must exploit the distinctive linguistic properties of the appropriate sublanguage; in fact, a precise description of these properties, incorporated into a sublanguage grammer and lexicon, is what enables the system to build a representation of the information (meaning) conveyed by the text.

Sublanguages which appear insufficiently closed for semantic processing often carry an important component of information which is encoded in a linguistically well-behaved way and is hence computationally separable. By way of illustration, a procedure is outlined for processing stock market reports into a predicate-argument representation of their content, for that part of the report which refers to the stock exchange activity. The procedure may have applications beyond information retrieval, in particular to the synthesis of informative stock market reports in one or more languages.

1. SEMANTIC PROCESSING OF "REAL" TEXTS

Computational linguistics as a (more or less well-defined) discipline can now be considered about 30 yr old (the first experiments in machine translation were carried out in the early 1950s). But is is only in the last few years that significant advances have occurred in processing the content (or meaning) of texts.

Substantial progress has been made both in constructing theoretical models for the meaning representation of texts and in implementing these models in experimental computer systems. In the early 1970s, impressive semantic capabilities were demonstrated in systems whose input was restricted to examples constructed by the experimenters. But since then it has proved quite difficult to extend those results to large samples of "real" (naturally occurring) texts, such as those which must be processed in many commercial applications. The reason for this seems to be that no powerful semantic model has been worked out in sufficient detail to accommodate the overwhelming variety of words and structures that one typically finds in arbitrary real texts.

In certain application areas, the problem of incomplete semantic modelling can be partially circumvented. For example, in the case of systems for querying restricted data bases, a "semantic grammar"[1, 2] can be set up to describe and interpret a subset of sentences which is adequate for the particular purposes of the system. Each sentence pattern recognized by the system is formulated in terms of semantic word classes, a fact which greatly reduces the possibility of misunderstanding queries. During dialogs with a human user the system provides instant feedback which helps the user to stay within the predefined limits. For example, when the system receives queries which are not formulated in accordance with its grammar or vocabulary, it may guide the user to rephrase his input. Human linguistic performance is therefore constrained in the direction of the system's capacities.

In other application areas, however, there may be no possibility of reformulating the natural language input. This is typically the case in automatic translation and information retrieval from documents, where the wide variety of semantic problems posed by real texts must be tackled head-on. Because of this, there is a growing consensus among researchers in these areas that (a) only texts from highly restricted domains will be amenable to semantic processing in the near future, and that (b) any practical system must be based on a thorough empirical description of the language as it is actually used in the subfield in which the texts originate.

In this paper we set out to do two things. First, we summarize briefly some recent results in the semantic processing of real texts for the purposes of automatic translation and information retrieval. These results illustrate the needs for restricting the domain and for carrying out a detailed linguistic analysis within the appropriate sublanguage. Second, we outline a procedure for automatically deriving semantic representations of texts in certain restricted sublanguages. To illustrate the procedure, we give an example of the analysis of a stock market report into a predicate-argument representation of the data contained in the report. Our illustration suggests direct application to problems of information retrieval from texts. But since many of the individual steps are reversible in principle, it also suggests how one might approach the problems of automatic translation and automatic synthesis of text from data, at least in such restricted sublanguages.

2. THREE PRACTICAL APPLICATIONS OF SEMANTIC PROCESSING TO REAL TEXTS

Computational linguists are achieving some initial successes in processing the content of technical sublanguages by basing each applied system on the linguistic analysis of a large corpus of representative texts. Before discussing the methodology of this approach, we survey briefly the scope and limitations of sublanguage processing of three kinds of text.

2.1 Automatic translation of weather bulletins

Automatic translation may have been the earliest practical goal of computational linguistics but it was not until recently that translation systems began to actually ease the load on human translators. One of the most successful cases has been the TAUM-METEO system, developed at the Université de Montréal, which since 1977 has been translating English weather bulletins into French of 10,000 words/day for the Canadian environment ministry [33].

METEO is designed to translate only those sentences in weather bulletins which are in telegraphic style such as (1).

(1) RAIN OCCASIONALLY MIXED WITH SLEET TODAY CHANGING TO SNOW THIS EVENING.

This is because more than 99% of bulletin sentences conform to this style and those sentences can be translated with virtually no errors. But weather bulletins may occasionally contain non-telegraphic sentences such as (2).

(2) PERSONS IN OR NEAR THIS AREA SHOULD BE ON THE LOOKOUT FOR THESE SEVERE WEATHER CONDITIONS AND WATCH FOR UPDATED WARNINGS.

In the presence of dangerous or unusual weather conditions, forecasters tend to abandon telegraphic style and resort to full sentence forms. The METEO parser rejects such sentences; instead, the system sends them to a terminal where a human translator provides the French equivalents, which are then inserted into the computer-translated text to give the complete French bulletin.

It is no coincidence that METEO, one of the most reliable systems for automatic translation, is limited to one of the most restricted, stereotyped sublanguages known. Successful translation depends on the fact that weather reports normally carry only a few kinds of information, and this information is encoded linguistically in very predictable ways, both in English and in French. The two languages have similar telegraphic styles in their respective sublanguages. Even if words cannot be mapped one-to-one between the two sublanguages, the semantic word classes and relations between classes define structures which are roughly isomorphic. The linguistic predictability which the system exploits in normal texts breaks down only in sentences where unusual kinds of information are being conveyed. In fact, the occasional shift from telegraphic to non-telegraphic style is an unmistakable sign of a shift from normal to abnormal (i.e. less predictable) information type.

2.2 Automatic translation of aircraft maintenance manuals

A second, far more difficult type of technical text has been the subject of a 5-yr research and development effort in automatic translation at the Université de Montréal. The TAUM-AVIATION system [4] is designed to translate English aircraft maintenance manuals into French in the field of aviation hydraulics The sublanguage of these manuals is linguistically quite complex, with a vocabulary of over 10,000 words (not counting proper or compound nouns) and a wide variety of problematic syntactic structures.

The domain of reference of hydraulics manuals is more complex than that of weather forecasting by several orders of magnitude. The possible physical objects which must be named in these texts number in the millions and their possible functions are also quite varied. As a consequence, the system of noun compounding is quite rich. For example, a general grammar of English will permit the "empilage" in (3) to be parsed in many ways, including (3a) and (3b):

(3) wing fold logic tree diagram
(3a) ((wing fold) ((logic tree) diagram))
(3b) (((wing fold) logic) (tree diagram))

where the left member of each parenthesized pair is taken to modify the right member.

A related and equally serious problem, which may intersect the empilage problem, concerns the scope of conjunction. The string of words in (4) may be taken to denote one (4a) or two (4b) separate objects:

(4) swivel joint and door hinge center line
(4a) (((swivel joint) and (door hinge)) (center line))
(4b) (swivel joint) and ((door hinge) (center line))

The proper analysis, and hence translation, of these compounds presupposes that we can establish a small set of semantic noun-noun relations which are at least partially domain-dependent. Although much progress has been made towards discovering and representing such relations, general and complete solutions to these and other problems do not appear imminent.

In recent tests[5] the TAUM-AVIATION system demonstrated the ability to produce an acceptable translation for somewhat more than half of a new 200-page text for which only the vocabulary list had been seen in advance. A small percentage of the remaining sentences were mistranslated, the others failing the parse. Output quality for translated sentences was judged at roughly 80% that of a first-draft human translation.

In view of the complexity of the domain, it is perhaps surprising that these texts should be relatively amenable to automatic translation. That this is so appears attributable to the fact that the domain is quite well-defined. The sets of objects, categories and relations in the domain are viewed from a similar functional perspective by technicians (whatever their language) and this coherent, precise view of a particular subworld is reflected in the structure of the language used. Whether for reasons of logical necessity or professional contact, the style for presenting maintenance procedures and system descriptions is also quite similar in English and French.

2.3 Information retrieval from medical texts

Many of the same challenges that impede progress in automatic translation also show up in research aimed at retrieving information from scientific and technical documents. In both cases real texts must be analyzed into content representations which are appropriately structured and sufficiently nuanced for the purpose at hand. Moreover, both automatic translation and information retrieval must deal with the analysis of continuous texts (as opposed to dialogs), and thus face the same set of primary linguistic problems (e.g. scope of conjunction and modification).

In one respect, however, the work in information retrieval faces a problem not encountered as such in automatic translation. Of primary concern for information retrieval is a way of comparing (and contrasting) the information (meaning) of different sentences from one or more documents in a functionally homogeneous set, and in storing together those units of information which have the greatest similarity among them. These requirements have been favorably met by the development, over the past decade, of the notion of INFORMATION FORMAT as a linguistically justified encapsulation of text content. Instrumental in the evolution of this notion has been the work of Sager *et al.*[6–8] on the information formatting of texts in certain narrow sublanguages of pharmacology and medicine.

Basically, an information format is a tabular structure in which each row represents the information contained in a simple sentence or a part of a sentence which corresponds semantically to a simple proposition. A single text sentence may correspond to one or many rows in a format. The theoretical origins of information formats can be found in Harris' work on discourse analysis[9], including the use of grammatical transformations (or their inverses) to

PATIENT	V-PT	BODY-PART	LAB	EXAM-TEST	V-SHOW	NEG	NORMALCY	QUANT	SIGN-SYMPTOM	LAB-RES
			TEST				RESULT		QUAL	
1.		[urine]	urin-alysis		showed	no			abnormalities	
2.		lungs			revealed				bilateral rhonchi	
3.		abdominal		felt		no			masses	
4.		liver		palpable				4 cm		
5.		right lung		to per-cussion			clear			

[ ] Material in square brackets reconstructed from other entries in the row.

Sentence 1: Urinalysis showed no abnormalities.
Sentence 2: Lungs revealed bilateral rhonchi.
Sentence 3: No abdominal masses felt.
Sentence 4: Liver palpable 4 cm.
Sentence 5: Right lung clear to percussion.

Fig. 1. Partial information format illustrating syntactic variations in the TEST-RESULT relation. (From Hirschman and Sager "Automatic Information Formatting of a Medical Sublanguage".)

decompose one complex sentence into two or more elementary sentences (i.e. format entries). But Sager's work has considerably refined the formatting procedure and developed it for the purposes of retrieval.

Figure 1 gives a simple information format, taken from recent paper by Hirschman and Sager[8]. Note that each word of the five formatted sentences is assigned to a column in the format in such a way that semantically similar words in structurally dissimilar sentences are aligned under the same heading. As a result, the constituents of sentences 3 and 5 are not in original order and some row-column positions are left empty. Columns are grouped together hierarchically under larger headings. What the format does, in a sense, is provide a maximal framework in which to fit all the sentences of a certain class. The class may be defined in terms of distributional regularities, but the members have a semantic unity in terms of underlying relations.

Sager *et al.* have developed a number of techniques for mapping texts into information formats. Texts are first analyzed syntactically using a general English parser[10] which is based on Harris' string grammar[11]. Most sentences receive multiple analyses, but these are then filtered by a "restriction grammar", which embodies a set of word co-occurrence restrictions valid only for the given sublanguage. (The restrictions state which semantic classes of nouns may serve as logical subject of which semantic classes of verbs, which adjectives may modify which nouns, which adverbs may modify which adverbs, etc.). The semantically characterized lexical restrictions for the sublanguage are usually compatible with only one of the syntactic parses. The output of the parse is therefore a grammatical structure for each input sentence, where each word in the structure is tagged with the labels of the semantic subclasses to which it belongs. These word subclasses can then be used to map the sentence onto the information format. Before this can be done, however, the sentence structures identified by the parser (and restriction grammar) must be put into a more canonical form. This essentially requires removing the effect of any grammatical transformations (e.g. passive sentences are converted to active form; nominalized clauses are replaced by the corresponding full sentences).

Experiments have been conducted in automatically mapping sentences of various kinds of medical texts onto information formats[12]. In general more than one format must be used to represent the content of an entire text. Once formatted, a text may serve as a kind of relational data base for purposes of automatic question answering or statistical analyses. It has proved possible to summarize information on hospital patients by formatting doctors' radiology reports and discharge summaries[13].

3. SUBLANGUAGE

3.1 *The importance of word co-occurrence patterns*

Each of the applied systems cited in the preceding section is oriented towards a particular processing goal, and limited to the particular sublanguage associated with a single knowledge domain. In order to process the content of a text, three things are required: (1) representations of meanings which make clear and computationally accessible both the differences and the similarities (e.g. equivalence, consequence, etc.) between meanings required by the processing goal, (2) ways of associating with each input word string a set of possible meanings on the basis of meaning representations for individual words and some combinatory rules which can operate on word representations, and (3) ways of isolating intended meanings from among the possible ones on the basis of axioms of common non-linguistic knowledge, some of which may be particular to the domain.

On the first of these requirements, very little is known of a general nature since only a few practical systems for real texts have incorporated anything near to a satisfactory general solution to the meaning representation problem. More can be said about the second and third requirements, at least in the case of sublanguage processing, since successful real-text semantic processors have relied heavily on a precise grammar of the possible elementary sublanguage sentence patterns, formulated in terms of the classes of words that are actually found in equivalent environments in a corpus of texts.

At the moment, linguists are quite incapable of specifying the semantic restrictions on word co-occurrence for the language as a whole, and it is not even clear that this is a worthwhile goal, for to do so would amount to an attempt to delineate what can be said in the language. But the situation is quite different in relatively fixed scientific and technical sublanguages, where there are fairly sharp restrictions on what is "sayable" (meaningful), at least with respect to the primary subject matter of the technology or science. The members of a given technical community share certain knowledge about sets of objects, their properties, and possible relations between them that consititute the common domain of discourse within the community. These common conceptual categories are directly reflected in the semantic word classes and grammatical configurations of these classes, found in a sample of texts in the sublanguage. A distributional analysis of a corpus of texts puts words into functionally similar equivalence classes that happen to mirror the accepted taxonomy of the associated subworld. A grammar of the sublanguage, when stated in terms of the semantic word classes, reflects the possible relationships between objects. It is important to realize that a precise study of a sublanguage grammar can thus reveal an important part of the structure of knowledge of the subworld.

3.2 *Factors giving rise to sublanguages*

Sublanguages have been characterized in various ways, but there is no widely accepted definition of the term. There is, however, a consensus as to the factors which are usually present when a subset of a natural language is restricted enough for efficient semantic processing[14].

● RESTRICTED DOMAIN OF REFERENCE. The set of objects and relations to which linguistic expressions can refer is relatively small.

● RESTRICTED PURPOSE AND ORIENTATION. The relationships among the participants in the linguistic exchange are of a particular type and the purpose of the exchange is oriented towards certain goals.

● RESTRICTED MODE OF COMMUNICATION. Communication may be spoken or written, but there may be constraints on the form because of "bandwidth" limitations (e.g. telegraphic style).

● COMMUNITY OF PARTICIPANTS SHARING SPECIALIZED KNOWLEDGE. The best, canonical examples of sublanguages are those for which there exists an identifiable community of users who share specialized knowledge and who communicate under restrictions of domain, purpose, and mode by using the sublanguage. These participants enforce the special patterns of usage and ensure the coherence and completeness of the sublanguage as a linguistic system.

3.3 *Sublanguages as infinite subsystems*

Harris has noted that sublanguages resemble mathematical subsystems in that they are sets closed under certain grammatical transformations[15]. Thus, for example, if the sublanguage of analysis in mathematics contains sentence (5a), it will also contain many others including (5b–f), which differ from (5a) only by grammatical changes which leave invariant the meaning relationship of "content words" (i.e. nouns, verbs, adjectives).

(5a) This theorem provides the solution to the boundary value problem.

(5b) It is this theorem that provides the solution to the boundary value problem.

(5c) What this theorem does is provide the solution to the boundary value problem.

(5d) The solution to the boundary value problem is provided by this theorem.

(5e) Does this theorem provide the solution to the boundary value problem?

(5f) This theorem does not provide the solution to the boundary value problem.

Certain sublanguages may not use all the grammatical transformations of the whole language, but most are closed under one or more recursively applicable operations (such as conjunction or relative clause formation). Since there is no limit in principle to the number of applications of such operations, it follows that most sublanguages are infinite sets of sentences (for the same reasons that whole languages are).

3.4 Sublanguages as imperfectly homogeneous systems

The very notion of sublanguage is introduced on the assumption that certain subsets of the language have special characteristics (regularities) that are not discernible in the language as a whole. But this appearance is a matter of degree. As we have already seen, even weather reports are not perfectly homogeneous, showing occasional departures from the familiar telegraphic style. Under ususual conditions the domain of reference can be extended and viewed from a different perspective. As a consequence, the set of linguistic forms used is also expanded to include forms which bear little resemblance to those habitually employed. Fortunately, separating the "habitual" sentences of weather reports from the "emergency" sentences is a simple task for a parser, because telegraphic sentences obey special constituent structure rules.

But sublanguages which are less stereotyped than weather bulletins may also have non-homogeneities of style or grammatical structure which can still present problems during computational treatment. Preliminary indications are that these linguistic singularities can be correlated with a shift of subject matter or viewpoint within the text. To the extent that the non-homogeneities can be detected automatically, we may improve the performance of semantic processing programs by calling up different sub-programs to operate on the separable components of the text. When, as often happens, only one component (i.e. the more homogeneous portion of the text) is computationally tractable, the information carried in that component may still be of interest even without the information of the less accessible remainder. The next two sections are devoted to a particular sublanguage where this is in fact the case.

4. STOCK MARKET REPORTS

4.1 Two worlds of reference

The sublanguage of daily stock market summaries affords a simple, yet revealing case study of the relationship between language and information. In the most common variety of these reports, we can distinguish two principal domains of reference:

THE PRIMARY DOMAIN—one or more stock exchanges and the trading activity (price changes, volume of shares traded, halt in trading, etc.) taking place during well-defined business hours (e.g. 10 a.m.–4 p.m. on the Montreal Stock Exchange).

THE SECONDARY DOMAIN—the less clearly defined world of economic and political events in which the causes of market changes can be perceived. Included in the secondary domain are other relatively well-defined sites of economic activity which bear a resemblance to the stock exchanges (e.g. the gold market, bond markets, commodity exchanges, etc.). Also included are wars, strikes, nuclear power plant accidents—in short, nearly any event of interest to investors.

Stock reports come in different varieties, depending on the expertise of the intended reader. Reports from some sources may refer only to the primary domain. In contrast, highly analytical reports may be concerned more with the economy in general than the stock market itself, treating the latter mainly as a barometer of the former. Reports of the kind considered here may be called INFORMATIVE, in that they describe the day's trading activity, interspersed with a certain number of comments about events in the outside world (i.e. the secondary domain). In such reports, the primary domain is normally viewed from the perspective of a single stock market. Reference to other markets is usually made in a way which reveals the relative importance and causal relationships between movements on the separate markets.

4.2 *Grammatical subordination reflects separation of domains*

Stock market reports have an interesting and useful property which can be exploited during semantic processing. The semantic division between the two major domains is reflected in the sublanguage syntax in the way subordination is used. To a large extent, text segments which refer to market activity constitute non-subordinate (independent) clauses. Text segments referring to the outside world usually occur in grammatically subordinate structures.

Grammatical subordination of propositions is usually indicated by one of the following five devices in this sublanguage (in each case, the italicized portion encodes a proposition which is considered to be grammatically subordinate to the remainder):

● CLAUSE INTRODUCED BY SUBORDINATING CONJUNCTION
(6) Seabord World Airlines plunged 4 1/2 to 12 5/8 *after Flexi-Van Corporation disclosed it had abandoned plans to take over the airline for about $18.25 a share.*

● COMPLEMENT OF NOUN IN THE CLASS N-news
(7) C.I.T. climbed 9 3/4 points *on rumors of an impending merger offer.*

● NON-RESTRICTIVE RELATIVE CLAUSE
(8) Superior Oil, *which had been hit by profit taking recently,* rocketed ahead 15 to 480.

● SENTENCE OR NOMINALIZATION AS COMPLEMENT OF VERB OR PRE-POSITION

(9a) The advance occurred despite *a fairly sharp rise for short-term rates in the credit market.*
(9b) Analysts said *a number of concerns are weighing on the market.*

● NON-INITIAL SENTENCE IN A "COMPANY NEWS" PARAGRAPH (a sublan-guage-specific device—certain paragraphs at the end of a report give trading activity in shares of single companies, with explanations)
(10) Reliance Electric held steady at 58. *The Federal Trade Commission has indicated that it will try to block Exxon Corporation's* $1.17 *offer for Reliance.*

Certain subordinate constructions may also serve to downplay one primary domain event to a second such event because of remoteness in time, space, etc. For example:

(11a) The MSE industrial index was down a fraction *while the Toronto composite index held a small gain.*
(11b) *The continuing downturn on Wall Street* pulled Canadian stock markets lower in the early going today...

Such occurrences, which can be distinguished on the basis of their formal properties, obscure an otherwise strong tendency to correlate subordinate constructions with secondary domain reference. In any case, one rarely finds secondary domain references in independent clauses. We are therefore motivated to distinguish a sub-sublanguage within stock market reports. This "core" sublanguage has interesting linguistic properties which can be exploited for computational purposes.

4.3 *Properties of the "core" sublanguage of stock market reports*

If we remove from a typical stock market report the portion which refers to the outside world (plus any subordination connectives such as *on news of*) the remaining portion can still be read as a coherent text. (When excising a nominalization, however, we must leave behind a pronoun). Let us refer to the sublanguage of stock market reports as L_s and to the "core" component which refers to the primary domain, as l_s. It turns out that l_s has a number of properties which make it much more tractable computationally than L_s as a whole. The lexicon of l_s is far simpler and more closed than that of L_s. The number of semantic word classes needed for a grammatical description is smaller, the words fall more neatly into distributional classes, and words in the same class have greater semantic homogeneity (and thus more predictable meanings). This is of course natural in view of the fact that l_s refers to a far more tightly constrained domain than does L_s in general.

The grammar of l_s is simpler and more predictable than that of L_s. Verbs denoting value change (*climb, jump, turn higher*) have corresponding event nominalizations (*climb, jump, upturn*) which are semantically regular. There are relatively few basic sentence patterns, describable in terms of word classes which are semantically homogeneous. To these patterns correspond the few basic kinds of information carried by l_s. What is striking about l_s, however, is the rich variety of vocabulary and locutions used to encode the few basic types of information carried. A major challenge in the computational processing of l_s is therefore a proper model for the syntactic and lexical means of expressing the same meaning through different forms (paraphrases). Although such models are available, their discussion is beyond the scope of this paper. In what follows, we will assume their existence and present only the few details necessary for outlining the computational procedures.

5. AUTOMATIC EXTRACTION OF CONTENT REPRESENTATIONS

In this section, we illustrate a general procedure for automatically deriving semantic representations for texts in the relatively straight-forward sublanguage of informative stock market reports. The content representations which result can be used to constitute a relational data base for a set of reports, an intermediate representation in an automatic translation system, or the starting point for the linguistic component of a text generation system. The procedure has sufficient generality to be applied in a number of sublanguages. The sublanguage l_s has been chosen for illustration purposes because it is linguistically non-trivial, yet amenable to computational treatment in the framework of the proposed procedure. (Whether or not the procedure can be implemented economically in a given application is a separate question which we do not attempt to answer here.)

Figure 2 gives a fragment of the kind of stock market report on which we illustrate our procedure:

Stocks were narrowly mixed in the early going on Canadian exchanges today as the pace-setting New York market slumped on news of a higher-than-expected rise in July's producer prices.
The MSE industrial index after the first hour of trading was down a fraction while the TSE composite index of 300 key stocks held a small gain. Financial service and metal issues sagged while oil, paper and utility stocks edged ahead. ...
Dom Stores edged up 1/4 to 19 after posting higher profits. CP, a recent high flyer, was off 1/8 at 33 5/8. Gaz Metro, which posted lower profits and filed for a rate increase, was unchanged...

Fig. 2. An informative daily stock market report. (Source: *Montreal Star*, 9 August 1979.)

If we are interested in processing "real" texts and in exploiting the special properties of a given sublanguage, we must first manually prepare a grammar and lexicon based on a detailed examination of a large corpus of texts considered to be representative of the field. We apply the techniques of distributional analysis, noting all the environments in which each word occurs. It quickly becomes clear that we can improve the description if, before comparing environments, we remove the effect of certain general grammatical transformations[9]. We may make use of automatic clustering techniques to discover important tendencies of distribution[16]. Since our sublanguage is relatively restricted, we find that classes of words which are equivalent in their distribution have a great deal of semantic homogeneity (e.g. noun classes designate functionally similar objects in the domain, verb classes designate functionally similar actions or states, etc.).

Once the important word classes have been established, at least in the first approximation, sentence patterns are stated in terms of these classes. Consider the elementary case of stock market sentences of the form $N_{stock} V_m \Omega$, where $N_{stock} = \{golds, industrials, IBM, \ldots\}$ and $V_m = \{plunge, add, gain, \ldots\}$ and Ω is an appropriate object string (possibly empty). The sentences of (12) are acceptable in L_s but the very similar sentences of the form $NV\Omega$ in (13), while normal in general English, are unacceptable in L_s.

(12) (a) Golds plunged.

(b) IBM added 1/2 to 64 3/4.

(c) Industrials chalked up a 10-point gain. (Derived from: Industrials gained 10 points.)

(13) (a) ● Analysts plunged (on news of lower brokerage profits).

(b) ● Traders added 1/2 to 64 3/4 (to get 65 1/4).

(c) ● Corporations chalked up substantial gains.

Even though the three nouns *analysts*, *traders* and *corporations* are used in L_s, they are not used as subjects of verbs of the class V_m. Information of the kind contained in the sentences of (13) is simply never communicated in stock market reports.

For the sublanguage l_s within L_s, only a few word classes are required to state the basic sentence patterns. The most important sentence structures cover information on (i) price changes in individual stocks or in group indices, (ii) volumes of shares traded for individual stocks or for the entire daily market, (iii) comparisons in the number of stocks moving up and stocks moving down in price, and (iv) halts and resumptions in trading. The most important part of the grammar of l_s, therefore, will be a "syntactic" statement of the form of the most elementary sentences, in terms of semantic word classes such as N_{stock} and V_m. In a separate part of the grammar will be a statement of the grammatical transformations (including conjunction and relative clause formation) which are allowed to operate on the various patterns. Some transformations will normally be particular to the sublanguage and their scope of application will be defined in terms of the semantic word classes. Even the more general transformations, which may have correlates outside the sublanguage, may be semantically restricted.

The lexicon of l_s will give information about the semantic class and subclass membership of each word. This information, as well as the description of sentence patterns and transformations on those patterns, need not have any validity outside the sublanguage in question, although the grammatical information may resemble that of the whole language or of other sublanguages in important respects.

5.1 Stage 1: *automatic separation of the "core" text*

Let us assume that the grammar and lexicon of l_s are described in detail, but that no similar precision can be brought to the description of L_S (this does in fact appear to be the case). The problem in gaining access to the information stored in the l_s component of a text in L_s is first of all that of determining the boundaries between text segments in l_s and those in the complement $L_S - l_s$ (henceforth $-l_s$). Vocabulary alone is not enough, since some words appear both in l_s and in $-l_s$ (e.g. *drop* is an intransitive verb in the class V_m in l_s but also appears as an intransitive in $-l_s$). Fortunately, we know that sentences can be divided grammatically into clauses (we include among clauses the nominalizations of sentences which occur superficially as noun phases and infinitives): clauses encode propositions, and simple propositions are either entirely in l_s or entirely in $-l_s$. Thus the problem of determining boundaries between segments in l_s and $-l_s$ is greatly reduced to the problem of identifying clause boundaries and then finding a way to verify, for each subordinate clause (encoded proposition) whether or not it belongs to l_s. (*Remember that main clauses are normally in* l_s.) Again fortunately, it turns out that the number of clause boundary types is quite small and easily recognizable (the syntactic recognition routine is easy to write).

The problem of determining which clauses belong to l_s is also not difficult. Although there is some lexical overlap between l_s and $-l_s$, no simple clause rule for l_s will "fit" a clause in $-l_s$ because the rules of grammar for l_s are stated in terms of tight semantic subclasses of words. Thus a clause which is successfully parsed with the subgrammar and a sublexicon of l_s MUST be in l_s; otherwise (if our grammar is good), we may assume it is in $-l_s$.

5.2 *Stage 2: mapping core clauses onto entries in an information format*

Given that we have succeeded in extracting from a text in L_s the sub-text consisting of all clauses in l_s, we are in a position to use the grammar of l_s to operate on the form of the subtext sentences in such a way as to lay bare the information structure of that text. Within this stage we can distinguish two steps: (1) segmenting each sentence into its grammatical constituents, and (2) assigning each constituent to a "slot" (column) of a specific kind of information format. Each elementary sentence structure is mapped to a specific format (e.g. there is one format for price-change sentences, one for trading volume sentences, etc.). In principle, as a sentence is segmented, enough structure must be recognized by the parsing program to discriminate sentences whose structure has been altered by grammatical transformations, and separate mapping rules applied to such sentences, or else the transformations must be reversed before mapping applies.

Consider now the stock market report and its resultant mapping onto the information format of Fig. 3. Text segments which refer to the secondary domain (i.e. segments belonging to $-l_s$) are set off in square brackets. The first sentence has the structure of (14):

(14) S1: Stocks were narrowly mixed in the early going on Canadian exchanges
S2: (As the pace-setting New York market slumped
S3: (on news of a higher-than-expected rise in July's producer prices))

S2 is the subordinate part of S1. S3 is the subordinate part of S2. The first line of S1 (i.e. its independent part) belongs to l_s. The independent clause of S2 also belongs to l_s. S3, as the nominalization of a sentence referring to the outside world, is clearly in $-l_s$.

A parser can easily segment the independent clause of S1, using the grammar of l_s, as follows:

(15) Stocks / were narrowly mixed / in the early going / on Canadian exchanges / today

For the purposes of information formatting, we need to extract certain types of modifier (place, degree, time, etc.) which may occur as a part of a larger consitituent. We face exactly this problem with *narrowly*, which occurs inside *were narrowly mixed*. The same grammatical rules

Text (from the Montreal Star, August 9, 1979):

    Stocks were narrowly mixed in the early going on Canadian exchanges today as the pace-setting New York market slumped [on news of a higher-than-expected rise in July's producer prices]
    The MSE industrial index after the first hour of trading was down a fraction while the TSE composite index of 300 key stocks held a small gain. Financial service and metal issues sagged while oil, paper and utility stocks edged ahead.   ...
    Dom Stores edged up 1/4 to 19 [after posting higher profits]. CP [, a recent high flyer,] was off 1/8 at 33 5/8. Gaz Metro [, which posted lower profits and filed for a rate increase,] was unchanged. ...

CONJ	N-STOCK	EXCHANGE	PRICE TREND			TIME	
			V-CHANGE	AMOUNT	END VALUE	DAY	INTERVAL
	stocks	on Canadian exchanges	were mixed	narrowly		today	in the early going
as	the pacesetting market	(in) New York	slumped				
	the industrial index	(at/on the) MSE	was down	a fraction			after the first hour of trading
while	the composite index of 300 key stocks	(at/on the) TSE	held a gain	small			
	financial service and metal issues		sagged				
while	oil, paper and utility stocks		edged ahead				
	Dom Stores		edged up	1/4	to 19		
	CP		was off	1/8	at 33 5/8		
	Gaz Metro		was unchanged				

Fig. 3. One information format used to represent the "core" component sentences of an informative stock market report. Text segments in square brackets are outside the core component. Degree and location modifiers are separated from the constituents they modify. Row entries can still be read as sentences (allowing for small paraphrastic changes such as addition of prepositions in the EXCHANGE column).

which permit *narrowly* to be recognized in this structure, however, can separate it as a format entry, moving it to the right of its parent constituent, since both actions require the lexical information that *narrowly* belongs to a certain distributional subclass (of degree adverbs). This same general principle, using subclass information to trigger the appropriate rules, is what allows us to write a set of general formatting transformations which recognize constituents and map them to column locations in the format in the same operation. Each clause in l_s can thus be given a canonical form and entered in the format, in essentially the same way as Sager *et al.* have done for medical texts.

By arranging the columns of the format properly, we may give a canonical order to constituents which retains the property of each row entry's being readable as a sentence. Note that at least three permutations are required to construct the first table entry from the clause form, yet this entry retains sentencehood. Although this property is not essential to our procedure, it appears that formats can usually be chosen which have it. We may, however, be required to insert grammatical constants (such as *in* which is added when *the pace-setting New York market* is transformed to *the pacesetting market/in New York*. Such additions are a normal part of linguistic transformations in general.

Since we have not changed the order of clauses in the original text (and we have preserved the conjunctions for the moment), and since the deletion of material from $- l_s$ does not destroy the cohesion of the text, our information format can be viewed as a kind of regularized text in which the recurrence of one basic sentence pattern is emphasized by separating the constituent classes (i.e. columns) and giving them semantic labels. One property of the information format of Fig. 3 is worth noting here. Only two columns have constituent entries for every sentence: *N*-stock and *V*-change. It is these two distributional classes which define, in a sense, the associated sentence pattern. So it is in fact obligatory that each clause have a constituent entered in each of these columns.

5.3 *Stage* 3: *normalization by means of paraphrase*

The formatted text of Fig. 3 is still not in a form appropriate for efficient semantic processing. In a third stage of our procedure, we must NORMALIZE the text so that entries in the same column have maximum conformity, within the limits of general rules of linguistic and non-linguistic knowledge formalizable for the sublanguage. Some of the most important steps in this stage are:

(i) Replacing semantically complex words by their most regular and semantically transparent paraphrases within the sublanguage (e.g. *sagged* becomes *moved down slightly*).

(ii) Eliminating redundant words or phrases which carry no new information in the context; this can be regarded as a kind of paraphrasing operation also, since meaning is preserved (e.g. *the pacesetting New York market* becomes *the (New York) market* since the two phrases have similar distribution, and their equivalence is confirmed on the basis of non-linguistic knowledge).

(iii) Expanding sentences with conjoined constituents into two or more separate sentences. For example, *financial service and metal issues sagged* becomes *financial service issues sagged and metal issues sagged*. (This is a traditional formatting operation which could have been carried out in creating a more regular version of Fig. 3.)

(iv) Recovering adverbials of time and place for each elementary row entry (normalized sentence) on the basis of rules of text structure. For example, in the third sentence of the text, it may not be clear on which market *financial service and metal issues sagged...* since the preceding sentence refers to both the Montreal (MSE) and Toronto (TSE) exchanges. But since the place adverbial of the main clause takes precedence over that of the subordinate clause, it is the former which is copied onto all following sentences which lack an explicit place adverbial (until the next occurrence of one).

It could be argued that the normalizing operations sketched above should be carried out prior to formatting, since their explicit formalization may occasionally depend on the structure of the original text. Suffice it to say here that (1) normalization and formatting are conceptually quite separate, and that (2) the order proposed here can be maintained in an algorithm with the aid of simple non-*ad hoc* devices.

Figure 4 gives a normalized information format for the text of Fig. 2. One of the most radical operations on the text has been the replacement of *stocks were mixed/narrowly* by a

CONJ	N-STOCK	EXCHANGE	V-CHANGE	AMOUNT	END VALUE	DAY	INTERVAL
	some stocks	(on) Canadian exchanges	moved up	slightly		today	(by) 11:00
and	some stocks	(on) Canadian exchanges	moved down	slightly		today	(by) 11:00
as	the market	(in) New York	moved down	moderately		today	(by) 11:00
	the industrial index	(in) Montreal	moved down	a fraction		today	(by) 11:00
while	the composite index	(in) Toronto	moved up	slightly		today	(by) 11:00
	financial service stocks	(in) Montreal	moved down	slightly		today	(by) 11:00
and	metal stocks	(in) Montreal	moved down	slightly		today	(by) 11:00
while	oil stocks	(in) Montreal	moved up	slightly		today	(by) 11:00
and	paper stocks	(in) Montreal	moved up	slightly		today	(by) 11:00
and	utility stocks	(in) Montreal	moved up	slightly		today	(by) 11:00
	Dominion Stores	(in) Montreal	moved up	1/4	(to) 19	today	(by) 11:00
	Canadian Pacific	(in) Montreal	moved up	1/8	(to) 33 5/8	today	(by) 11:00
	Gaz Metro	(in) Montreal	moved	0		today	(by) 11:00

Fig. 4. A normalized information format derived from the format of Fig. 3 by replacing text words by their most freely occurring synonyms *in the sublanguage*. Note that conjoined index names have been separated in otherwise identical sentences. The verb phrase *were mixed* in Fig. 3 has been paraphrased using a conjunction of *moved up* and *moved down* with separate subjects. Values for the place (EXCHANGE) and TIME are filled in on the basis of general rules of text structure. The linguistic value under INTERVAL should be as in Fig. 3, but the absolute value is inserted here to save space (paraphrases based on non-linguistic knowledge should not appear at this point). Values are obligatory in all columns except CONJ and END VALUE. Note that the whole table is still readable as a coherent (but uninteresting) text, although the vocabulary is now substantially reduced to a certain key subset. The CONJ values can be dropped without loss of information except for *as*, which indicates a causal link in this sublanguage: S_1 *as* S_2 means S_1 *as a result of* S_2.

complex paraphase using a conjunction of two sentences in which the generic quantification of *stocks* has been broken into two disjoint subsets: *some stocks moved up slightly and some stocks moved down slightly*. Such paraphrases are uncommon, but fully justified within the method. As a result of the four normalization operations, all rows have entries in each column except for the column labelled END VALUE. There is no basis for reconstituting specific values on the basis of the text given.

5.4 *Stage* 4: *conversion to a relational data base*

As a result of the normalization procedure given above, the format of Fig. 4 now contains a set of sentences still readable as a coherent text. But the vocabulary of these sentences is now quite reduced, and the words used have a very direct and obvious relationship to the central concepts of the domain. From the normalized format it is evident that each of the normalized sentences expresses a relation between entities of very restricted types. If we now give a name to this relation, using the highly regular verb *MOVE*, and fix the order of its arguments (according to their most regular surface order, to stay close to linguistic form), we may represent each basic proposition in the format as a formula of predicate logic, with the general form:

MOVE (⟨index or stock⟩, ⟨direction⟩, ⟨amount⟩, ⟨final value⟩, ⟨place⟩, ⟨date⟩, ⟨time interval⟩)

In order to make this transition, we must drop the conjunctions *and*, *as* and *while* which appear in the first column of Fig. 4. This amounts to a loss of foregrounding information which would be needed to reconstitute a well-formed text in the stock market sublanguage. But such information is irrelevant to the enterprise of comparing and collecting propositional content in the sum-total of all text clauses in l_s.

Figure 5 gives one possible representation for the thirteen propositions which concern the primary domain and which are derivable from the text of Fig. 2 by means of our procedure. Taken together, the set of propositions constitutes a relational data base for the text. We could

```
MOVE(some stocks,up,slightly,--,{MSE,TSE},1979/08/06,10:00-11:00)

MOVE(some stocks,down,slightly,--,{MSE,TSE},1979/08/06,10:00-11:00)

MOVE(stocks,down,moderately,--,NYSE,1979/08/06,10:00-11:00)

MOVE(industrial index,down,a fraction,--,MSE,1979/08/06,10:00-11:00)

MOVE(composite index,up,slightly,--,TSE,1979/08/06,10:00-11:00)

MOVE(financial services,down,slightly,--,MSE,1979/08/06,10:00-11:00)

MOVE(metals,down,slightly,--,MSE,1979/08/06,10:00-11:00)

MOVE(oils,up,slightly,--,MSE,1979/08/06,10:00-11:00)

MOVE(papers,up,slightly,--,MSE,1979/08/06,10:00-11:00)

MOVE(utilities,up,slightly,--,MSE,1979/08/06,10:00-11:00)

MOVE(Dominion Stores,up,1/4,19,MSE,1979/08/06,10:00-11:00)

MOVE(Canadian Pacific,down,1/8,33 5/8,MSE,1979/08/06,10:00-11:00)

MOVE(Gaz Metro,--,0,--,MSE,1979/08/06,10:00-11:00)
```

$$\text{MOVE}(\langle \begin{smallmatrix}\text{index or}\\\text{stock}\end{smallmatrix} \rangle, \langle\text{direction}\rangle, \langle\text{amount}\rangle, \langle\begin{smallmatrix}\text{final}\\\text{value}\end{smallmatrix}\rangle, \langle\text{place}\rangle, \langle\text{date}\rangle, \langle\begin{smallmatrix}\text{time}\\\text{interval}\end{smallmatrix}\rangle)$$

Fig. 5. The thirteen sentences of the normalized information format of Fig. 4 are here represented as propositions in predicate-argument form using the seven-place predicate MOVE. Order of arguments may differ from column order of the related format. Taken as a set, these propositions constitute a relational data base for the core sentences of the stock market report of Fig. 1, and can be interrogated in a question-answer system. Argument representations are convenient memonics, but could be coded differently, in particular in a way closer to some more standard data representation at the stock exchange where *metals*, for example, may refer to a specific index for metal stocks (note that in this case what appears to be a quantified plural is actually treated as an individual). Where a plural noun-phrase argument contains a genuine quantification (e.g. *some stocks*), it would be necessary to introduce a more complex propositional formula using an appropriately defined and interpreted quantifier *some* (different from ∃) for the purposes of formal theorem proving. Degree adverbs such as *slightly* could be defined as (fuzzy) intervals in a percentage change gradient. Such definitions are discoverable from the textual data by comparing use of each adverb with quantity changes given in the same sentence or accompanying quotations. It is not difficult to imagine how such propositions could be automatically generated from the relevant raw data.

imagine interrogating such a database either in relational or natural language form. Asking "Which stocks moved up in the first hour on 6 August 1979" would amount to asking for the set of all x such that MOVE $(x, \text{up}, y, z, w, 1979/08/06, 10:00-11:00)$ is in the database for any values of y, z and w. Many refinements and extensions are of course possible. In particular, degree adverbs such as *slightly* could be given definitions in terms of some fuzzy range of percentage change (defined somewhat differently for indices than for stocks). By processing queries through the same procedure as texts, we could allow queries to exploit the full paraphrastic range of the sublanguage. We would thus process a query such as "Did any issue nosedive today?" by first paraphrasing to "Did any stock move down sharply today?", then normalizing and converting to logical form. We would then reply "no" to the query if we find no x such that MOVE $(x, \text{down}, y, z, u, v, w)$ where y/z as a percentage change is defined as being large, u and w are any values, and v is equal to the date of the query.

6. CONCLUDING REMARKS

Sublanguages which can be analyzed semantically according to the procedure outlined above will almost certainly be good candidates for one or more types of automatic processing.

The applications to information retrieval are several. The propositional form of text content can be used for queries of a cumulative data base of texts. Statistical analyses can also be carried out directly on these forms. Or, the forms could serve an intermediate role in a system for automatic abstracting of sublanguage texts. Since we have shown that some sublanguages may have separable components, it is clear that we are not obliged to have a complete grammar and lexicon in order to extract useful data from texts. Indeed, perfect separability may not be a requirement. This approach would seem useful for extracting selected kinds of information from semantically complex texts if the sublanguage in question is well-defined and the relevant parts of the grammar are known (i.e. the semantic word classes for the sentence patterns of interest).

In the case of stock market reports, the most interesting application might be to generate the reports from data (i.e. the price quotations at different times of the day). This would require some domain-based principles for selecting "interesting" data (a non-linguistic problem). But the problem of sequencing the propositions and integrating more than one proposition in the same sentence is already partly solved on the basis of the linguistic description used in extracting propositional content.

It is obvious that the procedure could serve to design a semantic analyzer which would represent the first stage of an automatic translation system. The propositional form could serve as a kind of intermediate representation between two languages (provided the languages "speak in the same way about the same things" in their respective sublanguages—this often appears to be the case for technical sublanguages[17]).

But if two (or more) languages have the same propositional forms for their text content in some sublanguage (and if the corresponding semantic subclasses are indeed comparable), a further step is immediately suggested: co-synthesizing texts in those languages from the same data representation. In the case of simple texts which are as well-behaved as the "core" of stock market reports, this may indeed be a viable alternative to automatic translation.

Acknowledgements—This research was supported in part by the Social Sciences and Humanities Research Council of Canada under grants 410–79–0070 and 410–81–0249.

The main ideas of Section 4 were first presented at the COLING80 conference (Eighth International Conference on Computational Linguistics, Tokyo, Sept. 1980) as a talk entitled "Embedded sublanguages and natural language processing". The procedure of Section 5 was outlined in a report to a panel on natural language text processing at ASIS81 (American Society of Information Science, Washington, Oct. 1981). Discussions with conference participants led to improvements in both content and presentation Special thanks are due to Igor Mel'čuk for detailed comments on earlier drafts of this paper; his feedback has forced me to be much more precise about things I have always taken for granted.

REFERENCES

1. R. Burton, Semantic Grammar: An Engineering Technique for Constructing Natural Language Understanding Systems. *BBN Rep.* No. 3453 (1976).
2. G. Hendrix, E. Sacerdoti, D. Sagalowicz and J. Slocum, Developing a natural-language interface to complex data. *ACM Trans. Data Base Systems* 3(2) 105–147 (1978).
3. Chevalier, J. Dansereau and G. Poulin, TAUM-METEO. Groupe de Recherches pour la Traduction Automatique, Université de Montréal (1978).
4. L. Bourbeau (Ed.), Linguistic documentation of the computerized translation chain of the TAUM-AVIATION System. Groupe de Recherches pour la Traduction Automatique, Université de Montréal (1981).
5. Final Report—Evaluation of the TAUM-AVIATION machine translation pilot system. Secretary of State, Government of Canada (1980).
6. N. Sager, Syntactic formatting of science information. *AFIPS Conf. Proc.* 41 (1972).
7. N. Sager, Natural language information formatting: the automatic conversion of texts to a structured data base. *Advances in Computers* (Edited by M. Yovits), pp. 17, 89–162. Academic Press, New York (1978).
8. L. Hirschman and N. Sager, Automatic information formatting of a medical sublanguage, In *Sublanguage: Studies of Language in Restricted Semantic Domains* (Edited by R. Kittredge and J. Lehrberger), pp. 27–69. de Gruyter, Berlin (1982).
9. Z. Harris, *Discourse Analysis Reprints.* Mouton, Paris (1963).
10. N. Sager, *Natural Language Information Processing.* Addison–Wesley, New York (1981).
11. Z. Harris, *String Analysis of Sentence Structure.* Mouton, Paris (1962).
12. N. Sager, L. Hirschman and M. Lyman, Computerized language processing for use of narrative discharge summaries. *Proc. 2nd Ann. Symp. Computer Applications in Medical Care* (Edited by F. Orthner), pp. 330–343. New York (1978).
13. L. Hirschman and R. Grishman, Fact retrieval from natural language medical records. *Proc. 2nd World Conf. Medical Informatics* (Edited by D. Shires and H. Wolf), pp. 247–251. North-Holland, Amsterdam (1977).
14. R. Kittredge, J. Bachenko, R. Grishman, D. Walker and R. Weischedel, Sublanguage panel report, NSF/NRL Workshop on Applied Computational Linguistics in Perspective, Palo Alto (1981).
15. Z. Harris, *Mathematical Structures of Language.* Wiley–Interscience, New York (1968).
16. L. Hirschman, R. Grishman and N. Sager, Grammatically-based automatic word class formation. *Inform. Proc. Management* 11, 39–57 (1975).
17. R. Kittredge, Variation and homogeneity of sublanguages, *Sublanguage: Studies of Language in Restricted Semantic Domains* (Edited by R. Kittredge and J. Lehrberger), pp. 107–137. de Gruyter, Berlin (1982).

Comp. & Maths. with Appls. Vol. 9, No. 1, pp. 59–70, 1983
Printed in Great Britain.

0097–4943/83/010059–12$03.00/0
Pergamon Press Ltd.

THE CONTROL OF INFERENCING IN
NATURAL LANGUAGE UNDERSTANDING

Abe Lockman

Rutgers University, New Brunswick, NJ 08901, U.S.A.

and

David Klappholz

Polytechnic Institute of New York, Brooklyn, NY 11201, U.S.A.

Abstract—The understanding of a natural language text requires that a reader (human or computer program) be able to resolve ambiguities at the syntactic and lexical levels; it also requires that a reader be able to recover that part of the meaning of a text which is over and above the collection of meanings of its individual sentences taken in isolation.

The satisfaction of this requirement involves complex inferencing from a large database of world-knowledge. While human readers seem able to perform this task easily, the designer of computer programs for natural language understanding faces the serious difficulty of algorithmically defining precisely the items of world-knowledge required at any point in the processing, i.e. the problem of *controlling inferencing*. This paper discusses the problems involved in such control of inferencing; an approach to their solution is presented, based on the notion of determining where each successive sentence "fits" into the text as a whole.

1. INTRODUCTION

The topic of this paper is one aspect of the algorithmic "understanding" of natural language texts. In operational terms we will define "understanding" as the ability to answer those questions concerning the contents of a text which a typical human reader would be able to answer after having read the text. While this is clearly not a precise formal criterion—different human readers might "understand" a text somewhat differently from one another—it will suffice for the purposes of this discussion.

In what follows we will not be concerned with the process whereby questions relating to a text might be answered, but rather with that part of the understanding process which immediately precedes question answering: the sub-process whereby a text is reduced to a (logic-like) formal representation from which the attempt to answer specific questions would proceed. The language in which such a formal representation is expressed is typically referred to as a semantic representation language (SRL).

Suppose, then, that we have a text T consisting of sentences $S_1, S_2, \ldots S_n$ in that order. The long-recognized existence of levels of regularity in language[1–3] suggests the following fairly traditional model for the computation of the formal representation of T. Each sentence S_i, in turn, goes through the following three steps:†

(1) S_i is processed by a *parser* to expose the hierarchy (tree-structure) of syntactic categories which constitutes its syntactic structure.

(2) The "meaning" of each lexical item in S_i, i.e. the item's representation in the *SRL*, is substituted for that item in the parse tree.

(3) The resulting parse tree is processed in bottom-up fashion by an interpreter to produce the "meaning" of each phrase (non-terminal node in the parse tree) from those of its constituents, terminating, ultimately, with that of the entire sentence; we shall term this product (an *SRL* expression) the *semantic interpretation* of S_i, abbreviated $SI(S_i)$.

The set $\{SI(S_1), SI(S_2), \ldots, SI(S_n)\}$ is then taken to constitute the "meaning" of text T. Example 1 illustrates this process for a single simple sentence.

The insufficiency of this traditional model for achieving understanding has been evident since the very earliest attempts at implementing computational natural language understanding. In the first place, a sentence taken in isolation can be ambiguous on both the grammatical and lexical levels, as is illustrated by Examples 2 and 3.

---

†This division of the understanding process into steps does not imply that these steps must occur in the indicated order or that there is no communication between them.

He killed Harry. ==>

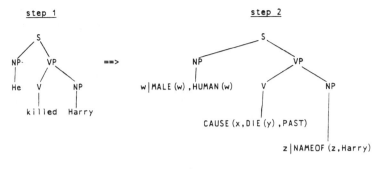

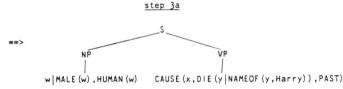

Example 1. Parsing and interpretation in the traditional model.

Today they are flying planes.

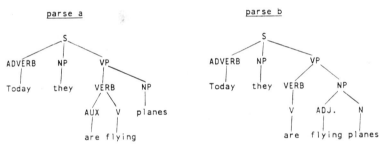

Example 2. Syntactic ambiguity (slightly modified from Chomsky 1957)

Yesterday he shot two bucks.

interpretation a: Yesterday he shot two male deer with a gun.

interpretation b: Yesterday he squandered two dollars.

Example 3. Lexical ambiguity (from [13]).

Thus the output of step 3 of the traditional model is not *the* semantic interpretation of S_{Li}, but is rather, in the general case, *a number of possible* semantic interpretations of S_i.

In the second place, the set $\{SI(S_1), SI(S_2), \ldots SI(S_n)\}$, even if all of its elements have been disambiguated, rarely constitutes the full interpretation which a reader would place on the text. In Example 4, for example, we see (indicated in square brackets) instances of additional information which a reader would extract upon reading each of the two-sentence texts.

Pronomial reference:
    I got together with Mike yesterday. He told me what he had been doing for the past four years. [*He* "is identical to" *Mike*]
Pro-adverbial reference:
    I was in Chicago last week; Bill was there also. [*there* "is identical to" *Chicago*]
Verb-phrase to verb-phrase reference:

John got a real workout yesterday. He swam four miles. [*swam four miles* "is the manner in which" *got a real workout*]
Noun-phrase to noun-phrase reference:
    All great men have problems. War heroes have to live with their emotional wounds for the rest of their lives. [The set of *war heroes* "is a subset of" the set of *great men*]
Sentence to sentence reference:
    I missed the meeting yesterday. I broke my leg just as I was about to leave home. [The (event of/fact that the) *second sentence* "is the cause of" the (event of/fact that the) *first sentence*]

Example 4. *Some types of contextual reference.*

In what follows we will use the term "contextual reference" to refer to the phenomenon (illustrated in Example 4) whereby the author of a text, for the sake of brevity, omits explicit mention of certain relations (e.g. "is identical to", "is the manner in which", etc.) intended to hold between items occurring in the text;[†] we shall use the term *full interpretation* of a sentence S_i, abbreviated $FI(S_i)$, to denote the result of resolving all ambiguities in $SI(S_i)$ and augmenting the resulting $SI(S_i)$ with all instances of contextual reference which a human reader would recover when reading S_i in the context of the preceding sentences of T. It is this full interpretation of all of the sentences of a text that is the goal of natural language understanding. How, then, might one compute $FI(S_i) - SI(S_i)$?   It has long been realized that the solution to the problems of disambiguation and contextual reference recovery lies in[‡]

- Codifying a large amount of world-knowledge (pragmatic information)[§] into a database.
- Using an *inferencing mechanism* which operates on $SI(S_i)$, on the full interpretations of $S_1, S_2, \ldots S_{i-1}$, and on the database of world-knowledge to perform complex chains of reasoning which end in the disambiguation of $SI(S_i)$ and in the determination of that part of $FI(S_i)$ which is over and above the interpretation of S_i taken in isolation.

Consider, for instance, the last example of 4:

    I missed the meeting yesterday.
    I broke my leg just as I was about to leave home.

The recovery of the intended "cause" reference from the second sentence to the first might involve a chain of inferencing from the following type of world-knowledge:

    (a) A meeting is a type of activity which has a precise setting in time and in location.
    (b) Participating in an activity which has a precise setting in time and in location requires being at the indicated location during the indicated time period.
    (c) Being in a particular physical location during a particular time period requires moving oneself from one's previous location to the indicated location by the beginning of the indicated time period.
    (d) When one intends to arrive at a particular location by a particular time one begins the process of moving oneself to the indicated location sufficiently in advance so that one will arrive by the indicated time.
    (e) Breaking a leg is (typically) an unexpected (accidental) occurrence.
    (f) When one experiences an unexpected occurrence one must often divert one's efforts from one's previous plans and spend time dealing with it.

Example 5. The type of world-knowledge required for the recovery of an instance of contextual reference

Continuing in this vein, Example 6 below gives two different preceding texts for each of the syntactically/lexically ambiguous sentences of Examples 2 and 3; when combined with world-knowledge, the full interpretation of each preceding text would allow the disambiguation of the second sentences, which would otherwise (in isolation) be ambiguous. Details of the required types of world-knowledge are omitted for the sake of brevity.

- *Syntactic ambiguity*
    (1) Before the salvage crews got to work, those aircraft which you see were just parts in junkyards. Today they are flying planes.
    (2) John and Betty are addicted to fast transportation. Yesterday they were driving sports cars. Today they are flying planes.

[†]We include in this phenomenon the phenomena of anaphora and definite noun phrase reference, as well as notions such as "implicature"[4]; see Lockman and Klappholz[5] for a more complete discussion of the notion of contextual reference.
  [‡]See [6–9] for explications of this process.
  [§]For a natural language understander with full human-equivalent capabilities over a wide range of texts, the contents of this database would seem to have to approach all of a human's knowledge concerning the world.

● *Lexical ambiguity*

(1) John is always gambling but never risks very much money. Yesterday he shot two bucks.

(2) John has been out in the woods hunting for the past three weeks. Yesterday he shot two bucks.

Example 6. Contexts within which inferencing can resolve ambiguity.

Now the type of inferencing required may be thought of as akin to deriving (in some logic) a set of conclusions from a set of axioms. The set of axioms in this case would be:

(a) The disjunction of the set of possible interpretations of S_i which is provided by the interpreter.

(b) $FI(S_1), FI(S_2), \ldots, FI(S_{i-1})$.

(c) The set of propositions constituting the world-knowledge database.

The rules of inference would be some set allowing us to combine propositions from (a), (b) and (c) to produce new propositions.

In its simplest form we may think of an inferencing algorithm as recursively "applying" (i.e. combining as allowed by the rules of inference) propositions from (c) to those in (a) and (b), as well as to those already inferred, until $FI(S_i)$ has been produced. The resolution of instances of ambiguity would result from contradictions derived from unintended interpretations of S_i; instances of contextual reference would be newly inferred propositions linking items in $SI(S_i)$ with items in the full interpretation of the preceding part of the text.

The above is, however, a simplification. We agree with many researchers that the inferencing process should not be viewed as deduction in a two-valued logic, but rather as something closer to probability-like reasoning about the relative "*plausibilities*" of various propositions. This requires the following modifications:

● A "plausibility" value is attached to each axiom in the world-knowledge database.

● The rules of inference are augmented by a "calculus of plausibility", so that each derived proposition has a plausibility which is a function of those of the propositions used in its derivation.

● The notions of "validity" and "contradiction" are replaced by suitable notions of high and low plausibility.

In the next section we will discuss some of the difficulties inherent in the construction of an inferencing mechanism, and point out problems with certain of the proposed approaches to this task. In Section 3 we will discuss what we believe to be the proper approach, namely the use of text structure to control inferencing. In Sections 4 and 5 we will sketch the natures of (respectively) the data structure and algorithm that the proposed approach would require.

2. THE CONTROL OF INFERENCING

The major problem which immediately arises when we consider doing world-knowledge based inferencing is that, if we simply recursively "apply" every piece of world-knowledge to every part of each $SI(S_j)(j \leq i)$ to which it can be applied, then we will be faced with a combinatorial explosion of derived conclusions. The "understanding" of Example 7(a) for example, requires a very different chain of reasoning from that required for Example 7(b).

(a) John has been out in the woods hunting for the past three weeks. His girlfriend won't go near him until he takes a shower.

(b) John has been out in the woods hunting for the past three weeks. Yesterday he shot two bucks.

Example 7. Sentences requiring different reasoning from the same context.

Moreover, there is a vast number of sentences S^j for which the two-sentence text

T^j: John has been out in the woods hunting for the past three weeks. S^j

is a coherent text. Each such T^j would require a different chain of reasoning for its understanding. But if the first sentence, "John has been out in the woods hunting for the past three weeks," caused the inferencer to pursue all of these (potentially necessary) chains then it would very likely be swamped before it was at all close to understanding a particular text.

A second major problem is that of how the inferencing mechanism decides that it has completed the processing of $SI(S_i)$, i.e. how it concludes that all instances of ambiguity have been resolved and all contextual references have been recovered. That this is in fact a problem may not be obvious. Given the definition of $FI(S_i)$, one might propose the following termination condition: halt when (a) the most plausible parse has been chosen for S_i; (b) the most plausible word sense has been chosen for every word in S_i; and (c) the most plausible referent has been found for each referring item in (the now disambiguated) $SI(S_i)$.

The problem with termination condition (b) is that in the general case it is not possible to include a complete set of word senses for every word in the lexicon. Rather, even in very prosaic texts, words are used in highly metaphoric senses (as in "The towns were *scattered* across the peninsula"), senses which must be determined through the use of world-knowledge based inferencing. There is, therefore, no fixed set of senses to choose from; as a result the inferencer cannot conclude that it has determined the correct sense when only one of the original lexical entries remains uncontradicted.

The problem with termination condition (c) is that, in general, by examining only $SI(S_i)$, one cannot detect all items in S_i which refer to (i.e. are intended by the author to be interpreted as bearing some relation to) items in the full interpretation of the preceding part of the text; in fact, almost any item in any sentence can be a referring item for some suitable previous text.† Thus the only way to formulate termination condition (c) would be: "every item in $SI(S_i)$ has been checked against every item in the full interpretation of the preceding sentences and for each such pair either an intended relation has been found or none exists." Attempting to satisfy such a condition would only aggravate the combinatorial explosion.

What is clearly needed then, is some method of *controlling* the inferencer, i.e. some method for deciding:

● which portions of the world-knowledge database are relevant to the processing of S_i;

● which of the derived propositions are, at any point in the inferencing process, relevant to that part of the processing of S_{Li} which still remains to be done, and which others should simply be discarded;

● when the inferencer has derived $FI(S_i)$ and may halt.

One proposal for the control of inferencing is that the world-knowledge database be *pre-organized* in such a way as to expose those of its parts which are inherently most likely to be useful in the inferencing process and should therefore be applied before other, less-relevant, parts of world knowledge; typical of such proposals are the notions of "natural salience" in Hobbs[11] and the "items to be foregrounded" in Chafe[10]. A more refined version of this type of approach proposes that world-knowledge be pre-organized into clusters of commonly associated ideas and/or events (e.g. [12, 13/35]). The motivation for such clustering is the hypothesis that those clusters associated with items occurring in $SI(S_i)$ or in the interpretations of the previous sentences of the text contain exactly the world knowledge that need be "applied" in the processing of S_i.

The problem with considering pre-organization of knowledge to be the solution to the control of inferencing is that this approach presumes the possibility of effectively *anticipating* (when pre-organizing the database) all associations which will be required in the full interpretation of any text. What it frequently leads to is the design of a recognizer of a relatively small set of texts involving a relatively small set of ideas and/or events which were anticipated by the builder of the database. The problem is that there is as yet no workable general notion of how to do such pre-organization, i.e. of how to decide how large such clusters should be and exactly what they should contain. Some researchers attempt to attack this problem by proposing a very large set of fairly small clusters which may be "triggered" (i.e. brought in as applicable) by other clusters, as well as by items in the semantic interpretation of the text (e.g. [14–17]). This simply reintroduces the combinatorial explosion and termination problems of the

---

†We refer the reader to Lockman and Klappholz[5] for evidence on this point.

original naive inferencer, although the larger units of world-knowledge used might mitigate the problem somewhat.

3. INFERENCING AND TEXT STRUCTURE

A major problem with the approaches to inferencing sketched thus far is that they make little use of a very important aspect of what there is to work with, namely the *structure* of the text; by this we mean the manner in which the text itself introduces and expands upon the items (ideas) with which it deals. The simplest text-structural feature is just the order in which the sentences of a text appear. To see its effect on the recovery of contextual references consider, e.g. Example 8 below. As its sentences are currently ordered, the phrase "to that effect" in sentence (*f*) is clearly a reference to the "fact that"/"event of" sentence (*e*). Yet in any reordering one might choose to make of sentences (a)–(e), "to that effect" in sentence (f) would always refer to the "fact that"/"event of" the last sentence in that reordering.

(a) It was a dark moonless night.
(b) We were camped on the banks of the Walapaloosa.
(c) The fire had just gone out.
(d) I remember that the crickets were making an incredible racket.
(e) We were all tired from the day's exertions.
(f) Jack said something to that effect.

Example 8. The effect of sentence order on full interpretation: contextual reference resolution.

Similarly, Example 9 illustrates the effect of text order on the resolution of lexical ambiguity.

(a) John drove across the country this summer.
(b) His first stop was in Chicago where he visited some friends.
(c) He then drove to Montana to go hunting.
(d) After a week there he went to Las Vegas to gamble.
(e) Surprisingly, he shot only two bucks.

vs

(a) John drove across the country this summer.
(b) His first stop was in Chicago where he visited some friends.
(c) After a week there he went to Las Vegas to gamble.
(d) He then drove to Montana to go hunting.
(e) Surprisingly, he shot only two bucks.

Example 9. The effect of sentence order on full interpretation: lexical ambiguity.

Clearly, then, an inferencer should attempt to detect and make use of the clues which the text itself provides in determining: (a) which parts of the world-knowledge database might be relevant to the processing of the sentence at hand; (b) which parts of the full interpretation of the *previous text* are of importance.

The linguistic notion of "focus" attempts to capture the latter. A focus is maintained dynamically as part of the processing of sentences S_1 through S_{i-1}, and consists of a *small subset* of the set of items occurring in their full interpretation. In the processing of S_i, the inferencer "applies" the world-knowledge database only to items in this focus or in $SI(S_i)$† Attempts to define such a "focus" have typically made use of syntactic structure, order of appearance in the text, semantic case markers, and the "newness" of the items in each sentence's interpretation; the problem is, however, that such techniques attempt to extract the focus of S_1 through S_{i-1} *independently of* S_i, i.e. before $SI(S_i)$ has been seen by the algorithm. Now it is certainly true that such focusing effects exist in the use of language, in the sense that the factors just mentioned may predispose a reader to a particular choice of referent from among otherwise (i.e. semantically and pragmatically) equally likely alternatives. However, while any such small focus may suffice for the full interpretation of many possible next sentences S_i, there will always be many other possible S_i's whose full interpretation requires the use of (i.e. inferencing from) items from outside the small extracted focus.‡ This approach to text structure is, therefore, insufficient.

†Typical of focus definitions are those found in [10, 18–21]. Attempts to use foci as part of computational algorithms for contextual reference recovery may be found in [22–25], among others.
‡See Lockman[24] for substantiation of this claim.

Recognizing that text structure should play a significant role in resolving instances of ambiguity and recovering contextual references still leaves open the problem of exactly how it might be used to effectively control inferencing to this end. What we propose as a solution requires that we first consider exactly what it is that makes texts understandable, i.e. that enables a human reader to successfully recover the missing portion of each $FI(S_i)$.

We first recall the very basic fact that the process of writing a text consists of introducing ideas/events and elaborating upon ideas/events which have already been introduced. In adding each new sentence to a text the author must follow certain structural conventions—not as yet very well understood—if the reader is to be able to determine *either*: (a) *that* the new sentence is meant to introduce something new; or (b) *how* the new sentence is meant to elaborate on some idea(s)/event(s) previously introduced. If such conventions were not observed, then the human reader would not be able to recover the full interpretation of the text; in fact, he/she would probably not even consider the text coherent.

We propose, therefore, that the inferencer be driven by the goal of determining the most plausible way in which each new S_i can be interpreted as "fitting in" to $FI(S_1)$, $FI(S_2), \ldots FI(S_{i-1})$, i.e. which portion(s) of the (already interpreted) preceding text S_i elaborates on and the nature of the elaboration. The claim is that the recovery of $FI(S_i) - SI(S_i)$ emerges from this process in the following way. The highest level task of the inferencer is the generation and evaluation of hypotheses concerning where and how $SI(S_i)$ "fits in" to the full interpretation of the preceding part of the text. The evaluation of each such hypothesis devolves into the generation and evaluation of a set of sub-hypotheses concerning particular resolutions of ambiguity and the recovery of particular contextual references, a set which, if assumed to be true, would support the "fit" of S_i into a particular part of the preceding text. The most plausible such set of sub-hypotheses which does not contradict (in the system of plausibility reasoning) anything in the world-knowledge database (or in the full interpretation of the preceding part of the text) is *assumed* to have been intended by the author to be inferred by the reader, and constitutes the missing part of $FI(S_i)$. If such an inferencer could be constructed, it would offer a solution to the termination problem: the mechanism would terminate, and would have produced $FI(S_i)$, exactly when it has found a coherent "fit" to the previous text for S_i.

In the next two sections we consider:

● The nature of the text-structural clues which should be maintained in processing a text in the manner just proposed, and the type of data structure which they naturally fit into.

● The nature of an algorithm for hypothesizing and testing possible "fits".

4. A DATA STRUCTURE FOR CONTEXT

In discussing just what sort of text-structual clues should be maintained during the processing of a text (for use in processing later parts) we shall concentrate on the requirements induced by the need to recover intended contextual references. Let us assume, then, that $FI(S_1), FI(S_2), \ldots FI(S_{i-1})$ have already been determined, and that we are about to start the inferencing process on $SI(S_i)$. Since an item in $SI(S_i)$ may, in general, refer to almost any item in the full interpretation of the text,† a minimal requirement for the data structure is that it contain $FI(S_1), FI(S_2), \ldots FI(S_{i-1})$. What else, though, is necessary to enable the inferencer to find the point(s) at which S_i "fits in" to the preceding text?

As we have noted above, the order of appearance of the sentences of a text can have an effect on the recovery of contextual references. Simply keeping track of sentence order, however, is by no means sufficient. In text A of Example 10 below, most readers would interpret "these particles" of sentence 5 as referring to "Zilchons" of sentence 2; in text B (which is identical to text A save for sentence order) the same phrase seems to refer to "The Blipons" of sentence 4. Yet in both of these texts Blipons are mentioned *after* Zilchons in linear text order. Clearly the implicit (via "high seriosity") reference to Zilchons in sentence 4 of text A affects a reader's picture of the structure of this text, which in turn effects the different resolution (from that made for text B) of the reference in sentence 5.

---

†We refer the reader to [5] for arguments in support of this claim.

Text A

(1) Consider the common pseudo-atomic particles.
(2) Zilchons exhibit high seriosity.
(3) The Blipons, however, have a low seriosity level.
(4) Herkimer attributed the high seriosity to extreme multifluicity.
(5) This explains why these particles are so hard to detect.

Text B

(1) Consider the common pseudo-atomic particles.
(2) Zilchons exhibit high seriosity.
(3) Herkimer attributed the high seriosity to extreme multifluicity.
(4) The Blipons, however, have a low seriosity level.
(5) This explains why these particles are so hard to detect.

Example 10. Non-linear text-structural effects on reference resolution.

Since linear order does not completely capture those clues to preferred "fit position" which an author has built into a text, the data structure must also include the pattern of sentence-to-sentence connections (e.g. via "high seriosity" above) which the text establishes, i.e. the pattern in which the author has introduced new concepts and expanded on already introduced concepts. Some clues to this pattern are explicitly marked in texts: paragraph breaks and introductory words such as "Now", "As for", or "Anyway" indicate a "pop" from the latest topic discussed to either some earlier, more general, topic or to something quite new; parenthetical phrases indicate a more detailed exploration of some component of a more general topic before returning to the more general topic. Most of this pattern, however, is extracted as part of the inferencing on the previous text, i.e. as part of the process whereby each of the previous sentences has itself been fitted into *its* preceding text.

We propose representing this pattern by organizing the full interpretation of the text into a "context graph" whose nodes are the $FI(S_j)$ for $j < i$ (where S_i is the current sentence). The nodes are connected by two types of link. The first type connects each (established) referring item to its referent; such links, however, capture only part of what is necessary. The second type of link, termed an *inter-sentence relation*, connects each $FI(S_j)$ to the nodes representing the (those) sentence(s) to which S_j was fitted when it was itself processed; we will elaborate further on this type of link in Section 5. Informally, each node of the context graph may be thought of as representing a "topic" which its descendents in the graph have "expanded upon". Example 11 below depicts such a context graph for text A of Example 10. The single arrows (labelled on the left) indicate the first (reference to referent) type of link, while double arrows indicate inter-sentence relations. Again, no attempt is made here to suggest a suitable semantic representation language; the $FI(S_j)$ are represented here by abbreviations of the original sentences.

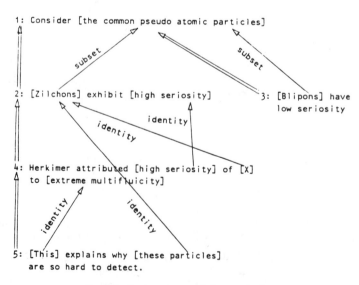

Example 11. A context graph for text A of 4-1.

From the point of view of contextual reference recovery the utility of these links is clear in the following sense. While it is certainly not the case that a reference from some item in S_i must have its referent in $FI(S_{i-1})$, it is the case that $FI(S_{i-1})$ should be the starting point of the search for any such reference, and that the ancestors of $FI(S_{i-1})$ in the context graph are logical continuation points for pursuing the search. The links in the context graph thus provide a notion of "discursive proximity" which may be used in fitting S_i to the "closest point(s)" to S_{i-1} to which it may reasonably be interpreted as belonging.

5. THE NATURE OF THE FIT ALGORITHM

In this section we sketch an algorithm for fitting $SI(S_i)$ into the context graph just described. Now the goal of "fitting" the current sentence S_i into its context amounts to deciding which (of the) node(s) of the context graph S_i can best be interpreted as an "expansion of" or "further elaboration on". We shall use the notation $EXPANDS(S_i, S_j)$ to denote that S_i expands on or elaborates on S_j. Our contention is that the attempt to find the "most suitable" sentence $S_j (j < i)$ in the context graph such that EXPANDS(S_i, S_j) is plausible should be the overall controlling goal of world-knowledge based inferencing. We contend, further, that the determination of $FI(S_i) - SI(S_i)$ will result from the achievement of this goal.†

The algorithm which we propose for finding the "most suitable" S_j makes use of the context graph in the following manner: we first attempt to fit $SI(S_i)$ to the node representing $FI(S_{i-1})$, i.e. to show that EXPANDS(S_i, S_{i-1}) is sufficiently plausible to be accepted; if we fail, i.e. if we cannot generate a set of assumptions which would (in the light of our world-knowledge database and the full interpretation of the preceding text) make EXPANDS(S_i, S_j) sufficiently plausible, then we move up the context graph to the immediate ancestor(s) of S_{i-1}; for each immediate ancestor S', we attempt to show that EXPANDS(S_i, S') is sufficiently plausible. The process of moving up the context graph continues until either we find an appropriate node (or nodes) or we reach the top of the context graph without a successful fit. In the former case we add the necessary supporting assumptions to $SI(S_i)$ to form $FI(S_i)$; in the latter we conclude that S_i is incoherent in its context.

In order to complete the picture we will sketch:

● How EXPANDS(S_i, S_j) can be algorithmically defined, i.e. how to generate a set of assumptions which will make it sufficiently plausible (or decide that there is no such set).

● How the determination of $FI(S_i) - SI(S_i)$ results from finding, in the manner sketched above, an S_j such that EXPANDS(S_i, S_j) meets the plausibility criterion; i.e., why $FI(S_i) - SI(S_i)$ is exactly the set of assumptions which enables EXPANDS(S_i, S_j) to meet the plausibility criterion.

The intuitive notion of "expansion" or "elaboration" denoted by the predicate EXPANDS can be viewed as the disjunction of a number of inter-sentence relations. A number of researchers concerned with the question of text coherence have proposed such relations. (In particular, we refer the reader to [28–31, 22, 27, 24]. Typical of the type of relation proposed are:

(1) EXAMPLES(S_i, S_j)
● *Definition*: The event/state described by S_i is a particular instance of or subclass of the events/states described by S_j.
● *Example*: All great men seem to have special emotional problems. War heroes have to live with their emotional wounds for the rest of their lives.

(2) RESULT(S_i, S_j)
● *Definition*: The event/state described by S_j is (in at least a contributory way) a cause of the event/state described by S_i.
● *Example*: John was late to work yesterday. He missed the meeting.

---

†An earlier version of this approach may be found in Klappholz and Lockman[26] and in Lockman[24]. Also, in Hobbs[11, 27] it is suggested that some of what we define as $FI(S_i)-SI(S_i)$ may be resolved as a by-product of determining the type of fit between a sentence S and the (previously occurring) sentence S' to which it fits.

(3) CAUSE(S_i, S_j)

● *Definition*: The event/state described by S_i is (in at least a contributory way) a cause of the event/state described in S_j.

● *Example*: John invited Bill to the conference. He thought that he might have something to contribute.

(4) DETAIL(S_i, S_j)

● *Definition*: S_{Li} gives further elaboration of some aspect of the event/state described in S_j (e.g. manner adverbial).

● *Example*: John mowed the lawn. He did an excellent job.

(5) SEQUENCE(S_i, S_j)

● *Definition*: The event described by S_i takes place in the same general spatial context as S_j and follows it in time sequence.

● *Example*: He decided to call the Police. The sergeant took down all the details.

Assuming that one can define a set of relations whose disjunction defines the predicate EXPANDS, our goal of generating the set of propositions which will support EXPANDS(S_i, S_j) (or demonstrating that there is none) becomes one of finding a set of propositions which will support at least one of the sentence relations between S_i and S_j. The "fit" algorithm thus amounts to utilizing the structure of the text to generate a specific goal for the inferencing mechanism. Once the goal has been generated the inferencer must attempt to *generate* a set of assumptions which will achieve the goal, i.e., from which one of the inter-sentence relations can be demonstrated to be plausible.

Essentially this process is analogous to a top-down inference proof-procedure (as discussed in [32–34] in that we start from a goal proposition and work backwards via rules of inference to axioms. The essential difference is that here the axiom-equivalents terminating the "proof" process are generally *not in the world-knowledge database*; rather they are *any* set of propositions whose inclusion in the database *would not cause a (plausibility-logic) contradiction*. When such a set is found, it is *assumed to be true* (actually intended by the author of the text), and added to the database. This set is, then, $FI(S_i) - SI(S_i)$.

To illustrate the point that the propositions so derived constitute the missing portion of $FI(S_i)$, we sketch their derivation for the following two sentences text:

(1) All of the common pseudo-atomic particles exhibit unusual behavior.
(2) Blipons spontaneously change their turgidity from positive to negative.

Assume that S_2 is the sentence currently being processed, and that we are examining the possibility of establishing EXPANDS(S_2, S_1). In particular, we will investigate the possibility of establishing the inter-sentence relation EXAMPLE(S_2, S_1). In order to do so we must first elaborate on the sketchy definition of EXAMPLE which was given earlier. We shall use the following schema as an approximation to such a definition.†

If sentences S_i, S_j have the forms

$$S_i:\ (\delta x)[P(x) \rightarrow Q(x)]$$

$$S_j:\ (\delta y)[P'(y) \rightarrow Q'(y)]$$

where δ is the *SRL* equivalent of any of the English quantifiers "all", "most", "many", etc.

Then EXAMPLE(S_i, S_j) (i.e. the event/state described by S_i is a particular instance of or subclass of the events/states described by S_j) holds if and only if it is plausible that:

$$(\delta v)[P(v) \rightarrow P'(v)]$$

and

$$(\delta w)[Q(w) \rightarrow Q'(w)].$$

†Note that in this definition P, Q, P', and Q' are arbitrarily complex well-formed formulas.

The application of this definition to the sentences under consderation is as follows:

- $P(x) = x$ is a Blipon.
- $Q(x) = x$ spontaneously changes its turgidity from positive to negative.
- $P'(x) = x$ is a common pseudo-atomic particle.
- $Q'(x) = x$ exhibits unusual behaviour.

In order to support $\text{EXAMPLE}(S_i, S_j)$, our inferencing mechanism would have to find support for the propositions:

- Blipons are common pseudo-atomic particles.
- Spontaneously changing turgidity from positive to negative is unusual behavior.

Now in general, $(\delta v)[P(v) \to P'(v)]$ and $(\delta w)[Q(w) \to Q'(W)]$ may or may not be inferable from the basic world knowledge of a particular reader; in this particular example they cannot possibly be, since we have deliberately chosen fictitious terms. However in order to give this text a coherent interpretation, a reader *must assume that the auther intended to communicate* that "Blipons are common pseudo-atomic particles" and that "Spontaneously changing turgidity from positive to negative is unusual behavior", and must add these propositions to his $FI(S_2)$ unless they contradict some other aspects of his world-knowledge. In this example, as is usual when reading about some hitherto unfamiliar topic, a reader possesses no relevant world-knowledge and takes the author on faith.

6. CONCLUSIONS

The approach presented above is, clearly, just the beginning of a theory of inference control. A number of serious problems remain to be solved. The first is the compilation of a far more complete catalog of formally defined inter-sentence relations. If, in fact, the theoretical framework proposed here is a workable approach, one can reasonably expect that the details of these specifications will delimit exactly what the power of the inferencer must be, and therefore provide clues concerning the rules of inference which it should use and the appropriate organization for the world-knowledge database which it must utilize.

In addition, the procedure for traversing the context graph must be refined, since we are already aware of text-structural effects which are not taken into account by the procedure proposed in Section 5. Consider, for example, the short text of Example 12:

I walked into the room.
The chandelier was the largest I had ever seen.

Example 12. Coherent text: DETAIL.

There is no question that this text is coherent, and the that second sentence is a DETAIL of the first, i.e. an elaboration of a particular aspect ("the room") of the first. Consider, however, Example 13, which is created by simply inserting an intervening sentence between the sentences of Example 12.

I walked into the room.
John approached me and began to complain about his salary.
The chandelier was the largest I had ever seen.

Example 13. Incoherent text.

Example 13 is clearly incoherent; in particular the third sentence does not seem to "fit". The algorithmic sketch of Section 5, however, would have no problem fitting this third sentence to the preceding text as follows. We first attempt to fit it to the immediately preceding, second, sentence; it is hard to devise any plausible assumptions which would relate the two, so we reject this and move up the context graph to the first. And as Example 12 demonstrated, the third sentence is easily interpreted as a DETAIL of the first, under the not unreasonable assumption that "the chandelier" of the former hangs in "the room" of the latter.

Clearly what is occurring is some sort of "blocking" effect, in that *certain types* of intervening material may prevent the interpretation of following sentences as "expanding upon" preceding (to the blocking material) sentences. The particular explanation for what occurs in Example 13 is something like: after a sentence which describes a change of state it is acceptable to further elaborate upon details of the new state; however after such elaboration has stopped, it may not be resumed without explicit reminders of the change of state or of the new state. The codification of such rules (which are really text structural conventions) is a prerequisite to further elaboration of a fit algorithm.

Finally, of course, there is the problem of how the inferencer will generate and test supporting assumptions for a particular hypothesis of fit. Both the definition of EXPANDS(S, S') as a disjunction of inter-sentence relations and the different possible instantiations of each inter-sentence relation create a complex disjunction as the goal to be supported. This, of course, creates the immediate problem of how to decide when to "cut off" the inferencing process down any one of these disjunctive paths; i.e. how to decide that *any* possible set of supporting assumptions for it is unlikely to meet the minimal (for coherence) plausability requirement.

We hope, however, that we have convinced the reader that the most likely source of control for the inferencing required in understanding natural language text is information embedded in the structure of the text itself.

REFERENCES

1. N. Chomsky, *Syntactic Structures*. Mouton, Paris (1957).
2. N. Chomsky, *Aspects of the Theory of Syntax*. M.I.T. Press, Mass. (1965).
3. J. J. Katz and J. A. Fodor, The structure of a semantic theory. *Language* **39** (1963).
4. H. Clark, Bridging. In *Theoretical Issues in Natural Language Processing* (Edited by R. Schank and B. L. Nash-Webber). Cambridge (1975).
5. A. D. Lockman and A. D. Klappholz, Toward a procedural model of contextual reference resolution. *Discourse Proc.* **3**, 1 (1980).
6. C. Rieger, Conceptual memory: a theory and computer program for processing the meaning content of natural language utterances. Doctoral dissertation, Computer Science Department, Stanford University (1974).
7. R. Schank, Understanding paragraphs. *Tech. Rep.* 6, Instituto per gli Studi Semantici e Cognitive, Castagnola 1975.
8. Y. Wilks, A preferential, pattern-seeking, semantics for natural language inference. *Artificial Intell.* **6** (1975).
9. T. Winograd, Understanding natural language. *Cognitive Psych.* **3** (1972).
10. W. Chafe, Discourse structure and human knowledge. In *Language Comprehension and the Acquisition of Knowledge* (Edited by J. B. Carroll and R. O. Freedle). Vinton (1972).
11. J. Hobbs, Selective inferencing. *Proc. 3rd Biennial Conf. Canadian Society for Computational Studies of Intelligence*. Victoria B.C. 1980.
12. R. E. Cullingford, Script application: computer understanding of newspaper stories. Ph.D. thesis, Computer Science Department, Yale University (1978).
13. C. Riesbeck, Computational understanding: analysis of sentences and context. Doctoral dissertation, Computer Science Department, Stanford University (1974).
14. C. Bullwinkle, Levels of complexity in discourse for anaphora disambiguation and speech act interpretation. *Proc. Int. Joint Conf. Artificial Intelligence*, M.I.T. (1977).
15. B. J. Grosz, The representation and use of focus in a system for understanding dialogs. *Proc. 5th Int. Joint Conf. Artificial Intelligence*, M.I.T. (1977).
16. C. Rieger, Conceptual overlays: a mechanism for the interpretation of sentence meaning in context. *Proc. 4th Int. Joint Conf. Artificial Intelligence*, Tbilisi 1975.
17. R. Schank, Language and memory. *Cognitive Sci.* **4**, 3 (1980).
18. M. A. K. Halliday, Notes on transitivity and theme in English: Part 2. *J. Linguistics* **3** (1967).
19. M. A. K. Halliday, Language structure and language function. In *New Horizons in Linguistics* (Edited by J. Lyons) (1970).
20. E. V. Paduceva, On the structure of the paragraph. *Linguistics* 131 (1974).
21. P. Sgall, E. Hajicova and E. Benesova, *Topic, Focus, and Generative Semantics*. Kronberg/Ts (1973).
22. J. Hobbs, A computational approach to discourse analysis. Computer Science Department, City University of New York, *Res. Rep.* 76-2 (1976).
23. A. D. Klappholz and A. D. Lockman, Contextual reference resolution. In *Proc. 13th Ann. Meeting of the Association for Computational Linguistics* (Edited by T. C. Diller), *Am. J. Computat. Linguistics* (1975).
24. A. D. Lockman, Contextual reference resolution in natural language processing. *DCS-TR-70*, Dept. of Computer Science, Rutgers University (1978).
25. C. L. Sidner, Focusing for interpretation of pronouns. *Am. J. Computat. Linguistics* **7**(4) (1981).
26. A. D. Klappholz and A. D. Lockman, The use of dynamically extracted context for anaphoric reference resolution. *Proc. 5th Int. Joint Conf. Artificial Intelligence*, M.I.T. (1977).
27. J. Hobbs, Coherence and coreference. *Cognitive Sci.* **3**, 1 (1979).
28. R. Alterman, Seven relations for representing conceptual coherence of events, *TR-188*, Computer Sciences Department, University of Texas, Austin (1981).
29. E. J. Crothers, Inference and coherence. *Discourse Proc.* **1**, 1 (1978).
30. M. A. K. Halliday and R. Hasan, *Cohesion in English*. Longman (1976).
31. G. Hirst, Discourse-oriented anaphora resolution: a review. *Am. J. Computat. Linguistics* **7**, 2 (1981).
32. R. Kowalski, *Logic for Problem Solving*. North Holland, Amsterdam (1979).
33. D. W. Loveland, Mechanical theorem proving by model elimination. *JACM* (April 1968).
34. D. W. Loveland, A simplified format for the model elinination procedure. *JACM* (July 1969).
35. R. Schank and R. Abelson, Scripts, plans, and knowledge. *Proc. 4th Int. Joint Conf. Artificial Intelligence*, Tbilisi 1975.

Comp. & Maths. with Appls. Vol. 9, No. 1, pp. 71–82, 1983
Printed in Great Britain.

0097–4943/83/010071–12$03.00/0
Pergamon Press Ltd.

WHAT THE SPEAKER MEANS: THE RECOGNITION OF SPEAKERS' PLANS IN DISCOURSE

Candace L. Sidner

Bolt Beranek and Newman Inc., 10 Moulton St., Cambridge, MA 02238, U.S.A.

Abstract—Human conversational participants depend upon the ability of their partners to recognize their intentions, so that those partners may respond appropriately. In such interactions, the speaker encodes his intentions about the hearer's response in a variety of sentence types. Instead of telling the hearer what to do, the speaker may just state his goals, and expect a response that meets these goals at least part way. This paper presents a new model for recognizing the speaker's intended meaning in determining a response. It shows that this recognition makes use of the speaker's plan, his beliefs about the domain and about the hearer's relevant capacities.

1. INTRODUCTION

Human conversational participants depend upon the ability of their partners to recognize their intentions, so that those partners may be capable of responding appropriately. For instance, in the dialogue below, the speaker's desires are encoded in a variety of sentence types.

D1–1 S1: I want to see the drawing of the new design layout.

2 S2: OK. Here it is. (Shows sheet with new design.)

3 S1: There isn't room to put in the color code charts at the bottom of the picture. Can you move up the main layout?

4 S2: Sure, I'll bring back the new design in half an hour.

Instead of telling the hearer what to do, the speaker stated his goals, and expected a response that met them, at least part way. The sentence forms used were not simply commands, but rather declaratives that described a desired state or a new difficulty, or commented on progress. This paper presents a model in which recognizing the speaker's intended meaning plays a fundamental part in determining a response. First I describe the methodological and theoretical approaches to this problem, and then I describe a model that enables us to tell what the speaker's intentions are. I will illustrate the model on two examples and compare it to previous work.

The model presented here is particularly powerful because it provides necessary linguistic capabilities to a system that understands natural language and presents information on a graphics display. In particular, it makes it possible for a system to reason about utterances that express errors in planning, to acknowledge those errors and respond to them just as people do in conversation.

2. BACKGROUND FOR A NEW MODEL

One of the goals of the Knowledge Representation and Natural Language group at BBN has been to provide powerful general tools for natural language processing and to build a language understanding system for a decision maker using a graphics display. We envision a decision maker accessing information from a database that can be represented visually; he/she needs to collect information from the database, add to it, change it, and define new features. In accessing information, the decision maker must be able to express him/herself naturally. S/he must be free to use imperatives, declaratives and interrogatives in whatever way is most convenient and expressive.

Natural communication with a language system is possible, however, only if it can be reason both about the intent behind the speaker's utterances and about its own responses to those utterances. Such reasoning involves—at least—(1) bringing to bear the kinds of knowledge people have before they enter into a given discussion, and (2) making use of the knowledge they gain in the discussion.

As part of our research to provide a sophisticated natural language and graphics-oriented system (NLGO) for a decision maker, I collected protocols of users communicating with a simulated version of the system. The simulated system was actually a person communicating in English over a terminal and computer link to a user. For graphics we used an overhead viewgraph projector to project the drawings that the person simulating the machine drew. Using an arrangement reported in[1], the user was able to point at the display and make changes as needed. The protocols consisted of the transcript of communications, all the pictures drawn during a session, and notes indicating deictic references to screen objects.† When I analyzed those collections of protocols, I recognized that a NLGO system would require the ability to understand declaratives that:

● Describe a desire (e.g. "I want to see a drawing of the new layout").

● State a problem (e.g. "There isn't room to put color code charts in.").

● Or function as a comment on progress (e.g. "I'm almost done this part of the layout.").

An organizing framework for a system that can reason about the speaker's intentions has been explored in our group and is reported elsewhere[2]. In that framework the group experimented with an implementation of Allen's model[3] of a plan-based approach to speech act recognition. This model provided us with a perspective within which to use models or speaker's beliefs and wants[4] as well as a framework for reasoning about the speaker's plan[3]. To include all the types of declaratives given above within the framework I found that I needed to expand the existing model for reasoning about plans in two ways: (1) by recognizing a richer form of plans than Allen's model permitted, and (2) by making explicit the connection between the speaker's intentions as structured by his plans and the response intended by the speaker.

3. DEFINING INTENDED SPEAKER MEANING

My goal is to provide a computational model of the hearer's interpretation of the speaker's intended meaning. The *intended meaning* of an utterance I define as that set of pairs of propositional attitudes (e.g. belief, want, intend), and propositional contents that the speaker wants the hearer to hold by means of the utterance.

The notion of the intended meaning of an utterance can be illustrated by contrasting it with that of semantic meaning. The semantic meaning of a declarative utterance is the propositional content assigned to that type of utterance by the semantic rules of the language. For instance, if someone says, "You're a prince", the semantic meaning is that the person addressed by the speaker is the son of a king. By contrast, the intended meaning depends on the psychological state of the speaker at the time and place of utterance. The speaker may mean that he thinks the hearer is a really nice guy and wants to tell him so, or he may be saying something quite different. The speaker, using irony, may mean that the addressee is just the opposite of a nice guy.

This example demonstrates that the speaker's intended meaning, though correlated, is not in general identical with semantic meaning. Comprehending the semantic meaning of the utterance forms the basis for discerning the intended meaning, but understanding the intended meaning also requires the hearer to use:

(1) The characteristics of the current situation.

(2) The speaker's beliefs and goals.

(3) The context of discussion (the *discourse context*) as a special aspect of (1).

(4) Conventions for action that exist between the speaker and hearer.‡

(5) The mutual beliefs of the speaker and hearer (those beliefs the hearer knows to be shared with the speaker) concerning (1)–(4).

A sample exchange will indicate the role of these kinds of information. In the example below, the user is interacting with our NLGO system to display some information about ATN grammars. The user's first two utterances are simple, direct imperatives that indicate that the user wants the NLGO system to display a part of the net and then move the focus to a subpart of the display.

D2–1 U: Display the clause level network.

    2 S: ⟨display of network⟩ OK.

---

†A deictic reference is one where a person uses a linguistic phrase to refer to something by pointing at it. The person may actually point his finger, cock his head or otherwise physically point or he may simply use a phrase that makes clear he's pointing.

‡This, of course, is relevant only to a special class of situations, a class that includes the kind of interaction the BBN system must handle.

3 U: Now focus on the preverbal constituents.

4 S: ⟨display of subnet, not including S/AUX⟩ OK.

5 U: No, I want to see S/AUX.

What does the user mean by his/her third utterance (D2-5)? The answer depends on what s/he believes about the network objects to which s/he referred. Suppose s/he thinks that S/AUX is part of the preverbal constituents (which it actually is). Then s/he is communicating that the display is wrong and what's wrong with it; s/he intends for S/AUX to be included in the display with the other constituents. Suppose, alternatively, that s/he thinks that S/AUX is not part of the preverbal constituents. S/he is still indicating that s/he wants to see S/AUX, but also that s/he has changed his/her mind about the display and intends S/AUX to be visible, perhaps without any other objects on the screen. This discourse, similar to one discussed in [2], could be handled by the prototype discussed there only by including S/AUX with other constituents on the screen. Reasoning about the user's overall task and the relation of S/AUX to it was not considered.

In choosing among its available responses, the NLGO system must use its model of the user's beliefs about the domain and its model of what the user takes to be mutually believed between the two of them about that domain. For example, the user might have thought that S/AUX was one of the preverbal constituents, and thought the NLGO system believed this also. S/he would then have expected and intended the NLGO system to include that state in the display. If the user had been right about this belief, the NLGO system would indeed have included it. Since it did not, the user's "No" indicates to the NLGO system some bug in the communication, a bug stemming either from the user having a faulty model of the domain (because S/AUX is not defined as a preverbal constituent) or from faulty expectations about the NLGO system's model (because S/AUX is a preverbal constituent, but the system does not know this).

Suppose alternatively that the NLGO system doesn't conclude that the user thinks S/AUX is among the preverbal constituents, and it believes that s/he takes *that* idea to be mutually believed. Then it must again use its models of the user and of the user's model of itself to determine what action *is* intended. For example, does the user intend the system to compress the current display to make room for S/AUX, or should it erase the current display and bring up a new one, centered on S/AUX? This decision may depend on the kinds of conventions alluded to in (4) above. In general, of course, people's behavior in conversational situations also depends on the relative status of the conversational partners, on what the participants think will benefit themselves, as well as not harm others and the like. These social considerations are significant to human interaction, but for the remainder of this paper, let us assume that the NLGO system responds in a slavishly cooperatine way, i.e. it has no interest beyond serving the user.

There are two ways to view the intentions of another agent. The first is simply in terms of one's beliefs about what the other person wants and believes. This is keyhole recognition (see [5]). One person decides what he thinks another intends simply by observing him through a keyhole; e.g. I decide that you are looking for your umbrella, because you look around the room with your coat on, when I believe you believe that it's raining outside). Keyhole recognition of a user's wants is central to Genesereth's MACSYMA advisor[6]; it also forms the basis of plan recognition in both Schmidt *et al.*'s[7] work on BELIEVER system and in Wilensky's story understanding[8].

The intended recognition of what someone is doing, on the other hand, is relevant for communicative situations[9, 3]. A speaker says something to a hearer and intends the hearer to recognize the intention that lies behind the utterance. The speaker is attempting to "give the hearer a piece of its mind" and it's essential to the success of the speaker's attempt that the hearer recognize it as such. In Allen's terms, the shared recognition by the hearer of intention occurs when the speaker says something to the hearer because the speaker wants the hearer to believe the speaker wants something. That is, *H* believes *S* wants *H* to think (believe) that *S* wants something (*HBSWHBSW*). In the example D2-5 above, shared recognition is involved in the fact that the user wants the NLGO system to believe her statement, a statement about the user's wants. Generally the hearer, in responding to the speaker, must take into account not only the shared recognition of the speaker's intentions but also the beliefs that the speaker assumes are shared with the hearer (in Cohen's model[4] these are beliefs in the context *H*B*S*B*H*B*S*B). Occasionally the hearer's own beliefs about a situation will differ from the shared beliefs (called mutual beliefs hereafter) and influence the hearer's response. Just how this occurs will be illustrated later.

4. MODEL OF RECOGNITION OF INTENDED MEANING

The hearer's task in recognizing what the speaker meant by an utterance is to be understood as follows:

(1) To produce an explanation for the utterance, stated in terms of the speaker's beliefs and wants.

(2) To use the explanation as a basis for a response.

I use the term "explanation" because the hearer is trying to answer the question "why did the speaker say that to me?" The answer to this question—the proffered explanation of the speaker's act in uttering what s/he did—in turn produces new beliefs about the speaker; these will form part of the basis of the hearer's response.

The explanation, in general, will have the form of a set of pairs of propositional attitudes and propositional contents attributed by the hearer to the speaker [E.g. ⟨belief, that S/AUX is part of the preverbal constituents⟩ ⟨Want, that I display all components of the preverbal constituents⟩, etc.] Certain beliefs play a central role in explaining why the speaker said what he did:

EXPLANATORY BELIEFS

(1) Beliefs about the speaker's goal and the plan to achieve it,

(2) Beliefs about the hearer's capacities,

(3) Beliefs about the hearer's dispositions to act given information about the speaker's wants.

To produce an explanation, the system must have a model that infers beliefs of these kinds and that distinguishes between the speaker's intended responses and some helpful but unintended responses. I want the NLGO system to recognize and produce the intended response whenever possible, and to be able to produce a helpful response when appropriate.

To model the construction of the required explanation, we begin with Grice's theory of speaker meaning[9, 10]. Grice notes that there are certain kinds of evidence normally available to an audience on the basis of which the audience is intended to draw certain conclusions about the speaker's intended meaning. These kinds of evidence include (1) the features of the utterance, and (2) mappings between those features and propositional attitude-propositional content pairs that the audience (assumed to be a competent speaker/hearer of the language) is supposed to be able to grasp, and *is intended to* grasp. For example, the feature; DECLARATIVE, will be mapped to the speaker's wanting the hearer to believe the speaker believes the propositional content of the utterance; while imperatives will be mapped to the speaker's wanting the hearer to believe the speaker wants the hearer to bring about the state of affairs expressed by the propositional component of the utterance.

Somewhat more formally; an audience who, for the utterance of a certain sentence *S*, the speaker believes to have certain attributes† *A*, is expected to be able to recognize certain features of the utterance and to be able to draw from those features certain conclusions about what the speaker intended in uttering *S* in that context. These conclusions include:

Intended conclusions

(1) *S* has certain features (call them *F*1 . . . *Fn*).

(2) *S* is correlated, in virtue of such features and the rules of the language, with the pair (*p*, *PC*(*S*)).

(3) The speaker intends the audience to believe that the speaker *p*'s that *PC*(*S*).

(4) By sincerity (see below), the speaker does *p* that *PC*(*S*).

---

†One such audience attribute, of course, is competence in the language of *S*; others are both interesting and more specific to the situation.

5. THE SPEAKER INTENDED THAT THE HEARER $p†$ THAT $PC(S)$

[In the above, "p" is a schematic letter that takes verbs of propositional attitude as arguments; "PC", a schematic letter that takes declarative sentences as arguments.] We can apply this theory directly to the sample dialogue. For example, let us consider a sample utterance from the dialogue D2, understood, however, as the initial utterance of a discourse:

$S1$: I want to see S/AUX.

Intuitively, we would like the theory to allow us to show how a computer system (call it S) would conclude that the user (U) wants to see S/AUX, and the user wants it to believe that s/he has this desire.

The set of relevant features F, attributes A and mappings C include:

● $F1 = S1$ is in declarative mood.
● $F2 = S1$ was uttered intentionally by U.
● $F3 = S1$ was intentionally directed at S.
● $A1 = S$ is a computer system with a graphics display, and U knows this.
● $A2 = S$ believes U is sincere.
● $C1 =$ is a rule that maps $F1$ to U's wanting S to believe that U believes that U wants to see S/AUX.‡

The system will make default assumptions about $F2$, $F3$, $A1$ and $A2$, recognize that $F1$, and apply $C1$ to $S1$. The NLGO system can then use the intended conclusions and infer directly that:

(1) U intended (S to recognize) that $S1$ is correlated with U's wanting S to believe that U believes that U wants to see S/AUX (derived from intended conclusion 3 and $C1$).

In order for the NLGO system to conclude that simply U wants to see S/AUX, it must apply two additional rules§ it has available. The first, a sincerity rule, allows it to deduce: U believes that U wants to see S/AUX. By a rule of reliability, it can conclude: U wants to see S/AUX. This, of course, is what, on intuitive grounds, we wanted the NLGO system to conclude. Now we must ask what it will do with this conclusion.

5. EXTENDING THE MODEL

While the Gricean framework provides a starting point for recognizing the speaker's communicative intentions, it does not provide a recipe for inferring the intended response. Given, for example, that the user wants the NLGO system to believe that the user wants to see S/AUX, and nothing more, the system could simply say "Yes, I understand", (or "Let me add that to my data base of beliefs about you")—a behavior the user probably did not intend. At the same time, the NLGO system *could* decide to provide a lot of information by showing the whole ATN network and highlighting S/AUX. Such behavior might even be helpful; but it is not, we can presume, the intended response.

To determine the response the user intended, the NLGO system must consider the utterance in a larger situational context. This context is determined by what (it thinks) the user is doing, what (it thinks) the user thinks the NLGO system can do, and how cooperative (it thinks) the user takes the NLGO system to be. The system will generate explanations that take into account the larger situational context as a means for responding as intended. We have augmented the Gricean framework to enable the NLGO system to derive a situation-specific explanation for the user's having the wants and beliefs s/he is believed to have. In particular, the system can be viewed as asking itself for an explanation of some of the beliefs it attributes to the user. The explanation is like that given earlier. For example, to explain why the user

---

†Actually the hearer may be intended to have a different propositional attitude p' toward a related proposition. For simplicity, I'll assume these are the same.

‡The general form of the $C1$ rule is: for declarative sentences map to U wants audience to believe that U believes $PC(S)$; for imperative sentences map to U wants audience to believe that U wants audience want $PC(S)$.

§Simply stated, these rules, for the case of belief, are: *Sincerity*: If x wants y to believe that x believes that q, then x believes that q. *Reliability*: If y believes that x believes that q and that x is reliably informed about q, then y will believe that q. The basis for these rules is the intuition that the speaker is sincere about his beliefs, and that what he believes he believes reliably, at least for certain subject matters, such as his own present state of mind.

wants the system to perform some action, the system would infer that the user is pursuing a plan in which that action is a step.

An example will illustrate what I have in mind. For utterance S1 above and the conclusions about the user's wants regarding S/AUX given previously, the NLGO system seeks to explain

(1) Why the user wants the NLGO system to believe that the user wants to see S/AUX.

(2) Why the user wants to see S/AUX.

To answer the first question, the system determines whether any of the plans it has provisionally attributed to the user contains this step; and if so, it determines what relevant capacities the user believes it to have. For the case at hand, suppose that the system has knowledge of several plans a user may undertake concerning S/AUX. These include getting the system to delete S/AUX from the screen, getting the system to change the arcs on S/AUX and finding out what other nodes its arcs connect to. To explain (1), the system will look to see if it has attributed any one of these plans to the user. Since S1 is the first utterance in an exchange, we can suppose the system has not attributing any plans to the user.

Since no plan is known, it can try to decide if one of the possible plans could be in effect on the evidence that the user wants the system to have beliefs about the user wanting to see S/AUX. However, this want offers too little evidence to determine which plan could be in effect. Since no plan explanation is available to the system, it turns to explanations about it capacities that may be relevant to seeing S/AUX. Should it find one that the user is also aware of, it can conclude that this is the intended response. Among its capacities, it will find one that will enable the user to see S/AUX, namely, to display it on the screen. So the system concludes that the user intends this capacity to be used, and since the system is cooperative, the system produces a display.

When the system turns to explaining (2), its task is rather simple—certain user desires are primitive to the system. For such desires the system does not try to generate any further explanation.

This extended theory depends not only on the Gricean framework but also on the ability to create an explanation based on the user's plans. This last involves:

(1) Recognizing the correlations between utterance features and pairs of propositional attitudes and propositional content.

(2) Using the attributes (A) of the NLGO system (described above in Grice's theory).

(3) Determining the goals of the user from the propositional attitudes, where the goals are structured in a hierarchy of goals and subgoals.

(4) Deciding on the capacities of the NLGO system (mutually believed to be capacities) that are relevant to the speaker's goals.

(6) Using the speaker's recognized goals as an expectation model for the remaining part of the discourse.

To implement this model, I am using a number of available A.I. tools (the implementation is not complete). The NLGO system must have definitions of a number of plans, so I am using Sacerdoti-based procedural networks of plans[11]. Beliefs and wants must also be represented, and this I am relying on Allen's and Conen's models of belief and want contexts. A crucial aspect of this model is a method of "parsing" the user's wants as steps in plans; I am currently studying algorithms using an ATN formalism, but modified to allow for bugs in a plan, recognizable with a small bug library (see [12]). This model bears some similarity to Genesereth's plan recognizer[6]; it is distinguished because it recognizes plans incrementally and can proceed with only a partial plan and several possible additional plans. This method makes it possible to use a plan, once selected from the collection of plans by unique substeps, as an expectation device for the remaining part of a discourse. Finally, I use standard antecedent reasoning for deducing the correlations between utterance features and propositional attitudes, and for relating user plans and the NLGO system's capacities.

6. REASONING ABOUT A USER'S "BUGGY" PLANS

In the previous discussion, I have shown the utility of explanations reflecting (among other things) beliefs about the speaker's goals and about his beliefs about the NLGO system's capacities. Now I will demonstrate what additional reasoning such a model enables. In particular, I will show that such explanations provide a NLGO system with a means of discerning bugs in a user's plan. I will show how the system can understand that a declarative utterance can express a bug in the user's plan; that declaratives may state problems about the user obtaining what s/he and expects, or that may describe difficulties in proceeding to the next part of what the user plans to accomplish. The model of speaker meaning presented so far makes it possible to interpret such utterances.

The example concerns the first part of a scenario where the NLGO system is interacting with a user when a graphics display is available for representing information about a database.

D3–1 *U*: I want to see the Generic Concept named employee.
  2 *S*: OK. (Display concept in mid-screen.)
  3 *U*: I can't fit a new Individual Concept below it.
  4 *U*: Can you move it up?
  5 *S*: Sure. (Moves up the Generic Concept.)
  6 *U*: OK. Now make an Individual Concept for employee whose first name is "Sam" and whose last name is "Jones".

In this dialogue, the user wants to view a kind of database concept called a Generic Concept. The database has generic concepts for many things, including employee, company, office, and the like. Then the user indicates a difficulty with Individual Concepts, which are particular examples of Generic Concepts. His intent is to have the system create a new Individual Concept of an employee and insert some particular information about it.

To respond to the user's "Can you move it up?" the NLGO system must determine whether the user meant his/her utterance directly as a question about the system's abilities, or whether the user intended to direct the system to move the concept under discussion. Its choice depends on inferring the speaker's plan and, in particular, on what it believes the user thinks its own capacities are.

This example illustrates a feature of natural interchanges: a user may have a plan in mind, and carry out a part of it, without considering possible undesired side effects; when one occurs, s/he may recognize and eliminate it. In D3 the user is carrying out the plan of accessing the Concept for EMPLOYEE so that s/he can add a new employee to the database. S/he wants the system to display the EMPLOYEE Concept, but has not foreseen that its display location might be inappropriate. After the inappropriateness is discovered, the user indicates the difficulty and expects it to be corrected. Just how the bug that is reflected in D3 is corrected depends on whether the user already believes that the system can move things up and intends the system to do so, or whether s/he has to find this out first.

From the NLGO system's point of view, the decision about what the user means may cause it to respond differently in various cases. Suppose the system thinks the user believes that the system is able to move up concepts on the screen. Then when the user indicates that his/her plan has a flaw (D3–3), the system must conclude that the user's plan is blocked by the lack of space for a new concept. When the user asks about being able to move the employee concept, the NLGO system will conclude that the user intends to tell the system to perform the move by asking about a precondition of the action that the user wants, since the system is *intended* to move up the concept, not simply to answer the question.

A different scenario is as follows. Suppose the NLGO system thinks the user is unaware that the system is capable of moving up the concept. Then, when the user indicates that his/her plan has a flaw and asks about the employee concept, the system will conclude that the user intends to find out whether it has that ability, as part of finding a means of resolving the block. In this case, if the system moves the concept, that is a bit of *helpful* behavior, one not intended to be recognized as intended by the user.

I will outline in some detail how the NLGO system reasons in such contexts by showing what plans are deduced, what rules are needed, and how the reasoning proceeds in the case of D3–3 and D3–4. The relevant user plan is:

Add-Data⟨User⟩⟨netpiece⟩⟨data⟩⟨screen-location⟩
  step 1: Consider-aspect ⟨User⟩⟨netpiece⟩
  step 2: Put User ⟨data⟩ at ⟨screen-location⟩

The Add-Data plan states that to add data, a user must consider some aspect of a network part (netpiece) and then put some data at a screen location. Even after recognizing from D3–1 that the user wants some data displayed, the system cannot deduce that Add-Data is the user's plan. Since there are many ways to consider some aspect of a net (ask for a display, think about it, ask to be informed about its contents), as well as many other plans for which displaying a netpiece is a first step, the user cannot be understood to have intended the system to recognize that his/her plan was to Add-Data from the utterance D3–1. All the system can conclude is that the user wants the employee concept displayed, and it responds accordingly.

In reasoning about D3–3, "I can't fit a new Individual Concept below it", the NLGO system concludes that among the user's intentions mutually presumed to be recognized is that the user produced a declarative utterance with the propositional content that the user cannot fit a new Individual Concept (abbreviated indiv2) below the Generic Concept (abbreviated generic1):

BELIEF1: (Say User System (Declarative (Not (Can User (*Fit* User indiv2 (below generic1))))))

From this, the system concludes that the user wants the system to believe that the user believes that it can't fit indiv2 below generic1, and that the user in fact believes that he can't. The system then infers the embedded proposition [(Not (Can . . .))], and that the user intended that that proposition be mutually believed. The system uses a (default) rule NOTCAN below,

> NOTCAN: Whenever a user says that s/he can't bring about a certain state of affairs or perform a certain typical action, then the user is telling the system that it wants that state of affairs brought about.

and concludes that it is intended to believe that the user wants it to believe WANT1: (Fit User indiv2 (below generic1)).

The system seeks a partial explanation of this intention. As in other cases, it seeks an explanation realting the intention to the user's plans, its own capacities and the assumptions of cooperation. So far it knows the user has enacted a plan to consider an aspect of the network (D3–1 is evidence for this), and it knows of several plans for which the first step is considering an aspect of the network. By examining those plans for the role of WANT1, it can notice that in the add-data plan, step 2 is the user putting some data at a screen location, and that fitting indiv2 below generic1 is a specific means for putting. It uses this information to decide that of all the plans it knows of the add-data plan is the intended plan.

Now the system can bring to bear a rule to the effect that it believes that the user has informed it that s/he can't perform a certain action which s/he wants to perform (as part of some plan s/he is pursuing), then it should conclude that (1) the user wants to unblock the action, (2) as part of unblocking, the user will get the system to perform an action that does the unblocking. Here the user wants the Put action unblocked.

How the system is expected to respond depends upon whether the system believes that the user believes there is some action available to the system relevant to this unblocking. In fact, the NLGO system might have several relevant capacities for making room (such as moving up screen objects or erasing the screen). Two responses are possible in this situation. First if the system believes the user knows it has several capacities and hence believes that the user wants to exploit one of them, it must await further information to determine which one was meant. When the user asks "Can you move it up?" on the basis of having attributed to the user the unblock plan, the system can interpret the user's question as a way of bringing about a move-up action rather than simply a desire for information. Even if no such request as "Can you move it up?" were to follow, the NLGO system would have a basis for asking about the user's intent ("Do you want me to move up the concept or empty the screen?").

An alternative response will result from different belief about the user. If the NLGO system believed that the user was unaware of its capacities to move screen objects up, it would reason no further on D3–3 (again, because it has not recognized any intention on the part of the user that it act). D3–4 allows the system to deduce that the user wants to know if it can move generic1 up, since yes–no questions are taken as signalling intensions to know if. The system, in seeking an explanation, can conclude that this is the first step of a plan to find an agent with the capacity to move up screen objects. The system also knows that once such an agent is found, it can be asked to move-up as a means of unblocking the put action. To produce this explanation the system must piece together evidence for several plans in just the same way it did to determine that the Add-Data plan was in effect.

The system will use its explanation about finding an agent with a move-up capacity to determine that it must respond by telling the user it can move up the display. It may also decide to move up generic1, but this choice is made as helpful behavior† because the system has only recognized that the user may ask for a move-up but s/he has not stated any intention to move up yet.

In both of the above cases, the plan to Add-Data to the screen is known to be in effect. Hence once the bug is cleared away, the NLGO system is prepared to interpret subsequent utterances in light of this plan. The user's subsequent utterance in D3 requests that the system make an Individual Concept with a Role first name "Sam" and last name "Jones", without stating where the concept is to be put. Because the system knows that this request is part of Add-Data, it can determine the intended location for the Individual Concept on the screen— below the Generic Concept for EMPLOYEE. In this way, the plan creates expectations for the next portion of the conversation.

This example illustrates not only that mutual beliefs about the NLGO system's capacities affect the system's determination of the user's intentions, but also that the full explanation of each utterance depends the system's understanding of the user's goals and subsequent utterances.

7. COMPARISON WITH AN EARLIER APPROACH

In this section, I present one short example of how Allen's algorithms, which form the basis of my previous work on speaker meaning, proceed on utterances from the domain of information about trains in [3]. I will show how my model would proceed and discuss the differences in the two approaches. The general framework of considering a speaker's plans in understanding speaker meaning was inspired by Allen's work. However, my approach differs because it uses the knowledge of what the speaker is doing (i.e. his plan) and knowledge of the hearer's (i.e. the system's) capacities to determine a response. Allen's model relies largely on invoking general rules true for any action; while my model uses some general rules about actions, it also brings to bear its knowledge of particular actions the speaker is executing and its knowledge of its own beliefs as a hearer about its capacities. Because the model brings these kinds of knowledge to bear, it explicitly connects the speaker's intentions with the response intended by the speaker.

Figure 1 illustrates the processing of Allen's model for the utterance, "Can you tell me if there is a bus to E. Watertown?" Notice that the algorithm assumes that this question maps to an *s.* request‡ by actor A to hearer H of an informif by H to A of whether H can do an informif of the existence of a bus to E. Watertow. The reader should observe that two speech acts, both requests, are identified during the processing (they are underlined in the figure). The model, after deducing all the propositions (called the plan), uses them to determine obstacles in this plan, obstacles it should overcome. One obstacle it might recognize is: (A Knowif ($\ni$ bus to E. Watertown)). This obstacle can be overcome by an informif.

By comparison, my model will reason as follows. For the question "Can you tell me if there's a bus to E. Watertown?" H will ask itself why A said that to H and will conclude on the basis of "can you" questions that:

Want0: A wants to know if I (H) can tell him (A) if there's a bus to E. Watertown.

Such a want causes the system to ask itself for an explanation of that want. To do so, H uses a rule that states that if someone wants to know something and asks a question to a person who is believed able to answer that type of question, then an answer is wanted, i.e.

Want1: A wants H to tell A if H can tell A if there's a bus to E. Watertown?

---

†This choice is based on rules about helping out when one has an appropriate capacity. As with other heuristics, it may be wise to monitor carefully what the system does to be helpful, since some helpful actions can be easily undone, but others have serious side-effects.

‡For definitions of *s.* request and informif, see [3].

Can you tell me if there is a bus to E. Watertown?
(*S.* Request *A H* (Informatif *H A* (Can do *H*
(Informif *H A* (∃ bus to EW)))

  | |

                   | | body (body-action
                       \\/

  | | *(Request A H (Informif H A*
                          <u>*(Cando H (Informif . . .))))*</u>

  | |
  | | effect
  \\/

(HBAW (Informif *H A* (Cando *H* (Informif . . .))))

  | | deduce-action (effect)
  \\/

(HBAW (Knowif a (Cando *H* (Informif . . .)))

  | | deduce (known-prop +)
  \\/

(HBAW (Cando *H* (Informif *H A* . . .)))

  | | deduce (precondition-action (Informif))
  \\/

(HBAW (Informif *H A* (∃ bus to EW)))

  | | body (body-action)
  \\/

<u>*(Request A H (Informif H A (∃ bus to EW)))*</u>

  | | effect
  \\/

(HW (Informif *H A* (∃ bus to EW)))

  | | enable (want action)
  \\/

(Informif *H A* (∃ bus to EW))

  | | effect (action-effect)
  \\/

(*A* Knowif (∃ bus to EW))

  | | deduce (known-prop +)
  \\/

(∃ bus to EW)

  | | body (body-action)
  \\/

(Determine *A* modes-of-transportation)

Fig. 1. Sample processing for Allen's model.

Now *H* asks why does *A* want this? *H* turns his attention to what *A* is doing and deduces *A* is a stranger in a train station. Such people, *H* reasons, are usually interested in modes of transportation, such as trains and buses, and for getting to places. To find a means of travel one can look at a travel book or ask a person who has knowledge such matters. If one chooses to ask a person, then one must identify a person with such knowledge. *H* believes that he is one such person and W0 indicates that *A* has decided to find out that *H* is. Hence *H* is able to conclude that *A* needs information about modes of travel, rather than just information about *H*'s capacities. Then, by looking at the internal structure of Want1, *H* can determine just which modes of travel *A* wants to know about, and conclude that *A* has Want2:

Want2: *A* wants me to tell him if there is a bus to EW.

Before going further with *H*'s reasoning, it is important to see that the particular situation of the speaker and hearer are significant to the deductions the hearer can make. The inference to

Want2 depends on the fact that both speaker and hearer know that A is a stranger in a train station and that such a person wants to know about transportation modes. Furthermore, the capacities of the hearer, which are mutually known to hearer and speaker, help the hearer explain what the speaker says. Hence H is not merely good at guessing what A wants, but rather A intends that H conclude Want0, Want1 and Want2.

Just as with Want0 and Want1, H must ask himself why A wants Want2. Here the answer brings to an end any further explanations. A wants information about buses (call that Want3) but H cannot draw further conclusions (such as answer to why A wants Want3) because such conclusions would involve guessing about S's wants and desires. There is no reason to believe that such guessing is intended by A, so H suspends reasoning further about A's wants.

Now that H has established several of A's wants, we can ask, what does H do with his explanation? Two of A's wants (Want1 and Want2) involve H as the agent of an action wanted. H brings to bear knowledge about what A knows of H's capacities to determine that A intends for H to act on these. For the other wants, Want0 and Want3, H may act, as a helpful person, in some way H believes appropriate, but his actions are not intended by the communication. In carrying out Want1 and Want2, H must reason that if he performs the telling of Want2, he will also perform the one for Want1, so that only one action is necessary.

The major difference in these two models is use of the speaker's plan. Allen, who takes all the conclusions inferred in his model to be part of the plan, does not use the speaker's overall goal in reaching those conclusions. Instead, that goal is the last conclusion reached in his model. By contrast, in my model the speaker's overall goal (to determine a mode of transportation and find someone who knows about it) is used early in the processing, in addition to rules about the reasons for actions.

The two approaches also differ on what the hearer takes the intended response to be. For Allen's work, the response consists of overcoming any obstacles that another component of his model can identify. Overcoming these obstacles is taken to be the intended act because in general the speaker wants the hearer to be as helpful as possible. In my model, helpful behavior is distinguished from more directly intended responses such as Want2. These responses must be explicitly related to the speaker's intentions viewed as a plan. In addition, my model takes into account the hearer's specific capacities, known to speaker and hearer, in determining an intended response.

A final distinction between the two models concerns the utterance and initial conclusions drawn from it. Allen assumes that utterances can be mapped into surface speech act forms (such as s. request) for his model. I have chosen rules that map from the utterance to the NLGO system's first conclusion by conventions about how English is used. The type of conclusion drawn is not one that identifies an act that A wants H to perform, but rather states some want that A has about his own concerns.

One difference between the two approaches cannot be easily illustrated in the domain of information about trains. I have expanded on the notion of plans originally given in Allen's work to include multistep and interrupted plans. Allen's model cannot recognize these kinds of plans because the model's plan language is not equipped with a means of describing them.

In summary, I have presented in this paper a model of the interpretation of speaker meaning which takes into account several different kinds of belief: about the current situation of the speaker, about the speaker's goals, about the discourse context, about the speaker's knowledge of the hearer's capacities, and about the hearer's conventions for acting. The model, both in the abstract and in its computational form, infers an intended response on the basis of these beliefs by producing an explanation for each of these beliefs and using that explanation for further conclusions about speaker intentions. This model makes possible the recognition of the speaker's intended meaning not only of imperative and interrogative utterances but also of declaratives that serve as statements of desires, comments, complaints about problems, checks on progress, and announcements of bugs in the speaker's attempts to achieve his/her goal.

Acknowledgements—I want to thank David Israel for his participation in the research presented here and also the BBN Knowledge Representation and Natural Language Group for their discussions and support.

The research reported in this paper was supported in part by the Advanced Research Projects Agency and was monitored by the Office of Naval Research under Contract No. N00014-77-C-0378.

REFERENCES

1. C. L. Sidner, Protocols of users manipulating visually presented information with natural language. Unpublished manuscript, Bolt, Beranek & Newman Inc. (May 1980).
2. R. J. Brachman, R. J. Bobrow, P. R. Cohen, J. W. Klovstad, B. L. Webber and W. A. Woods, Research in natural language understanding—annual report: 1 Sept. 78–31 Aug. 79, *BBN Rep. No.* 4274, Bolt, Beranek & Newman Inc. (August 1979).
3. J. F. Allen, A plan-based approach to speech act recognition. *Tech. Rep.* 131, Dep. of Computer Science, University of Toronto (Jan. 1979).
4. P. R. Cohen, On knowing what to say: planning speech acts. Ph.D. dissertation, University of Toronto, *Tech. Rep. No.* 118, Dept. of Computer Science (Jan. 1978).
5. P. Cohen, R. Perrault and J. Allen, Beyond question answering. *Strategies for Natural Language Processing* (Edited by Lehnart and Ringle). Lawrence Erlbaum Assoc., Hillsdale, New Jersey (1981).
6. M. R. Genesereth, Automated consultations for complex computer systems. Ph.D. dissertation, Department of Computer Science, Division of Applied Sciences, Harvard University (Sept. 1978).
7. D. F. Schmidt, N. S. Sridharan and J. L. Goodson, The plan recognition problem: an intersection of artificial intelligence and psychology. *Artificial Intell.* **10**, 45–83 (1979).
8. R. Wilensky, Understanding goal-based stories. Ph.D. dissertation, Dept. of Computer Science, Yale University, *Res. Rep. No.* 140 (1978).
9. H. P. Grice, Meaning, *Philosophical Rev.* **66**, 377–388 (1957).
10. H. P. Grice, Utterer's meaning and intentions. *Philosophical Rev.* **68**(2), 147–177 (1969).
11. E. Sacerdoti, *A Structure for Plans and Behavior*. American Elsevier, New York (1977).
12. G. Sussman, *A Computer Model of Skill Acquistion*. American Elsevier, New York (1975).

Comp. & Maths. with Appls. Vol. 9, No. 1, pp. 83–95, 1983
Printed in Great Britain.

0097–4943/83/010083–13$03.00/0
Pergamon Press Ltd.

FORMAL SEMANTIC AND COMPUTER
TEXT PROCESSING, 1982

J. G. Meunier and F. Lepage

Université du Québec à Montréal, Montreal, Quebec, Canada

Abstract—Computer processing of large non-preedited natural language texts has often been limited either to managing and editing or to analysing basic levels of content (indexes, concordances, clusters, etc.). Few systems approach syntactic information, even less semantic information. Because of the complexity and the originality of the underlying semantic information of any text it is not possible to import directly the A.I. and computational semantic concepts. It is necessary to explore news paths. The research presented here is oriented toward the understanding of certain semantic aspects in computer text processing (words and meaning representation and inference patterns). This is done through a model theoretic approach embedded in an algebraic language. The hypothesis which governs the concepts and the distinctions is the following: discourse in a text constitutes a semantic space built of an ordered set of sentences which are of different logical types and which present a specific pattern of coherence expressible in a syntactic manner.

1. INTRODUCTION

From 1960 to the seventies many of the advanced uses of the computer in the field of humanities and social sciences, except for the statistical packages, were concentrated on building more and more sophisticated systems capable of storing, parsing and analysing natural language texts. These systems produced indexes, concordances, content analysis etc. (EYE-BALL, GENERAL INQUIRER, COCOA, SATO, JEUDEMO, CONCORD, SYNTOL).

Many of these systems shared the common paradigm of working on a large, minimally pre-edited text. The challenge met by these systems was in copying, editing, classifying, managing and analysing a large amount of natural language information. They were, in a sense, text information retrievers. But most of them were limited to processing the basic level of information, i.e. the word. They were seldom sensitive to the syntactic level, even less to the semantic one. Compared with the artificial intelligence understanding systems of the seventies, they were quite simple. However, in their simplicity they were useful for scholarly research and simple editorial tasks, as the market shows by the success of word processing packages, packages that are but a pale shadow of the original text processors. Limited to tasks of editing, these latter systems never attain the content except for indexes. Scholarly research, as well as text database documentary systems, now demand more and more sophisticated retrieval and analysis techniques.

In the seventies, and in the wake of A.I success, some systems attempted to integrate more complex levels of analysis. Always working in the paradigm of *large, non pre-edited natural language texts* (hereafter NPNL texts), these later systems explored mainly the syntactic level (description and analysis); some attained a high level of success in parsing sentences of a specific natural language (EYEBALL, DEREDEC, PHLIQA1). But to our knowledge, no significant attempt has been made to build NPNL text processors sensitive to the semantic aspects, except through basic lexical categories (as in classical content analysis) or through general classification schemes of lexical or discourse content (summaries, resumés, database, representations, etc.).

Now, it is true that many AI projects have worked on NPNL texts (e.g. Wilks, Schank, Charniak); however, these texts were quite limited in size (5 pages at the most). In addition, their focus of research was to define the structure of information (lexical meaning, world representation, etc.) necessary for the presumed "understanding" (or paraphrasing) of certain sentences of the texts. Nowhere but in some translating projects have large NPNL texts been accepted. Still, these projects were not oriented for content analysis of for information retrieval and mainly were limited to a specific domain. These A.I. systems aimed at exploring a NPNL text in such a way as to extract complex structured information; this task does not necessarily demand a full understanding of the text. We should stress that many users in the field of the humanities and social research prefer the computer not to "understand" the text. What they are looking for is much more an intermediary structured information that would permit more exhaustive or complex analysis, such as thematic, lexical, textual structure, etc. Something similar could be said for the user of NPNL data based documentary systems. Often, they only have a vague idea of the content, (e.g. journals, legal or medical texts, library reports, office documents). The request here is much more related to an exploration of these documents than to a translation, paraphrase, deduction, etc.

Some systems have attempted to explore such higher levels of structured information through the paradigms of artificial intelligence. But often they failed, because the paradigm was not applicable on such large texts. In effect, how could a system ever store all the information necessary for understanding "the complete works of Shakespeare"? More even, how could we provide information about texts for which we have but a small idea of their content (e.g. parsing the criminal code, the *daily journal*, etc.).

Thus, a clear theoretical definition of what tasks are involved in text information retrieving is essential. Too often the categories of understanding systems are used directly to model text processing system. This inevitably leads to their failure because text information processors cannot be text understanders!

The research we report on in this paper is oriented towards the understanding, through model theoretic concepts, of some aspects of the semantics involved in the processing of a non-preedited natural language text. For instance: "What is the logical status of the meaning representation, the compositional processes and the inference rules underlying the questions and answers on and from a NPNL texts? For example, given a natural language text of a few hundred pages, how can we interrogate it in such a manner as to find in it the pertinent sentence as answer to a specific question? (E.g. if a text has a sentence "John murdered Mary" can it be found as an answer to the question: Is Mary dead?)

These theoretical considerations are related to a concrete conversational text processor we are building. This system, called ACTO (Analyse conversationnelle de textes par ordinateur), through a complex managing and parsing system called DEREDEC, can economically store a large text (a few hundred pages), do the basic editing and managing, and parse each sentence as well as deliver a syntactic surface structure with indications of its basic grammatical dependencies, (subject-predicate determination, etc.). Finally, it can, in a recursive manner, reparse the syntactically structured text for either complex content analysis of question answering experiments[1]. If this system is to be sensitive to certain semantic information (synonyms, paraphases, inferences) it must develop a semantic grammar.

2. TEXT AND DISCOURSE

As the literature on text processing and understanding has shown, one should distinguish between a *text* and a *discourse*. What is printed is a *text*, what is understood is a *discourse*. A *text* expresses a *discourse*. *Texts* can be printed, not *discourses*. The same *discourse* can be present in different *texts*. A *discourse* is to a text, what a proposition is to a sentence. *Texts* and discourses do not have the same identity criteria.

When transferred to the field of computer text processors, this distinction becomes slightly more complicated. As any human must do in reading a text, a text processing system (hereafter called *P*-system) must have access to the discourse. It is there that it finds the syntactic, semantic and pragmatic information necessary for more sophisticated text parsing. But what is a discourse in a computer?

To be clear about what we are referring to we shall define some basic concepts: We shall call the original text, i.e. the one that is printed, typed or the manuscript of the original text, the *o*-text, and the discourse related to it, the *o*-discourse.

In the computer, the *o*-text and *o*-discourse will be transcribed into what we shall call an electronic script, or *e*-script (as opposed to manuscript). In this *e*-script we shall find the *t*-script (or computer transcripts) for all the *t*-sentences of the original text. We shall also find a *d*-script containing the computer transcripts of any information pertaining to the *o*-discourse or the *o*-text. This *d*-script may be about the underlying syntactic structures of each *t*-sentence (deep, shallow or surface). It also could be about their propositional content together with their lexical composition, their inclusion in conceptual schemata, etc. Others could be about some possible state of affairs in the world, and even meaning postulates for a specific language. This d-script and t-script hence form an ordered set of sentences of some sort, that is the e-script. Let us then represent these simple distinctions in Fig. 1.

In the world	In the computer
o-discourse o-text	e-script $\begin{cases} d\text{-script} \\ t\text{-script} \end{cases}$

Fig. 1.

Having reduced a text and a discourse to an e-script, let us now reflect more deeply on its composition. As an e-script is but a list of sentences, two basic questions arise, (a) where do they come from? and (b) what is their logical status?

(a) *The origin of the* e-*script and* e-*sentences*

For the t-script, the problem of its origin is simple. All t-sentences are but the transcriptions of the original text. The transcription function that takes an o-sentence and produces a computer version of it is theoretically simple, but it is often materially a complex one, i.e. a copying and storing program.

The question of the origin of d-sentences is more complex, and it is often at this point that the difference between these text processing systems and A.I. text understanding systems (U-systems) appears. If these latter systems are to parse specific sentences for some underlying information (propositional content, logical structure, possible inferences) they should have access to higher order information (semantic nets, schemata, hierarchies, frames, etc.). And it is from this higher order information that they will compositionally infer the "semantic" structure of a particular sentence.

But how are these U-systems informed of this higher-order information? The answer is quite obvious. In most systems this is done by stipulation. This information is never learned. In fact, these higher types of information are part of the essence of the understanding program and are defined in a stipulative manner long before any processing has actually started.

In a P-system this information must also exist in order for a sentence token to receive a semantic representation. But why should it be given way before any processing has started, and why should it be given by one source? There are many conceivable ways by which a particular t-sentence can receive or infer d-sentences expressing their various semantic components and structures.

In our system, ACTO, we define both the content and the inferential pattern in a conversational manner, from which ACTO can afterwards generalize and hence "learn" from the text itself.

The preceding remarks are important for defining the task involved in P-systems. They distinguish clearly the generic problem from the logical one. By "generic problem" we mean the origin of the higher-order information from which can be compositionally infered specific semantic information for each token sentence. By "logical problem" we mean the role and function of this higher order information, in the overall discourse explicitation. What we here maintain is that as with any A.I. -system, a P-system must have some semantic information having the same logical function or status but it may acquire it in a quite different manner.

(b) *The logical status*

Independently, then, of how a P-system can acquire this higher order information one must be clear about its logical role and function. Be it the A.I. or the computational approach to semantics, it's that a P-system can parse a sentence, choose the pertinent interpretation, if not informed of this higher order information. But this does not give us the logical type of the information. What is the role of a world representation? Of a lexical meaning representation? Are they identical? What is their logical status?

In these areas, the literature does not offer the clearest theories. One encounters here more operational definitions than really logical ones. If a lexical decomposition or a world representation manages to output the right inferences, it will then often be said to be adequate for that purpose. This leaves us in the dark as to the logical status of then semantic informations as to their real logical status.

So in order to clarify this status as others have done [2–5], we shall try here to translate some of the A.I. concepts of world representation and frames or the computational-interpretative semantics in model-theoretic terms.

In this line of thought, a world representation can be understood as a model for a set of sentences; that is, it is a description (predicative or procedural) of an actual or possible state of affairs in which a particular sentence can be said to be true of false. Often, though, a concrete world representation is not only a model. It contains something else, as well. In fact, one will often find not only information about the word but also the "meaning" of the word, meaning that will be expressed either in the Katzian manner or the Quillian way.

But whatever the semantic representation advanced, be it the interpretative, (à la Katz-Fodor, Weinreich, Miller John-Laird, Jackendoff, etc.), or the computational one (à la Wilks, Schank, Winograd, Rumelhart, Charniak, Schubert) independently of their formalization and notational variants, either can be seen as trying to express the truth conditions of an NL language disambiguated sentence. In one sense, as maintained Kempson[6] and Hayes[2], these are semantic representations of the Tarskian T-convention. They could even be understood as the meaning postulates for a set of d-script sentences. Hence from a logical point of view, the status of a set of d-sentences that express the underlying discourse information may be of two different sort; i.e. first, these sentences can express the truth conditions of T-sentences, while secondly, at the same time they can refer to models retained in the t-script.

For example, the t-sentence "John kills Mary" can be said to have its truth conditions expressed in this possible d-sentence "(John CAUSES Mary Be Dead)" which in turn, because it originates in an o-text, is said to be asserted in a possible world.

These remarks bring us to the related problem of the formalization of semantic information. Considerable debate in A.I. semantic theories has taken place on the subject of the logical and the procedural representation of semantic information, and the various interpretations of these concepts have not always been of the clearest kind. We are of the opinion that this debate stems from a confusion between logical *status* and logical *formalization*. Having a logical status does not necessarily mean logical formalization; that is, the main quality semantic information must have is characterizable by a specific role and function in a system (i.e. it must present definite criteria of identity).

Compared with logical *status*, formalization is secondary. It is true that for some systems the representation of semantic and inferential information should be the least ambiguous sort possible and the most rule-governed. But for others, it may be just the opposite. But even if one chooses between a strict predicate language, a relational net language (e.g. a semantic and hierarchical net) or a fuzzy set one, these particular meta-languages and their notational variants do not define the logical status of the semantic information. They help only to describe, in a controllable fashion, their logical or semi-logical structure. They embody differently the semantic information, and some render processing more easily than others[7]. Some have a higher degree of expressive adequacy than others.

As Woods[8] and Katz[9] have shown, the literature on this subject has often confused the logical status with the formalization, notational and computational problem. Whatever the semantic representation chosen, it must have a logical status, and this status must not be confused with its expression in a formal language which, in turn, can have notational variants (e.g. Polish vs Russellian notation, set theoretical or algebraic).

So, in building a P-system for processing NPNL texts one should be clear about the logical status and structure of the semantic information involved. This may seem quite obvious, yet in the practice of text processing as compared with A.I. understanding systems, the various levels and types of semantic information involved are not clearly understood, as has been shown in the large literature on text linguistics[10, 11, 5]. As an illustration, if one simulates in a Gedanken experiment some of the possible d-sentences to be related to a t-sentence, one would easily see the complexity of the logical status and structure of these d-sentences. They would immediately show their various differences in identity. Some d-sentences are a representation of the syntactic structure, others of the lexical information, of the logical structure (quantifiation, modalisation, etc.), of inference patterns, of the pragmatic-performative dimension, etc. As an example, for the *t*-sentence "John killed Mary" a *P*-system could be given by a function (stipulative or computational), a transcription or a *d*-sentence in the form of its categorical syntactic structure S(N(John) S/NN (kill) N(Mary)) a predicative categorical semantic representation of some sort such as: ((John DO X) CAUSE (Mary Be Dead)) or in any Schubert[12], Miller and Johnson-Laird[13] or Dowty[14] manner.

As can be seen, these two sentences or *d*-transcripts are expressions of some aspects of the discourse content. They are in one sense related to the truth conditions of the *t*-sentence. They were both generated in some way (by stipulation). They do not have the same logical level and are not even in the same formal language. Hence it follows that our *d*-script is composed of many *d*-sentences or *d*-transcripts, all having a specific logical status and having some mutual relations.

The question we shall now address is how to understand and formalize some aspects of the structure of these *d*-scripts. What appears now to be the case is that the discourse representation is not just one type of semantic information (e.g. a complex hierarchical semantic net) but a whole structure of various *d*-sentences and set of *d*-sentences belonging to different levels of languages and logical types. Hence the semantic information now looks more like an algebraic structure than a classical semantic net. It is some of the formal structures of these algebraic *d*-sentences that we shall now explore and discuss.

3. *E*-SCRIPT AND GRAMMAR

From a formal point of view, an *e*-script can now be seen as a set of sentences, each of which in turn can be thought of as belonging to a different language (hereafter called transcription language or LT); i.e. all sentences of the *e*-script are either sentences that are transcriptions of the original text or sentences that are statements about the various aspects involved in the semantics of the *t*-sentences. Each *t*-language and its sentences can be of various logical status.

But even if all each sentences can have in this "semantic space" different logical status, it is possible to think of them as being formed or generated from a common grammar, by which we mean that all languages have the same types of rules. So before discussing the possible rellations between the various sentences we shall briefly define this common grammar.

Each sentence of the *e*-script can theoretically be thought of as a well-formed sentences of a categorical language, such as the one defined in the literature by Adjukiewiczs[15], Bar Hillel[16] and mainly reused by Montague[17] and Cresswell[18]. The definiton we will call upon here is influenced by the Montague one from *Universal Grammar.*†

The language for each *e*-sentence is then defined as a quintuple:

$$\langle A, F_\gamma, X_\delta, S, \Delta \rangle_{\gamma \in \Gamma, \delta \in \Delta}$$

where (a) X_δ is the set of basic expressions for each δ, i.e. for each category. (b) The set Δ of categories can be defined recursively as the smallest set such that:

(1) $N \in \Delta$ (category of names).

(2) $S \in \Delta$ (category of sentences).

(3) if σ and τ are in Δ then $\langle \sigma, \tau \rangle$ is also in Δ so the categories of a transcription language are the categories of the classical categorial languages. The set A is the set of proper expressions.

This set A can be defined in the following manner. Consider first the free monoid M generated by finited concatenation of members of $\cup_{\delta \in \Delta} X_\delta$. The F_γ being *n*-place operations on the set of the members of M (i.e. the underlying set of M), let A be the smallest set such that:

(1) $\cup_{\delta \in \Delta} X_\delta \subset A$

(2) if $x = \langle x_0, \ldots, x_{n-1} \rangle$ and F_γ is an *n*-place operation, then $F_\gamma(x) \in A$. The F_γ may (and sometimes must) vary from one language to another. Here are a few examples of these

---

†*Universal Grammar* (1970).

functions F_γ.

$$F_0(x, y) = xy \qquad \text{2-concatenation}$$

$$F_1(x, y) = x = y \quad \text{identity}$$

$$F_2(x, y) = \wedge \, xy \quad \text{function introduction}$$

$$F_3(x) = {}^{\cdot}x \qquad \text{negation}$$

$$F_4(x, y) = x \vee y \quad \text{disjunction}$$

$$F_5(x, y) = x \wedge y \quad \text{conjunction}$$

$$F_6(x, y) = x \rightarrow y \quad \text{implication}$$

$$F_7(x, y) = x \equiv y \quad \text{equivalence}$$

$$F_8(x, y) = \forall xy \quad \text{universal quantification}$$

$$F_9(x, y) = \exists xy \quad \text{existential quantification}$$

$$F_{10}(x, y) = !xy \qquad \text{description}$$

$$F_{11}(x) = \hat{x} \qquad \text{meaning insertion}$$

$$F_{12}(x) = \square x \qquad \text{necessity}$$

$$F_{13}(x) = Tx \qquad \text{time}$$

(d) and where S is a set of grammatical rules. The general form of these rules is the following:

$$\langle F_\gamma, \langle \delta_i \rangle_{i<n}, \epsilon \rangle$$

where F_γ is an n-place operation, δ_i is a category for each i and ϵ is also a category.

These rules mean that if the operation $F\gamma$ is applied to a sequence of expressions $\langle x_i \rangle_{i<n}$ each of them belong to δ_i then the resulting expression belongs to the category ϵ. In order to make the preceding definitions more concrete let us here give a few examples. In our T-script we could have the t-sentence T_1: "Peter sees a man". This English sentence can be described as being generated by a grammar of the preceding type, that is: G_{L1} will contain a set of category assigning rules:

$$RC_1: \; S/SN \rightarrow \text{man}$$

$$RC_2: \; S/NN \rightarrow \text{sees}$$

$$RC_3: \; N \rightarrow \text{Peter}$$

a set of operational rules

$$OR_1: \; \langle F_1, \langle N, S/NN \rangle, S/SN \rangle$$

$$OR_2: \; \langle F_2, \langle N, S/NN \rangle, S/N \rangle$$

$$OR_3: \; \langle F_3, \langle S/N, S/SN \rangle, S \rangle.$$

These rules are formally equivalent to the following phrase structured rules:

$$R_1: \; S \rightarrow VP + NP$$

$$R_2: \; VP \rightarrow N + V\text{trans}$$

$$R_3: \; NP \rightarrow \text{a man}$$

$$R_4: \; N \rightarrow \text{Peter}$$

$$R_5: \; V\text{trans} \rightarrow \text{sees}.$$

Both set of rules will generate the following structure on the T-sentence.

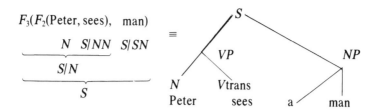

Now our e-script does not contain only t-sentences, but also d-sentences representing various aspects of the semantic involved, such as

$$d_1: \exists x \text{ (Peter Sees } x \wedge \text{ Man } x)$$

$$d_2: \text{(with PERCEIVE) (Peter, Man, Eyes)}$$

(à la Miller/Johnson-Laird[13]). There could be many other d-sentences inspired by the various semantical theories. As said before, we could use the formulations of the Schank conceptual dependencies, the Wilks templates and primitives, the Charniak frames, the Metzing stereo-types and even representation of the time structures of Aqvist and Guenthner[14], the performatives of Searle–Vandervecken and so forth. But the important thing is that they all ought to be generatable by a categorical language of the kind here defined. (For such a possibility see [14, 4, 20–22]).

For the purpose of illustration let us show that the preceding d-sentence could also be generated by a specific categorical grammar GL_2.

GL_2 will contain:

$$RC_1': S/SN \rightarrow \text{Man}$$

$$RC_2': S/NN \rightarrow \text{sees}$$

$$RC_3': N \rightarrow \text{Peter}$$

and

$$OR_1': \langle F_4', \langle S/N \rangle, S \rangle$$

$$OR_2': \langle F_2', \langle N, S/NN \rangle, S/N \rangle$$

$$OR_3': \langle F_5', \langle S/N \rangle, S \rangle$$

$$OR_4': \langle F_6', \langle S, S \rangle, S \rangle$$

$$OR_5': \langle F_7', \langle S \rangle, S \rangle$$

and will generate the following structure

$$F_1'(\text{Peter sees, man}) = (F_7'(F_6'(F_5'(\underset{N}{F_2'(\text{Peter sees}}), \underset{S/NN}{F_4' \text{ man}})))).$$

Now we can define F_3' such that

$$F_1'(\text{Peter, sees, man}) = F_3'(F_2'(\text{Peter, sees}), \text{man}) = \exists x(\text{Peter Sees } x \wedge \text{Man } x).$$

As can be seen from the preceding definitions and examples, it is theoretically possible to think of all the d-sentences of the e-script as well-formed sentences of a common grammar defined in the Montague fashion. And we stress that the "theoretically possible" aspect of this task is mainly realizable if empirically one can find a good working hypothesis for the syntactical and conceptual structure involved. The important thing here is to underling the possibility of expressing these conceptual-semantical structures in well-defined grammar and not just in a conglomerate of primitives. Because these sentences will be so expressed, their logical status and structure will be more evident and hence permit a better understanding of the various relations involved.

4. THE TRANSCRIPTIONS

Having now defined an e-script as a complex set of t- and d-sentences all embedded in common grammar and constituting various different languages, is it possible to find a certain relational structure among them? This question is a subquestion of what the text-grammarians call the "coherence" problem [23] and overlaps what text-understanding systems call the plan, scenario and frames [24] or the mapping languages of Petofi [10]; i.e. a discourse is not a simple amalgam of sentences. It presents a proper structure. Our intention here is not to summarize or to criticize some of the attempts made to solve this problem. We intend only to show how the theoretical frameworks of the transcription languages treat some aspects of this problem for P-systems for NPNL texts. What we shall specifically present here concerns some of the formal properties of the rules permitting a set of e-sentences to relate to each other. Let us consider two languages L_i and L_j. Each language contains a set of sentences S_i and S_j. Each of which expresses a specific aspect of the e-sentence. We then can define a relation T between these two sets such that T is a transcription or mapping from L_1 into L_2. This transcription will be in fact a function defined as the triplet such that the transcriptoin T_{12} is a morphism between two languages L_1 and L_2. This morphism is represented in the following commutative diagram

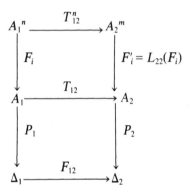

where T_{12} is a transcription, F_{12} maps the category of L_1 on categories of L_2 and L_{12} maps n-place operations of L_1 on a corresponding n-place operation of L_2. These rules mean:

(1) That a transcription between two languages preserves categorial properties, or, in other words, two expressions of the same category have their transcription in a same category.

(2) That if an expression results from an operation on other expressions, the transcription of the first expression is the result of a corresponding operation on the transcriptions of the other expressions.

Let us illustrate this transcription function on our previous example: Recall the two e-sentences:

$$t_1: \text{Peter sees a man.}$$

$$d_1: \exists x(\text{Peter sees } x \ \& \ \text{man } x).$$

We want d_1 to be a transcription of t_1. The transcription function on this example can be formally defined as: $\langle T_{12}, F_{12}, L_{12} \rangle$ such that:

$$T_{12}(\text{Peter}) = \text{Peter}$$

$$T_{12}(\text{sees}) = \text{sees}$$

$$T_{12}(\text{man}) = \text{man}$$

$$L_{12}(F_1) = F_1'$$

$$L_{12}(F_2) = F_2'$$

$$L_{12}(F_3) = F_3'$$

$$F_{12}(N) = N$$

$$F_{12}(S/NN) = S/NN$$

$$F_{12}(S/SN) = S/N$$

This function can be illustrated in the following transcription.

$$T_{12}(\text{Peter sees a man}) =$$

$$T_{12}(F_3(\text{Peter sees})\text{man}) =$$

$$T_{12}(F_3(F_2(\text{Peter, sees}))\text{man}) =$$

$$F_3'(F_2'(\text{Peter, sees})\text{man}) =$$

$$\exists x(\text{Peter sees } x \ \& \ \text{man } x).$$

We can easily verify that this transcription is a good one and satisfies all the intended properties. As can be seen by this example, t_1 is the transcription of the logical structure of d_1. It does not exhibit any other information possibly expressive in other d_n sentences. But because these sentences are now defined (in a *stipulative manner*) as transcriptions of one into the other, it is possible to show their compatibility. This compatibility is always assured by the rule that says: the composition of a morphism is a morphism. In other words, the successive application of transcription functions is itself a transcription function. Hence the coherence problem is here translated in terms of compatible algebraic transcription.

For instance, after having exhibited the logical structure in a d-transcript, we now could exhibit some of the lexical structure of certain components of this d-sentence by another transcription function that would produce a d_3 transcript also compatible with d_2 and so forth. Hence by means of the transcription functions we could render compatible a subset of sentences in the whole set of d-sentences or d-script.

We could now summarize the theoretical postulate of our transcription framework in the following terms: All hypotheses for representing the semantic (and possibly the pragmatic) content of a t-sentence must be expressed in a categorial grammar as defined above and be produced by a transcription function (algorithmicly or stipulatively). This postulate is but one translation of the Fregean principle of compositionality. It follows then that the coherence relations between the discourse sentences can be expressed by syntactic relations.

5. DEFINITIONS OF SOME INTERESTING PROBLEMS

Having built a syntactical structure of the related d-languages we shall now analyse some correlative properties of this "compatible" structure.

First, among all these languages, we shall build a tree-type structure in the following manner: let us consider a set of transcriptions that maps a first node L_ϕ into many. From each L_α and down there can exist many other transcriptions that also map each L_α into their subordinates $L_{\alpha\beta}$. Let us represent this tree of language in the following diagram.

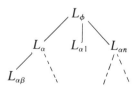

The preceding tree can be formally defined as a partially ordered set of languages where the ordering principle is the transcription functions between the languages. The languages in the tree are indexed by a sequence of ordinals where the top node is associated with the null sequence. The other sequence wil be recursively defined in the following manner: the top language is associated with the nul sequence; if L_α is a language, where α is a sequence of ordinals, consider all the languages into which there exists a transcription of L_α. This class can be well-ordered, i.e. we can give an ordinal number to each of these languages. The index of each of these languages will be the sequence of ordinals α followed by the ordinal associated with this language by the well-ordering relation.

So we have a language L_β that follows immediately L_α if and only if there is an ordinal γ such that: $\beta = \alpha\gamma$.

This relation will be noted $\ll$ and the transcription between L_α, L_β, $T_{\langle\alpha\beta\rangle}$. The partial ordering relation is obtained by taking the transitive closure of $\ll$. This new relation will be noted $\leq$ and a tree of transcription languages will appear to be like this:

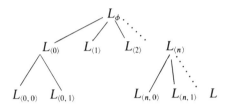

The language tree will be noted $[\![L_\alpha]\!]_{\alpha \in A}$ where A is the set of sequences of ordinals which serve as indexes for the tree. We define in a similar way the transcription functions tree and we note it $[\![T_{\langle\alpha, \beta\rangle}]\!]_{\langle\alpha, \beta\rangle \in B}$ where B is the set of pairs of indexes $\langle\alpha, \beta\rangle$ such that there exists a transcription between L_α and L_β. These notations serve mainly to distinguish trees from sets in the same way that we need to distinguish sequences from sets.

Let us now turn to each language L_α in our tree, and consider their internal deduction rules (i.e. for each language L_α, there is a token set of sentences S_α). Within this language a set of rules is given which allows derivation of some members of S_α from others (i.e. the subset of proper syntactic rules of each language which permit the internal derivation of sentences from sentences—they are purely syntactic consequences). A simple example would be the following. Consider a set of classical propositional calculus sentences. Given any set X of sentence these rules generate another set Y containing the formes and which can be considered as a set of consequences independent of any king of interpretation of the sentences. The function of these rules is to represent what we could call a particular deductive structure for these sentences.

This example may seem very trivial. A less trivial example would be the addition to these of transformational rules, deplacement rules about quantification[25], etc. admitting, as their defenders do, that these rules belong to the logic of the language, i.e. their conditions of applicability are purely syntactic and universal.

Let us call $C_\alpha(X_\alpha)$ the set generated from X_α, and let it be read as the set of consequences of X_α at the level α. Suppose now that there is a transcription from L_α into L_β that is to say $L_\alpha \leq L_\beta$. We now define the set of consequences of X_α at the level β as the set

$$C_\beta(X_\alpha) = C_\alpha(T_{\alpha\beta}^{-1}[C_\beta(T_{\alpha\beta}[X_\alpha])]).$$

In other words, the set of consequences of X_α at the level β is the set of consequences at the level β of the largest set that has the same transcription as X_α in L_β.

An illustration of this would be lexical decomposition of a given type (lexical decomposition is certainly not a part of the logic of a language). So we suppose that we have rules of transcription of expressions of a language L_1 into another language L_2 and that these transcription correspond to lexical decomposition. Let the two sentences S_1 and S_2 be such that they are not consequence one of the other (in the first language) but that after lexical decomposition the first becomes a consequence of the second, i.e.

$$T_{\langle\alpha, \beta\rangle}(S_2) \Rightarrow T_{\langle\alpha, \beta\rangle}(S_1).$$

Applying the definition we will have

$$T_{\langle\alpha, \beta\rangle}(S_1) \in C_\beta(\{T_{\langle\alpha, \beta\rangle}(S_2)\})$$

But this means that S_1 is a consequence of S_2 at the level β because we have

$$C_\beta(\{S_2\}) = C_\alpha(T_{\alpha\beta}^{-1}[C_\beta(T_{\alpha\beta}(\{S_2\}))])$$
$$\supset C_\alpha(T_{\alpha\beta}^{-1}[\{T_{\alpha\beta}(S_1), T_{\alpha\beta}(S_2)\}])$$
$$\supset C_\alpha(\{S_1, S_2\})$$
$$\supset \{S_1, S_2\}$$

and hence

$$S_1 \in C_\beta(\{S_2\}).$$

So we see that each analysis, i.e. each transcription, may enrich to set of consequences of a given set of sentences.

The above formal description is an attempt to capture logical relations and it shows how semantic inferences could be given their possible transcription as t-sentences.

Let us now introduce the notion of consistency. This notion will be considered here in a relative sense, i.e. a set of sentences can be consistent at a certain level of analysis, but reveal itself to be inconsistent in a further analysis.

More precisely, a set of sentences X_α will be called α-consistent if for any sentence S, X_α does not contain simultaneously this sentence and its negation. This corresponds to the classical notion of consistency. Now we will say that a set X_α is β-consistent (for $L_\alpha \ll L_\beta$) if $T_{\langle\alpha,\beta\rangle}(X_\alpha)$ is β-consistent. This last definition means that a set of sentence is consistent at any level if the transcription of the set of sentences at this level does not reveal a contradiction. For example, suppose that the language L_β is a language used for lexical decomposition and that in this language the sentence "John killed Mary" has a transcription something like "John CAUSE Mary BECOME dead". Suppose further that the syntactic rules of this language are such that from a sentence like "A CAUSE (B BECOME P)" we can infer by syntactic rules a sentence like "B IS P". In that case, if the sentence "Mary is alive" receives as transcription the sentence "Mary IS NOT dead", then the set "John killed Mary", "Mary is alive" will be β-inconsistent.

These definitions can be generalized. Let $[\![L_\alpha]\!]_{\alpha \in A}$ be a tree of languages, and $[\![T_{\langle\alpha,\beta\rangle}]\!]_{\langle\alpha,\beta\rangle \in B}$ be the corresponding tree of transcription functions. What we now want to define is not consistency in relation with one analysis but for the entire analysis expressed here by all the transcriptions of the tree. So we define the consistency of a set of sentences of the top language in relation with a tree of transcription functions in the following manner. If X_ϕ is a set of sentences of the top language, we will say that X_ϕ is consistent in relation with $[\![T_{\langle\alpha,\beta\rangle}]\!]_{\langle\alpha,\beta\rangle \in B}$ if $\bigcup_{\alpha \in A} C_\alpha(X_\phi)$ is ϕ-consistent. This means that a set of sentences is consistent in relation with a tree of transcriptions not only if none of these transcriptions leads to a contradiction, but also if all these transcriptions are compatible.

The notion of consistency in relation with a tree of transcription functions permits us to introduce the concept of world representation. A world representation is an ordered pair $\langle[\![T_{\langle\alpha,\beta\rangle}]\!]_{\langle\alpha,\beta\rangle \in B}, X_\phi\rangle$ where X_ϕ is consistent in relation with $[\![T_{\langle\alpha,\beta\rangle}]\!]_{\langle\alpha,\beta\rangle \in B}$.

A world representation will play the role of what is classically called a possible world. The main difference is the following: first, a world representation is always partial, i.e. an under-determination of what it is the case; second, a world representation is not only determinated by a set of sentences, but a set of sentences with their specific analysis. We could even venture to say that a sentence with its specific analysis is a material correspondent of what philosophers call propositions.

The notion of truth in a world representation follows naturally. We will say that a sentence S is true for the world representation $\langle[\![T_{\langle\alpha,\beta\rangle}]\!]_{\langle\alpha,\beta\rangle \in B}, X_\phi\rangle$ if $\langle[\![T_{\langle\alpha,\beta\rangle}]\!]_{\langle\alpha,\beta\rangle \in B}, X_\phi \cup \{\ S\}\rangle$ is not a world representation. This means that a sentence is true for a world representation if, when adding his negation to this world representation, we obtain a contradiction.

We see that the notion of truth is relative to the analysis of a sentence. Furthermore, the definition of a world representation as a pair has consequences that two *different* world representations may have the same set of true sentences because they do not have the same tree of transcription functions. Intuitively, this corresponds to the fact that we can agree on certain sentences, and be justified to do so, without having the same knowledge of the content of the sentence. An example will illustrate this point. Consider the sentence "It is raining". A child, a philosophy teacher and a meteorologist may agree on the truth value of this sentence just by looking through the window but they certainly do not have the same analysis of the situation. And this does not mean that one of them has a false representation of "It is raining".

CONCLUSIONS

As it may be seen by the preceding analysis, our research intention is to explore the possible integration of some of the concepts of formal theories of semantics into the specific problems of computer processing of a non pre-edited natural language text. In this report, we have presented some distinctions which allow us to give to each sentence of the original text and of the underlying discourse a formal representation and a logical status. As we have shown, each sentence is transcribed in an algebraic form that has its proper syntactic inferences. Each sentence also receives a logical status expressive of either the truth conditions of another sentence or a possible state of the world for a set of sentences.

Sentences, thus have different logical types; some express intensions others extensions and, as such, build up a complex system.

The character of the descriptions presented above may seem very abstract, but we believe that they are essential for understanding the various types of information involved in text processing. And in the specific paradigm in which we are working no system will have access to a semantic level if these distinctions are not made.

REFERENCES

1. P. Plante, Le système DEREDEC. *3rd Int. Conf. Computing in the Humanities, Waterloo,* 1977.
2. J. Hayes, On semantic nets, frames and associations. *Proc. 5th Int. Joint Conf. Artificial Intelligence,* pp. 99–107, 1977.
3. S. P. J. Landsbergen, Syntax and formal semantics of English. *PHLIQ,AI, Coling, Art.* 21 (1976).
4. T. Ballmer and W. Brennenstuhl, An empirical approach to frame theory (Verb Thesaurus Organization). In *Words, Worlds and Context* (Edited by H. J. Eikmeyer and H. Rieser). de Gruyter, Berlin (1982).
5. De Beaugrande, *Text, Discours, and Process.* Longman, London (1980).
6. R. M. Kempson, *Semantic Theory.* Cambridge University Press, Cambridge (1977).
7. N. J. Cercone, The nature and computational use of a meaning representation for word concepts. *Am. J. Computat. Linguistics* 2(Microfiche 34), 64–81 (1975).
8. W. A. Woods, What's in a link: foundations for semantic networks. In *Representation and Understanding* (Edited by D. Bobrow and A. Collins), pp. 35–82 (1975).
9. J. Katz, *Semantic Theory.* Harper & Row, New York (1972).
10. J. S. Petofi, Beyond the sentence, between linguistic and logic. In *Style and Text.* Stockholm, Skiptor (1975).
11. T. A. Van Dijk, *Some Aspects of Text Grammars.* Mouton, The Hague (1972).
12. L. K. Schubert, Extending the expressive power of semantic networks. *Advance Papers of the 4th Int. Joint Conf. on Artificial Intelligence,* 1975, pp. 158–164. (This is a condensed version of Schubert, 1976.)
13. G. A. Miller and P. N. Johnson-Laird, *Language and perception.* Cambridge University Press, Cambridge (1976).
14. R. D. Dowty, *Word Meaning and Montague Grammar.* Reidel, New York (1979).
15. K. Ajdukiewicz, Die Syntaktische Konnexitat. *Studia Philosophica* 1, pp. 1–27; Translated as, Syntactic Connection. In *Polish Logic* (Edited by S. McCall), pp. 207–231. Oxford (1967). Part I published as, On syntactic coherence. *Rev. Metaphys.* **20**, 635–647 (1935).
16. Y. Bar-Hillel, Logical syntax and semantics. *Language* **30**, 230–237 (1954).
17. R. Montague, *Formal Philosophy: Selected Papers of Richard Montague* (Edited by R. Thomason). Yale University Press (1973).
18. M. J. Cresswell, *Logic and Languages.* Methuen, London (1973).
19. L. Aqvist and F. Guenthner, Fundamentals of a theory of verbs aspects and events within the setting of an improved tense logic. In *Studies in Formal Semantics* (Edited by F. Guenthener and C. Rohrer). North Holland, Amsterdam (1976).
20. G. Carlson, Reference to kinds in English. Doctoral dissertation, Univ. of Massachusetts (1977).
21. W. Kummer, *Grundlagen der Text theorie.* Rowohlt, Reinbek (1975).
22. E. L. Keenan, *Formal Semantics of Natural Language.* Cambridge University Press, Cambridge (1975).
23. M. Bierwisch, On classifying semantic features. In (Bierwisch and Heidolph), pp. 27–50 (4) (1970).
24. R. C. Schank and R. P. Abelson, *Scripts, Plans and Understanding.* Lawrence Erlbaum Assoc., Hillsdale, New Jersey (1977).
25. N. Chomsky, *Lectures on Government and Binding.* Foris, Dordrecht (1981).
26. S. Arikana, A study of syntactical structures of documents and its application to indexing systems. *Res. Rep. No* 63, Res Inst. Fund. Inform Scie, Kyvshu Univ. (1976).
27. C. Bourrelly, *Le Système Documentaire SATIN. Description Générale et Manuel d'Utilisation.* CNRS, Paris (1974).
28. P. Bratley, P. Lusignan and F. Ouellette, *JEUDEMO, A package for Scholars in the Humanities, Siglash News letters.* ACM, New York (1974).
29. W. Burghart and K. Holker, *Text processing, Papers on text Analysis and Text description.* de Gruyter, Berlin (1978).

30. E. Charniak, Towards a model of children's story comprehension (AI, TR 266). Cambridge, Mass., M.I.T. Artificial Intelligence Laboratory (1972).

31. R. C. Cros, J. C. Gardin and F. Levy, *L'automatisation des Recherches Documentaires, un Modèle Général le SYNTOL. Gauthier-Villars*, Paris (1968).

32. N. Hamilton-Smith, CONCORD, user's specification. Edinburgh Regional Computing Center (1970).

33. J. Hayes, In defence of logic. *Proc. 5th Int. Conf. Artificial Intelligence*, pp. 559–565 (1977).

34. P. W. J. Medema, H. G. Bronnenburg, S. P. J. Bunt, R. J. H. Landsbergen, W. J. Scha, E. P. C. Scoenmakers and Van Utteren, PHILIQAI: a multilevel semantics in question answering. *Am. J. Computat. Linguistics*, Microfiche 32 (1975).

35. D. Metzing, Frame representation and lexical semantic. in *Words, Worlds, and Context* (Edited by H. J. Eikmeyer and H. Risser). de Gruyter, Paris (1981).

36. J. G. Meunier and F. D'Aoust, The SATO system: a system for content analysis. *Comput. Humanities* (1974).

37. B. H. Partee, Some transformational extensions of Montague grammar. *J. Philosophical Logic* **2**, 509–534 (19??).

38. M. R. Quillian, Semantic memory. In *Semantic Information Processing* (Edited by M. Minsky), pp. 227–270. M.I.T. Press, Cambridge, Mass. (1968).

39. D. Ross and R. Rasche, Eyeball: A computer program for description of style. *CHUM* **6**, 213–21 (1972).

40. D. B. Russell, COCOA, A manual. Chilton, Atlas Computer Laboratory (1967).

41. R. C. Schank, Conceptual dependency: a theory of natural language understanding. *Cognitive Psych.* **3**, 552–631 (1972).

42. L. K. Schubert, Extending the expressive power of semantic networks. *Artificial Intell.* **7**, 163–198 (1976).

43. L. K. Schubert, L. K. Goebel and N. J. Cercone, The structure and organization of a semantic net for comprehension and inference. *Associative Networks*. Academic Press, New York (1979).

44. A. Tarski, The semantic conception of truth and the foundations of semantics. *Phil. and Phenom. Res.* **4**, 341–376 (reprinted in *Semantics and the Philosophy of Language* (Edited by L. Linsky), University of Illinois Press, Urbana, 1952, pp. 13–47; also in *Readings in Philosophical Analysis* (Edited by M. Feigl and W. Sellars), Appleton, New York (1949).

45. T. A. Van Dijk, *Text and Context: Explorations in the Semantics and Pragmatics of Discourse*. Longmans, London (1977).

46. Y. Wilks, An artificial intelligence approach to machine translation. In *Computer Models of Thought and Language* (Edited by R. C. Schank and K. M. Colby), pp. 114–151. Freeman, San Francisco, Calif. (1973).

47. J. Searle and D. Vandervecken, *Foundations of Illocutionary Logic*. Oxford University Press (1983).

Comp. & Maths. with Appls. Vol. 9, No. 1, pp. 97–109, 1983
Printed in Great Britain

0097–4943/83/010097–13$03.00/0
Pergamon Press Ltd.

ARGOT: A SYSTEM OVERVIEW†

JAMES F. ALLEN

Computer Science Department, University of Rochester, Rochester, NY 14627, U.S.A.

Abstract—We are engaged in a long-term research project that has the ultimate aim of describing a mechanism that can partake in an extended English dialogue on some reasonably well specified range of topics. The fundamental assumption in this project is that conversants in a dialogue are constantly recognizing and monitoring the goals of the other participants. To do this, they must have a rich body of knowledge about the topic, about the goals and beliefs of the other participants, and about the structure of dialogues in general.

This paper described progress made towards these goals and outlines the current research areas in which the project is focused. It describes the basic theory underlying our work and an initial system built according to this theory. It then considers some deficiencies in this system built according to this theory. It then considers some deficiencies in this system and describes the new system, called ARGOT, currently under development. Finally, various specific research efforts within the group are described.

1. BACKGROUND

Most current natural language understanding systems do not engage in a dialogue in any general sense. The "conversations" with these systems consist of a series of single question/answer pairs that are analyzed without any consideration of the user's overall goals. Knowledge of the inter-relations between succeeding questions is very limited, typically providing a mechanism for resolving anaphoric reference and possibly some forms of ellipsis. There is no sense of a continuing interaction in which a topic is developed and tasks are accomplished.

Some story comprehension systems (e.g.[1–3]) analyze the intentions of characters in the story being understood, and answer questions about these characters' goals. But these techniques are not used to analyze the questioner's intent, or to make the system an active participant in the question answering dialogue that tests the system's comprehension of the story.

Consider Dialogue 1, a sample fragment of a dialogue that serves to motivate our work. This is a slightly cleaned up version of an actual dialogue between a computer operator and a user communicating via terminals.

(1) User: Could you mount a magtape for me?
(2)   It's tape xxx.
(3)   No ring, please.
(4)   Can you do it in five minutes?
(5) System: Sorry, we are not allowed to mount that magtape, you will have to talk to [Operator yyy] about it.
(6) User: How about tape zzz?

Dialogue 1.

We are building a computer system called ARGOT that plays the role of the operator in extended dialogues such as the above. This dialogue illustrates some of the many issues that must be addressed in building such a system. For instance, the first utterance, taken literally, is a query about the system's (i.e. the operator's) abilities. In this dialogue, however, the user intends it as part of a request to mount a particular magtape. Utterance (2) identifies the tape in question, and the third and fourth add constraints on how the requested mounting is supposed to be done. These four utterances, taken as a unit, can be summarized as a single request to mount a particular magtape with no ring within five minutes.

Furthermore, once the above is inferred, the system generates an answer (5) that not only denies the request but provides additional information that may be helpful to the user. The operator believes that talking to the other operator will be of use to the user because he has recognized the user's goal of getting a tape mounted. Utterance (6) taken in isolation is

†The preparation of this paper was supported in part by the National Science Foundation under Grant IST-8012418, the Office of Naval Research under Grants N00014-80-C-0197 and N00014-82-K-0193, and the Defense Advanced Research Projects Agency under Grant N00014-78-C-0164.

meaningless; however, in the context of the entire dialogue, it can be seen as an attempt to modify the original request by changing the tape to be mounted.

Another problem facing the system is deciding when to speak. In another dialogue the user might not have provided the additional information (such as whether to use a ring) in later utterances, and the system would have had to ask the user for clarification.

We are currently building a system that provides some answer to each of the above difficulties. It is based on the following assumptions:

—The participants in the dialogue are goal-directed reasoning systems that can perform both physical actions (including linguistic communication) and mental actions such as inference.

—Much of language arises in an attempt to achieve some goal (e.g. obtain information, get the other to do some task).

—Each participant attempts to understand the other's utterances in part by recognizing the goals that motivated them. They mutually develop a common base of knowledge about the task under discussion as the dialogue progresses.

–A large part of the cooperative behavior observed between the participants occurs because one participant accepts a goal of the other as his or her own goal.

In order to develop this model further we need to investigate the nature of the goals and actions in such a setting. This is not the place to examine such issues in detail (see [4]), but a brief summary is necessary to understand the remainder of the paper.

Most goals in this setting involve acquiring beliefs and influencing other's beliefs and goals. These goals are typically achieved using linguistic actions (speech acts) such as *informing*, *requesting*, *warning*, etc. Speech acts are defined by specifying the prerequisites and effects which typically are conditions on the beliefs of the speaker and hearer.

To give an idea of the necessity for this analysis, consider a set of situations in which two agents, S and H, discuss a secret. The situations differ only in what the agents know about each other's knowledge of the secret. In each, we shall consider the plausible interpretations of the utterance "Do you know the secret?"

Setting 1. If S knows the secret and believes that H doesn't know the secret, then "Do you know the secret?" is probably an *offer* to tell H the secret.

Setting 2. If S doesn't know the secret and believes that H does know the secret, then "Do you know the secret?" is probably a *request* that H tell S the secret.

Setting 3. If S knows the secret and doesn't know if H knows the secret, then "Do you know the secret?" is probably either a literal yes/no question or a conditional offer to tell H the secret.

The only changes in the above settings involves S's and H's beliefs about each other. The interpretations of the utterance arise from considering what goals are plausible given what S and H know about each other.

Formalizing adequate models of belief and action is a difficult task, but initial attempts have been made (e.g. [4, 5]) that provide a basis for future work. Our recent efforts in this area will be discussed later in the paper.

This paper summarizes our progress in transforming this theory into a system that actually can participate in dialogues. In Section 2, an early implementation by Allen [6] is described which produces some helpful responses and is successful in analyzing some noun phrase sentence fragments and indirect speech acts. The major deficiencies of this system are considered in Section 3: it has no knowledge of discourse structure, which prevents it from comprehending extended dialogues, and its representation of actions, beliefs, and time is inadequate. These issues are discussed in Sections 4 and 5 respectively.

One of the major advances made in ARGOT is that it recognizes multiple goals underlying utterances. For example, consider the user's goals underlying utterance (2). From the point of view of the task domain, the user's goal is to get the tape mounted (by means of identifying it). From the point of view of the dialogue, the user's goal is to elaborate on a previous request's, i.e. the user is specifying the value of a parameter in the plan that was recognized from the first utterance. In the ARGOT system, we recognize both these goals and are investigating the relationship between them. The need for this type of analysis has been pointed out by many researchers (e.g. [7–10]).

2. A SIMPLE DIALOGUE MODEL

Given this background, let us consider a simple model of a participant in a dialogue. This model was implemented in a system that simulated a clerk in an information booth in a train station[6]. The model uses the above theory and outlines four major steps in modeling a participant. These are:

(1) Identify the linguistic actions performed by the speaker using syntactic and semantic analysis, taking the utterance *literally*.

(2) Recognize at least part of the speaker's plan by finding an inference path connecting the observed linguistic action(s) to an expected goal in the context.

(3) Choose a set of goals by identifying the key steps in the other's plan that cannot be achieved without assistance (i.e., the *obstacles*).

(4) Plan a response that achieves the goals identified in Step (3).

In the train station dialogues, the goals of the users were assumed to be one of the following:

—boarding a train;
—meeting an arriving train;
—other (chosen only if above two are eliminated).

Let us consider it operating on the simple question
                "When does the Montreal train leave?"

In Step (1), this was analyzed to be an instance of the action
        User REQUEST that
            System INFORM user of the departure time.

A simple outline of the plan recognized in Step (2) is shown in Fig. 1. Reading the plan from the bottom to the top, we see the following connections. An eventual effect of the user's REQUEST is that the system performs the requested action, namely the INFORM. The effect of the INFORM action is that the user will KNOW the departure time. This knowledge is necessary for the user to achieve the goal of being at the departure location at the departure

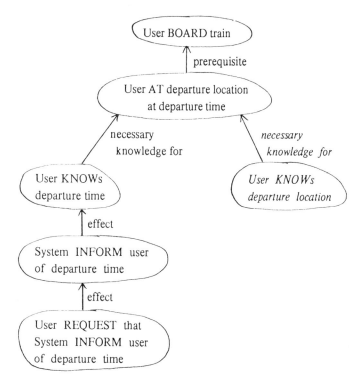

Fig. 1. The (simplified) plan recognized from "When does the Montreal train leave?"

time, which in turn is a prerequisite for boarding the train. Since boarding the train is an expected goal in this context, we are done.

In Step (3), the system examines the user's plan and finds two obstacles. The first is directly on the path outlined above: the user needs to KNOW the departure time. The second is implicit from general knowledge about the structure of plans: the user also needs to know the departure location. If the context were slightly different, say the station had only one track, then the system would have believed that the user already knew the departure location, and thus it would not be an obstacle. In this context, however, the system believes that users do not generally know this information. The system's response from Step (4) addresses both these goals, and the answer is:

"4:00 at gate 7."

Thus we have seen how a helpful response can be generated. The exact same mechanism can also account for comprehending many indirect speech acts as well as simple noun phrase sentence fragments.

Dialogues 2 and 3 give an indication of these abilities:

User: The 3:15 train to Windsor?
System: Gate 10

Dialogue 2: A Simple Noun Phrase.

In Dialogue 2, the user's utterance is not a complete sentence, yet the noun phrase can be analyzed appropriately because the only reasonable plan that involves such a train (in this context) is the boarding plan. The answer is generated from the obstacles detected in the plan as in the first example.

User: Do you know when the Rapido leaves?
System: 4:20.

Dialogue 3: A Simple Indirect Speech Act.

In Dialogue 3, the user's utterance is literally a yes/no question, yet "yes" is not an appropriate response. The appropriate response results from recognizing that the user has goals that go beyond the literal interperation. The plan recognized in this case includes the goal of the user knowing the departure time. The most important point to remember in this example is that the user's plan is recognized starting from the literal interpretation of the utterance. The indirect interpretation falls out naturally from the plan analysis (see [11] for details).

3. THE ARGOT SYSTEM

In the current system we are extending the previous work in a number of ways. Most importantly, the earlier model has no knowledge of discourse structure, so can not partake in an extended dialogue. The only constraints on what is said arise from the structure of the plans that are constructed. Also, the parsing model is too weak to analyze any fragments more complicated than simple noun phrases. Many sentence fragments are considerably more complex than this. Finally, the theoretical work on the formal models of belief, action, goals, and plans needs strengthening.

The architecture of the current system can be motivated best by considering the first problem introduced above. Consider the beginning of Dialogue 1:

User: Could you mount a magtape for me?
        It's tape xxx.

The first of these utterances can be analyzed in the old system. Let us assume it is recognized as an indirect request and that the user's goal is to get a magtape mounted, What is the user's goal in the second utterance? From one viewpoint, it is still to get the tape mounted. From another viewpoint, however, the important goal to recognize is that this sentence is intended to elaborate on the previous request, i.e. it is specifying the value of a parameter in the plan that was recognized from the previous utterance. The goals at this level of analysis are only indirectly related to the goal of mounting the tape. Thus we find that there are at least two levels of goal analysis that must be considered. Recognition of intention then proceeds at both these levels of analysis.

The two levels that we have identified are the *task level*, which includes goals such as mounting tapes, restoring files, etc. and the *communication level*, which includes such goals as introducing a topic, clarifying or elaborating on a previous utterance, modifying the current topic, etc. In the dialogues we consider, the topics generally concern some task that the user needs assistance in performing.

Given this distinction, we can see where other recent dialogue systems fit into this framework. The work at SRI[12] in the expert-apprentice dialogues monitored the goals of the user at the task level. The only analysis at the communicative goal level was implicit in various mechanisms such as the focusing of attention[13]. This work ties the task structure and communicative structure too closely together for our purposes.

The work of Mann *et al.*[14] and Reichman[15] both can be seen as analyses of the communicative goals underlying sentences. Thus these give a clue to the set of high-level goals in the communicative goal plan recognition. Neither of these analyses describe in detail the process of recognizing the communicative goals from actual utterances.

The system described in Section 2 and the work at BBN[16] have both levels of analysis but collapse them into one level, and thus do not allow knowledge of the dialogue structure to be utilized in the analysis. In fact, if we reconsider the analysis made above of the utterance "When is the Windsor train?", we can identify a tension where the two levels interact. In particular, all the relationships (i.e. the arcs) in plans arise from a theory of problem solving, independent of linguistic actions. Thus we have arcs such as "effect of," "prerequisite," "part of," etc. However, there is one class of arcs indicated in the example as "knowledge necessary for" arcs. (In[6], these links were introduced by the knowledge inferences, *knowif, knowref,* etc.) These relate steps in a plan to prerequisite knowledge on the part of the actor, but are hard to motivate within the general problem solving theory. It is exactly at these links that the transition between communicative goals and task goals is made. In the new model the utterance "When does the Montreal train leave?" would be recognized at the communicative goal level as a *bid goal* to obtain information (about the departure time). This analysis allows the task level analysis to recognize the user's ultimate goal of boarding the train.

The overall architecture of the system is depicted in Fig. 2. Included as well is the generative side of the system which is not currently being implemented. Each level of analysis is considered to be running in parallel, and to be passing partial analyses of the utterances and the plans as they are produced. Using this figure, let us consider what the system behavior would be if the user had said only the opening utterance of Dialogue 1.

The utterance "Could you mount a magtape for me?" could be analyzed at the linguistic level as either a yes/no question or an indirect request. The indirect request interpretation arises because of the idiomatic nature of the utterance. Note that since the communicative goal reasoner is able to take the literal and infer the indirect act as well, the indirect request need not be recognized at the linguistic level. These observed linguistic acts are sent to the communicative goal level. Using this input, the communicative goal recognized is a *bid goal* to mount the magtape, which is sent to the task reasoner. The task reasoner analyzes the communicative goal and produces a plan for the task. In this simple example, it could simply introduce a top level mutual goal of mounting the tape.

This goal can then be expanded by the task reasoner and the resultant plan inspected for obstacles. Assuming the user says nothing further, there is an obstacle in the task plan, for the system does not know which tape to mount. This generates a system goal to identify the tape parameter, which is sent to the communicative goal reasoner. A speech act (or acts) is planned that will lead to accomplishing the goal and which obeys the constraints on well-formed discourse. This would be sent to the linguistic level where a response would be generated, such as "which tape?"

The interactions are considerably simplified in the above example. In order to be able to recognize sentence fragments, and to recognize linguistic clues as to the discourse structure, the parser must send partial descriptions as the utterance is being analyzed. Example messages could be "a noun phrase referring to a tape was mentioned," or "the utterance was preceded

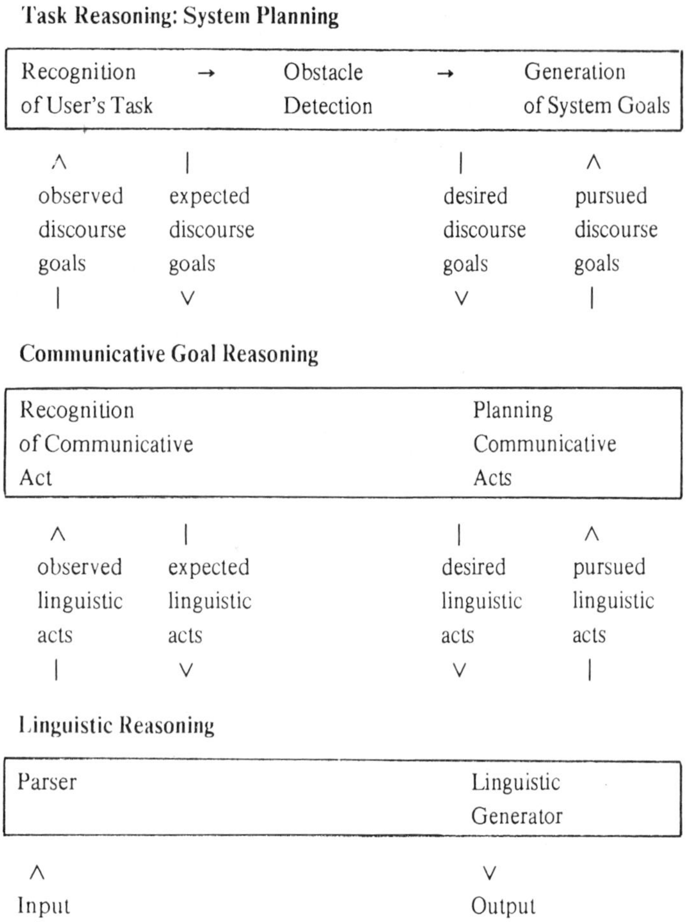

Task Reasoning: System Planning

Recognition of User's Task	→	Obstacle Detection	→	Generation of System Goals

```
    ∧              |                    |              ∧
 observed      expected             desired        pursued
 discourse     discourse            discourse       discourse
 goals         goals                goals          goals
    |              ∨                    ∨              |
```

Communicative Goal Reasoning

Recognition of Communicative Act		Planning Communicative Acts

```
    ∧              |                    |              ∧
 observed      expected             desired        pursued
 linguistic    linguistic           linguistic      linguistic
 acts          acts                 acts           acts
    |              ∨                    ∨              |
```

Linguistic Reasoning

Parser	Linguistic Generator

```
    ∧                                  ∨
  Input                              Output
```

Fig. 2.

with a 'but'" (indicating topic change). One design objective is to make it possible for the system to generate a reasonable response even if the parser fails to generate a complete analysis of the utterances. To allow such behavior we view each of the levels of analysis as running in parallel. In the implementation, each level is implemented by one or more processes and the levels interact using message passing (e.g.[17]). Thus, although we have separated out various stages of analysis, the utterances are not processed by one stage at a time in sequence.

In the actual dialogue we saw the user identify the tape before the system had a chance (or possibly realized the need!) to generate a request to identify it. It is not plausible to allow the system to ignore such new information and generate the response anyway. On the other hand, some system responses, especially those that correct a bad assumption on the part of the user, should be generated anyway and the input effectively ignored. To make such a decision the system needs to know both the import of the user's new utterance and the goals underlying its response to the original utterance.

Our initial solution to this problem is to have the linguistic generation level check with the task level just before the response is actually generated to see if the goal that motivated the response is still valid. Thus the task level of the system is responsible for some coordination of behavior between the other levels. This of course, makes the processing speed an important aspect of the model. If utterances are presented too rapidly, they will not be fully comprehended. If they are presented too slowly, the system will generate many requests for elaboration and clarification. These issues have not been investigated extensively at this stage, but will eventually be a major area of research.

Finally, each module is connected to a knowledge of base of facts. We have developed a representation language which is a variant of the first order predicate calculus (FOPC) that allows knowledge to be structured in a manner akin to semantic networks. Associated with the representation is a specialized limited inference mechanism that mimics the role of a network matcher and provides the system with general inference behavior such as the inheritance of properties and limited reasoning about coreference, time, and beliefs. This will be considered in detail in Section 5.

4. COMMUNICATIVE GOAL REASONING

Given that the new system splits the analyses of intention into two levels, the question arises as to what are the high-level goals at each, and how do they relate to each other. The high-level goals at the task level are dependent on the domain, but correspond to the high-level goals in the earlier system. The high-level communicative goals were not present previously, and must satisfy two constraints. First, they must reflect the structure of English dialogue. Second, though, they must be useful as input to the task level reasoner. In other words, they must specify some operation (e.g. introduce goal, specify parameter) that indicates how the task level plan is to be manipulated.

Our initial set of high-level communicative goals is based on the work of Mann, Moore and Levin[14]. In their model, conversations are analyzed in terms of the manipulation of goals in the task domain. Thus, typical communicative goals are reflected by the actions:

Bid-Goal—introduction of a task goal for adoption by the hearer;

Accept-Goal—acceptance by the hearer of a bid goal;

Parameter Specification—identification of a parameter in an already accepted task;

Termination—end of a discussion and pursuit of an already accepted goal.

These are suitable for our analysis, for each specifies some specific operation that the task level reasoner should perform. Of course, since the task level reasoner is a general plan recognizer as well, it may infer beyond the immediate effect of the specific communicative action inferred at any one stage. For example, if a goal is bid to mount a tape, the system might infer that the user has a higher-level goal of restoring a file, or possibly backing up a file.

We have specified these comunicative goals as actions in our plan model, outlining their prerequisites, effects, and methods for accomplishing them. These tie in with the speech act analysis in the original system easily. Thus, using the same plan recognition algorithm as before, we can recognize the communicative goals.

Not all of these communicative actions are possible at any given time. For instance, at the start of a dialogue, one may either bid a goal or get the other agent's attention (a summons). In order to capture this knowledge we have a context-free grammar which has these communicative acts as terminals, along the lines of Horrigan[18]. The grammar indicates what acts are legal at any particular time for both participants. In order to produce such a grammar, we needed to extend the set of communicative acts to include acts such as summoning attention, acknowledgments, etc. which are included in[18]. This model is currently being implemented and tested on some sample dialogues, including Dialogue 1. We are currently considering incorporating a more general model of discourse that can handle a wider range of dialogues, including topic change, clarification dialogues, and repair.

One of the successes of the previous system is that some utterances consisting of a single noun phrase can be understood appropriately. The context is sufficient to identify one plausible plan for the speaker. We hope to extend this success to ungrammatical utterances. As the linguistic analysis progresses, the linguistic level can notify the communicative goal level of the various noun phrases that appear as they are analyzed. This allows the other levels to start analyzing the speaker's intentions before the entire sentence is linguistically analyzed. Thus, sometimes an interpretation may be found even if the linguistic analysis eventually "fails" to find a complete sentence. (Failure is not quite the correct word here, since if the utterance is understood, whether it was "correct" or not becomes less relevant.)

In addition, the rest of the system may be able to provide the linguistic level with strong enough expectations as to the content of the utterance that is able to construct a plausible analysis of what was said.

We are currently investigating what other partial information could be useful for the communicative goal recognizer. One area that is obvious is the recognition of *clue* words to the discourse structure[15]. For example, if the next user utterance begins with the word "but", this gives a clue as to what communicative goal the user is performing. In particular, the system should expect the user to modify the current topic in some way. Similarly, if an utterance contains the word "please," then the intent behind the utterance will involve a *request* at some level of analysis.

5. ISSUES IN KNOWLEDGE REPRESENTATION

One of the more important first tasks in designing a system is to specify a system-wide language in which facts could be expressed and transmitted in messages. One of the methodological goals in this development has been not to introduce any constructs into this language until they were rigorously defined. We started with a standard version of the first order predicate calculus and have since introduced notational abbreviations and defined a wide range of predicates at two separate levels of analysis. The first level, corresponding to the epistemological level in[16], consists of predicates that are used to define the structure of knowledge. The initial set of these has been determined by investigating what types of inferences we want to be able to do efficiently and automatically. Given these predicates and the set of desired inferences, we have defined a retrieval component acting on a knowledge base of facts. The current retriever implements inferences such as those that produce semantic network-like inheritance of properties. This work is considered in more detail in Section 5.1.

The other level of analysis corresponds to the conceptual level of[16]. At this level we have outlined basic theories of the structure of actions, events, plans, times, and beliefs. Using these theories, we then have specified hierarchies of actions and events, eventually arriving at predicates that are specific to the domain being modeled. Some of the theoretical underpinnings of this work are outlined in Section 5.2.

5.1 *The epistemological primitives and the retriever*

Ever since Woods's[19] "What's in a Link" paper, there has been a growing concern for formalization in the study of knowledge representation. Several arguments have been made that frame representation languages and semantic-network languages are syntactic variants of the first-order predicate calculus (FOPC). The typical argument (e.g.[20, 21]) proceeds by showing how any given frame or network representation can be mapped to a *logically isomorphic* (i.e. logically equivalent when the mapping between the two notations is accounted for) FOPC representation. We emphasize the term "logically isomorphic" because these arguments have primarily dealt with the content (semantics) of the representations rather than their forms (syntax). Though these arguments are valid and scientifically important, there is another side to the story.

For the past two years we have been studying the formalization of knowledge retrievers as well as the representation languages that they operate on. This study has led to the conclusion that the form of a representation is crucial to the design of a retriever. We are designing a representation language in the notation of FOPC whose form facilitates the design of a semantic-network-like retriever.

Elsewhere[22], we have demonstrated the utility of viewing a knowledge retriever as a specialized inference engine (theorem prover). A specialized inference engine is tailored to treat certain predicate, function, and constant symbols differently than others. This is done by building into the inference engine certain true sentences involving these symbols and the control needed to handle these sentences. The inference engine must also be able to recognize when it is able to use its specialized machinery. That is, its specialized knowledge must be coupled to the *form* of the situations that it can deal with.

For illustration, consider an instance of the ubiquitous type hierarchies of semantic networks:

FORDS

↑

| subtype

|

MUSTANGS

↑

| type

|

OLD-BLACK

By considering the types *FORDS* and *MUSTANGS* to be predicates, the following two FOPC sentences are logically isomorphic to the network:

(1.) $\forall \times MUSTANGS(\times) \to FORDS(\times)$

(1.2) MUSTANGS(OLD-BLACK)

However, these two sentences have not captured the form of the network, and furthermore, not doing so is problematic to the design of a retriever. The subtype and type links have been built into the network language because the network retriever has been built to handle them specially. That is, the retriever does not view a subtype link as an arbitrary implication such as (1.1) and it does not view a type link as an arbitrary atomic sentence such as (1.2). Rather, they are recognized specially and enable specialized inferences.

In our representation language we capture the form as well as the content of the network. By introducing two predicates, *TYPE* and *SUBTYPE*, we capture the meaning of the type and subtype links. $TYPE(i, t)$ is true iff the individual u is a member of the type (set of objects) t, and $SUBTYPE(t_1, t_2)$ is true iff the type t_1 is a subtype (subset) of the type t_2. Thus, in our language, the following two sentences would be used to represent what was intended by the network:

(2.1) SUBTYPE(FORDS, MUSTANGS)

(2.2) TYPE(OLD-BLACK, FORDS)

It is now easy to build a retriever that recognizes subtype and type assertions by matching predicate names. Contrast this to the case where the representation language used (1.1) and (1.2) and the retriever would have to recognize these as sentences to be handled in a special manner.

But what must the retriever know about the SUBTYPE and TYPE predicates in order that it can reason (make inferences) with them? There are two assertions, (A.1) and (A.2), such that {(1.1), (1.2)} is logically isomorphic to {(2.1), (2.2), (A.1), (A.2)}. (Note: throughout this paper, axioms that define the retriever's capabilities will be specially labeled A.1, A.2, etc.)

(A.1) $\forall t_1, t_2, t_3 \; SUBTYPE(t_1, t_2) \wedge SUBTYPE(t_2, t_3) \to SUBTYPE(t_1, t_3)$
     (*SUBTYPE* is transitive.)

(A.2) $\forall 0, t_1, t_2 \; TYPE(0, t_1) \wedge SUBTYPE(t_1, t_2) \to TYPE(0, t_2)$
     (Every member of a given type is a member of its supertypes.)

The retriever will also need to know how to control inferences with these axioms, but this issue is not taken up in this paper.

The design of a semantic-network language often continues by introducing new kinds of nodes and links into the language. This process may terminate with a fixed set of node and link types that are the knowledge-structuring primitives out of which all representations are built. Others have referred to these knowledge-structuring primitives as epistemological primitives[16] and structural relations[23]. If a fixed set of knowledge-structuring primitives is used in the language, then a retriever can be built that knows how to deal with all of them.

The design of our representation language very much mimics this approach. Our knowledge-structuring rimitives include a fixed set of predicate names and terms denoting three kinds of elements in the domain. We give meaning to these primitives by writing domain-independent axioms involving them. A retriever has been built that reasons with these axioms and thus knows how to deal with all the primitives of our language. Thus far in this paper we have introduced two predicates (*TYPE* and *SUBTYPE*), two kinds of elements (individuals and types), and two axioms ((A.1) and (A.2)).

This type of analysis can be continued to introduce roles, distinguished types, and limited forms of equality (see[24]).

The important point to notice here is that once we have selected our predicates and given the axioms defining them, we have a precise characterization of what inferences we would like the retrieval component to perform. We have used this approach to define a prototype knowledge base retrieval mechanism that is currently being used in the system. It is implemented in a Horn clause theorem prover and has approximately the same capabilities as the partitioned networks of Hendrix[25], and makes retrievals reasonably efficiently.

5.2 Formal aspects of the conceptual level of representation

An important part of this research over the last two years has been the investigation of some basic issues in representation. In particular, the existing models of action have proven inadequate to represent many of the concepts talked about in even simple dialogues, as well as being inadequate for a more general plan reasoning. This problem has mainly been caused by an inadequate treatment of time in existing knowledge representations. The other major problem has been the precise specification of a representation of belief that did not lead to theoretical difficulties. Progress has been made on all of these issues.

An interval-based temporal logic has been defined[26] and is currently being incorporated into our knowledge representation. Relationships between intervals are maintained in a hierarchical manner and an inference process based on constraint propagation has been developed and implemented. This representation is notable in a few areas:

—It allows one to efficiently represent the present moment (i.e. "now") so that it can be continually updated without making major changes to the knowledge base.

—It is designed using relative information about how intervals are related. Thus it doesn't depend on a date line which is often found in temporal representations. This is particularly important in a dialogue system for most temporal information does not have a precise time.

—It allows time intervals to extend indefinitely into the past or future, and supports a limited type of default reasoning.

This representation of time has been used to produce a general model of events and actions[27]. Rather than concentrating on how actions are performed, as is done in the problem-solving literature, this work examines the set of conditions under which an action or event can be said to have occurred. In other words, if one is told that action A occurred, what can be inferred about the state of the world?

Consider an example investigated in detail in[27]. What are the conditions under which one might say that an actor hid a book from another actor? Certainly, this can't be answered in terms of the physical actions the actor did, for the actor might have hidden the book by

—putting it behind a desk;
—standing between it and the other agent while they are in the same room; or
—calling a friend and getting him to do one of the above.

Furthermore, the actor might hide the object by simply not doing something s/he intended to do. For example, assume Sam is planning to go to lunch with Carole after picking Carole up at her office. If, on the way out of his office, Sam decides not to take his coat because he doesn't want Carole to see it, then Sam has hidden the coat from Carole. Of course, it is crucial here that Sam believe that he normally would have taken the coat. Sam couldn't have hidden his coat by forgetting to bring it.

This example brings up a few key points that may not be noticed from the first three examples. First, Sam must have intended that Carole not see the coat. Without this intention (i.e., in the forgetting case), no such action occurs. Second, Sam must have believed that it was likely that Carole would see the coat in the future course of events. Finally, Sam must have acted in such a way that he then believed that Carole would not see the coat in the future course of events. Of course, in this case, the action Sam performed was "not bringing the coat," which would normally not be considered an action unless it was intentionally not done.

I claim that these three conditions provide a reasonably accurate definition of what it means to hide something. They certainly cover the examples presented above. It is also important to note that one does not have to be successful in order to have been hiding something. The definition depends on what the hider believes and intends at the time, not what actually occurs.

However, the present definition is rather unsatisfactory, as many extremely difficult concepts, such as belief and intention, have been thrown about casually.

In the last two years, we have developed a model of belief by viewing BELIEVE as a predicate between an agent and a description of a sentence. To do this, we must introduce quotation into the logic. Thus the assertion "John believes Sam lives on 4th Street" would be expressed as

$$\text{BELIEVE(JOHN, ``LIVES(SAM, 4th STREET)'').}$$

Introducing quotation into a logic does not cause any difficulties until one tries to relate the quoted formula to the formula it names. To do this, we need a truth predicate, and an axiom such as: for any sentence α

$$(*) \quad \text{TR(``}\alpha\text{'')}\langle = \rangle\alpha.$$

Thus,

$$\text{TR(``LIVES(SAM, 4th STREET)'')} \langle = \rangle \text{LIVES(SAM, 4th STREET).}$$

Unfortunately, such an axiom leads to paradoxes. Perlis[28], however, has shown that one can define a truth scheme that intuitively gives us the behavior above but which is provably consistent. There is not the space to examine this here, but suffice to say that (*) does not get us into trouble unless α contains a negation outside a "Tr" predicate.

Using this formalism, we can safely introduce the BELIEVE predicate and examine its behavior. One of the initial difficulties concerns representing the fact that someone knows something that the believer does not know. For instance, if it is not known where Sam lives, we would still like to be able to represent the fact that John knows where Sam lives. This is typically handled by quantifying in. Thus we get a formula such as

$$(**) \quad \exists \times \text{BELIEVE(JOHN, ``LIVES(SAM, }\times\text{)'').}$$

I have been deliberately loose here about quotation. Actually the variable $\times$ ranges over quoted expressions and must not be quoted. So we need a more elaborate quotation scheme that gives us the abilities of Quine's corner quotes. Leaving these details aside, however, the above formula does not capture the required knowledge. Presumably, everyone believe that Sam lives where Sam lives, so the description "the place where Sam lives" satisfies(**) but does not capture that John knows where Sam lives.

One way out of this problem is to assume there is a *standard name* for every object (e.g. Moore[29]). This is inadequate, however, for the name that will satisfy the above knowledge changes as the context changes. For example, if John were a customs officer at the border, the description "Rochester" would be enough to claim that John knows where Sam lives. If John were a friend going to Sam's house, however, directions to the house (e.g. an address) would be required. Thus to solve this problem we need to be able to assert what descriptions are useful for what task, and then knowing what something is depends on what task is being considered.

Within a logic with quotation, however, predicates that operate on the syntactic form of formulas are perfectly acceptable, and one can specify exactly what form of description is necessary for any task. Thus for JOHN the customs officer at the border, he knows where Sam lives if

$$\exists \times \text{BELIEVE(JOHN, ``LIVES(SAM, }\times\text{)'') \& CITY-NAME(}\times\text{)}$$

where CITY-NAME is a predicate on expressions and is true if $\times$ is the proper name of a city. The interested reader should see[30] for further details.

One problem with quotation schemes that it also solved by Haas is that if one simulates another's reasoning by simulating inference rules on syntactic formulas, the length of the simulation with respect to the simulated reasoning grows exponentially with the depth of nesting of beliefs. An approach that avoids this involves collecting all the beliefs of the agent in question into a separate "data base" and then running the inference rules on only those facts. This technique, however, appears not to be able to handle beliefs that involve quantifying in or to use knowledge involving disjunctions of beliefs. Techniques have been devised to remedy these problems. By introducing the concept of *dummy constants* along the lines of[31], we can handle the quantifying in case. Haas[30] presents a rigorous treatment of these issues. Since the simulation technique is just another proof rule in a general inference system, disjunctions can be handled using the standard techniques.

6. CONCLUDING REMARKS

The ARGOT project is still in its infancy. Simple prototypes of the task level reasoner, communicative goal reasoner, and the knowledge base have been constructed, and more sophisticated versions are under development. Within the next few years we hope to understand the relationship between knowledge of discourse structure and the process of plan recognition, and to develop more sophisticated plan recognition methods based on our work in the representation of belief, action, and time. We consider these to be two major steps towards constructing truly conversant systems.

Acknowledgements—Many people have made significant contributions to the project so far. In particular, I would like to thank Gary Cottrell, Alan Frisch, Diane Litman, Andy Haas, Pat Hayes, Don Perlis, Steven Small, and Marc Villain.

REFERENCES

1. B. Bruce and D. Newman, Interacting plans. *Cognitive Science* 2(3), 195–233 (1978).
2. R. Wilensky, Understanding goal-based stories. Ph.D. Thesis, Yale University (1978).
3. J. G. Carbonell. POLITICS: Automated ideological reasoning. *Cognitive Science* 2(1), 27–51 (1978).
4. J. F. Allen and C. R. Perrault, Analyzing intention in utterances. *Artificial Intelligence* 15, 3 (1980).
5. R. C. Moore, Reasoning about knowledge and action, Ph.D. Thesis MIT, Cambridge, Mass. (1979).
6. J. F. Allen, A plan-based approach to speech act recognition. Ph.D. Thesis, Computer Science Dept., University of Toronto (1979).
7. D. Levy, Communicative goals and strategies: between discourse and syntax. (Edited by T. Givon), *Syntax and Semantics*, Vol. 12 Academic Press, New York (1979).
8. B. J. Grosz, Utterance and objective: issues in natural language communication. *Proc., 6th IJCAI*, Tokyo (1979).
9. D. Appelt, Planning natural language utterances to satisfy multiple goals. Ph.D. Thesis, Computer Science Dept., Stanford University (1981).
10. P. N. Johnson and S. P. Robertson, *MAGPIE: A goal-based model of conversation*. Research Report #206, Computer Science Dept., Yale University, May (1981).
11. C. R. Perrault and J. F. Allen, A plan-based analysis of indirect speech acts. *J. Assoc. Comp'l, Linguistics* 6, 3 (1980).
12. D. E. Walker, *Understanding Spoken Language*. North-Holland, Amsterdam (1978).
13. B. J. Grosz, Discourse knowledge. *Understanding Spoken Language* (Edited by P. E. Walker) Section 4. North-Holland, Amsterdam (1978).
14. W. C. Mann, J. A. Moore, and J. A. Levin, A comprehension model for human dialogue. *Proc. 5th IJCAI*, MIT, Cambridge, Mass. (1977).
15. R. Reichman, Conversational coherency. *Cognitive Science* 2 (1978).
16. R. J. Brachman, Taxonomy, descriptions, and individuals in natural language understanding. *Proc. 17th Ann. Meeting*. pp. 33–37. Assoc. for Computational Linguistics, UCSD, La Jolla, CA, August (1979).
17. J. A. Feldman, High-level programming for distributed computing, *CACM* 22(6), 363–368 (1979).
18. M. K. Horrigan, Modelling simple dialogues. *Proc. 5th Int. Joint Conf. on Artificial Intelligence*. MIT, Cambridge, Mass (1977).
19. W. A. Woods, What's in a link: Foundations for semantic networks. (Edited by Bobrow and A. Collins). *Representation and Understanding: Studies in Cognitive Science*. Academic Press, New York (1975).
20. Patrick J. Hayes, The logic of frames. *Frame Conceptions and Text Understanding*. (Edited by M. Dieter). de Gruyter, New York (1980).
21. N. J. Nilsson, *Principles of Artificial Intelligence*. Palo Alto, California: Tioga (1980).
22. A. M. Frisch, and J. F. Allen, Knowledge retrieval as limited inference. *Lecture Notes in Computer Science* 138: 6th Conference on Automated Deduction (Edited by G. Goos and J. Hestnanis). Springer-Verlag, New York (1982).
23. S. Shapiro, The SNePS semantic network processing system. *Associative Networks* (Edited by N. V. Findler). Academic Press, New York (1979).
24. J. F. Allen, and A. M. Frisch, What's in a semantic network? *Proc., 20th Meeting*. Assoc. for Computational Linguistics, Toronto (1982).
25. G. G. Hendrix, Encoding knowledge in partioned networks. *Associative Networks* (Edited by N. V. Findler) Academic Press New York (1979).
26. J. F. Allen, An interval-based representation of temporal knowledge. *Proc., 7th IJCAI*, Vancouver, B. C., August (1981a).
27. J. F. Allen, What's necessary to hide?: Reasoning about action verbs. *Proc. 19th Ann. Meeting*. pp. 77–81. Assoc. for Computational Linguistics, 77–81, Stanford University (1981b).

28. D. Perlis, Language, computation, and reality. Ph.D. Thesis, Computer Science Dept., University of Rochester, (1981).
29. R. C. Moore, Reasoning about knowledge and action. *Proc., 5th IJCAI.* MIT, Cambridge Mass. August (1977).
30. A. Haas, Mental states and mental actions in planning. Ph.D. Thesis, Computer Science Dept., University of Rochester (1982).
31. Cohen, P. R., Planning speech acts. Ph.D. Thesis and TR 118, Dept. of Computer Science, University of Toronto (1978).

Comp. & Maths. with Appls. Vol. 9, No. 1, pp. 111–129, 1983
Printed in Great Britain.

0097–4943/83/010111–19$03.00/0
Pergamon Press Ltd.

DESCRIPTION DIRECTED CONTROL: ITS IMPLICATIONS
FOR NATURAL LANGUAGE GENERATION

David D. McDonald†

Department of Computer and Information Science, University of Massachusetts at Amherst, MA 01003,
U.S.A.

Abstract—We propose a very specifically constrained virtual machine design for goal-directed natural language generation based on a refinement of the technique of data-directed control that we have termed "description-directed control". Important psycholinguistic properties of generation follow inescapably from the use of this control technique, including: efficient runtimes, bounded lookahead, indelible decisions, incremental production of the text, and inescapable adherence to grammaticality. The technique also provides a possible explanation for some well known universal constraints, though this cannot be confirmed without further empirical investigation.

In description-directed control the controlling data structure is the surface-level linguistic description of the very text being generated. This constituent structure tree is itself generated depth first by the incremental realization of a hierarchical description of the speaker's communicative goals (neutrally termed a "realization specification") organized according to the scope and importance of its components. The process of traversing the surface structure gates and constrains the realization process; all realizations are thus subject to the grammatical constraints that accrue to the surface structure at which they occur, as defined by the grammatical annotation of the surface structure tree.

1. INTRODUCTION: COMPUTATIONAL HYPOTHESES IN A.I.

In the early stages of Artificial Intelligence research into a new phenomena, we normally do our modeling with the most powerful and general purpose computational tools at our disposal. This is because we do not yet know what will be required in the processing and need to retain maximum flexibility to experiment with variations in our model. Once the phenomena is better understood however, we can develop hypotheses about exactly what representations and operations on them the process requires. The primitive tools can then be tailored and restricted to accommodate just those requirements and no more, transforming the computational architecture from general purpose and powerful to particular and limited. The type of architecture adopted—the design of the virtual machine on which the modeling is based—becomes a *direct manifestation* of our hypotheses about the phenomenon under study.

This tactic, the limitation of primitive algorithms, representations, and operations to just those required to support the hypothesized processing and no more, is the strongest means available to us within the discipline of Artificial Intelligence for expressing a hypothesis about a psychological process. Its precision makes the hypothesis easier to disprove, either through the discovery of internal inconsistencies that can no longer be hidden behind vague definitions, or by finding ourselves unable to fit pretheoretically expected elaborations of the hypothesis within the stipulations of the design. (In this regard a restricted architecture acts as a "safety check" while the hypothesized model is being completed, since it makes an inadvertent or disguised extension of the system's computational power impossible because it is impossible to formulate.)

We have seen this methodological pattern at work during this last decade in research on natural language parsing. The initial exploratory work of Thorne *et al.*[1], Winograd[2] and Woods[3] was based on tools that could almost implement completely general type zero rewriting systems (e.g. augmented transition networks). The information gathering ability and possible control paths of these systems were constrained only by the informal conventions of the people writing the rules. After experience with these all-powerful systems had been accumulated however, we saw some researchers making a shift to a very specific hypotheses about the computational requirements of the parsing task, e.g.[4–7], the core of their hypotheses being the specification of the carefully limited machine on which the parsing process was to run.

†Preparation of this paper was supported in part by the National Science Foundation under Grant IST-8104984.

In this paper we will look closely at a virtual machine for goal-directed natural language generation and consider its implications. The computational hypothesis that this design embodies has evolved during the last eight years according to the same sort of progression as has taken place in the treatment of parsing: Its first instantiations were based on very general tools that permitted free and easy modification of the design; it became clear however that the full power of the tools was not being used, and, after adjustments to a few of the grammatical analyses (interesting in their own right), a far more restricted set of tools was found to perform just as well. In addition, the restricted design was found to lead inescapably to behavioral properties of the virtual machine with important psycholinguistic consequences, some of which will be discussed at the end of this paper.

We will begin by defining the role that the hypothesized control structure plays in generation. This will entail making certain assumptions which, while appealing, cannot now be proven. We will then look at the control structure algorithm and the representation of surface structure on which it is based. This will lead to a discussion of the computational constraints that the control structure imposes on generation, and to some of their linguistic and psycholinguistic implications. For concreteness a short example taken from one of the applications of the current implementation will be woven throughout the discussion.

2. THE ROLE OF THE CONTROL STRUCTURE IN GENERATION

What are the actions that take place during language generation? What is it that a control structure must organize? This is the most basic question that one can ask about the generation process: if we are drastically wrong in our answer (i.e. if people function on some other basis), then regardless of how effective the virtual machine may be it will be an improper model for people.

Regrettably there is no direct evidence from psycholinguistic studies that we can bring to bear on this question. Deliberate studies aimed for example at determining how work load varies during generation[8] or at determining how much advance planning there must be[9] can to date yield only indirect evidence, and must be placed in a theoretical framework before they can be interpreted. They define phenomena that a successful computational theory must be able to account for, but they do not themselves provide the basis for such a theory. Even studies of spontaneous speech errors[10–14]—the richest source of evidence on generation that we presently have—can yield hard evidence only about the kinds of data that the generation process must be manipulating and not about the process itself.

In the absence of hard evidence about human processing, one must rely on intuitions derived from studies of linguistic competence and from what we know about efficient computation. This leads us to a set of kernal assumptions, which we make precise by developing into a specification of a virtual machine. Space does not permit a discussion of why these particular assumptions were adopted (cf.[15, 16]), nor would any discussion at this point convince the skeptical reader since assumptions have the status of postulates and as such are difficult to argue about. The enterprise is instead to use them as the basis of a theoretical account of generation that is rich enough computationally to make it possible to derive and test its empirical consequences and have the assumptions stand or fall accordingly.

There are three principle assumptions of the present research, each with its corollaries and fine points:

Goal-directed natural language generation is best characterized as a decision-making process. This is a matter of point of view and emphasis: it means that the control structure is to be concerned with, e.g. what dictates what decisions are to be made, what kinds of things are decided upon, what information the decisions are based on and how it is made accessible, or what should be the form of the result. Computationally, emphasizing decision-making might be contrasted with emphasizing the space of a heuristic search, or the stages of a perceptual process, or the adaptive relaxation process that sets an organism's global state.

I assume that all decisions either contribute directly to the substance of the text under production or constrain it, i.e. the choices to be made are between alternate surface-level linguistic forms: alternate words, idioms, sentence structures, rhetorical or intonational effects, etc. (N.B. this means that there is no notion of "grammatical derivation" in this theory, in direct contrast with models of production based on transformational generative grammar ("TG") such as Fay's[13].

All decisions "count". Every decision that a speaker makes is assumed to contribute to the processing effort expended. Consequently if deliberative effort is to be minimized, then the control structure must ensure that every decision is compatible. With every decision adding to the text (or imposing constraints on its structure), compatibility becomes equated with grammaticality—all that we know about the elaborate systems of grammatical dependencies in natural language can be brought over into our study of the generation process. In particular, any decision that is made before all of the other decisions on which it is dependent have been made runs the risk of selecting a choice that is incompatible with those other decisions, leading either to a mistake or to wasteful backup. Under this assumption the order in which decisions are made has real consequences and provides a means, albeit indirect, of testing whether the dependencies proposed in a given grammar are psychologically real.

Only a limited part of the text is planned at a time. The structures that are selected in a decision† are typically greater than one word in length and can involve grammatical relations among widely separated parts of the output text. It must therefore be possible to represent planned but not yet uttered text and grammatical relations. It must also be possible to represent *planned but unexecuted decisions* as well, since decision-making continues as a text is actually being uttered. One can, and in unpracticed conversation usually will, begin a text without having totally decided how it will end. Consequently, later decisions may be restricted in the choices open to them since the text they select must be grammatically compatible with what has already been spoken. The common experience of "talking oneself into a corner"—leaving out things we should have mentioned and even making grammatical errors—suggests that we are unable to appreciate all of the grammatical consequences of early decisions upon later ones, and that we are unable to rescind earlier problematic decisions short of aborting any planned but unspoken text and starting over (another way of saying that all decisions count).

This assumption means that the control structure must support a representation of pending decisions and selected but not yet uttered linguistic structures. In doing this however, the design must very carefully regulate access to the information that is latent in such a representation, and must tie this regulation in with independently justifiable systems such as the grammar if phenomena such as "talking oneself into a corner" are to be captured in a non-*ad hoc* way.

The virtual machine that I shall describe in this paper—based on description-directed control—manifests a sharpened version of these assumptions as an inescapable consequence of its design, i.e. it cannot behave otherwise. Thus if the assumptions are correct, this virtual machine is a *prima facie* candidate to be the one that people actually use; more precisely, we can put this machine forward as transparently functionally isomorphic to the architecture of the human language generation process at the computational level (cf. [17]). Methodologically there are two kinds of test that must be passed before we can believe such a claim. First, the design must be shown to be internally consistent: there must be a successful implementation actually exhibiting the posited behaviors, and it must be possible to consistently incorporate refinements to the behavior as they become known through empirical study. Second, we must look for evidence (presumably indirect) that the functional divisions posited in the virtual machine are in fact the ones that people have. This will certainly include considering whether the design can account for the classes of speech-errors that people make, and possibly the behavior of aphasic patients or the results of online psycholinguistic experiments. (N.B. in judging whether any such account is satisfactory, it is essential to appreciate that all "confrontations" between competence theories (even computational ones) and observed psychological data are mediated by a theoretical account of the functional mapping between them

†To avoid confusion it is important here to distinguish the process of making a decision from what one has decided once the decision has been made. I will refer to what is decided upon as the *choice*, and reserve the term *decision* for the process by which the choice is arrived at. Formally such a "decision" is a function which when evaluated in a given environment returns a "choice". Decisions are implemented in the current computer implementation of the generator by schematically specifying a decision-tree of predicates to be tested (i.e. a set of nested conditionals), with the alternative choices explicitly given as the decision-tree's leaves.

(i.e. which device in the competence theory is to be responsible for which observed effect), and this account must be independently argued for; see[18] for discussion.)

3. ASSUMPTIONS ABOUT THE INPUT TO THE GENERATION PROCESS

The "generation process' that the virtual machine defines is *not* assumed to include the initial "urge to communicate" that sets the process in motion; its focus is instead on the process of deciding the linguistic form of the text and of actually uttering it. The bulk of the decisions not connected with form, e.g. when to speak, what information to include and what to leave out, or how to organize the presentation on a large scale, are assumed to have preceded the initiation of the generation process, and to have resulted in the construction of a specification of the speaker's communicative goals. Such a *realization specification*† (abbreviated "*r*-spec") would include the propositions and references that the audience is to be made aware of, the connotations and affective overtones that are to be maintained, any assumptions about what the audience already knows or about what kinds of rhetorical tactics work best with them, and other things of that sort.‡

Since the actual form of realization specifications within the human mind is not known§ (we do not even know whether they would have to exist as explicit entities), the framework makes only minimum assumptions about them. Specifically:

● A realization specification is a *composite* structure that is brought together for a specific communicative situation.

● Consequently, the determination of what decisions a particular specification implies can not be precomputed; it must instead be uncovered through some kind of recursive decomposition of the structure, this process presumably being ordered by the relative importance of the individual goals and mental objects involved (for convenience also termed "*r*-specs") and the relations between them.

● At any one moment the total set of atomic relations, objects, properties, etc. from which a realization specification can be composed is *fixed*. The correspondence between each available atomic "term" in an *r*-spec and the possible natural language phrases, syntactic relations, etc. that could realize it in context can therefore be known before hand and drawn upon as the raw material of the generator. (This formulation would allow for changes in the correspondences or the addition of new base terms, but only over time as the use of the language changes or as new concepts are learned.)

To be concrete, let me introduce an actual *r*-spec from one of the computer programs that use this generator. This program and the design behind it are discussed in[20]. The computer speaker is a scene-description system written by Jeff Conklin that takes a database of objects and spatial relations produced by the UMass VISIONS system analysing a photograph of a suburban street scene and plans paragraph of text in English describing the scene. The example paragraph in the 1982 paper is:

> "*This is a picture of a white house with a fence around it. The door of the house is red, and so is the gate of the fence. There is a mailbox across the street in front of the fence, and a large tree obscures part of a driveway on the right. It is a cloudy day in summer.*"

---

†I have elected to coin a functionally descriptive term, "realization specification" ("the specification of what is to be realized in the text"), rather than to use a more common term such as "message", in order to emphasize the interpretive, context-sensitive nature of the relationship between an *r*-spec and the text that results from it. The metaphor of "messages" carries with it a notion of generation (and interpretation) as a translation process where the audience reconstructs in its mind the very same expression—the "message"—as the speaker starts with. This metaphor is fraught with difficulties both practical and philosophical (for discussion see[19]), and has largely been abandoned in A.I. research in favor of the view of generation as a planning process with plan realization as its last phase.

‡The point of declaring that the planning and construction of such specifications is external to the processing of the generator is to avoid any claim that such processing has to use the generator's control structure. This is a precaution based on the fact that while I see good reasons for adopting a very restricted but efficient virtual machine design for orchestrating linguistic reasoning, I have no evidence as yet to suggest that the conceptual planning of goals for natural language generation is comparably restricted.

§For computer programs we presume that there is some flexibility in the design of whatever expert program is serving as the speaker for this generator and that these assumptions can be met. Without such flexibility, there is no guarantee that a generator of this design will perform as desired for an arbitrary expert progam: it cannot make a silk purse from a sow's ear.

Let us look at the *r*-spec that gave rise to the second sentence of that paragraph. (This data structure is an LISP list with five embedded lists as indicated by the parentheses and indentation. Each of the embedded lists represents and individual "sub-" *r*-spec which can be referred to by the unique symbol at the beginning of the list (e.g. "*r*-spec2"). The order of the embedded *r*-specs reflects their importance to the composite *r*-spec as a whole.)

```
(r-spec1
    (r-spec2   color-of (door-3 red))
    (r-spec3   part-of (door-3 house-1))
    (r-spec4   condense-on-property (r-spec2 r-spec5 red))
    (r-spec5   color-of (gate-4 red))
    (r-spec6   part-of (gate-4 fence-2)))
```

Fig. 1. An example realization specification.

Decision-procedures for realizing the terms in an r-*spec.* Of equal stature with a speaker's knowledge of their grammar is their knowledge of the correspondence between the terms they use in their realization specifications and the linguistic structures that could serve as their realizations. This is the "raw material" of the generation process, which itself could be characterized as the process of selecting and combining the realizations of *r*-specs in such a way that the grammar of the language is obeyed and the overall goals of the speaker are met.

I will stipulate that every term in an *r*-spec is associated with a set of alternative choices of linguistic realization plus a decision procedure that selects between them according to constraints that hold at the time the decision is to be made. The relation "color-of" for example would have one realization when it functioned as an independent proposition (e.g. "⟨object⟩ is ⟨color⟩"), and another when it functioned as part of an object's description (e.g. "⟨color⟩⟨object⟩" or "⟨object⟩ which is ⟨color⟩"). The form and internal behavior of these decision procedures is not important for the purposes of this paper. Our concern is only with how they interact with the rest of the generation process, and in our assumption (number three above) that decision procedures are fixed and thus will contribute not more than a predictable, bounded amount of effort to the overall process.

Planning vocabulary. Our rescarch on scene description has set aside the question of lexical choice, allowing us to represent the contents of these *r*-specs as simple relations for which the English vocabulary choices are deliberately obvious. (The terms and relation names are taken from a simulation of the object-level spatial data base that is the output of the VISIONS system's analysis.) We have instead concentrated our efforts on the design of the speaker's rhetorical planning vocabulary. "R-spec4" is a token of this vocabulary. Its content is a rhetorical goal that Conklin has called "condense-on-property". It represents an observation by the planner that two of the objects it wishes to describe share a common salient property, in this case their color. Notice that condense-on-property is a relation over other *r*-specs (*r*-spec2 and *r*-spec5) rather than just objects in VISIONS' data base. Consequently its realization will not result in text, but will *impose constraints* on the realization of *r*-spec2 and *r*-spec5, in this case coordinating them and forcing an ordering on their constituents that emphasizes their shared color. (That is, it forces the realization to be something like "The door of the house is red and so is the gate of the fence", rather than say "A red door is part of the house. The fence has a red gate.")

A major part of our on-going research is the formalization of rhetorical effects like condense-on-property (others we have looked at include focus, ordering by new vs old information, restrictions on the extent of a description, and coordinated emphasis and contrast). We believe that rhetorical effects are a key part of a speaker's planning vocabulary—one which we must understand thoroughly if we are to make sense of the structure of human discourses. This is because terms at the rhetorical level can serve the *r*-spec planner as a compact and expeditious model of the lower-level syntactic resources of the language, simplifying the planning process by encapsulating the complexities of syntactic variations into manageable packages, thereby reducing what the planner has to know about. Complementary to the question of identifying the rhetorical vocabulary is the question of how that vocabulary is realized—by what means is condense-on-property to impose its constraints on *r*-spec2 and *r*-spec5? This, it turns out, is neatly handled under description-directed control, as we will see when we continue this example at the end of the next section.

With the assumptions laid out, we can now move on to the heart of this paper, the definition of description-directed control and its ramifications. One cautionary note before leaping in: readers with linguistic training may be skeptical, once they see the workings of this design, that it would possibly be able to produce certain basic natural language constructions such as wh-movement or raising to subject. Their concern is appropriate since the design does impose a severe bias on the "direction" in which grammatical dependencies can be noticed and acted positions within a sentence back to early and high positions might seem to be impossible to capture. There is of course a way out, namely to develop new, alternative theories of what the speaker-internal sources of these constructions are, adopting sources where the dependencies flow in the proper direction. The motivation for alternatives of this sort will be the subject of the last section.

4. DESCRIPTION-DIRECTED CONTROL

Description-directed control is a special case of *data-directed* control, where the controlling data structure is the evolving description of the final product. In the case of generation we have two such descriptions: an abstract description given in the speaker's planning vocabulary (the realization specification), and a much more concrete, linguistic description that is built up from the first by successively realizing its components (the surface structure). Both are used to control the process, with the linguistic description being most important since it provides the primary constraints on realization and organizes the recursive decomposition of the original *r*-spec into its component *r*-specs so as to match the order in which the text is to be incrementally produced.

We will begin this section by sketching the basics of data-directed control and how it has been used in generation; this corresponds to control by the first of our two descriptions, the realization specification. The motivation for introducing a level of linguistic description into the control structure will then be discussed, and the interleaving of the two descriptions described by returning to our example of the house scene. We end the section by giving a careful description of the mechanisms of description directed control, elaborating on the concept of surface structure as program.

4.1 *Data-directed control*

In a data-directed system there is no fixed program. Instead, the knowledge the system has is distributed into many relatively small modules, with the execution order of the modules dictated by an external data structure (typically the input to the system) as interpreted by a simple controller algorithm. The controller treats the data structure as though it were a program in a very high-level language, interpreting the terms and relations that it reads as instructions to execute particular system modules. This technique of associating program modules with specific terms or cannonical events as interpreted by some controlling algorithm is known as *procedural attachment*, and it lies at the heart of any data-directed system.

To specify a data-directed system given a specification of the class of data structure that is to be in control, one must specify (1) how the structure will be traversed, (2) the mapping between terms in the data structure and modules in the system, and (3) the computational environment that the modules will be allowed to access—can they for example examine other parts of the data structure than those the controller currently "has its fingers on"? Is there an independent record of past actions? Where do the modules put the results of their computations?

Data-directed control is a natural technique for an interface system such as a natural language generator. It permits a flexible and efficient response to a speaker's specifications which a system based on a fixed program can not match. Several well-known generators besides my own have used data-directed control, e.g. [21–23]; it is the basis of the technique that Mann *et al.*[28] in their review have termed "direct translation". To use direct translation, the speaker program selects one of its own internal data structures to be the basis of the text and passes it to the generator to be traversed via *recursive descent* and rendered into English term by term. Such a system might for example answer a "how" question by selecting and passing to the generator the internal procedure that actually performed action. Conditionals in the procedure might be rendered by "if-then" clauses, test predicates as clauses, and so on, with the overall pattern of the text exactly matching that of the internal procedure since the procedure served directly as the template that organized the generator's translation.

4.2 *The need for control by a linguistic description*

In the terminology of this paper, the "modules" that contain a data-directed system's knowledge are (principally) the decision procedures, and the realization specification is the input to the system that serves as (part of) the data that directs control. However, the speaker's realization specification does not exhaustively determine all of the decisions that must be made. The demands of the language's grammar must be taken into account, as well as the constraints due to any text that has already been produced. This leads us to the special contribution of my technique for natural language generation, which is otherwise very similar to direct translation. This is the design decision to *embed* the process of realizing the speaker's specifications within *another* process—also data-directed—this second, enfolding process being responsible for ensuring that the output text is grammatical and that it includes those details that are important because the text is English rather than some other natural language.

The controlling data structure that I have chosen for this second process is *the text's own linguistic description*. This description is of course the output of the decision procedures as they realize the r-specs. It is a tree-structured, surface-level syntactic description, based on the form of the text as it will actually be produced rather than as it would look at some more abstract linguistic level. (In terms of Chomsky's most recent formulation[24], the level of this description corresponds to his "R-structure", the level at which any optional "stylistic" transformations that may apply have done so, and which is the input to the phonological component.) Part of what the surface structure does is to define the path of the traversal; it fixes the order in which the linguistic "program" that it defines will be executed. This is the function of the hierarchical pattern of the nodes and the sequential order of their immediate constituents. The other part of what the surface structure does is to define the "content" of this program, this being done by the grammatical labels that have been selected to annotate the parts of the tree.

The form of the surface structure. The surface structure tree is created incrementally from top to bottom and from left to right by the realization of successive embedded r-specs (see next section). In the "finished" syntactic trees that we are accustomed to looking at, the nodes specify syntactic constituents and the leaves are the words of the text. Here however we are dealing with trees that are "in progress" and whose force in the algorithm is to specify where they can be extended and what grammatical constraints they impose on those extensions. Thus while the tree's nodes will always denote constituents, its leaves may all be r-specs in the early parts of the process. Later, after the first of those r-specs had been decomposed through the action of several successive realizations, that part of the tree will probably have been developed down to the clause and NP level and most of its leaves will be words. The surface structure tree is not exceptional in form. Nodes are labeled to indicate their categories and other grammatical properties (e.g. "clause", "VP", "possible-sentence-start"). Nodes by definition have immediate constituents; every nonterminal constituent must be a node: legal terminal constituents can be only words or r-specs. One significant extension to the usual formalism for tree structure has been made in this design, namely that the positions daughter constituents can take with respect to their mother node have been reified. These "position objects" are called *slots*, and are labeled with the terms that linguists normally use for grammatical relations between constituents, e.g. "subject", "object-of-a-preposition", "head", etc.

This grammatical "annotation" represented by the labels is very conventional at the sentence level and below (reflecting the author's background in transformational generative linguistics and systemic grammar). At the discourse level on the other hand, while it maintains the same form, i.e. a strict tree, the relationship of the structure of the tree to the structure of the output text is less fixed than at lower levels. For example one sentence in the text might actually span several nodes at the discourse level because it was realized from several r-specs in sequence.

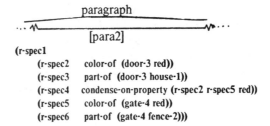

```
(r-spec1
      (r-spec2    color-of  (door-3 red))
      (r-spec3    part-of   (door-3 house-1))
      (r-spec4    condense-on-property (r-spec2 r-spec5 red))
      (r-spec5    color-of  (gate-4 red))
      (r-spec6    part-of   (gate-4 fence-2)))
```

Fig. 2. Snapshot after the *r*-spec arrives at the generator.

4.3 *Embedding r-specs within a syntactic description*

To illustrate how the two descriptions are interleaved, let me return to the example of the second sentence of the house scene. The *r*-spec that led to that text (shown in Fig. 1) was the second in a stream of five. By the time it was passed to the generator, the decision that it was to be part of a paragraph had been made and the first *r*-spec put in place as the paragraph's first constituent and its utterance begun. (We assume that planning and realization are asyncronous.) The second *r*-spec is thus already embedded in a linguistic context, albeit a relatively unconstraining one, which we can diagram as shown below in Fig. 2. In this style of diagram, syntactic nodes are shown as trapezoids labeled on top by their category and with their positions for constituents running along the bottom as functional labels enclosed in brackets. (Only the second constituent position ("slot") with the *r*-spec is shown. The first slot at this point contains the complete surface structure tree corresponding to the first sentence; following slots as needed will contain the succeeding *r*-specs as the planner constructs them and passes them over.)

As will be discussed in detail later, the generation process is directed by a depth-first traversal of the surface structure tree: words are spoken as soon as they are reached, and the grammatical labels on the tree are interpreted for the constraints and low-level grammatical actions that they imply. As the second constituent of the paragraph, the *r*-spec is now also a part of the surface structure—a planned realization decision waiting to be made once the traversal reaches its position. Let us say that that position has just been reached, the first sentence having just been uttered. All *r*-specs are realized according to the same schematic procedure, which can be summarized as follows. (Details can be found in [15] or in [16].)

The Realization Procedure

● Every realization specification is either a single, composite structure or with a loosely related set of other *r*-specs as in the present example. In both cases the *r*-spec is passed to its associated decision-procedure which will either be one that is specific to that kind of composite or be a very general procedure that will try to find a realizable unifying linguistic relation among the *r*-specs of the set, and realize the other *r*-specs in terms of it.

● All *decision-procedures* that realize *r*-specs are organized in the same way. Formally they are functions from *r*-specs to surface structure. (Except for minor grammatical adjustment rules, they are the *only* source of syntactic relations and content words.) They have two parts: a set of predetermined choices (see below) and a set of tests (the actual "decision procedure") which are organized into a tree with the choices at its leaves. They are always preconstructed rather than being the result of a dynamic planning process. They may (and typically do) anticipate dynamic contingencies by incorporating context-sensitive tests within their conditions, however they are selected—associated with the appropriate classes of *r*-specs—on a strictly context-free basis that is computed locally to the individual *r*-spec.

● The output of one of these decision-procedures will always be a *choice* selected from among its predetermined set of alternatives. A choice is a minimal, schematic description of some linguistic structure. The structure may be of any size from an entire paragraph to a single word, and may contain any amount of detail from a completely "canned" phrase to just a constraint on later-realized *r*-specs, for example that one particular part of the *r*-spec under realization is to precede another in the text.

● When a choice is selected, it is "instantiated", and a well-formed subtree is constructed to meet the schematic description. A choice may be parameterized, i.e. some of the constituents it specifies may be given as variables that are filled on instantiation with selected sub-components of the original r-spec.

The result of realizing our example r-spec is thus to cause a new fragment of the surface structure of the text to be created and then *installed in the r-spec's place* as the paragraph's second constituent. This is how the surface structure grows: via the replacement of r-specs by the surface structures that realize them. The new surface structure typically incorporates other r-specs that were components of the original; these are reached and realized in turn as the traversal process continues, the whole procedure exactly matching the intended recursive decomposition of the original r-spec.

Figure 3 shows the relevant section of the surface structure just after the example r-spec has been realized and replaced. The example was a *set* of r-specs, and as sketched above, its realization was performed by looking for a unifying linguistic relation (in this case the rhetorical goal "condense-on-property") and basing the realization just on it. In the computer program there were two choices available to the decision procedure for condense-on-property: the first was to merge the subjects of the relations (e.g. "Both the door of the house and gate of the fence are red"), and the second is to use some form of what in the TG tradition is known as "verb phrase deletion" (e.g. "The door of the house is red and so is the gate of the fence."). The second is chosen because a "standing order"† concerning the proper style of a scene description has not been overridden. This standing order is to avoid constructions that make the "chaining" of discourse topics difficult. The selected sentence, because it ends mentioning the fence, can be coherently followed by a subsequent sentence elaborating on the fence's other properties. The blocked sentence on the other hand ends by emphasizing the color "red" and has bunched the scene objects up in the subject, making it awkward to continue describing them.‡

The conjunction node, the "modifies" relations appended to the two embedded r-specs, and the special "VP-deletion" label on the conjunction's second slot are all reflexes of the decision to realize condense-on-property using a form of verb phrase deletion. Decision procedures are forbidden from looking ahead to anticipate the effects of later embedded realizations to expand several levels of an r-spec at once (as would have been required if the textual effects of verb phrase deletion were to have been produced at the very moment the decision to use it was made). Instead, the decision procedures are given the ability to specially mark the surface structure that they do produce with special labels whose effect will be to bring about the desired effects when the relevant part of the tree is reached by the traversal. Such annotations are

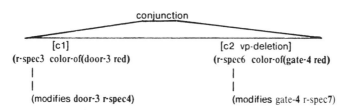

Fig. 3. Snapshot after realizing the initial r-spec.

---

†The idea behind the notion of a "standing order" is that the planner should be able to impose constraints on what is said which will apply universally (unless specifically overridden) and thus not need to be thought about while constructing each and every r-spec. Standing orders are effectively default components of every r-spec, which for convenience are instead incorporated directly into the decision-procedures.

‡As it happens, the next sentence in this paragraph does not continue to chain on the fence but instead changes the topic completely and talks about the mailbox. This is not a mistake: it is rather a reflection of the fact that the planner's deliberations as it constructs a realization specification are very local. The planner had not looked ahead to the third sentence before it sent off the r-spec for the second; as far as it knew, the third sentence might have been more about the fence and the standing order thus to the point. Even though it turns out that the third sentence starts an entirely new discourse unit (signalled by the "there is" construction), the use of verb phrase deletion did not do any harm. If it had, we would have had evidence that the scope of the planner's deliberations was too narrow.

another way in which the needs of the generation process have introduced variations in the form of surface structure from what linguists are accustomed to.

4.4 *Traversing the surface structure: syntactic trees as programs*

Given what has been said about the organization of data-directed systems, the explanation of how a text's surface structure is used to control its generation should include a specification of how the surface structure is traversed, a specification of the kind of "modules" that there are and how the terms in the surface structure map to them, and finally a specification of the overall computational environment to which the modules have access; these are the subject of the rest of this section. The specifications that will be given are not the only ones that one could imagine given only the notion of a surface structure tree as a controlling representation. They reflect *additional design constraints* that are intended (1) to enforce a very strict constraint on the rate at which the generation process proceeds, and (2) to support a minimalist position on the amount of information that is required moment to moment to support linguistic decisions. We will take up these issues after the fundamentals of the traversal's operation have been established.

The traversal algorithm. The surface structure tree is traversed in the classic depth-first pattern, i.e. top-down and left-to-right starting from its root-node. The traversal is performed by a trivial skeleton algorithm that spends the bulk of its time dispatching to the procedures attached to the grammatical labels (see below). Its only other important function is to define what happens to the contents of each slot as it is reached:

● If the slot contains a word then it is a leaf and the traversal will return back up the tree. The word is passed to a morphological routine for specialization according to the labels on its slot; thense it is passed to the output stream (i.e. it is "spoken").

● If the slot contains a syntactic node then it is a nonterminal and the traversal continues down into that subtree.

● If the slot contains a realization specification then it is (for the moment) a leaf. The r-spec is passed to the decision-procedure to which it maps for realization. This process will return either a node or a word which is then knit into the tree in the r-spec's place and the dispatch-on-contents process done again.

Attached grammatical procedures. The key to the data-directed use of the tree is the definition of reference "events" within the traversal. These events provide the same kind of "hooks"—points at which to attach procedures—as are provided in many knowledge representation systems by the operations that add or remove assertions from the data base. Just as we can have "if-added" or "if-removed" procedures that are associated with the patterns of assertions in a knowledge base, we here have procedures associated with the grammatical labels that annotate the surface structure and have them triggered by the occurrence of well-defined events in the traversal. Five such events have been found to be important:

(1) *Entering a node* from above, having traversed all of the tree above it and to its left.
(2) *Leaving a node* from below, having traversed all of its constituents.
(3) *Entering a slot*, having traversed all of its sister constituents to its left.
(4) *Leaving a slot*, having just traversed the constituent (or word) that it contains.
(5) *After realizing a r-spec* when the subtree that was chosen for it has been constructed and just been knit into the tree (in the r-spec's place), but not yet traversed. Since embedded r-specs appear only as the contents of slots, procedures associated with this "After-realization" event are attached only to slot-annotating labels.

Attached grammatical procedures perform several kinds of functions. A major one is to provide the staging grounds for decisions that the grammar requires but that the speaker's specifications do not provide for. Relative pronouns and complementizers are a clear case in point: The fact that one must include the word "that" in a phrase like "the report *that* the island's sovereignty had changed" is a fact about the English language and not about the information that has to be conveyed. Consequently one wants the decision to say "that" (or to decide between "that" and "which", or to decide whether to leave it out when it is optional) to be incorporated as an action of the grammar independent of the speaker's specifications. That is done by making the "relative pronoun decision" part of a procedure associated with the label that marks post-nominal NP constituents, identifying it with the "enter-slot" event in the transition algorithm so that the decision is made and the pronoun said (or not) just after the head of the NP is said (the "head" being the previous constituent), and before any of the relative clause is said.

Uninteresting but necessary matters such as putting commas after the items of a conjunction or periods at the end of sentences are readily implemented by making them part of procedures attached to the labels that identify those subtrees as such in the surface structure. The "of" of the genitive or the "to" of the infinitive are done similarly. In a description-directed system, such lexical or morphological correlates of syntactic constructions are efficiently and economically incorporated into the process since the fact that they are "piggybacked" onto the very labels that define the constructions means that they will automatically be incorporated when their constructions are used and will never be thought about when they are not.

The grammatical operation of subject-verb agreement brings up another, very important function of the attached procedures: the maintenance of *pointers* to grammatically significant parts of the surface structure tree. The English rule that subject and (tensed) verb must agree in person and number is understood in generation as a constraint of the form of the verb rather than of the subject. That is, we presume that a speaker does not first decide that the verb should be, say, second person singular and then select a subject to match! The rule is manifest as a trivial decision procedure, positioned within the morphology routine, that is activated whenever the morphology routine is passed a word that is identified as the first word of a tensed verb group (the identification having been set up by the action of earlier labels). In order to select a form of the verb that matches the subject in person and number, this decision procedure clearly needs to be able to identify and query the subject constituent, which it does by accessing a pointer to it that was set by the action of a procedure attached to the label "subject" and that has been maintained in the computational environment ever since. (Such a pointer is implemented in the computer program as a global variable of a given name and is incorporated into the body of the decision-maker on that basis.)

The human grammar writer is permitted to declare pointers freely and to have attached procedures assign them to whatever structures in the tree that the procedures can access (typically just the contents of the current slot if done at an "enter-slot" or "leave-slot" event, or the current node if at an "enter-node" or "leave-node" event; the "after-realization" event can access both the *r*-spec the current slot originally contained and the new node that replaces it). The pointers are recursive, permitting them to be assigned relative to the current grammatical context and then reassigned (with the former values saved) when the traversal recursively enters another grammatical unit of the same sort. For example one would have the value of the pointer to the "current-subject" rebound when the traversal enters an embedded clause, and then have it restored to its former value when the traversal finishes the embedding and returns to the original clause.

4.5 *Constraining decisions: the rest of the example*

As the purpose of this paper is to illustrate a control structure rather than to explore possibly controversial linguistic analyses, I will not dwell on this example more than necessary. We left it at the point of the snapshot in Fig. 3 taken just after the initial *r*-spec had been realized. This corresponds to the third condition of the traversal algorithm (beginning of previous section), and the next step is to continue the traversal down into the conjunction and then to the *r*-spec embedded as its first constituent, i.e. "(*r*-spec2 color-of(door-3 red))". Realizing it gives us its next level of terms embedded in a predicate adjective clause, essentially "[(door-3)--(modifies door-3 *r*-spec3)] is ⟨red⟩".

As already discussed, lexicalization in this task domain is deliberately trivial: all of the properties of an object that are to go into its description are given explicitly in the *r*-spec, and the decision as to what determiner to use has been simplified to just "the" for already mentioned objects, and "a" for when they are introduced. The realization of the first constituent thus goes very simply; the embedded *r*-spec "*r*-spec3" (i.e. "part-of(door-3 house-1)") is realized as genitive construction because of its function as a modifier.

Once the completed first noun phrase is traversed (causing the words "the door of the house"

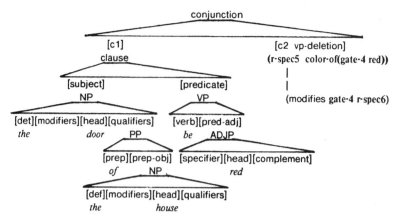

Spoken so far: *The door of the house is red, and //*

Fig. 4. Snapshot just before VP-deletion.

to be spoken), the traversal moves back up the tree and on into the verb phrase. When its traversal is complete the surface structure looks as shown in the snapshot in Fig. 4.

At this point there are two strong sources of constraint on the realization of "*r*-spec5": the fact that it is in a conjunction, and the fact that it (or rather its slot—the effect is the same) has been marked to undergo VP-deletion. As another standing order on text style, we have decided that all of the clauses of a conjunction should employ parallel constructions. This is translated for purposes of generation into the constraint that all decisions made in later clauses should automatically make the same choice as was made in the first. Thus decision processes for the second instance of the "color-of" relation will be pre-empted: Color-of will automatically be realized as a predicate adjective clause, and the second "part-of" will automatically come out as a genitive.

The force of the directive to perform VP-deletion is to transform the selected predicate adjective construction into either a "predicate-preposed" form where the repeated predicate can pronominalized as "do so" (e.g. "The casualties were heavy and *so were* the material losses."), or to keep the order the same and add an adverb such as "too" or "also" ("... and the material losses were too."). Here again the stylistic standing order applies and selects the predicate-preposed form preferentially. (Actually it does not do a "selection", rather it filters out the other choice. Since it is only a stylistic heuristic, it cannot be allowed to block all alternatives, thus if the "too" form had been the only one possible no filtering would have been done.)

The rest of the traversal proceeds the same way as the traversal of the first conjunct had gone. The actual mechanism of the verb phrase deletion is to first invoke a transformation (so to speak) to cause the "color-of" relation to be realized in copula-shifted order (i.e. "⟨red⟩ is ⟨gate-4⟩"), and then to "pronominalize" the predicate-adjective as the word "so".

5. IMPLICATIONS OF THE ALGORITHM

Regardless of how effective a computational system may be, success as an abstract system does not automatically imply success as a psychological theory. The latter can only be accessed by projecting the behavior of the system onto observed human behavior and attempting to formulate a coherent accounting of it with predictive consequences. Section 5.1 of this section introduces the key computational constraints that the design imposes on the generator's behavior. Since the design itself does not specify what the grammar and pragmatic decision-criteria are to be, only how they can be used within the process, these constraints are likely to be the key points of leverage in eliciting predictions. Section 5.2 lays out the most immediate matches between the behavior of the system and of humans, while 5.3 discusses alternative ways to analyse certain linguistic phenomena that might otherwise be problematic. Section 5.4 looks at the status of the traditional notion of constraints in transformational generative grammars and suggests that the phenomena these capture would be more satisfactorally accounted for by looking to the computational properties of the processor. Section 5.5 carries this further by examining some actual human speech errors and considering how they might have arisen.

5.1 Computational constraints

The use of pointers to positions of interest within the surface structure tree alludes to several constraints imposed by the generator's computational environment that have been implied by the discussion so far but not made explicit:

● No computations of any sort take place in the generator except those that are directed by the actions of the traversal algorithm.

● Computations are therefore local to a single location in the tree at a time.

● No parts of the tree other than the present location of the traversal are accessible to a decision-maker (except for those expressly pointed to). In particular, there are deliberately no provisions for operations that could "walk" through the tree looking for arbitrary landmarks or patterns (One cannot, for example, have a grammatical rule that refers to "the subject of the clause two embeddings up and one back from the present position").

These constraints follow directly and inescapably from the data-directed basis of the generator. They act to guarantee two very attractive run-time properties, namely that the algorithm is "on-line", and executes in linear time at a constant (bounded) rate.

On-line transduction. Formally the algorithm can be viewed as two cascaded transducers, a realization process converting realization specifications couched in the speaker's internal representation into a surface structure tree, and a traversal process "converting" that tree (with words at its leaves) into a text. An "on-line" transducer is one that converts the current token in its input stream completely into tokens of the output stream before moving on to the next input token. An on-line transducer thus faithfully reflects the ordering of its input stream in its output, and does not accumulate unconverted parts of its input. This definition must be complicated somewhat to accommodate the fact that the input *r*-specs and output subtrees of the realization process are both nested structures; however since the transduction preserves proper nesting, there is no problem.

Linear time/constant bounded rate. The linearity of the algorithm and its bounded rate are guaranteed by the fact that the second transducer—the one from the surface structure to the output text—is the one that dictates the overall flow of control. Since control is based on a one-pass traversal of an acyclic tree, the process is guaranteed to be linear in the number of nodes (i.e. each node and each slot will be entered and left only once). Since the only sources of subtrees in the surface structure is the realization of successive *r*-specs as they are "exposed" in the recursive decomposition of the speaker's original *r*-spec, the number of nodes in a given surface structure will be dictated by the number of embedded *r*-specs that are realized. The side of the subtree that results from any one realization is fixed in advance, and thus can be no larger than some bound determined by the available choices. (Recall that all choices are precomputed—realization is basically just a process of filtering out ungrammatical choices and selecting from what is left.) Overall then, we can establish that no more than a bounded number of nodes will have to be traversed per element in the initial composite *r*-spec. Therefore given the completely data-directed nature of the computation, there can be no more than a bounded number of operations per input element, or, for that matter, per word of output text.

To insure that the linear time—bounded rate—constraint is adhered to, one must guarantee that none of the modules that are dispatched to are capable of performing operations that could potentially require processing time proportional to the length of one of controlling data-structures. Prohibiting predicates that can perform tree-walking operations (or that can perform arbitrary scans of the realization specifications) is a key part of this guarantee. Maintaining a fixed set of pointers, on the other hand, does not perturb the constraint at all, since they are set only when the traversal is directly on top of the place of interest.

5.2 A natural match with human phenomenology

These purely computational properties of description-directed control in generation lend themselves to a very attractive phenominological interpretation—a "match" with the way that the generation process appears to us as human beings that should be exploitable as a point of leverage in formal psycholinguistic experiments.

Incremental production. Since each word is spoken as soon as the traversal reaches it at a leaf of the tree, texts are produced in their natural order and in increments that correspond to the size of the units (the input r-specs) by which they were planned conceptually.

Indelibility. Once this generator has spoken a word, it cannot take it back; once it has decided to use a certain construction and made it part of the surface structure, it cannot change its mind short of aborting the entire process and starting over. This "indelibility" of the output text and grammatical context is again an inescapable consequence of the use of description-directed control.

Limited lookahead. Since embedded realization specifications are never elaborated before the point in the text where they are to appear has been reached by the traversal, decision-makers never can have more than a sketchy notion of what decisions will happen after theirs. In the tree behind the current position of the traversal, all structures are described in an entirely linguistic vocabulary and the grammar writer may arrange to have the system remember (through pointers) any class of information that they wish. In front of the current position however, the specificity of the linguistic plans in place so far becomes increasingly vague since none of their details have been decided yet. This is suggestive of the common experience that people have of starting to speak without knowing how they will finish beyond knowing that they will try and speak about such and such a relation or make a certain reference.

Enforced grammaticality. Though not discussed in this paper, the labels on the surface structure also serve to define "filters" that restrict the choices available for realizing an r-spec to just those that are grammatical in the context defined by its position in the tree. (Details can be found in[15]). For example when an r-spec whose *a priori* choices include realization both as an adjective and as a predicate adjective (e.g. both "the X *is red*" and "the *red* X") has been embedded in the surface structure at a position that permits only the adjective form, then the labels on that position will act to suppress the predicate adjective choice, leaving the r-spec's decision procedure to decide only between variations on the adjective choice.

The effect of this kind of filtering action is to insure that the output text will be grammatical regardless of the organization of the original specification. We have always presumed that the original r-spec was deliberately planned and constructed; we can make the further assumption that the speaker has so structured the r-spec that its most important components will be realized first. This means that since grammatical constraints are minimal at the beginning of a text but built up as the traversal goes further along or become more deeply embedded, it will be the least important (or last thought of) components of the r-spec that will be most in danger of being omitted from the text for grammatical reasons—exactly our experience as human speakers.

5.3 *The direction of grammatical dependencies*

The fact that this generator is based on a description-directed control technique with its attendant constraints on the computational environment has the effect of imposing a discipline on the analyses of the human grammar writer that forces significant departures from those commonly seen. Some of this may just involve alternatives in methodology, but some may indicate substantive ontological differences in what the nature of grammar is taken to be that should be ammenable to psycholinguistic tests.

Natural language constructions involve syntactic dependences between their parts that must be captured by the grammar that is written for the generator. The usual way of expressing these rules in the past, at least for main-stream American linguistics, has involved the use of a procedural calculus—transformational generative grammar—in which the relationship between surface texts and their corresponding semantic representations are "derived" by a cyclic, bottom-up process from schematic syntactic base structures. As a result, some of the grammatical dependencies most significant for linguistic theory are couched in terms of procedural analyses that are completely the reverse of those required for a psychologically plausible generator that is actually to be used by a speaker. Examples of such dependencies include the relation between the WH word and its "gap" in questions or relative clauses, the relation between subject noun phrases and the deep case structure of the complements of so-called "raising verbs" such as "*expect*" or "*seems*", or generally speaking any grammatical dependency where a marked feature high and to the left in a text apparently depends upon circumstances that are only manifest lower and to its right.

The effect in the present design of adopting a depth-first traversal pattern on the emerging surface structure tree is to impose an inescapable bias on the flow of information, grammatical or otherwise, within it. Those parts of the surface structure that are high and to the left are constructed first: decisions made there impose constraints on all decisions made later in the tree down and to the right. For the bulk of the grammatical dependencies in English, this is exactly the right direction: pronouns depend upon their antecedents; extraposition and heavy-phrase shift "move" their phrases to the right; the various kinds of conjunction-reduction occur only after the first conjunct has appeared; subjects precede their verbs.

The cases of dependencies that apparently move "against the current" so to speak are undeniable however, and to deal with them this generator must impose certain conventions on the way that speakers organize their realization specifications if the computational constraints of the description-directed control structure are to be preserved. The control structure does not allow the generator to "hold off" on a grammatical decision while it extends the surface structure down and to the right in order to find out some critical later decision is going to turn out—such an operation cannot possibly be formulated in this generator. Instead, the speaker must provide the requisite information as part of its r-spec. In[16], I refer to this as the *constraint-proceeds* stipulation. It is a prediction that must be borne out by independent examination of human r-spec's if the present virtual machine is to prove valid.

The use of a description-directed generator encourages *planning* by the speaker as the way to achieve the most effective texts. There are no restrictions in the design on the *passing down* of linguistic information that has been determined by an early decision-maker; consequently, if speakers plan their use of marked linguistic constructions and signal them explicitly at the appropriate points in their realization specifications, then linguistically "redundant" information can be provided to dependencies top-down to make up for information down and to the right would otherwise not be available until it was too late to use it.

WH-movement is a clear case in point. Under the generative grammar analysis, questions are derived from specifically marked D-structures by a process of transformationally moving a WH-word (e.g. "who", "what", "why", etc.) up to the front of the sentence from the position it would have held in the declarative version of the same sentence, leaving a "gap". This analysis "captures" the generalization that the form of the WH-word is dictated by the position of the gap.[†] In the analysis for generation, on the other hand, questions arise from r-specs that begin with the internal representation of the questioned element (the source of the WH-word) *and* that of the body of the question (a lambda abstraction), both at the same level. No motion within the constituent structure is required since the WH-word is available from the start. (The gap is created by what amounts to a form of pronominalization at the point when the recurrence of the questioned element is reached during the traversal of the question matrix.) By adopting this alternative analysis of the "source" for questions and other WH constructions, we are making the assumption that in deciding to use a question a speaker already knows three items before starting to speak: (1) what is going to be questioned, (2) how the question will be framed (the source of the body), and (3) how the question relates to that frame (information from which to make a decision like "who" vs "whom"). This does not seem unreasonable; indeed, it is hard to imagine how it could be otherwise.

This example of questions points to a methodology for dealing with natural language constructions whose dependencies appear to go in the wrong direction. First we must ask why a speaker would want to use the construction: is there some special rhetorical effect that it achieves? a special emphasis? a special stylistic pattern in the text? Asking this question is a critical step since one cannot formulate a grammatical analysis for a generator without first deciding what the non-linguistic source of the analyzed construction is, e.g. an apparently minor change in the information in the realization specification can make an enormous difference in how the construction must be analyzed linguistically. If the construction is one that is

---

[†]Consider the use of "who" vs "whom". "Who" is used when the questioned item would have been a subject or direct object (as in "Who did the islander's think _____ should have soverignty?"), while "whom" is used when the item would have been the object of a preposition ("For whom was the loss more important?"). This phenomena is very weak in English, but in languages with strong case markings such as Russian or Finnish, the question word must match the grammatical properties of the position of the gap in every respect.

"marked" (i.e. realizes a rhetorical goal that a speaker might plan for in a realization specification), then we can reanalyze right-to-left linguistic dependencies as top-down dependencies, by arranging that speakers place the goal that triggers the construction sufficiently early in the r-spec that the text of the construction has not yet been started when that goal is considered. This will give the decision-makers sufficient "warning" that they will not inadvertently select realizations that would make the construction impossible.

Consider how we would use this methodology to analyze the tough-movement construction, one that would be impossible for the generator under its usual analysis. ("Tough-movement" is what is said to have happened in the grammatical derivation of a sentence like "Economics is tough for John to study".) Step one is to ask why a speaker would ever want to use it; or better, why they would want to use tough-movement in favor of the other two alternatives usually included in that paradigm, i.e. the extraposed form "It's tough for John to study economics", and the (putatively) unmarked case "For John to study economics is tough". One very comfortable answer for why to use it would be "in order to focus on 'economics'". That being the case, then if that goal is ordered in the speaker's r-spec before the goal to express the proposition "tough(study(John,economics))", the required top-down information flow of the re-analysis can be carried forward (see [15] for details).

5.4 Alternatives to stipulated constraints

One of the most important hypotheses one can make in linguistic theory is to propose a universal constraint. Such constraints apply "across the board", controlling the actions of all individual rules and thereby simplifying their statement. Early constraints, such as those proposed by Ross[26], proposed limitations on the structural descriptions (i.e. constituent trees) to which transformations could be applied. His "complex noun phrase constraint" for example stated that no transformation was permitted to move a constituent from inside a relative clause to outside. This for instance blocks the "extraction" that would lead to the ungrammatical question: "What treasure did Sigfried kill the dragon that guarded?".

For all its comprehensiveness however, a stipulated constraint is just that, stipulated. One has no explanation of why the grammar of a natural language should include it, other than that it is necessary if the grammar is to generate only grammatical sentences—a conclusion that does not sit well with many computational linguists. Marcus's treatment of syntactic parsing with a computationally restricted virtual machine[5] demonstrated how the restrictions on his machine lead inescapably to behavior that satisfied certain universal constraints that had been stipulated for competence grammars (i.e. Chomsky's "specified subject" and "tensed-S" constraints[25]). The same kind of demonstration can be made with this description-directed treatment of language generation.

Note however that nothing is necessarily "proved" by such demonstrations in and of themselves. They establish that if such and such a virtual machine were in use then the behavior captured by the constraint would occur without the need for any stipulation in the grammar that the virtual machine employs. There still remains the problem of establishing that said virtual machine is actually functionally isomorphic to the one that people use—a demonstration that is not yet possible given the indirect nature of the available evidence.

With the grammar and realization procedures used in the present computer implementation, this generator appears to have non-stipulative explanations for at least the following constraints: the A-over-A principle, complex-NP and prohibited extractions from islands generally, right-node raising, and the "that-deletion" filter of [27]. However, rather than extend this paper to several times its present length by presenting detailed arguments in support of that claim (some appear in [15], the rest will appear in [29]), I prefer to end here with a discussion of how I believe the question of "constraints" should be approached by those who would study natural language generation. Detailed arguments will always be contingent on what grammatical analyses one believes in and on "boot-strapped" assumptions about the form and content of the speaker's internal sources, neither of which can be taken to any firm conclusions until considerably more empirical work has been done on the processes involved in language use rather than just on the description of language competence.

5.5 Constraints: what do people actually do?

People violate grammatical constraints regularly. The frequency is low—perhaps one or two occurrences per day among the people I regularly listen to—nevertheless violations occur often enough that one can characterize what happens and try to make hypotheses about it. Consider the following actually occurring texts: (These were written down immediately after they occurred and checked for veracity against what the speaker remembered having said.)

[Said in reference to the speaker's cluttered bedroom]
"There are all sorts of assorted things here that should be found a place for."

[Said about a roadmap that had a poor index]
"It's not a map that you can use to find a street that you don't know where it is."

[Said while trying to coordinate vacations]
"I wonder if we could find an expedition that we would both be interested in and the leader would both be interested in us."

The first text is strange because the speaker has "passivized" a verb which does not allow it, i.e. "find a place for". The second is strange because it violates Ross's Complex NP Constraint: the NP "a street" has been modified with a relative clause in which "street" occurs in a place where it is not legal to leave a gap and a resumptive pronoun has been used instead. The third has arranged for a parallelism in the placement of the word "both" while ignoring the fact that the word can not be used in its intended meaning when in that position in the second conjunct (i.e. the text should have been "...interested in both of us").

The most important thing about these texts is that the speakers *did not stop* when faced with a violated constraint. In a generative grammar, constraints act to block illegal derivations; in actual use however, these "illegal" texts are produced in spite of the constraint and with the same fluency and intonation as normal texts. The speaker is typically very aware of having said something strange and may well immediately say the text over again correctly formed, but the original ill-formed text does appear—the grammar is *not* an all or nothing filter.

The story that such texts suggest to me revolves around failures in planning: speakers have a very strong ordering on their communicative goals but they have neither the time, nor perhaps the ability, to evaluate the linguistic consequences of all of their goals taken together. They begin their text as though there was not going to be any problem and only afterwards find that their later *r*-specs cannot be realized properly in the linguistic context that their earlier *r*-specs have established. At this point human speakers do not go catatonic. They have already planned the text that would follow (or rather positioned the *r*-specs it derives from and made some decisions about its linguistic character), and thus they have the option of continuing. The grammar will in fact support them as they continue, making the best of a bad situation, because *the grammar is not a censor but a mediator*—it shapes what is said but does not dictate it.

In the production of the second text about finding streets on the badly indexed map (one of my own errors), the goal was first to characterize the map and second to say about it that you couldn't use it to find a street if you didn't already know where the street was. The first goal led to the use of extraposition ("It's not a map that..."); the second was fundamentally a fact about streets and the difficulty of finding them, hence its realization as a complex NP centered on "a street". Only at the last minute did I become aware of the grammatical bind in which I had placed myself, and, being among friends, I decided to complete my sentence and assume that they could figure it out rather than stop and restructure the whole utterance.

This grammatical "horizon effect" has a natural explanation in the context of description-directed generation. The meaning of a grammatical constraint is to force a selection between alternative realizations: one uses the legal form and does not consider its illegal alternative. However, this action can occur only if the linguistic parameters required to recognize that the constraint applies are available at the time that the two alternatives must be decided between. When a violation occurs, it is because one or more of the needed parameters was unknown when the choice-point was reached, e.g. the choice required knowing how a *r*-spec embedded further on in the tree was going to be realized. The speaker assumes that everything will work out correctly, but is unable to actually prove it because of limitations in the kinds of information that can be acquired about an *r*-spec's realization without actually producing it. When the realization eventually occurred, it turns out to be "out of phase" with the actual grammatical environment; the grammatical procedures attached to that environment are unable to perform their usual functions; and the resulting text "violates" the constraint.

6. CONCLUSION: PROPERTIES OF THE VIRTUAL MACHINE

As this is a concepts paper rather than a technical report, it would be inappropriate here to develop the background necessary for presenting a formal specification of the virtual machine: there is not yet anything resembling a universal notation or universally understood set of primitives that could be appealed to in representing the definitions. Let me instead attempt to present the key ideas in prose, leaving the compact† symbolic definition to [29].

Surface structures as processes

The key concept of this design is that the surface structure selected for the text defines the steps to be taken in producing it. The node pattern of the surface structure defines the order of the steps, and its grammatical labels define the constraints that are to be imposed on any embedded decisions. As a computational object, the surface structure is all action and no representation: i.e. it defines the processing that takes place but does not itself need to be examined. This means that the most natural implementation of such surface structure is as *a process, not a buffer*—an object that performs a series of actions, but whose internal structure is not accessible or modifiable from outside it.

Enumeration and association. After control by the surface structure description of the text, the other concept the virtual machine must support is a capability for enumerating the components ("sub" r-specs) of the realization specification as dictated by its recursive decomposition by the process of realization. The enumeration—the sequential stream of r-specs being realized one after the other—defines the timing and "chunk size" of the transition from the speaker's conceptual vocabulary used for planning what they want to say and their linguistic vocabulary manifest in the surface structure procedures. R-spec's in the enumeration stream pass out of it by being realized, i.e. by causing the initiation of the surface structure process that the decision-procedure associated with them has selected.

Unlike the surface structure processes which are defined once and for all by the grammar and can thus be precomputed, enumeration cannot be implemented by a fixed process since each realization specification is specific to the speaking situation that motivated it and these situations constitute an unbounded set. However, the set of components from which r-specs can be composed is assumed to be fixed (at least over the short term), thus the associations between the individual components and the surface structures that can realize them does constitute a bounded set and could be manifested by a set of precomputed processes just like the surface structures. The enumeration would then be the output of a continuous function (here undefined) whose inputs would be the current situation and some (also here undefined) "urge to speak".

Coordinating the two. A critical requirement on the virtual machine is that it supports the gating of the enumeration and realization process by the surface structure processes. R-specs embedded within the selected surface structure are not realized until the traversal reaches the point where they appear, and the output of the realization, the new "sub" surface structure, is traversed immediately afterwards. The two processes must therefore be running in close coordination, with the timing of successive realizations dependent on the (virtual) text position reached by the active surface structure processes. The least assuming way to support this coordination is to have the surface structures syncronously control the enumeration; asyncronous coordination would not violate any of the design criteria of the generator, but would add a requirement for something like a buffer of pending r-specs tagged by the point in the surface structure at which they were to appear, which would not otherwise be required.

---

†What a specification language must provide is a clearly defined set of primitive operations and a calculus for their combination from which the meaning of any expression in the specification can be unambiguously and exactly determined. Any well-constructed computer programming language could play this role; though one would rarely want to accept the primitives that the programming language supplied as the primitives of any proposed psychological process. An "extended language" defined in terms of the original programming language could serve this process however, with the original language serving as a concrete instance of an implementation of specifications written in the extended language.

The LISP program presently instantiating the generator can in this sense serve as one definition of the virtual machine the generator requires, since it consists first of the definition (in LISP) of an extended language in which to define a grammar and pragmatic decision procedures, and then a specific set of primitives by which to interpret them. The program is quite cleanly written in terms of typed objects and a few compact algorithms, and is available to interested investigators for inspection and application. The LISP dialect used is Lispmachine lisp.

The virtual machine must thus support:

● The instantiation and execution of surface structure processes,

● The enumeration of the realization specification (i.e. its conversion from a hierarchical network to a sequential stream), and

● Coordination between these two, with the timing of the enumeration and realization dictated by the "position" that the surface structure processes had reached.

In order to run in real time, the processes maintained by the virtual machine *must* be precomputed, since the time required to construct them from primitives would be a polynomial function of the size of the constituents in the text (see [29]). This implies that the underlying physical machine (e.g. the human brain) must be able to contain latent processes in the hundreds of thousands if not the tens of millions. A sobering thought perhaps, but one which researchers in vision have become quite comfortable with[17], and which should not daunt us.

7. REFERENCES

1. J. Thorne, P. Bratley and H. Dewar, The syntactic analysis of English by machine. In *Machine Intelligence* **3** (Edited by Richie). American Elsevier, New York (1968).
2. T. Winograd, *Natural Language Understanding.* Academic Press, New York (1972).
3. W. Woods, Transition network grammars for natural language analysis. *CACM* **13**(10), 591–606 (1972).
4. M. Marcus, "A 'wait and see' theory of syntactic parsing. In *Proc. TINLAP*-1. ACM, New York (1975).
5. M. Marcus, *A Theory of Syntactic Recognition for Natural Language.* MIT Press, Cambridge, Mass. (1980).
6. R. Milne, Paper presented at the *Winter Meeting of the Association for Computational Linguistics,* 28–30 December 1981.
7. R. Berwick, Learning structural descriptions of grammar rules from examples. Master's Thesis, MIT (1980).
8. M. Ford and V. Holmes, Planing units and syntax in natural language generation. *Cognition* **6**, 35–53 (1978).
9. M. Ford, Sentence planning units: implications for the speaker's representation of meaningful relations underlying sentences. Occasional Paper No. 2, MIT Center for Cognitive Science (1980).
10. V. Fromkin, *Speech Errors as Linguistic Evidence.* Mouton, Paris (1973).
11. M. Garrett, The analysis of sentence production. In *Psychology of Learning and Motivation,* Vol. 9. Academic Press, New York.
12. M. Garrett, Syntactic processes in sentence production. In *New Approaches to Language Mechanisms* (Edited by Walker and Walker). North-Holland, Amsterdam (1976).
13. D. Fay, Transformational errors. In *Errors in Linguistic Performance* (Edited by Fromkin). Academic Press, New York (1980).
14. S. Shattuck-Hufnagel, Speech errors as evidence for a serial ordering mechanism in sentence production. In *Sentence Processing: Psycholinguistic Studies Presented to Merrill Garrett* (Edited by Cooper and Walker). Lawerence Erlbaum Assoc. New York (1979).
15. D. D. McDonald, Natural language generation as a process of decision-making under constraints. Ph.D. Thesis, MIT revision in preparation to appear as a Technical Report from the MIT Artificial Intelligence Lab. (1980).
16. D. D. McDonald, Natural language generation as a computational problem: an introduction. In *Computational Models of Discourse* (Edited by Brady). MIT Press, Cambridge, Mass.
17. D. Marr, *Vision.* Freeman, New York (1982).
18. R. Berwick and A. Weinberg, The role of grammars in models of language use. *Cognition* In press.
19. D. Appelt, Planning natural-language utterances to satisfy multiple goals. Ph.D. Thesis, Stanford University; available as SRI International Technical Note 259 (March 1982).
20. J. Conklin and D. D. McDonald, Salience: the key to the selection problem in natural language generation. In *Proc. 20th Ann. Meeting of the Association for Computational Linguistics,* pp. 129–135. University of Toronto, 16–18 June 1982.
21. W. R. Swartout, A digitalis therapy advisor with explanations. Technical Report TR-176, MIT Laboratory for Computer Science, Cambridge, Mass (1977).
22. W. Clancy, Transfer of rule-based expertise through a tutorial dialogue. Stan-cs-79-769, Dept. of Computer Science, Stanford University.
23. D. Chester, The translations of formal proofs into English. *Artificial Intell.* **7**(3) (1976).
24. N. Chomsky, *Lectures on Government and Binding.* Foris Publications, Dordrecht (1982).
25. N. Chomsky, Conditions on Transformations. In *A Festschrift for Morris Halle* (Edited by Anderson and Kuporsky). Holt, Rinehart & Winston.
26. R. Ross, Constraints on variables in syntax. Ph.D. Thesis, MIT; available from the Indiana Linguistics Club (1968).
27. N. Chomsky and H. Lasnik, Filters and control. *Linguistic Inquiry* **8**(3), 425–504 (1977).
28. W. Mann, M. Bates, B. Grosz, D. D. McDonald, K. McKeown and W. Swartout, Text generation: the state of the art and literature. Technical Report *RR*-81-101, Information Sciences Institute (1981).
29. D. D. McDonald, a revision of [15] in preparation to appear as a Technical Report from the MIT Artificial Intelligence Lab.

Comp. & Maths. with Appls. Vol. 9, No. 1, pp. 131–147, 1983
Printed in Great Britain.

0097-4943/83/010131-17$03.00/0
Pergamon Press Ltd.

UNDERSTANDING NOVEL LANGUAGE†

GERALD F. DeJONG and DAVID L. WALTZ

Coordinated Science Laboratory and Electrical Engineering Department, University of Illinois, Urbana,
IL 61801, U.S.A.

Abstract—In this article we treat in some detail the problem of designing mechanisms that will allow us to deal with two types of novel language: (1) text requiring scheme learning; and (2) the understanding of novel metaphorical use of verbs. Schema learning is addressed by four types of processes: schema composition, secondary effect elevation, schema alteration, and volitionalization. The processing of novel metaphors depends on a decompositional analysis of verbs into "event shape diagrams," along with a matching process that uses semantic marker-like information, to construct novel meaning structures. The examples we describe have been chosen to be types that occur commonly, so that rules that we need to understand them can also be used to understand a much wider range of novel language.

1. INTRODUCTION

Natural language understanding systems are interesting to the extent that they understand material that they were never explicitly programmed to handle. A system such as ELIZA[1] or PARRY[2], which operates primarily by pattern matching, is less interesting than a system which has a set of general rules that can be used to generate a meaning representation for unanticipated inputs. There are a wide variety of types of unanticipated input. Some examples are:

(a) New instances of known case frames, scripts, or plans. Each of these can be a kind of novel language in the sense that sentences never seen before can be processed appropriately. This may mean that information is retrieved from a data base on request, or that a representation of a news story is constructed and remembered, or that a question is answered about an earlier dialogue, and so on. If the general rules in a system are good ones, then a relatively small number of rules will allow a program to handle a wide variety of inputs, most of which were never explicitly anticipated by the programmer of the system. This is the simplest type of novel language, and is by now so familiar that it hardly seems to be a way of dealing with novel language at all.

(b) Isolated novel words that have to be understood in context. Some work has been done in this area by Granger[3]. Whenever we can extract a meaning structure for a sentence in context, we have some hope of guessing the meaning of a novel word. For example, if we were told:

When the tank got low, John filled his car with gasohol.

A system that had some scriptal knowledge in the automobile domain could guess that gasohol was a kind of fuel, or possibly a fluid to substitute for oil, water or antifreeze, or by some stretch of the imagination, gasohol might be something to put in a tank that just happens to be being transported by the car. Several types of information can be used to constrain the possible meanings for gasohol: it is something that can be the instrument of "fill", something that a car is filled with, probably its tank, that since the tank got low, something, probably the car or John, was using up the substance in the tank.

(c) Combinations of words that denote items never before known to a system. Examples in (a) above shade into others where concepts are referenced that are novel to a system. For example, complex noun phrases can use familiar words to construct novel items, as in the

†This work was supported in part by the Office of Naval Research under Contract N00014-75-C-0612, and in part by the National Science Foundation under Grants NSF IST 81-17238 and NSF IST 81-20254.

phrase (from Finin[4]):

> ...engine housing acid damage report summary...

Here, all the words (engine, housing, etc.) may be known, but the phrase taken as a whole denotes an item that may never have been encountered before by the system. A program that "understands" this phrase could create an internal representation for the item, and infer properties about the item, e.g. that the item was the summary part of a report, that the report was about engine housing acid damage, that the material of the engine housing is probably metal, that the acid damage was to the housing, that acid damage to metal is called "corrosion", and so on. From this information, a system could recognize paraphrases and a variety of references to the same item.

(d) Events that are novel, as in the example:

> My dachshund bit our postman on the ear.

Waltz[5] lays out mechanisms that would allow a system to generate the working equivalent of a mental image for this sentence, attempt to simulate the running of a "mental image" corresponding to the sentence, and from the difficulties encountered in running the mental image simulation, judge that the sentence was at least mildly implausible.

(e) New schemas, describing goal-oriented sequences of actions that may never have been encountered before, as in hearing and understanding the nature of skyjacking for the first time[6]. Here, the understanding consists of first untangling the motivations for each of the participants, accounting for each of the actions that are part of the overall schema, and generalizing the schema so that novel occurrences of similar schemas can remind the system of the original schema.

(f) Novel metaphors and analogies. Here the variety of language that requires explanation is staggering. Understanding metaphorical language first requires noting that the language *is* metaphorical, that is that it couldn't be literal descriptive text. (This in turn requires an internal model of what is ordinary, expected, or possible, that a system can use to judge the plausibility of novel language—see item (d) above.) Next, information from the "base domain", that is the domain in which the language has literal meaning, must be somehow transferred (with appropriate modifications) to the "target domain", i.e. the domain which is actually being described. As an example, given the sentence:

> John ate up the compliments.

we would want to transfer material such as pleasure, desire and "ingestion" (suitably modified) from the eating domain to the communication domain. The result can become the basis for learning about a new abstract domain or it may simply be that a metaphor allows one to express in a few words many notions about a target domain that would otherwise require a much lengthier exposition. In any case, a system should also keep some record of its metaphor understanding process, so that subsequent processing of similar metaphors would be eased.

In this article, we look in more detail at the problem of designing mechanisms that will allow us to deal with the types of novel language described in (e) and (f) above, namely schema learning and the understanding of metaphors. This work is just beginning. The examples we describe have been chosen to be types that occur commonly, so that rules that we need to understand them can be used to also understand a much wider range of novel language. However, we must note that there is only so far that rules can take us: ultimately the power of systems will depend on the sheer amount of knowledge they have, knowledge which can be used as the base domain for new metaphors, and schemas that can be used to build yet more schemas. Therefore, to really achieve something resembling common sense, we will have to *exercise* our rules on whatever base information we have, building a yet larger base on which the rules can operate recursively. This important process is meant to be a first-order model of the process of adult knowledge acquisition through language.

2. SCHEMA LEARNING

In this section we examine the problem of processing texts that express unfamiliar concepts. Acquiring some grasp of those new concepts is an essential aspect of processing such texts. This is different from learning new words from context. The distinction here is between unfamiliar words that express familiar concepts and familiar words that express unfamiliar concepts. The former problem has been somewhat studied (Selfridge, Granger, Anderson, Langley). The latter has not.

How can familiar words express unfamiliar concepts? After all, knowing a word entails knowing the set of concepts corresponding to its various word senses. While this is true, words in aggregate often can be used to express concepts beyond the simple composition of their meanings. These larger concepts have variously been termed frames[7, 8], schemas[9, 10], scripts[11] or MOPs[12]. Structures corresponding to these larger concepts are used to organize world knowledge in artificial intelligence systems, and play a crucial role in the understanding process in natural language systems (e.g. [13–17]. We will use the (relatively) neutral term "schema" to refer to these knowledge structures.

Very briefly, schemas are used in natural language processing as follows. A text is input to the system. The schemas relevant to the situations described in the text are selected and activated. Schema selection is a difficult problem, outside the domain of this paper. There have been several approaches (e.g. [17–19]).

After schema activation, text sentences are interpreted with respect to the chosen schemas. For each situation the corresponding schema supplies normal causal and temporal connections among events, a specification of what is important and what is not, preconditions and postconditions, etc. Thus, the use of schemas facilitates the task of constructing a unified conceptual representation for the text as a whole. In some systems[17, 20] the schemas are also used to aid in word and sentence interpretation.

Now we can ask a crucial question: What can a natural language system do if it does not have an appropriate schema for understanding a new input text? As a partial answer, we will introduce a new kind of learning called *Explanatory Schema Acquisition*. As the name implies, it is used to acquire schemas. It is not a universal learning technique. The method will be applied only to acquisition of volitional schemas, i.e. schemas used by people in problem solving situations. Furthermore, it builds on knowledge already in the system and so it is not immediately applicable to learning a system's first schemas. Even with non-schema and first schema learning ruled out, a very large and interesting class of learning remains. In fact, it seems that a very large fraction of human adult learning is of this kind. It encompasses learning schemas from instruction, from observation of others, from untutored examples, and from fortuitous accidents.

The main argument that will be advanced is that acquiring schemas involves generalizing structures made up of old and familiar schemas which are combined in novel ways. The generalizing process itself is performed through consideration of the interactions between the effects, preconditions and slot filler constraints supplied by the component schemas.

Thus, the method is a knowledge based one. It is capable of one trial learning. Moreover, it relies very little on inductively acquired correlational experience.

2.1 *An example*

To clarify the procedure, consider an example. This example is a story about a kidnapping, Let us assume that we, the readers of this example, do not yet have a schema for kidnapping or extortion or any similar notion. We do, however, assume the knowledge of a considerable quantity of background information about stealing, bargaining, the use of normal physical objects, and goals of people and institutions.

Example story:

Paris police disclosed Tuesday that a man who identified himself as Jean Maraneaux abducted the 12-yr-old daughter of wealthy Parisian businessman Michel Boullard late last week. Boullard received a letter containing a snapshot of the kidnapped girl. The next day he received a telegram demanding that 1 million francs be left in a lobby waste basket of the crowded Pompidou Center in exchange for the girl. Asking that the police not intervene, Boullard arranged for the delivery of the money. His daughter was found wandering blindfolded with her hands bound near his downtown office on Monday.

A KIDNAPPING schema, if we had one, would contain information to help us make sense of the story. With it, processing the story would be relatively easy.

But by assumption we do not know about kidnapping. Therefore some events in the story are incomprehensible. In particular we cannot explain why Maraneaux might steal Boullard's daughter. While this is quite clearly an instance of taking something that belongs to someone else, there is no motivation for it. The daughter has no apparent value to Boullard; a person, unlike money, cannot be used to acquire other valued goods. Any schema-based understander requires motivations for major volitional actions (such as a character invoking the STEAL schema). Therefore, this input seems anomalous.

The confusion is resolved by the next sentence. This input invokes the BARGAIN schema. We know immediately the motivation for Maraneaux trying to bargain with Boullard: he is trying to acquire money. Possessing money is a common goal that can be attributed to most people. Thus, it serves as an understandable motivation for the bargaining. Furthermore, stealing the girl is now motivated: Maraneaux used the STEAL schema to satisfy a precondition of the BARGAIN schema. The precondition states that the bargain is unlikely to work unless each party indeed possesses the item he plans to trade away.

Thus far we have done nothing new. Previous systems have proposed understanding new text inputs via analysis of goals and plans of the characters [2, 16, 21]. These systems tend to be more oriented toward "planning" or "problem solving" than "script application".

Once the story has been understood in this way it might already be viewed as a new schema. The system could file away the representation as a method by which a particular person (Maraneaux) can procure a particular amount of money (1 million francs) by a particular action (stealing Boullard's daughter and offering to trade her back for the money). This is a mistake for several reasons. The most important is that it is simply far too specific.

Our concern here is how a system might do better than to simply file away a very specific plan. Our contention is that the same knowledge used to process the input in the first place can be used to make the schema more general. For example, the system has the knowledge necessary to prove that if Maraneaux wanted 100,000 francs instead of 1 million, that the same plan would work. It can do this because the system knows the function of the million francs in Maraneaux's plan. It knows that the money is traded by Boullard for the return of his daughter. Also it knows that the preconditions for Boullard's acceptance of the proposed bargain are that (1) Boullard must value his daughter's safety more than the money and (2) that Boullard must have access to that amount of money. Clearly, since 1 million francs satisfies these requirements, any amount less than 1 million francs also satisfies the requirements and would have worked. Sums larger than a million francs might work as well provided they do not violate (1) or (2) above. We have been a bit sloppy in our analysis. To understand Maraneaux's actions it is not important in reality for Boullard to have access to the money but only for Maraneaux to *believe* he does, and for Maraneaux to *believe* Boullard values his daughter. Nonetheless, the point is well made: this event can be generalized through knowledge-based manipulations using information that had to be in the system anyway in order for the story to be understood. In a like manner the identity of Boullard, his daughter, and Maraneaux are not important. What is important are that these roles be played by people with certain relationships to other people and things. The required relationships are dictated by the volitional actions required of the people by the schema. After these knowledge-based generalizations have been made, the specific event can be transformed into a KIDNAP schema.

In general, the newly generalized schemas require further refinement. Due to eccentricities in the input story, the schema may lack information. For example, if the first kidnapping story seen by the system reported the kidnappers successfully escaping with the ransom even though they killed the hostage, the system might acquire a distorted concept of kidnapping. Even more frequent are cases where the first schema constructed is correct but incomplete. This might result from situations where there are alternate methods of achieving certain sub-goals, only one of which is reported. Clearly, schema modification is essential. Thus, the system's schemas must constantly be adjusted and refined in reaction to normal input processing.

2.2 The generalization process

There are two problems that the generalization process must face. The first is to know when it should be applied. Clearly, every input text ought not to cause the system to construct a new schema. Only "interesting" inputs should invoke the schema acquisition system. The second problem is how to perform the generalization. There are a number of subproblems here, for example, selecting which events and objects should be generalized, imposing limits on the extent of generalization, and actually carrying out the schema modification.

There are four situations which when recognized in the text either individually or in combination ought to invoke the generalization routines. They are:

Schema composition
Secondary effect elevation
Schema alteration
Volitionalization.

In the first part of this section we will illustrate each of these situations with an example.

2.2.1 Schema composition.

The first situation we will discuss is called *schema composition*. Basically, it involves composing known schemas in a novel way. Typically, this will involve a primary schema, essentially unchanged, with one or more of its preconditions satisfied in a novel way by other known schemas.

An example of this was seen in the above kidnapping story. In that story, the primary schema is BARGAIN, a schema which we assumed the system already knew. One of the preconditions specified in the BARGAIN schema is that each party to the bargain must convince the other that he can indeed deliver his side of the bargain. For Maraneaux, this corresponds to making Boullard believe that he (Maraneaux) has control of Boullard's daughter an can, therefore, relinquish the girl to him. Maraneaux achieves this by actually establishing control over the daughter (via an instance of the STEAL schema) and then sending Boullard a photograph. To the system, this is a novel way to satisfy BARGAIN's preconditions. We know this must be novel to the system because if it were not, the system would already have a schema in which this precondition of BARGAIN was satisfied by an application of STEAL. But by hypothesis, the system does not yet possess a kidnapping schema and therefore, cannot yet know of this method of satisfying the precondition. Thus, a precondition of a known schema has been satisfied in an interesting new way, and a new schema must be constructed to capture the underlying generalization.

2.2.2 Secondary effect elevation.

Consider the following scenario:

> Fred wanted to date only Sue, but Sue steadfastly refused his overtures. Fred was on the verge of giving up when he saw what happened to his friend, John: John wanted to date Mary but she also refused. John started seeing Wilma. Mary became jealous and the next time he asked her, Mary eagerly accepted. Fred told Sue that he was going to make a date with Lisa.

Here Fred has not acquired a new schema; he has used an existing schema (DATE) in a new way. This is called secondary effect elevation. Fred's DATE schema already contains all of the knowledge necessary for resolving his dilemma. The problem is that the normal DATE schema is organized in the wrong way. In secondary effect elevation situations an existing schema is annotated indicating that the schema may be used to achieve a result which is normally neutral or negative.

The main purpose of the DATE schema is to satisfy certain recurring social goals (like companionship, sex, etc.). DATE contains secondary effects as well. These are often undesirable effects accompanying the main, planned effects. For example, one is usually monetarily poorer after a date. Another secondary effect is that if one has an old girlfriend, she may become jealous of a new date.

What Fred learned from John's experience is that it is occasionally useful to invoke the DATE schema in order to cause one of its secondary effects (jealousy) while completely ignoring the usual main goal.

Just as with schema composition, the existing schema is changed to reflect a *generalization* made from a specific instance. In this case, the specific instance is John's interactions with Mary. Notice, however, that Fred did not simply copy John's actions. John actually made a date with Wilma while Fred only expressed an intention to date Lisa. This is not an earth-shaking difference, but in the context of dating it is extremely significant. In the normal DATE situation expressing an intention to date someone is not nearly so satisfying as an actual date. Once modified for the purpose of causing jealousy, however, expressing an intention for a date and actually carrying it out can be equally effective.

One might argue that the distinction between main and secondary effects of a schema is otiose and, in situations such as this, even deleterious. After all, DATE already had all of the information necessary for solving Fred's problem. If a system simply treats all of the effects of a schema the same, then any effect can be singled out during the planning process to be used as the main goal. There is, however, a strong argument against this position. The possible desired effects of a schema do not exist only within the schema itself. They are used to organize and select among schemas in both understanding and planning applications (see [14] and [18]). Many effects (like feeling more tired after a date than before) will not be used in the normal planning or understanding process. If they are treated the same as legitimate main goals the system will be swamped in a combinatorial quagmire of undifferentiated possibilities, most of which are wildly implausible. For example, we do not want our understanding process to predict that John will take a nap when it is told that John dated Mary. Given the input "John took a nap" the system ought to be able to justify it. However, it ought not actively predict it. Given the multiplicity of individual actions making up the DATE schema (each with its own set of effects) the vast majority of the effects from this scheme (and any other schema) are simply irrelevant to overall planning and understanding processes. Instead, we would like our system to single out the plausible volitional effects of its schemas and use only those for schema organization and selection. Thus, in our example, Fred has constructed, via secondary effect elevation, a new use of the DATE schema.

2.2.3 *Schema alteration.* Schema alteration involves modifying a nearly correct schema so that it fits the requirements of a new situation. The alteration process is guided by the system's world model. This is illustrated by the following brief anecdote:

Recently I had occasion to replace temporarily a broken window in my back door with a plywood panel. The plywood sheet from which the panel was to be cut had a "good" side and a "bad" side (as does most raw lumber). The good side was reasonably smooth while the bad side had several ruts and knot holes. I automatically examined both sides of the sheet (presumably as part of my SAWING or CUTTING-A-BOARD-TO-FIT schema) and selected the good side to face into the house with the bad side to be exposed to the elements. After I had cut the panel and fitted it in place I noticed that several splinters had been torn out leaving ruts in the "good" side. I immediately saw the problem. Hand saws only cut in one direction. With hand saws, the downward motion does the cutting while the upward motion only repositions the cutting blade for another downward motion. I had cut the wood panel with the "good" side facing down. The downward cutting action has a tendency to tear splinters of wood out of the lower surface of the board. Since the good side was the lower surface, it suffered the loss of splinters. If I had to perform the same action again, I would not make the same mistake. I would cut the board with the good side facing up. However, what I learned was not just a simple specialized patch to handle this particular instance of splintering. Since I knew the cause of the splintering, I knew that it would not always be a problem: it is only a problem when (1) the lumber is prone to splintering, (2) there is a "good" side of the board that is to be preserved, and (3) one is making a crosscut (across the wood's grain) rather than a rip cut (along the grain). Moreover, the solution is not always to position the wood with the good side up. My electric saber saw (also a reciprocating saw) cuts during the upward blade motion rather than the downward motion. Clearly, the solution when using the saber saw is the opposite: to position the board with the good side down. Now, these are not hard and fast rules: with a sufficiently poor quality sheet of plywood splintering would likely always be a problem. Rather, these are useful heuristics that lead to a refinement of the SAWING schema.

Note that this refinement to the SAWING schema is far more general than required to handle the particular problem that gave rise to it. The refinement contains contingencies relevant to the use of saber saws even though no saber saw was used in the immediate problem. This is possible because the refinement is driven by world model, not just the problem. The SAWING schema was altered by identifying and eliminating the offending cause in the underlying knowledge-based explanation of the phenomena.

2.2.4 *Volitionalization.* This situation involves transforming a schema for which there is no planner (like VEHICLE-ACCIDENT, ROULETTE, etc.) into a schema which can be used be a planner to attain a specific goal. Consider the following story:

> Herman was his grandfather's only living relative. When Herman's business was failing he decided to ask his grandfather for a loan. They had never been close but his grandfather was a rich man and Herman knew he could spare the money. When his grandfather refused, Herman decided he would do the old fellow in. He gave him a vintage bottle of wine spiked with arsenic. His grandfather died. Herman inherited several million dollars and lived happily ever after.

This story is a paraphrase of innumerable mystery stories and illustrates a schema familiar to all who-done-it readers. It might be called the HEIR-ELIMINATES-BENEFACTOR schema. It is produced via volitionalization by modifying the existing non-volitional schema INHERIT. INHERIT is non-volitional since there is no active agent. The schema simply dictates what happens to a person's possessions when he dies.

In this example, volitionalization parallels schema composition. One of the preconditions to INHERIT is that the individual be dead. The ELIMINATE-BENEFACTOR schema uses the schema MURDER to accomplish this. One major difference is that schema composition requires all volitional schemas. This parallelism need not always be present, however. Non-volitional to volitional transformation is also applicable to removing stochastic causal steps from a schema resulting in a volitional one.

2.3 *Limits on generalization*

Basically, the generalization process is based on certain data dependency links established during understanding.

After a story is understood, the understood representation can be viewed as an *explanation* of why the events are plausible. For example, take the case of a kidnapping. KIDNAP is an instance of schema composition, not unlike RANSOM. Thus, the first kidnapping story seen by the system is understood as a THEFT followed by a BARGAIN. If the kidnapper is successful, the ransom is paid. For a system to understand this, it must justify that the person paying values the safety of the kidnapped victim more than the ransom money. This justification is a data dependency[22] link to some general world knowledge (e.g. that a parent loves his children). Now the event can be generalized so long as these data dependency links are preserved. Clearly, as long as the data dependencies are preserved, the underlying events will still form a believable whole.

Consider again the secondary effect elevation example of Fred trying to date Sue. The observed specific instance is John's interactions with Mary. Notice, however, that Fred did not simply copy John's actions. John actually made a date with Wilma while Fred only expressed an intention to date Lisa. This is not an earth-shaking difference, but in the context of dating it is extremely significant. In the normal DATE situation expressing an intention to date someone is not nearly so satisfying as an actual date. Once modified for the purpose of causing jealousy, however, expressing an intention for a date and actually carrying it out can be equally effective. That is, they both maintain the data dependency link for why we believe that Sue is in fact jealous.

Likewise, in the alteration example the schema for preserving one side of a board while sawing can be generalized. The resulting schema is applicable to circular saws, jig saws, etc. as well as hand saws. Again this is due to the preservation of a data dependency link: we believe that the wood's surface is preserved because the surface is supported by the rest of the board during deformation due to the saw's teeth. As long as we know which direction the teeth point on a saw, we know how to orient the board to preserve its good side.

2.4 *Comparison to previous work*

How does this method compare to other learning systems? There are a number of previous learning systems that spring to mind: Schank's MOPs[12], Selfridge's language learning model[36],

Soloway's program to learn the rules of baseball[25] and SRI STRIPS system[37]. The system outlined is strikingly different from Schank's and Selfridge's. It has some interesting similarities to Soloway's and one part of the STRIPS system.

While the domain of Schank's MOPs is similar to the described system, the learning technique used with MOPs is very different. The systems of Kolodner[38] and Lebowitz[20] both made "generalizations" but these are all of the correlational variety and might better be termed "specializations". IPPS generalization that Italian terrorists tend to shoot people in the knee caps, for example, is actually a correlational constraint noticed in the pre-existing terrorism MOP. The result is actually a specialized terrorism MOP to be applied only to Italian terrorist stories which makes a prediction about shooting in knee caps. Learning in both IPP and CYRUS is of this variety. Their approach precludes the kind of learning that extends a system's range of processing. Lebowitz's general terrorism MOP could not in principle be learned by his system. In the example outlined, the system learned an EXTORT schema without having a more general version already built in.

Selfridge's system was concerned with learning sentence structure and the names of already existing concepts. It learned, for example, that the words "put on" can refer to the already defined algorithmic concept "get dressed in". The domain of my system is learning the original concepts. It might be interesting to explore how these ideas could be applied to language learning but that would not be the main thrust.

Soloway's system is similar to the one outlined here in that it has the flavor of one-trial or "insight" learning. Furthermore, he made use of general background goal information (in the form of notions such as competition) to aid in processing. However, the domain of learning baseball rules from game descriptions is very different from learning process schemata. Also, the purpose of his system is very different. It did not try to extend the range of its processing in an open-ended way. Rather, it tried to induce general rules from instances. In that sense it is more of an inductive inference system.

The MACROPS idea of SRIs are similar in that they result in new processing structures which can in turn be combined to form yet other structures. However, the domain of planning paths around blocks and through doors is much more constrained and simplified. Furthermore, the MACROPS structures were built from a successful planning search through the problem space, not in the midst of processing inputs. This makes STRIPS very inward motivated in its learning.

2.5 Conclusion

There are several concluding points:

(1) Explanatory schema acquisition does not depend on correlational evidence. Unlike some learning system (e.g. [23, 24]), it is capable of one trial learning. It is somewhat similar to Soloway's view of learning[25].

(2) The approach is heavily knowledge-based. A great deal of background knowledge must be present for learning to take place. In this respect explanatory schema acquisition follows the current trend in AI learning and discovery systems perhaps traceable to Lenat[26].

(3) The learning mechanism is not "failure-driven" as is the MOPs approach[12]. In that view learning takes place in response to incorrect predictions by the system. In explanatory acquisition learning can also be stimulated by positive inputs which encounter no particular problems or prediction failures.

(4) The absolute representation power of the system is not enhanced by learning new schemas. This statement is only superficially surprising. Indeed, Fodor[27] implies that this must be true of all self-consistent learning systems. Explanatory schema acquisition does, however, increase processing efficiency. Since all real-world systems are resource limited, this learning technique does, in fact, increase the system's processing power. Furthermore, it may indicate how Socratic method learning is possible and why the psychological phenomenon of functional fixedness is adaptive.

3. UNDERSTANDING METAPHOR

3.1 Importance of metaphor

Metaphors are pervasive. It is nearly impossible to avoid metaphor in language use, even if the language is technical. For example, hydraulic metaphors are common in economics (e.g. economic *pressure*, cash *flow*, *turning off* the money supply, *draining* of assets, etc.). It is not possible to talk about *love* except through metaphor: love can be likened to a journey together, a meeting of minds, complementary shapes (as in fitting or belonging together), madness, falling into an abyss, transmitting and receiving on the same wavelength, and so on. Jackendoff[28] has argued that metaphor is the basic process by which we acquire proficiency in abstract domains; he suggests that as infants, when we encounter a novel domain, we use existing sensory-motor schemas to form the basis of schemas suitable for understanding the abstract domain, and that this process can continue recursively, using existing abstract schemas as the basis for understanding novel abstract domains. Jackendoff therefore suggests that the surface similarity of "Mary kept the ring in a box" and "They kept the business in the family" reflects a deep similarity due to the derivation of the abstract domain of *possession* from the concrete domain of *position.*

Metaphors can be used to transfer complex combinations of information from one well-known domain to another less well known or completely unfamiliar one. Understanding metaphorical language first requires noting that the language *is* metaphorical, that is that it couldn't be literal descriptive text. This in turn requires an internal model of what is ordinary, expected, or possible, that a system can use to judge the plausibility of novel language (see for example item (d) in the Introduction). Next, material from the "base domain", that is the domain in which the language has literal meaning, must be used to understand the "target domain", that is, the domain which is actually being described. This could be done in a number of ways, for example, by establishing links between the base domain of the metaphor and the target (novel) domain that the metaphor is being used to describe, or by copying base domain structures into a target domain. The result can become the basis for learning about a new domain (by transferring knowledge from the base domain selectively) or it may simply be that a metaphor allows one to express in a few words many notions about a target domain that would otherwise require a much lengthier exposition. Consider for example:

(S1) John ate up the compliments.

or

(S2) Robbie's metal legs ate up the space between him and Susie.†

Assuming that these sentences represented novel uses of the words "ate up", we might want a system to infer that in the first sentence John desired the compliments, eagerly "ingested" them with his mind, thereby making them internal and being given pleasure by them, and that in the second sentence, the distance between Robbie and Susie was being reduced to zero, just as an amount of food is reduced to zero when it is "eaten up".

In the following sections I will show methods which will make the correct interpretations of the two examples above. First, however, I must introduce "event shape diagrams", a new representation scheme for verb meaning, which is used centrally in this method for understanding novel metaphors.‡

3.2 *Event shape diagrams*

In their simplest forms, event shape diagrams have a time line, a scale, and values on the scale at one or more points. Diagrams can be used to represent concurrent processes, causation, and other temporal relations by aligning two or more diagrams, as illustrated in Fig. 1 which shows the representation for "eat". Note that several simple diagrams are aligned, and that each has different kinds of scales, and different event shapes. The top scale corresponds to the CD primitive INGEST[29]. Causal relations hold between the events described in each simple

---

†This is a slightly modified sentence from Isaac Asimov's *I, Robot.*
‡Only verb-based metaphors will be treated here. These methods seem inappropriate for interpreting noun-based metaphors such as "John is a rat", or for "phenomenological metaphors", such as "I woke up in the morning with a sledge hammer banging in my head", as well as for others, no doubt. I have not attempted a taxonomy of metaphor types.

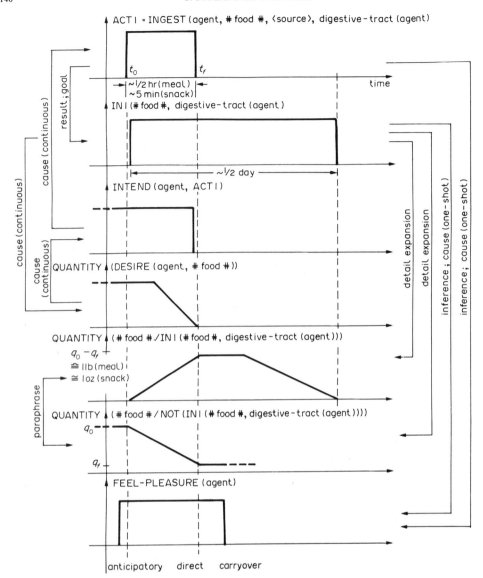

Fig. 1. Event shape diagram for "eat".

diagram. The names for the causal relations are adopted from Rieger's CSA work[30]. The action INGEST stops in this default case where "desire to eat" goes to zero. "Desire to eat" sums up in one measure coercion, habit, and other factors as well as hunger. Typical values for amounts of food, time required to eat, and so on are also associated with the diagram, to be used as default values.

Many adverbial modifiers can be represented neatly: "eat quickly" shrinks the value of $t_f - t_0$ with respect to typical values; "eat a lot" increases the values of $q_0 - q_f$ above typical values. Similarly "eat only half of one's meal", "eat very slowly", "eat one bite", etc. can be neatly represented. "Eat up" can be represented by making the

QUANTITY(food/IN 1 (food, digestive-tract (agent)))

go to zero before the DESIRE (agent, ACT 1) goes to zero. This representation is shown in Fig. 2.

The point of time from which events are viewed can also be clearly represented. Past tense (e.g. "we ate 3 hamburgers") puts "now" on the time line to the right of the action, while future tense puts "now" to the left of the action, and present progressive (e.g. "we are eating") puts "now" between t_0 and t_f.

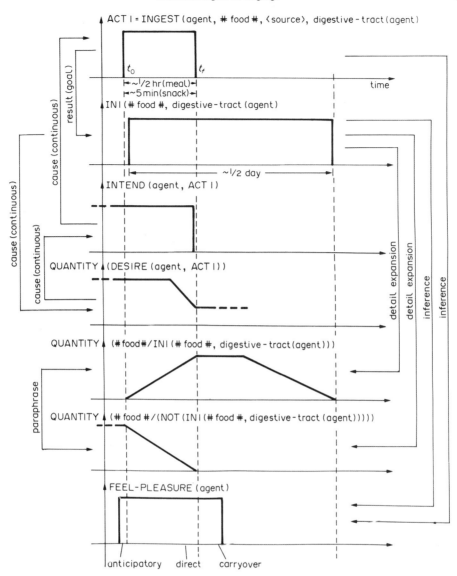

Fig. 2. Event shape diagram for "eat up".

More levels of detail can be added if needed. For instance, the action diagram for eating ought to have links to more general event shape diagrams representing the typical daily eating habits of humans (three meals, one in the early morning, one around noon, and one in the early evening, plus between-meal snacks, coupled with diagrams representing the gradual onset of desire to eat after a meal); the diagram for "eating" should also have links to more detailed event shape diagrams that expand upon the actions involved (eating involves many recurrences of putting food in one's mouth, biting, chewing and swallowing, and the diagram for the amount of food inside the agent can reflect a series of stepwise changes as each mouthful is ingested).

For more detail on event shape diagrams, see [31].

3.3 *Metaphor with event shape diagrams*

The interpretation of verb-based metaphors is based on the following general principles:

(1) Both verbs and nouns have inherent selection restrictions. Thus, for the purposes of this example, "eat (up)" prefers that its semantic object be food, and foods of various kinds are marked by a preference to appear with certain actions, such as "eat", "buy", "grow", "prepare", "throw away", etc. (See Finin[4] for discussion of "case frames" for nouns.)

(2) Nouns are far less likely to be metaphorical than verbs. If a verb and object do not

match each others' selection restrictions, the object should be taken as referring literally, and the verb as referring metaphorically. Thus, we can correctly predict that each of the following sentences is really about ordinary actions on food, even though literally these actions are very remote meanings for each of the verbs:

(S3) Mary destroyed the food. (= prepared badly or ate ravenously).
(S4) Sue made the food disappear. (= ate up rapidly).
(S5) John threw the food together. (= prepared rapidly).

(3) Understanding of a verb-based metaphor involves (a) selection of candidate meanings using the semantic object, (b) matching the event shape diagrams of the candidate meanings with both the current context and the event shape diagrams of the *actual* verb in the sentence.

If there is more than one basic meaning candidate for a metaphorically used work (as in S2 above) the most appropriate meaning is selected by testing the various basic meanings in the current context to see which fits best. Once a basic meaning is selected, the event shape diagrams of this meaning are matched with the event shape diagrams of the *actual* verb used, and some meaning is transferred. The meaning transfer can take two forms: (1) modifying the basic meaning, in a manner similar to adverbial modification; and (2) (more interestingly) superimposing certain portions of the event shape diagram for the verb actually used in the sentence onto the selected basic meaning.

This process should be clearer after I show examples of its operation on sentences (S1) and (S2).

3.4 *An example*

Consider the processing required to handle the metaphor in

(S1) John ate up the compliments.

Using principle (1) above, we first note that "ate up" prefers *food* of some kind as a semantic object, that "compliments" is not a food, and itself prefers an MTRANS-type verb[24], in particular either "tell" or "hear". Next, using principle (2), we can judge that "compliments" refers literally, and so either "tell" or "hear" is probably the true basic verb. The event shape diagrams for "tell" and "hear" are shown in Fig. 3. STM means "short term memory" and LTM means "long term memory". These terms are used here with their common sense (non-technical) meaning.

If the sentence appeared in context, we might be able to select the proper basic meaning by comparing the two possibilities with our current expectations, but in this case, we have to rely on event shape diagram matching to determine the best choice.

Let us look first at trying to match "tell" with "eat up". In order to judge the quality of the match, we must first describe a scoring scheme. The scoring scheme used here is rather simple: it looks for scales that are the same, and matches them, provided the shapes of the scale are the same (i.e. both are changes in the positive direction, or both are *occurrences*, where an occurrence is defined as a change on some scale from a zero to a non-zero value, followed by a change back to zero again. In this case, MTRANS matches INGEST—both are *occurrences*— *and*

INTEND (agent, MTRANS (agent, compliment, STM (agent), STM (hearer)))

matches

INTEND (agent, INGEST (agent, food, [source], digestive-tract (agent)))

—both are *negative changes*. There is a serious mismatch between these two, in that STM (hearer) does not match digestive-tract (agent) well, and these items are the goal portions of the DESIRE, the most important part.

Now consider the match between "hear" and "eat up". As before, MTRANS matches

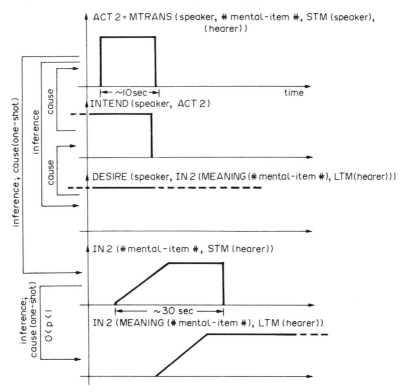

Fig. 3(a). Event shape diagram for "tell".

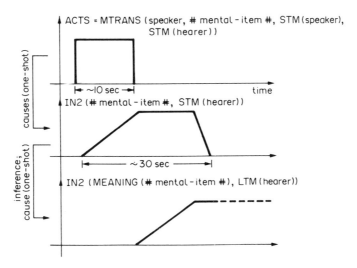

Fig. 3(b). Event shape diagram for "hear".

INGEST, but now the INTEND postion of "eat up" has no match. However, IN1 (compliment, STM (hearer)) matches IN2 (food, digestive-tract (agent)) very well—both are the major scales of their respective verbs, and both have the same "shape", namely the *occurrence* shape, and finally, IN1 and IN2 are closely related binary predicates.

The understanding of the metaphor can now be addressed. Understanding in this model is the transfer to *hear* of the "residue" of the meaning of *eat up*, where by "residue" I mean the portion of *eat up* that had no match with portions of *hear*. The residue in this case consists of the scales for DESIRE, INTEND, QUANTITY and FEEL-PLEASURE that were associated with *eat up*. Theoretically, there are two main options for the mechanism that makes the transfer: (1) the scales may simply be added to the meaning of *hear*, or (2) some of these scales may already be present in latent or potential form as part of our understanding of *hear*, and the transfer would then consist of boosting their prominence, assigning a polarity to them, etc. Even within this single example, there are three kinds of issues that lead me to believe that option (2) is the right choice in general: first, it is difficult to understand why INTEND cannot be transferred to *hear* unless one realizes that hearing a particular item is not something we can ever intend in a causal sense; second, the transfer cannot be literal in any event—for example we would not want to infer that compliments remain in our STM for a day, just because food may do so; and third, adverbial modification seems to already require scales to be present in latent form, as for example in

(S6) I heard the compliments with great pleasure.

Taking the second option, then, we can construct a meaning for (S1), as shown in Fig. 4. Figure 4(a) shows the enriched version of *hear* used to receive the transferred material from *eat up*. Note that although the items below the dotted line are truly part of the meaning of *hear*, these items would not ordinarily be evoked when understanding the word *hear*, and that really, this version of *hear* represents three meanings, corresponding to "hear", "hear with pleasure",

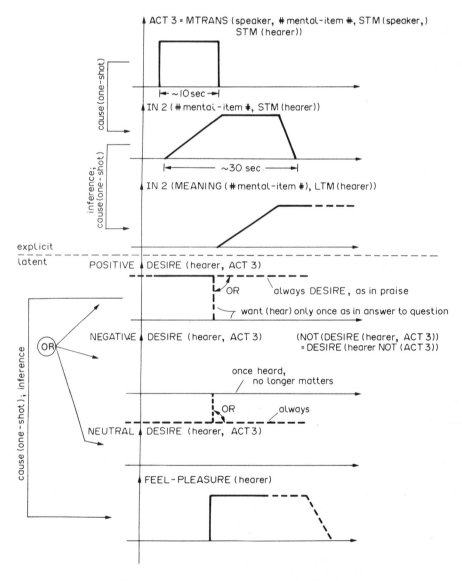

Fig. 4(a). "encircled" event shape diagram for "hear".

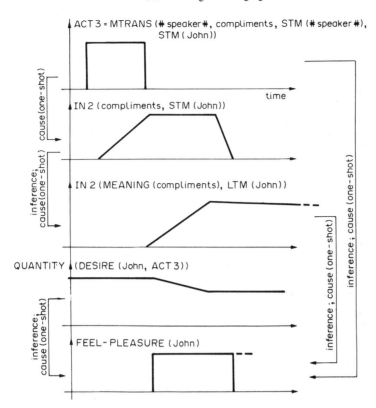

Fig. 4(b). Representation of (S1) "John ate up the compliments".

and "hear with displeasure". It would clearly not be difficult to select "hear with pleasure" by matching with "eat up". Figure 4(b) shows the final meaning representation for (S1).

Example (S2)

(S2) Robbie's metal legs ate up the space between him and Susie.

can be understood using similar methods, though there are some interesting differences. The object of the verb in this case is "space" which is again not an appropriate object for use with "eat up". Again taking the semantic object as the item most likely to refer literally, space suggests that the true basic verb in the sentence ought to be PTRANS, i.e. the physical transfer of an object through space. "Legs" also play an important part here, constraining the PTRANS to be either "run" or "walk" (this requires different processing methods that I have not yet investigated very thoroughly). For our purposes, "run" and "walk" look pretty much the same. There are some main variants that I believe ought to be represented differently, namely the meaning suggested by phrases such as run from (away from) x, run to (toward) y, run (without source or goal), run from x to y, and so on. These differ according to whether movement is stated with reference to a source, goal, neither or both, and whether or not the motion actually starts and/or ends at the source and goal points, or whether these specify only the direction of motion. In this case, the QUANTITY of food which goes to zero should make it possible to match the "run to" meaning.

So far, so good, but some interesting issues remain. First, there is little residue to transfer in this case, except for the intensification of the DESIRE to be at the goal. In fact, I don't think that this is bad, but there are some inferences that I make in hearing (S2) that cannot be easily accounted for using this model. In particular, there is an analogy between taking bites and taking steps, and perhaps more important (and possibly related) (S2) seems to focus on the past progressive aspects of the action; to my mind the sentence is better paraphrased as "Robbie was running toward Susie" than as "Robbie ran to Susie". Overall, however, the account of the understanding of the two metaphors seems to capture roughly the right meanings in a natural and (to me) quite satisfying manner; the problems seem to require refinements to the method rather than complete rethinking.

3.5 *Assessment*

I do not want to claim that all metaphors can be handled by methods of the sort that have been described above. I do believe that the mechanisms suggested above are particularly good and natural for a reasonably rich class of metaphors. There still are holes in the theory, however. Consider the following sentence (due to Gentner[32]):

(S7) The flower kissed the rock.

I have suggested that objects ought to be taken literally, and indeed, if we do so, we can obtain a reasonable reading, namely that a flower bent over and its "face" touched a rock gently. However, one could also take the verb literally, and take "rock" and "flower" metaphorically; in this case, the sentence could refer to a gentle woman literally kissing a tough man.

4. CONCLUSION

This work is just beginning. The examples we describe have been chosen to be types that commonly occur, so that rules needed to understand them can also be used to understand a much wider range of novel language. However, we must note that there is only so far that rules can take us: ultimately the power of systems will depend on the sheer amount of knowledge they have, knowledge which can be used as the base domain for new metaphors, and schemas that can be used to build yet more schemas. Therefore, to really achieve something resembling common sense, we will have to *exercise* our rules on whatever base of information we have, building a yet larger base on which the rules can operate recursively.

REFERENCES

1. Weizenbaum, ELIZA—a computer program for the study of natural language communication between man and machine. *Comm. ACM* **10**(8), 474–480 (1966).
2. K. M. Colby, B. Faught and R. Parkinson, Pattern matching rules of the recognition of natural language dialogue expressions. Stanford A.I. Lab., *Memo AIM-234* (1976).
3. R. H. Granger, FOUL-UP: a program that figures out meanings of words from context. *Proc. IJCAI-77*, M.I.T., Cambridge Mass., pp. 172–178, August 1977.
4. T. W. Finin, The semantic interpretation of nominal compounds. *Tech. Rep. T-96*, Coordinated Science Lab., Univ. of Illinois, Urbana, March 1980.
5. D. L. Waltz, Toward a detailed model of processing for language describing the physical world. In *Proc. IJAI-81*, Vancouver, B.C., Canada, pp. 1–6, August 1981.
6. G. DeJong, Automatic schema acquisition in a natural language environment. In *Proc. 2nd Annual Nat. Conf. Artificial Intell.*, Pittsburgh, Penn., August 1982.
7. M. Minsky, A framework for the representation of knowledge. M.I.T. AI. *Rep. TR-306*, M.I.T., Cambridge, Mass. (1974).
8. E. Charniak, A framed PAINTING: the representation of a common sense knowledge fragment. *Cognitive Sci.* **4**, 355–394 (1976).
9. D. Bobrow and D. Norman, Some principles of memory schemata. In *Representation and Understanding* (Edited by D. Bobrow and A. Collins). Academic Press, New York (1975).
10. W. Chafe, Some thoughts on schemata. In *Proc. Workshop on Theoretical Issues in Natural Language Processing*, Cambridge, Mass., June, 1975.
11. R. Schank and R. Abelson, *Scripts Plans Goals and Understanding*. Erlbaum, Hillsdale, New Jersey (1977).
12. R. Schank, Language and memory. *Cognitive Sci.* **4**, 243–283 (1980).
13. R. Cullingford, Script application: computer understanding of newspaper stories. *Res. Rep.* 116, Yale Computer Science Department, New Haven, Conn., (1978).
14. E. Charniak, MS. MALAPROP, a language comprehension system. In *Proc. 5th IHCAI*, Cambridge, Mass. (1977).
15. D. Bobrow, R. Kaplan, M. Kay, D. Norman, H. Thompson and T. Winograd, GUS, a frame driven dialog system. *Artificial Intell.* **8**(1) (1977).
16. R. Wilensky, Understanding goal-base stories. Ph.D. dissertation, Yale Computer Science Rep. 140, Yale University, New Haven, Conn. (1978).
17. G. DeJong, Skimming stories in real time: an experiment in integrated understanding. *Res. Rep.* 158, Yale Computer Science Department, New Haven, Conn. (1979).
18. E. Charniak, With spoon in hand this must be the eating frame. In *Proc. 2nd Workshop on Theoretical Issues in Natural Language Processing*, University of Illinois, Urbana, Ill. (1978).
19. S. Fahlman, *NETL: A System for Representing and Using Real-World Knowledge*. M.I.T. Press, Cambridge, Mass. (1979).
20. M. Lebowitz, Generalization and memory in an integrated understanding system. Computer Science, *Res. Rep.* 186, Ph.D. dissertation, Yale University, New Haven, Conn. (1980).
21. C. Schmidt and N. Sridharan, Plan recognition using a hypothesize and revise paradigm: an example. In *Proc. 5th Int. Joint Conf. Artificial Intelligence*, pp. 480–486, 1977.

22. J. Doyle, Truth maintenance systems for problem solving. M.I.T. A.I. *Tech. Rep. TR*-419, M.I.T., Cambridge, Mass. (1978).

23. P. H. Winston, Learning structural descriptions from examples. *Rep. AI TR*-231, M.I.T. A.I. Lab., Cambridge, Mass.

24. M. Fox and R. Reddy, Knowledge-guided learning of structural descriptions. In *Proc. 5th IJCAI*, Cambridge, Mass., 1977.

25. E. Soloway, Learning = interpretation + generalization: a case study in knowledge-driven learning. *COINS Tech. Rep.* 78-13, University of Massachusetts, Amherst, Mass. (1978).

26. D. B. Lenat, AM: an artificial intelligence approach to discovery in mathematics as heuristic search. *SAIL-AIM*-286, Standord University (1976).

27. J. Fodor, *The Language of Thought.* Crowell, New York (1975).

28. R. Jackendoff, A system of semantic primitives. In *Theoretical Issues in Natural Language Processing* (Edited by R. Schank and B. Nash-Weber). ACL, Arlington, Virginia (1975).

29. R. C. Schank, The primitive ACTs of conceptual dependency. In *Theoretical Issues in Natural Language Processing* (Edited by R. Schank and B. Nash-Webber). ACL, Arlington, Virginia.

30. C. Rieger, The commonsense algorithm as a basis for computer models of human memory, inference, belief and contextual language comprehension. In *Theoretical Issues in Natural Language Processing* (Edited by R. Schank and B. Nash-Webber), pp. 180–195. ACL, Arlington, Virginia (1975).

31. D. L. Waltz, Event shape diagrams. *Proc. 2nd Ann. Nat. Conf. Artificial Intelligence*, Pittsburgh, Penn., August 1981.

32. D. Genter, Talk presented to the *Conf. Cognitive Sci. Soc.*, Yale University, New Haven, Conn., June 1980.

33. N. Cercone, A note on representing adjectives and adverbs. In *Proc. IJCAI*-77, M.I.T., Cambridge, Mass., pp. 139–140, August 1977.

34. K. D. Forbus, Qualitative process theory. *A.I. Memo* 664, M.I.T. A.I. Laboratory, Cambridge, Mass. (1982).

35. C. R. Perrault and P. R. Cohen, It's for your own good: a note on inaccurate reference. In *Elements of Discourse Understanding* (Edited by Joshi, Sag and Webber), pp. 217–230, Cambridge University Press, Cambridge, Mass. (1981).

36. M. Selfridge, A process model of language acquisition. Yale Computer Science Res. Rep 172, Ph.D. dissertation, Yale University, New Haven Conn. (1980).

37. R. Fikes, P. Hart, and N. Nilsson, Learning and executing generalized robot plans, *Artificial Intell.* 3(3), (1972).

38. J. Kolodner, Retrieval and organizational strategies in conceptual memory: a computer model, Yale Computer Science Res. Rep. 187, Ph.D. dissertation, Yale University, New Haven, Conn. (1980).

Comp. & Maths. with Appls. Vol. 9, No. 1, pp. 149–184, 1983
Printed in Great Britain.

0097–4943/83/010149–36$03.00/0
Pergamon Press Ltd.

A COMPUTATIONAL APPROACH TO FUZZY
QUANTIFIERS IN NATURAL LANGUAGES†

Lotfi A. Zadeh

Computer Science Division, University of California, Berkeley, CA 94720, U.S.A.

Abstract—The generic term *fuzzy quantifier* is employed in this paper to denote the collection of quantifiers in natural languages whose representative elements are: *several, most, much, not many, very many, not very many, few, quite a few, large number, small number, close to five, approximately ten, frequently,* etc. In our approach, such quantifiers are treated as fuzzy numbers which may be manipulated through the use of fuzzy arithmetic and, more generally, fuzzy logic.

A concept which plays an essential role in the treatment of fuzzy quantifiers is that of the cardinality of a fuzzy set. Through the use of this concept, the meaning of a proposition containing one or more fuzzy quantifiers may be represented as a system of elastic constraints whose domain is a collection of fuzzy relations in a relational database. This representation, then, provides a basis for inference from premises which contain fuzzy quantifiers. For example, from the propositions "Most *U*'s are *A*'s" and "Most *A*'s are *B*'s," it follows that "Most² *U*'s are *B*'s," where *most²* is the fuzzy product of the fuzzy proportion *most* with itself.

The computational approach to fuzzy quantifiers which is described in this paper may be viewed as a derivative of fuzzy logic and test-score semantics. In this semantics, the meaning of a semantic entity is represented as a procedure which tests, scores and aggregates the elastic constraints which are induced by the entity in question.

1. INTRODUCTION

During the past two decades, the work of Montague and others[57, 67, 18] has contributed much to our understanding of the proper treatment of the quantifiers *all, some* and *any* when they occur singly or in combination in a proposition in a natural language.

Recently, Barwise and Cooper and others[7, 68] have described methods for dealing with so-called *generalized quantifiers* exemplified by *most, many,* etc. In a different approach which we have described in a series of papers starting in 1975[86–90, 92], the quantifiers in question— as well as other quantifiers with imprecise meaning such as *few, several, not very many,* etc.—are treated as fuzzy numbers and hence are referred to as *fuzzy quantifiers*. As an illustration, a fuzzy quantifier such as *most* in the proposition "Most big men are kind" is interpreted as a fuzzily defined proportion of the fuzzy set of kind men in the fuzzy set of big men. Then, the concept of the cardinality‡ of a fuzzy set is employed to compute the proportion in question and find the degree to which it is compatible with the meaning of *most*.

We shall employ the class labels "fuzzy quantifiers of the first kind" and "fuzzy quantifiers of the second kind" to refer to absolute and relative counts, respectively, with the understanding that a particular quantifier, e.g. *many*, may be employed in either sense, depending on the context. Common examples of quantifiers of the first kind are: *several, few, many, not very many, approximately five, close to ten, much larger than ten, a large number,* etc. while those of the second kind are: *most, many, a large fraction, often, once in a while, much of,* etc. Where needed, ratios of fuzzy quantifiers of the second kind will be referred to as *fuzzy quantifiers of the third kind*. Examples of quantifiers of this type are the likelihood ratios and certainty factors which are encountered in the analysis of evidence, hypothesis testing and expert systems[73, 24, 5].

An important aspect of fuzzy quantifiers is that their occurrence in human discourse is, for the most part, implicit rather than explicit. For example, when we assert that "Basketball players are very tall," what we usually mean is that "Almost all basketball players are very tall." Likewise, the proposition, "Lynne is never late," would normally be interpreted as "Lynne is late very rarely." Similarly, by "Overeating causes obesity," one may mean that

---

To Professor Kokichi Tanaka.

†Research supported in part by the NSF Grants IST-8018196 and MCS79–06543.

‡Informally, the cardinality of a fuzzy set *F* is a real or fuzzy number which serves as a count of the number of elements "in" *F*. A more precise definition of cardinality will be given in Section 2.

"Most of those who overeat are obese," while "Heavy smoking causes lung cancer," might be interpreted as "The incidence of lung cancer among heavy smokers is much higher than among nonsmokers."

An interesting observation that relates to this issue is that *property inheritance*—which is exploited extensively in knowledge representation systems and high-level AI languages[5]—is a *brittle* property with respect to the replacement of the nonfuzzy quantifier *all* with the fuzzy quantifier *almost all*.† What this means is that if in the inference rule‡

$$p \overset{\Delta}{=} all\ A\text{'s are } B\text{'s}$$

$$q \overset{\Delta}{=} all\ B\text{'s are } C\text{'s}$$

$$r \overset{\Delta}{=} all\ A\text{'s are } C\text{'s}$$

the quantifier *all* in p and q is replaced by *almost all*, then the quantifier *all* in r should be replaced by *none-to-all*. Thus, a slight change in the quantifier *all* in the premises may result in a large change in the quantifier *all* in the conclusion.§

Another point which should be noted relates to the close connection between fuzzy quantifiers and fuzzy probabilities. Specifically, it can be shown[86, 87] that a proposition of the form $p \overset{\Delta}{=} Q\ A$'s are B's, where Q is a fuzzy quantifier (e.g. $p \overset{\Delta}{=}$ most doctors are not very tall), implies that the conditional probability of the event B given the event A is a fuzzy probability which is equal to Q. What can be shown, in fact, is that most statements involving fuzzy probabilities may be replaced by semantically equivalent statements involving fuzzy quantifiers. This connection between fuzzy quantifiers and fuzzy probabilities plays an important role in expert systems and fuzzy temporal logic, but we shall not dwell on it in the present paper.

As was stated earlier, the main idea underlying our approach to fuzzy quantifiers is that the natural way of dealing with such quantifiers is to treat them as fuzzy numbers. However, this does not imply that the concept of a fuzzy quantifier is coextensive with that of a fuzzy number. Thus, in the proposition "Vickie is several years younger than Mary," the fuzzy number *several* does not play the role of a fuzzy quantifier, whereas in "Vickie has several good friends," it does. More generally, we shall view a fuzzy quantifier as a fuzzy number which provides a fuzzy characterization of the absolute or relative cardinality of one or more fuzzy or nonfuzzy sets. For example, in "Vickie has several credit cards," *several* is a fuzzy characterization of the cardinality of the nonfuzzy set of Vickie's credit cards; in "Vickie has several good friends," *several* is a fuzzy characterization of the cardinality of the fuzzy set of Vickie's good friends; and in "Most big men are kind," *most* is a fuzzy characterization of the relative cardinality of the fuzzy set of kind men in the fuzzy set of big men. There are propositions, however, in which the question of whether or not a constituent fuzzy number is a fuzzy quantifier does not have a clear cut answer.

A simple example may be of help at this point in providing an idea of how fuzzy quantifiers may be treated as fuzzy numbers. Specifically, consider the propositions

$$p \overset{\Delta}{=} 80\%\ of\ students\ are\ single$$

$$q \overset{\Delta}{=} 60\%\ of\ single\ students\ are\ male$$

$$r \overset{\Delta}{=} Q\ of\ students\ are\ single\ and\ male$$

---

†The brittleness of property inheritance is of relevance to nonmonotonic logic, default reasoning and exception handling.

‡The symbol $\overset{\Delta}{=}$ stands for "denotes" or "is defined to be."

§An example which relates to this phenomenon is: What is rare is expensive. A cheap apartment in Paris is rare. Therefore, a cheap apartment in Paris is expensive. This example was suggested to the author in a different connection by Prof. O. Botta of the University of Lyon.

in which r represents the answer to the question "What percentage of students are single males?" given the premises expressed by p and q.

Clearly, the answer is: $80\% \times 60\% = 48\%$, and, more generally, we can assert that:

$$p \stackrel{\Delta}{=} Q_1 \ of \ A\text{'s} \ are \ B\text{'s} \tag{1.1}$$

$$\underline{q \stackrel{\Delta}{=} Q_2 \ of \ (A \ and \ B)\text{'s} \ are \ C\text{'s}}$$

$$r \stackrel{\Delta}{=} Q_1 Q_2 \ of \ A\text{'s} \ are \ (B \ and \ C)\text{'s}$$

where Q_1 and Q_2 are numerical percentages, and A, B and C are labels of nonfuzzy sets or, equivalently, names of their defining properties.

Now suppose that Q_1 and Q_2 are fuzzy quantifiers of the second kind, as in the following example:

$$p \stackrel{\Delta}{=} most \ students \ are \ single$$

$$\underline{q \stackrel{\Delta}{=} a \ little \ more \ than \ a \ half \ of \ single \ students \ are \ male}$$

$$r \stackrel{\Delta}{=} ? \ Q \ of \ students \ are \ single \ and \ male$$

where the question mark indicates that the value of Q is to be inferred from p and q.

By interpreting the fuzzy quantifiers *most, a little more than a half*, and Q as fuzzy numbers which characterize, respectively, the proportions of single students among students, males among single students and single males among students, we can show that Q may be expressed as the product, in fuzzy arithmetic (see Appendix), of the fuzzy numbers *most* and *a little more than a half*. Thus, in symbols,

$$Q = most \otimes a \ little \ more \ than \ a \ half \tag{1.2}$$

and, more generally, for fuzzy Q's, A's, B's and C's, we can assert the syllogism:

$$p \stackrel{\Delta}{=} Q_1 \ of \ A\text{'s} \ are \ B\text{'s} \tag{1.3}$$

$$\underline{q \stackrel{\Delta}{=} Q_2 \ of \ (A \ and \ B)\text{'s} \ are \ C\text{'s}}$$

$$r \stackrel{\Delta}{=} Q_1 \otimes Q_2 \ of \ A\text{'s} \ are \ (B \ and \ C)\text{'s},$$

which will be referred to as the *intersection/product* syllogism. A pictorial representation of (1.2) is shown in Fig. 1.

The point of this example is that the syllogism (or the *inference schema*) expressed by (1.1) generalizes simply and naturally to fuzzy quantifiers when they are treated as fuzzy numbers. Furthermore, through the use of *linguistic approximation* [87, 45]—which is analogous to rounding to an integer in ordinary arithmetic—the expression for Q may be approximated to by a fuzzy quantifier which is an element of a specified context-free language. For example, in the case of (1.2), such a quantifier may be expressed as *about a half*, or *more or less close to a half*, etc. depending on how the fuzzy numbers *most, a little more than a half*, and *close to a half* are defined through their respective possibility distributions (see Appendix).

152   L. A. ZADEH

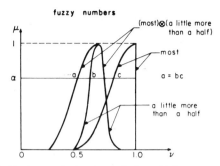

Fig. 1. The intersection/product syllogism with fuzzy quantifiers.

In our discussion so far, we have tacitly assumed that a fuzzy quantifier is a fuzzy number of type 1, i.e. a fuzzy set whose membership function takes values in the unit interval. More generally, however, a fuzzy quantifier may be a fuzzy set of type 2 (or higher), in which case we shall refer to it as an *ultrafuzzy quantifier*. The membership functions of such quantifiers take values in the space of fuzzy sets of type 1, which implies that the compatibility of an ultrafuzzy quantifier with a real number is a fuzzy number of type 1. For example, the fuzzy quantifier *not so many* would be regarded as an ultrafuzzy quantifier if the compatibility of *not so many* with 5, say, would be specified in a particular context as *rather high*, where *rather high* is interpreted as a fuzzy number in the unit interval.

Although the rule of inference expressed by (1.3) remains valid for ultrafuzzy quantifiers if $\otimes$ is interpreted as the product of ultrafuzzy numbers (see Fig. 2), we shall restrict our attention in the present paper to fuzzy quantifiers of type 1, with the understanding that most of the inference schemas derived on this assumption can readily be generalized to fuzzy quantifiers of higher type.

As will be seen in the sequel, a convenient framework for the treatment of fuzzy quantifiers as fuzzy numbers is provided by a recently developed meaning-representation system for natural languages termed *test-score semantics* [93]. Test-score semantics represents a break with the traditional approaches to semantics in that it is based on the premise that almost everything that relates to natural languages is a matter of degree. The acceptance of this premise necessitates an abandonment of bivalent logical systems as a basis for the analysis of natural languages and suggests the adoption of fuzzy logic [86, 90, 8], as the basic conceptual framework for the representation of meaning, knowledge and strength of belief.

Viewed from the perspective of test-score semantics, a semantic entity such as a proposition, predicate, predicate-modifier, quantifier, qualifier, command, question, etc. may be regarded as a system of elastic constraints whose domain is a collection of fuzzy relations in a database—a database which describes a state of affairs [11] or a possible world [44] or, more generally, a set of objects or derived objects in a universe of discourse. The meaning of a semantic entity, then, is represented as a test which when applied to the database yields a collection of partial test scores. Upon aggregation, these test scores lead to an overall vector test score, τ, whose components are numbers in the unit interval, with τ serving as a measure of the compatibility of the semantic entity with the database. In this respect, test-score semantics

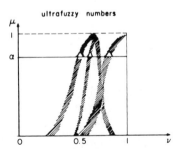

Fig. 2. The intersection/product syllogism with ultrafuzzy quantifiers.

subsumes both truth-conditional and possible-world semantics as limiting cases in which the partial and overall test scores are restricted to {pass, fail} or, equivalently, {true, false} or {1,0}.

In more specific terms, the process of meaning representation in test-score semantics involves three distinct phases. In Phase I, an *explanatory database frame* or EDF, for short, is constructed. EDF consists of a collection of relational frames, i.e. names of relations, names of attributes and attribute domains, whose meaning is assumed to be known. In consequence of this assumption, the choice of EDF is not unique and is strongly influenced by the knowledge profile of the addressee of the representation process as well as by the desideratum of explanatory effectiveness. For example, in the case of the proposition $p \overset{\Delta}{=}$ Over the past few years Nick earned far more than most of his close friends, the EDF might consist of the following relations:† *INCOME* [*Name*; *Amount*; *Year*], which lists the income of each individual identified by his/her name as a function of the variable *Year*; *FRIEND* [*Name*; μ], where μ is the degree to which *Name* is a friend of Nick; *FEW* [*Number*; μ], where μ is the degree to which *Number* is compatible with the fuzzy quantifier *FEW*; *MOST* [*Proportion*; μ], in which μ is the degree to which *Proportion* is compatible with the fuzzy quantifier *MOST*; and *FAR. MORE* [*Income 1*; *Income 2*; μ], where μ is the degree to which *Income 1* fits the fuzzy predicate *FAR. MORE* in relation to *Income 2*. Each of these relations is interpreted as an elastic constraint on the variables which are associated with it.

In Phase 2, a test procedure is constructed which acts on relations in the explanatory database and yields the test scores which represent the degrees to which the elastic constraints induced by the constituents of the semantic entity are satisfied. For example, in the case of p, the test procedure would yield the test scores for the constraints induced by the relations *FRIEND*, *FEW*, *MOST* and *FAR. MORE*.

In Phase 3, the partial test scores are aggregated into an overall test score, τ, which, in general, is a vector which serves as a measure of the compatibility of the semantic entity with an instantiation of EDF. As was stated earlier, the components of this vector are numbers in the unit interval, or, more generally, possibility/probability distributions over this interval. In particular, in the case of a proposition, p, for which the overall test score is a scalar, τ may be interpreted—in the spirit of truth-conditional semantics—as the degree of truth of the proposition with respect to the explanatory database ED (i.e. an instantiation of EDF). Equivalently, τ may be interpreted as the possibility of ED given p, in which case we may say that p *induces a possibility distribution*. More concretely, we shall say that p *translates into a possibility assignment equation* [88]:

$$p \to \Pi_{(X_1, \dots X_n)} = F, \tag{1.4}$$

where F is a fuzzy subset of a universe of discourse U, $X_1, \dots X_n$ are variables which are explicit or implicit in p, and $\Pi_{(X_1, \dots X_n)}$ is their joint possibility distribution. For example, in the case of the proposition $p \overset{\Delta}{=}$ Danielle is tall, we have

$$Danielle\ is\ tall \to \Pi_{Height(Danielle)} = TALL, \tag{1.5}$$

where *TALL* is a fuzzy subset of the real-line, *Height(Danielle)* is a variable which is implicit in p, and $\Pi_{Height(Danielle)}$ is the possibility distribution of the variable *Height(Danielle)*. Equation (1.5) implies that

$$Poss\{Height(Danielle) = u\} = \mu_{TALL}(u),$$

where u is a specified value of the variable *Height(Danielle)*, $\mu_{TALL}(u)$ is the grade of membership of u in the fuzzy set *TALL*, and $Poss\{X = u\}$ should be read as "the possibility that X is u." In effect, (1.5) signifies that the proposition "Danielle is tall," may be interpreted as an elastic constraint on the variable *Height(Danielle)*, with the elasticity of the constraint characterized by the unary relation *TALL* which is defined as a fuzzy subset of the real line.

---

†Generally, we follow the practice of writing the names of fuzzy subsets and fuzzy relations in uppercase symbols.

The same basic idea may be applied to propositions containing one or more fuzzy quantifiers. As a simple illustration, let us consider the proposition

$$p \overset{\Delta}{=} \text{Vickie has several credit cards,}$$

in which *several* is regarded as a fuzzy quantifier which induces an elastic constraint on the number of credit cards possessed by Vickie. In this case, X may be taken to be the count of Vickie's cards, and the possibility assignment equation becomes

$$\text{Vickie has several credit cards} \rightarrow \Pi_{Count(Cards(Vickie))} = SEVERAL, \qquad (1.6)$$

in which *SEVERAL* plays the role of a specified fuzzy subset of the integers 1, 2, ... 10. Thus, if the integer 4, say, is assumed to be compatible with the meaning of *several* to the degree 0.8, then (1.6) implies that, given *p* and the definition of *several*, the possibility that Vickie has four credit cards is expressed by

$$Poss\{Count(Cards(Vickie)) = 4\} = 0.8.$$

In the above example, the class of Vickie's credit cards is a nonfuzzy set and hence there is no problem in counting their number. By contrast, in the proposition

$$p \overset{\Delta}{=} \text{Vickie has several close friends}$$

the class of close friends is a fuzzy set and thus we must first resolve the question of how to count the number of elements in a fuzzy set or, equivalently, how to determine its cardinality. This issue is addressed in the following section.

1. CARDINALITY OF FUZZY SETS

In the case of a crisp (nonfuzzy) subset, A, of a universe of discourse, U, the proposition "u is an element of A," is either true or false, and hence there is just one way in which the cardinality of A, i.e. the count of elements of A, may be defined. However, even though the count may be defined uniquely, there may be some uncertainty about its value if there is an uncertainty regarding the membership status of points of U in A.

By contrast, in the case of a fuzzy subset, F, of U, the proposition "u is an element of F," is generally true to degree, with the result that the concept of cardinality admits of a variety of definitions. Among them, some associate with a fuzzy set F a real number, in which case the cardinality of a fuzzy set is nonfuzzy. Others associate with F a fuzzy number, since it may be argued that the cardinality of a fuzzy set should be a fuzzy number. A brief discussion of these viewpoints is presented in the following. For simplicity, we shall restrict our attention to finite universes of discourse, in which case a fuzzy subset, F, of $U = \{u_1, \dots u_n\}$ may be expressed symbolically as

$$F = \mu_1/u_1 + \dots + \mu_n/u_n$$

or, more simply, as

$$F = \mu_1 u_1 + \dots + \mu_n u_n,$$

in which the term μ_i/u_i, $i = 1, \dots n$, signifies that μ_i is the grade of membership of u_i in F, and the plus sign represents the union.†

Nonfuzzy cardinality

A simple way of extending the concept of cardinality to fuzzy sets is to form the *sigma-count* [17, 85], which is the arithmetic sum of the grades of membership in F. Thus

$$\Sigma Count(F) \overset{\Delta}{=} \Sigma_i u_i, \quad i = 1, \dots n, \qquad (2.1)$$

†For the most part we shall rely on the context to disambiguate the meaning of +.

with the understanding that the sum may be rounded, if need be, to the nearest integer. Furthermore, one may stipulate that the terms whose grade of membership falls below a specified threshold be excluded from the summation. The purpose of such an exclusion is to avoid a situation in which a large number of terms with low grades of membership become count-equivalent to a small number of terms with high membership.

As a simple illustration of the concept of sigma-count, assume that the fuzzy set of close friends of Teresa is expressed as

$$F = 1/Enrique + 0.8/Ramon + 0.7/Elie + 0.9/Sergei + 0.8/Ron.$$

In this case,

$$\Sigma Count(F) = 1 + 0.8 + 0.7 + 0.9 + 0.8$$
$$= 4.2.$$

A sigma-count may be *weighted*, in the sense that if $w = (w_1, \ldots w_n)$ is an n-tuple of nonnegative real numbers, then the *weighted sigma-count of F with respect to w* is defined by

$$\Sigma Count(F; w) \overset{\Delta}{=} \Sigma_i w_i \mu_i. \quad i = 1, \ldots n.$$

This definition implies that $\Sigma Count(F; w)$ may be interpreted as the sigma-count of a fuzzy multiset[†] $'F$ in which the grade of membership and the multiplicity of u_i, $i = 1, \ldots n$, are, respectively, μ_i and w_i. The concept of a weighted sigma-count is closely related to that of the *measure* of a fuzzy set[83, 75, 40–42].

Whether weighted or not, the sigma-count of a fuzzy set is a real number. As was stated earlier, it may be argued that the cardinality of a fuzzy set should be a fuzzy number. If one accepts this argument, then a natural way of defining fuzzy cardinality is the following[90].

Fuzzy cardinality[‡]

In this case, the point of departure is a stratified representation of F in terms of its *level sets*[84], i.e.

$$F = \Sigma_\alpha \alpha F_\alpha,$$

in which the α-level-sets F_α are nonfuzzy sets defined by

$$F_\alpha \overset{\Delta}{=} \{u | \mu_F(u) \ge \alpha\}, \qquad 0 < \alpha \le 1,$$

and

$$\mu_{\alpha F\alpha}(u) = \alpha \mu_F(u), \qquad u \in U.$$

In terms of this representation, there are three fuzzy counts, *FCounts*, that may be associated with F. First, the *FGCount* is defined as the conjunctive fuzzy integer[§][93]

$$FGCount(F) = 1/0 + \Sigma_\alpha \alpha / Count(F_\alpha), \qquad a > 0.$$

[†]A fuzzy multiset, $'F$, may be represented as $'F = \Sigma_i \mu_i/m_i \times u_i$, in which m_i is the *multiplicity* of u_i and μ_i is the grade of membership of u_i in the fuzzy set $F = \Sigma_i \mu_i/u_i$. The multiplicity, m_i, is a nonnegative real number which is usually, but not necessarily, an integer. Thus, a fuzzy multiset may have identical elements, or elements which differ only in their grade of membership.

[‡]Although it is perhaps a more natural extension of the concept of cardinality than the sigma-count, fuzzy cardinality is a more complex concept and is more difficult to manipulate. The exposition of fuzzy cardinality in this section may be omitted on first reading.

[§]It should be noted that the membership function of a conjunctive fuzzy number is not a possibility distribution.

Second, the *FLCount* is defined as

$$FLCount(F) = (FGCount(F))' \ominus 1$$

where $'$ denotes the complement and $\ominus 1$ means that 1 is subtracted from the fuzzy number $FGCount(F)$. And finally, the *FECount(F)* is defined as the intersection of *FGCount(F)* and *FLCount(F)*, i.e.

$$FECount(F) = FGCount(F) \cap FLCount(F).$$

Equivalently—and more precisely—we may define the counts in question via the membership function of F, i.e.

$$\mu_{FECount(F)}(i) \stackrel{\Delta}{=} sup_{\alpha}\{\alpha | Count(F_{\alpha}) \geq i\}, \qquad i = 0, 1, \ldots n, \tag{2.2}$$

$$\mu_{FLCount(F)}(i) \stackrel{\Delta}{=} sup_{\alpha}\{\alpha | Count(F_{\alpha}) \geq n - i)\} \tag{2.3}$$

$$\mu_{FECount(F)}(i) \stackrel{\Delta}{=} \mu_{FGCount(F)}(i) \wedge \mu_{FLCount(F)}(i), \tag{2.4}$$

where $\wedge$ stands for min in infix position.

As a simple illustration, consider the fuzzy set expressed as

$$F = 0.6/u_1 + 0.9/u_2 + 1/u_3 + 0.7/u_4 + 0.3/u_5. \tag{2.5}$$

In this case,

$$F_1 = u_3$$
$$F_{0.9} = u_2 + u_3$$
$$F_{0.7} = u_2 + u_3 + u_4$$
$$F_{0.6} = u_1 + u_2 + u_3 + u_4$$
$$F_{0.3} = u_1 + u_2 + u_3 + u_4 + u_5,$$

which implies that, in stratified form, F may be expressed as

$$F = 1(u_3) + 0.9(u_2 + u_3) + 0.7(u_2 + u_3 + u_4) + 0.6(u_1 + u_2 + u_3 + u_4) + 0.3(u_1 + u_2 + u_3 + u_4 + u_5),$$

and hence that

$$FGCount(F) = 1/0 + 1/1 + 0.9/2 + 0.7/3 + 0.6/4 + 0.3/5$$
$$FLCount(F) = 0.1/2 + 0.3/3 + 0.4/4 + 0.7/5 + 1/6 + \cdots \ominus 1$$
$$= 0.1/1 + 0.3/2 + 0.4/3 + 0.7/4 + 1/5 + \cdots$$
$$FECount(F) = 0.1/1 + 0.3/2 + 0.4/3 + 0.6/4 + 0.3/5$$

while, by comparison,

$$\Sigma Count(F) = 0.6 + 0.9 + 1.0 + 0.7 + 0.3$$
$$= 3.5.$$

A useful interpretation of the defining relations (2.2)–(2.4) may be stated as follows:

(a) $\mu_{FGCount}(i)$ is the truth value of the proposition "F contains at least i elements."

(b) $\mu_{FLCount}(i)$ if the truth value of the proposition "F contains at most i elements."

(c) $\mu_{FECount}(i)$ is the truth value of the proposition "F contains i and only i elements."

From (a), it follows that $FGCount(F)$ may readily be obtained from F by first sorting F in the order of decreasing grades of membership and then replacing u_i with i and adding the term $1/0$. For example, for F defined by (2.5), we have

$$F\downarrow = 1/u_3 + 0.9/u_2 + 0.7/u_4 + 0.6/u_1 + 0.3/u_5 \tag{2.6}$$

$$NF\downarrow = 1/1 + 0.9/2 + 0.7/3 + 0.6/4 + 0.3/5$$

and

$$FGCount(F) = 1/0 + 1/1 + 0.9/2 + 0.7/3 + 0.6/4 + 0.3/5,$$

where $F\downarrow$ denotes F sorted in descending order, and $NF\downarrow$ is $F\downarrow$ with *ith u* replaced by *i*. An immediate consequence of this relation between $\Sigma Count(F)$ and $FGCount(F)$ is the identity

$$\Sigma Count(F) = \Sigma_i \mu_{FGCount}(i) - 1,$$

which shows that, as a real number, $\Sigma Count(F)$ may be regarded as a "summary" of the fuzzy number $FGCount(F)$.

Relative count

A type of count which plays an important role in meaning representation is that of *relative count* (or *relative cardinality*)[87]. Specifically, if F and G are fuzzy sets, then the relative sigma-count of F and G is defined as the ratio:

$$\Sigma Count(F/G) = \frac{\Sigma Count(F \cap G)}{\Sigma Count(G)}, \tag{2.7}$$

which represents the proportion of elements of F which are in G, with the intersection $F \cap G$ defined by

$$\mu_{F \cap G}(u) = \mu_F(u) \wedge \mu_G(u). \tag{2.8}$$

The corresponding definition for the $FGCount$ is

$$FGCount(F/G) = \Sigma_\alpha \alpha \left/ \frac{Count(F_\alpha \cap G_\alpha)}{Count(G_\alpha)} \right., \tag{2.9}$$

where the F_α and G_α represent the α-sets of F and G, respectively. It should be noted that the right-hand member of (2.9) should be treated as a fuzzy multiset, which implies that terms of the form α_1/u and α_2/u should not be combined into a single term $(\alpha_1 \vee \alpha_2)/u$, as they would be in the case of a fuzzy set.

The $\Sigma Count$ and $FCounts$ of fuzzy sets have a number of basic properties of which only a few will be stated here. Specifically, if F and G are fuzzy sets, then from the identity

$$a \vee b + a \wedge b = a + b$$

which holds for any real numbers, it follows at once that

$$\Sigma Count(F \cap G) + \Sigma Count(F \cup G) = \Sigma Count(F) + \Sigma Count(G) \tag{2.10}$$

since

$$\mu_{F \cap G}(u) = \mu_F(u) \wedge \mu_G(u), \qquad u \in U$$

and

$$\mu_{F \cup G}(u) = \mu_F(u) \vee \mu_G(u).$$

Thus, if F and G are disjoint (i.e. $F \cap G = \theta$), then

$$\Sigma Count(F \cup G) = \Sigma Count(F) + \Sigma Count(G) \tag{2.11}$$

and, more generally,

$$\Sigma Count(F) \vee \Sigma Count(G) \leq \Sigma Count(F \cup G) \leq \Sigma Count(F) + \Sigma Count(G) \tag{2.12}$$

and

$$0 \vee (\Sigma Count(F) + \Sigma Count(G) - Count(U)) \leq \Sigma Count(F \cap G) \leq \Sigma Count(F) \wedge \Sigma Count(G). \tag{2.13}$$

These inequalities follow at once from (2.10) and

$$\Sigma Count(F \cap G) \leq \Sigma Count(F)$$

$$\Sigma Count(F \cap G) \leq \Sigma Count(G)$$

$$\Sigma Count(F \cup G) \leq \Sigma Count(U).$$

In the case of *FCounts* and, more specifically, the *FGCount*, the identity corresponding to (2.10) reads [92, 93, 23],

$$FGCount(F \cap G) \oplus FGCount(F \cup G) = FGCount(F) \oplus FGCount(G), \tag{2.14}$$

where $\oplus$ denotes the addition of fuzzy numbers, which is defined by (see Appendix)

$$\mu_{A \oplus B}(u) = sup_v(\mu_A(v) \wedge \mu_B(u - v), \qquad u, v \in (-\infty, \infty), \tag{2.15}$$

where A and B are fuzzy numbers, and μ_A and μ_B are their respective membership functions.

A basic identity which holds for relative counts may be expressed as:

$$\Sigma Count(F \cap G) = \Sigma Count(G)\Sigma Count(F/G) \tag{2.16}$$

for sigma-counts, and as

$$FGCount(F \cap G) = FCount(G) \otimes FGCount(F/G) \tag{2.17}$$

for *FGCounts*, where $\otimes$ denotes the multiplication of fuzzy numbers, which is defined by (see Appendix)

$$\mu_{A \otimes B}(u) = sup_v\left(\mu_A(v) \quad \mu_B\left(\frac{u}{v}\right)\right), \qquad u, v \in (-\infty, \infty), \quad v \neq 0. \tag{2.18}$$

An inequality involving relative sigma-counts which is of relevance to the analysis of evidence in expert systems is the following:

$$\Sigma Count(F/G) + \Sigma Count(\neg F/G) \geq 1 \tag{2.19}$$

where $\neg F$ denotes the complement of F, i.e. $= 1$ *if G is nonfuzzy*,

$$\mu_{\neg F}(u) = 1 - \mu_F(u), \qquad u \in U. \tag{2.20}$$

Note that (2.19) implies that if the relative sigma-count $\Sigma Count(F/G)$ is identified with the conditional probability $Prob(F/G)$[94], then

$$Prob\,(\neg\,F/G) \geq 1 - Prob(F/G) \qquad (2.21)$$

rather than

$$Prob\,(\neg\,F/G) = 1 - Prob(F/G), \qquad (2.22)$$

which holds if G is nonfuzzy.

The inequality in question follows at once from

$$\Sigma Count(\neg\,F/G) = \frac{\Sigma_i(1 - \mu_F(u_i)) \wedge \mu_G(u_i)}{\Sigma_i \mu_G(u_i)} \qquad (2.23)$$

$$\geq \frac{\Sigma_i(1 - \mu_F(u_i))\mu_G(u_i)}{\Sigma_i \mu_G(u_i)}$$

$$\geq 1 - \frac{\Sigma_i \mu_F(u_i)\mu_G(u_i)}{\Sigma_i \mu_G(u_i)}$$

$$\geq 1 - \frac{\Sigma_i \mu_F(u_i) \wedge \mu_G(u_i)}{\Sigma_i \mu_G(u_i)}$$

since

$$\Sigma Count(F/G) = \frac{\Sigma_i \mu_F(u_i) \wedge \mu_G(u_i)}{\Sigma_i \mu_G(u_i)}.$$

This concludes our brief exposition of some of the basic aspects of the concept of cardinality of fuzzy sets. As was stated earlier, the concept of cardinality plays an essential role in representing the meaning of fuzzy quantifiers. In the following sections, this connection will be made more concrete and a basis for inference from propositions containing fuzzy quantifiers will be established.

3. FUZZY QUANTIFIERS AND CARDINALITY OF FUZZY SETS

As was stated earlier, a fuzzy quantifier may be viewed as a fuzzy characterization of absolute or relative cardinality. Thus, in the proposition $p \overset{\Delta}{=} Q$ A's *are* B's, where Q is a fuzzy quantifier and A and B are labels of fuzzy or nonfuzzy sets, Q may be interpreted as a fuzzy characterization of the relative cardinality of B and A. The fuzzy set A will be referred to as the *base set*.

When both A and B are nonfuzzy sets, the relative cardinality of B in A is a real number and Q is its possibility distribution. The same is true if A and/or B are fuzzy sets and the sigma-count is employed to define the relative cardinality. The situation becomes more complicated, however, if an *FCount* is employed for this purpose, since Q, then, is the possibility distribution of a conjunctive fuzzy number.

To encompass these cases, we shall assume that the following propositions are semantically equivalent[89]:

$$\textit{There are Q A's} \leftrightarrow Count(A)\,\textit{is Q} \qquad (3.1)$$

$$\textit{Q A's are B's} \leftrightarrow Prop(B/A)\,\textit{is Q}, \qquad (3.2)$$

where the more specific term *Proportion* or *Prop*, for short, is used in place of *Count* in (3.2) to underscore that *Prop(B/A)* is the relative cardinality of B in A, with the understanding that both *Count* in (3.1) and *Prop* in (3.2) may be fuzzy or nonfuzzy counts. In the sequel, we shall assume for simplicity that, except where stated to the contrary, both absolute and relative cardinalities are defined via the sigma-count.

The right-hand members of (3.1) and (3.2) may be translated into possibility assignment equations (see 1.1). Thus we have

$$Count(A) \ is \ Q \rightarrow \Pi_{Count(A)} = Q \tag{3.3}$$

and

$$Prop(B|A) \ is \ Q \rightarrow \Pi_{Prop(B|A)} = Q, \tag{3.4}$$

in which $\Pi_{Count(A)}$ and $\Pi_{Prop(B|A)}$ represent the possibility distributions of $Count(A)$ and $Prop(B|A)$, respectively. Furthermore, in view of (3.1) and (3.2), we have

$$There \ are \ Q \ A\text{'s} \rightarrow \Pi_{Count(A)} = Q \tag{3.5}$$

$$Q \ A\text{'s} \ are \ B\text{'s} \rightarrow \Pi_{Prop(B|A)} = Q. \tag{3.6}$$

These translation rules in combination with the results established in Section 2, provide a basis for deriving a variety of syllogisms for propositions containing fuzzy quantifiers, an instance of which is the *intersection/product* syllogism described by (1.3), namely,

$$Q_1 \ A\text{'s} \ are \ B\text{'s} \tag{3.7}$$

$$\underline{Q_2(A \ and \ B)\text{'s} \ are \ C\text{'s}}$$

$$Q_1 \otimes Q_2 \ A\text{'s} \ are \ (B \ and \ C)\text{'s}$$

in which Q_1, Q_2, A, B and C are assumed to be fuzzy, as in

$$most \ tall \ men \ are \ fat \tag{3.8}$$

$$\underline{many \ tall \ and \ fat \ men \ are \ bald}$$

$$most \otimes many \ tall \ men \ are \ fat \ and \ bald.$$

To establish the validity of syllogisms of this form, we shall rely, in the main, on the semantic entailment principle [89, 90], and on a special case of this principle which will be referred to as the *quantifier extension principle*.

Stated in brief, the semantic entailment principle asserts that a proposition p entails proposition q, which we shall express as $p \rightarrow q$ or

$$\frac{p}{q},$$

if and only if the possibility distribution which is induced by p, $\Pi^p_{(X_1, \ldots X_n)}$, is contained in the possibility distribution induced by q, $\Pi^q_{(X_1, \ldots X_n)}$ (see (1.4)). Thus, stated in terms of the possibility distribution functions of Π^p and Π^q, we have [88]

$$\frac{p}{q} \ if \ and \ only \ if \ \pi^p_{(X_1, \ldots X_n)} \leq \pi^q_{(X_1, \ldots X_n)} \tag{3.9}$$

for all points in the domain of π^p and π^q.

Informally, (3.9) means that p entails q if and only if q is less specific than p. For example, the proposition $p \overset{\Delta}{=}$ Diana is 28 years old, entails the proposition $q \overset{\Delta}{=}$ Diana is in her late twenties, because p is less specific than q, which in turn is a consequence of the containment of the nonfuzzy set "28" in the fuzzy set "late twenties."

It should be noted that, in the context of test-score semantics, the inequality of possibilities in (3.9) may be expressed as a corresponding inequality of overall test scores. Thus, if τ^p and τ^q are the overall test scores associated with p and q, respectively, then

$$\frac{p}{q} \text{ if and } only \text{ if } \tau^p \le \tau^q, \tag{3.10}$$

with the understanding that the tests yielding τ^p and τ^q are applied to the same explanatory database and that the inequality holds for all instantiations of EDF.

In our applications of the entailment principle, we shall be concerned, for the most part, with an entailment relation between a collection of propositions $p_1, \ldots p_n$ and a proposition q which is entailed by the collection. Under the assumption that the propositions which constitute the premises are noninteractive[89], the statement of the entailment principle (3.9) becomes:

$$p_1 \text{ if and } only \text{ if } \pi^{P_1 \wedge} \cdots \wedge \pi^{P_n} \le \pi^{q'} \tag{3.11}$$
$$\vdots$$
$$\frac{p_n}{q}$$

where $\pi^{P_1}, \ldots \pi^{P_n}, \pi^q$, are the possibility distribution functions induced by $p_1, \ldots p_n, q$, respectively, and likewise for (3.10).

We are now in a position to formulate an important special case of the entailment principle which will be referred to as the *quantifier extension principle*. This principle may also be viewed as an inference rule which is related to the transformational rule of inference described in[91].

Specifically, assume that each of the propositions $p_1, \ldots p_n$ is a fuzzy characterization of an absolute or relative cardinality which may be expressed as $p_i \overset{\Delta}{=} C_i \text{ is } Q_i, i = 1, \ldots n$, in which C_i is a count and Q_i is a fuzzy quantifier, e.g.

$$p_i \overset{\Delta}{=} \Sigma \, Count(B/A) \text{ is } Q_i$$

or, more concretely,

$$p_i \overset{\Delta}{=} most \ A\text{'s } are \ B\text{'s.}$$

Now, in general, a syllogism involving fuzzy quantifiers has the form of a collection of premises of the form $p_i \overset{\Delta}{=} C_i \text{ is } Q_i, i = 1, \ldots n$, followed by a conclusion of the same form, i.e. $q \overset{\Delta}{=} C \text{ is } Q$, where C is a count that is related to $C_i, \ldots C_n$, and Q is a fuzzy quantifier which is related to $Q_i, \ldots Q_n$. The quantifier extension principle makes these relations explicit, as represented in the following inference schema:

$$C_1 \text{ is } Q_1$$
$$\underline{C_n \text{ is } Q_n} \tag{3.12}$$
$$C \text{ is } Q,$$

where Q is given by

$$If \ C = g(C_1, \ldots C_n) \ then \ Q = g(Q_1, \ldots Q_n),$$

in which g is a function which expresses the relation between C and the C_i, and the meaning of $Q = g(Q_1, \ldots Q_n)$ is defined by the extension principle (see Appendix). A somewhat more general version of the quantifier extension principle which can also be readily deduced from the extension principle is the following:

$$C_1 \text{ is } Q_1 \tag{3.13}$$

$$\underline{C_n \text{ is } Q_n}$$

$$C \text{ is } Q,$$

where Q is given by

$$\text{If } f(C_1, \ldots C_n) \le C \le g(C_1, \ldots C_n) \text{ then } f(Q_1, \ldots Q_n) \le Q \le g(Q_1, \ldots Q_n).$$

As in (3.12), the meaning of the inequalities which bound Q is defined by the extension principle. In more concrete terms, these inequalities imply that Q is a fuzzy interval which may be expressed as

$$Q = (\ge f(Q_1, \ldots Q_n)) \cap (\le g(Q_1, \ldots Q_n)), \tag{3.14}$$

where the fuzzy s-number $\ge f(Q_1, \ldots Q_n)$ and the fuzzy z-number $\le g(Q_1, \ldots Q_n)$ (see Appendix) should be read as "at least $f(Q_1, \ldots Q_n)$" and "at most $g(Q_1, \ldots Q_n)$," respectively, and are the compositions† of the binary relations $\ge$ and $\le$ with $f(Q_1, \ldots Q_n)$ and $g(Q_1, \ldots Q_n)$. In terms of (3.14), then, the relation between C and Q may be expressed as:

$$\text{If } f(C_1, \ldots C_n) \le C \le g(C_1, \ldots C_n) \text{ then } Q = (\ge f(Q_1, \ldots Q_n)) \cap (\le g(Q_1, \ldots Q_n)). \tag{3.15}$$

An important special case of (3.12) and (3.15) is one where f and g are arithmetic or boolean expressions, as in

$$C = C_1 C_2 + C_3$$

and

$$C_1 + C_2 - 1 \le C \le C_1 \wedge C_2.$$

For these cases, the quantifier extension principle yields

$$Q = Q_1 \otimes Q_2 \oplus Q_3$$

and

$$Q = (\ge (Q_1 \oplus Q_2 \ominus 1)) \cap \le (Q_1 \oslash Q_2),$$

where Q, Q_1, Q_2 and Q_3 are fuzzy numbers, and $\otimes$, $\oplus$ and $\oslash$ are the product, sum and min in fuzzy arithmetic.‡

We are now in a position to apply the quantifier extension principle to the derivation of the intersection/product syllogism expressed by (3.7). Specifically, we note that

$$Q_1 \text{ A's are B's} \leftrightarrow Prop(B/A) \text{ is } Q_1 \tag{3.16}$$

$$Q_2(A \text{ and } B)\text{'s are C's} \leftrightarrow Prop(C/A \cap B) \text{ is } Q_2 \tag{3.17}$$

---

†The composition, RoS, of a binary relation R with a unary relation S is defined by $\mu_{RoS}(v) = \vee_u (\mu_R(v, u) \wedge \mu_S(u))$, $u \in U$, $v \in V$, where μ_R, μ_S, and μ_{RoS} are the membership functions of R, S and RoS, respectively, and $\vee_u$ denotes the supremum over U. Where no confusion can result, the symbol o may be suppressed.

‡Where typographical convenience is a significant consideration, a fuzzy version of an arithmetic operation * may be expressed more simply as (*).

and

$$Q \text{ } A\text{'s } are \text{ } (B \text{ and } C)\text{'s} \leftrightarrow Prop(B \cap C/A) \text{ is } Q, \tag{3.18}$$

where

$$Prop(B/A) = \frac{\Sigma Count(B \cap A)}{\Sigma Count(A)} \tag{3.19}$$

$$Prop(C/A \cap B) = \frac{\Sigma Count(A \cap B \cap C)}{\Sigma Count(A \cap B)} \tag{3.20}$$

$$Prop(B \cap C/A) = \frac{\Sigma Count(A \cap B \cap C)}{\Sigma Count(A)}. \tag{3.21}$$

From (3.19) to (3.21), it follows that the relative counts $C_1 \overset{\Delta}{=} Prop(B/A)$, $C_2 \overset{\Delta}{=} Prop(C/A \cap B)$ and $C \overset{\Delta}{=} Prop(B \cap C/A)$ satisfy the identity

$$Prop(B \cap C/A) = Prop(B/A)Prop(C/A \cap B). \tag{3.22}$$

and hence

$$C = C_1 C_2. \tag{3.23}$$

On the other hand, from (3.16) to (3.18), we see that Q_1, Q_2 and Q are the respective possibility distributions of C_1, C_2 and C. Consequently, from the quantifier extension principle applied to arithmetic expressions, it follows that the fuzzy quantifier Q is the fuzzy product of the fuzzy quantifiers Q_1 and Q_2, i.e.

$$Q = Q_1 \otimes Q_2, \tag{3.24}$$

which is what we wanted to establish.

As a corollary of (3.7), we can deduce at once the following syllogism:

$$Q_1 \text{ } A\text{'s } are \text{ } B\text{'s} \tag{3.25}$$

$$\underline{Q_2(A \text{ and } B)\text{'s } are \text{ } C\text{'s}}$$

$$(\geq (Q_1 \otimes Q_2)) \text{ } A\text{'s } are \text{ } C\text{'s},$$

where the quantifier $(\geq (Q_1 \otimes Q_2))$, which represents the composition of the binary relation $\geq$ with the unary relation $Q_1 \otimes Q_2$, should be read as $at \text{ } least(Q_1 \otimes Q_2)$. This syllogism is a consequence of (3.7) by virtue of the inequality

$$\Sigma Count(B \cap C) \leq \Sigma Count(C), \tag{3.26}$$

which holds for all fuzzy or nonfuzzy B and C. For, if we rewrite (3.7) in terms of proportions,

$$Prop(B/A) \text{ is } Q_1 \tag{3.27}$$

$$\underline{Prop(C/A \cap B) \text{ is } Q_2}$$

$$Prop(B \cap C/A) \text{ is } (Q_1 \otimes Q_2),$$

then from (3.26) it follows that

$$Prop(B \cap C/A) \text{ is } (Q_1 \otimes Q_2) \Rightarrow Prop(C/A) \text{ is } (\geq (Q_1 \otimes Q_2)). \tag{3.28}$$

Thus, based on (3.28), the syllogism (3.7) and its corollary (3.25) may be represented compactly in the form:

$$Q_1 \, A\text{'s are } B\text{'s} \tag{3.29}$$

$$\underline{Q_2(A \cap B)\text{'s are } C\text{'s}}$$

$$\underline{(Q_1 \otimes Q_2) \, A\text{'s are } (B \text{ and } C)\text{'s}}$$

$$(\geq (Q_1 \otimes Q_2)) \, A\text{'s are } C\text{'s}.$$

As an additional illustration of the quantifier extension principle, consider the inequality established in Section 2, namely,

$$O \vee (\Sigma Count(A) + \Sigma Count(B) - Count(U)) \leq \Sigma Count(A \cap B) \leq \Sigma Count(A) \wedge \Sigma Count(B). \tag{3.30}$$

Let Q, Q_1 and Q_2 be the fuzzy quantifiers which characterize $C \overset{\Delta}{=} \Sigma Count(A \cap B)$, $C_1 \overset{\Delta}{=} \Sigma Count(A)$, and $C_2 \overset{\Delta}{=} \Sigma Count(B)$, respectively. Then

$$O \oslash (Q_1 \oplus Q_2 \ominus 1) \leq Q \leq Q_1 \oslash Q_2. \tag{3.31}$$

where, as stated earlier, $\oplus$, $\otimes$, $\oslash$ and $\oslash$ are the operations of sum, product, min and max in fuzzy arithmetic. Consequently, as a special case of (3.31), we can assert that in the inference schema

$$most \ students \ are \ single \tag{3.32}$$

$$\underline{many \ students \ are \ male}$$

$$Q \ students \ are \ single \ and \ male,$$

Q is a fuzzy interval given by

$$Q = (\geq (O \oslash (most \oplus many \ominus 1))) \cap (\leq (most \oslash many)). \tag{3.33}$$

Monotonicity

In the theory of generalized quantifiers[7], a generalized quantifier Q is said to be *monotonic* if a true proposition of the form $p \overset{\Delta}{=} Q \, A\text{'s are } B\text{'s}$, where A and B are nonfuzzy sets, remains true when B is replaced by any superset (or any subset) of B. In this sense, *most* is a monotonic generalized quantifier under the assumption that B is replaced by a superset of B.

In the case of fuzzy quantifiers of the first or second kinds, a similar but more general definition which is valid for fuzzy sets may be formulated in terms of the membership function or, equivalently, the possibility distribution function of Q. More specifically:

A fuzzy quantifier Q is *monotone nondecreasing* (*nonincreasing*) if and only if the membership function of Q, μ_Q, is monotone nondecreasing (nonincreasing) over the domain of Q. From this definition, it follows at once that

$$Q \ is \ monotone \ nondecreasing \Leftrightarrow \geq Q = Q \tag{3.34}$$

$$Q \ is \ monotone \ nonincreasing \Leftrightarrow \leq Q = Q, \tag{3.35}$$

where, as stated earlier, $\geq Q$ and $\leq Q$ should be read as "at least Q" and "at most Q," respectively. Furthermore, from (2.7) it follows that, if $B \subset C$, then

$$Q \text{ is monotone nondecreasing} \Leftrightarrow \quad (3.36)$$

$$Prop(B/A) \text{ is } Q \Rightarrow Prop(C/A) \text{ is } Q$$

and

$$Q \text{ is monotone nonincreasing} \Leftrightarrow \quad (3.37)$$

$$Prop(C/A) \text{ is } Q \Leftrightarrow Prop(B/A) \text{ is } Q.$$

If Q is a fuzzy quantifier of the second kind, the *antonym* of Q, *ant* Q, is defined by [89]

$$\mu_{antQ}(u) = \mu_Q(1 - u), \quad u \in [0,1]. \quad (3.38)$$

Thus, if *few* is interpreted as the antonym of *most*, we have

$$\mu_{FEW}(u) = \mu_{MOST}(1 - u), \quad u \in [0,1]. \quad (3.39)$$

A graphic illustration of (3.39) is shown in Fig. 3.

An immediate consequence of (3.38) is the following:

If Q is monotone nondecreasing (e.g. most), then its antonym (e.g. few) is monotone nonincreasing.

We are now in a position to derive additional syllogisms for fuzzily-quantified propositions and, inter alia, establish the validity of the example given in the abstract, namely,

$$\text{most } U\text{'s are } A\text{'s} \quad (3.40)$$

$$\underline{\text{most } A\text{'s are } B\text{'s}}$$

$$\text{most}^2 \ U\text{'s are } B\text{'s,}$$

where by U's we mean the elements of the universe of discourse U, and *most* is assumed to be monotone nondecreasing.

Specifically, by identifying A in (3.25) with U in (3.40), B in (3.25) with A in (3.40), C in (3.25) with B in (3.40), and noting that

$$U \cap A = A,$$

we obtain as a special case of (3.25) the inference schema

$$\text{most } U\text{'s are } A\text{'s} \quad (3.41)$$

$$\underline{\text{most } A\text{'s are } B\text{'s}}$$

$$\underline{\geq 0 \, (\text{most} \otimes \text{most}) \ U\text{'s are } B\text{'s}}$$

$$\text{most}^2 \ U\text{'s are } B\text{'s,}$$

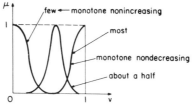

Fig. 3. The fuzzy quantifier *few* as an antonym of *most*.

where $most^2$ denotes $most \otimes most$. More generally, for any monotone nondecreasing fuzzy quantifiers Q_1 and Q_2, we can assert that

$$Q_1 \ U\text{'s are } A\text{'s} \tag{3.42}$$

$$\underline{Q_2 \ A\text{'s are } B\text{'s}}$$

$$(Q_1 \otimes Q_2) \ U\text{'s are } B\text{'s}.$$

If one starts with a rule of inference in predicate calculus, a natural question which arises is: how does the rule in question generalize to fuzzy quantifiers? An elementary example of an answer to a question of this kind is the following inference schema:

$$\frac{Q_1 \ A\text{'s are } B\text{'s}}{(\geq Q_2) \ A\text{'s are } B\text{'s}} \quad \text{if} \quad Q_2 \leq Q_1, \tag{3.43}$$

which is a generalization of the basic rule:

$$\frac{(\forall x)P(x)}{(\exists x)P(x)},$$

where P is a predicate. In (3.43), the inequality $Q_2 \leq Q_1$ signifies that, as a fuzzy number, Q_2 is less than or equal to the fuzzy number Q_1 (see Fig. 4).

To establish the validity of (3.43), we start with the inference rule

$$\frac{Q_1 \ A\text{'s are } B\text{'s}}{Q_2 \ A\text{'s are } B\text{'s}} \quad \text{if} \quad Q_1 \subset Q_2, \tag{3.44}$$

which is an immediate consequence of the entailment principle (3.9), since the conclusion in (3.44) is less specific than the premise. Then, (3.43) follows at once from (3.44) and the containment relation

$$Q_1 \leq Q_2 \Rightarrow Q_2 \subset (\geq Q_1) \tag{3.45}$$

which, in words, means that, if a fuzzy number Q_1 is less than or equal to Q_2, then, as a fuzzy set, Q_2 is contained in the fuzzy set which corresponds to the fuzzy number "at least Q_1."

In inferring from fuzzily-quantified propositions with negations, it is useful to have rules which concern the semantic equivalence or semantic entailment of such propositions. In what follows, we shall derive a few basic rules of this type.

The first rule, which applies to fuzzy quantifiers of the first kind, and to fuzzy quantifiers of the second kind when the base set, A, is nonfuzzy, is the following:

$$Q \ A\text{'s are } B\text{'s} \leftrightarrow (antQ) \ A\text{'s are not } B\text{'s}, \tag{3.46}$$

where $antQ$ denotes the antonym of Q (see (3.38)). For example,

$$most \ men \ are \ tall \leftrightarrow (ant \ most) \ men \ are \ not \ tall, \tag{3.47}$$

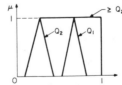

Fig. 4. The possibility distributions of Q_2 and Q_1, with $Q_2 \leq Q_1$.

and

$$most\ men\ are\ tall \leftrightarrow few\ men\ are\ not\ tall$$

if *few* is interpreted as the antonym of *most*.

To establish (3.46), we note that, in consequence of (3.6), we have

$$Q\ A\text{'s}\ are\ B\text{'s} \rightarrow \Pi_{\Sigma \text{Count}(B/A)} = Q. \tag{3.48}$$

The possibility assignment equation in (3.48) implies that the test score, τ_1, associated with the proposition "$Q A$'s are B's," is given by

$$\tau_1 = \mu_Q(\Sigma Count(B/A)). \tag{3.49}$$

where μ_Q is the membership function of Q.

Similarly, the test score associated with the proposition "$(antQ)\ A$'s *are not* B's," is given by

$$\tau_2 = \mu_{antQ}(\Sigma Count(\neg B/A)). \tag{3.50}$$

Thus, to demonstrate that the two propositions are semantically equivalent, it will suffice to show that $\tau_1 = \tau_2$.

To this end, we note that

$$\Sigma Count(\neg B/A) = \frac{\Sigma Count(A \cap (\neg B))}{\Sigma Count(A)} \tag{3.51}$$

$$= \frac{\Sigma_i \mu_A(u_i) \wedge (1 - \mu_B(u_i))}{\Sigma_i \mu_A(u_i)}$$

and, if A is nonfuzzy, the right-hand member of (3.51) may be written as:

$$\frac{\Sigma_i \mu_A(u_i) \wedge (1 - \mu_B(u_i))}{\Sigma_i \mu_A(u_i)} = 1 - \Sigma Count(B/A). \tag{3.52}$$

Now, from the definition of the antonym (3.38), it follows that

$$\mu_{antQ}(1 - \Sigma Count(B/A)) = \mu_Q(\Sigma Count(B/A)), \tag{3.53}$$

and hence that $\tau_1 = \tau_2$, which is what we had to establish.

In the more general case where A is fuzzy, the semantic equivalence (3.46) does not hold. Instead, the following semantic entailment may be asserted:

If Q is monotone nonincreasing, then

$$\frac{Q\ A\text{'s}\ are\ B\text{'s}}{(antQ)\ A\text{'s}\ are\ not\ B\text{'s}} \tag{3.54}$$

To validate (3.54), we note that in Section 2 we have established the inequality (see 2.19)

$$1 - \Sigma Count(\neg B/A) \leq \Sigma Count(B/A). \tag{3.55}$$

Now, if Q is monotone nonincreasing, then on application of μ_Q to both sides of (3.55) the inequality is reversed, yielding

$$\mu_Q(1 - \Sigma Count(\neg B/A)) \geq \mu_Q(\Sigma Count(B/A))$$

or, equivalently,

$$\mu_{antQ}(\Sigma Count(\neg B/A)) \geq \mu_Q(\Sigma Count(B/A)), \tag{3.56}$$

which establishes that the consequence in (3.54) is less specific than the premise and thus, by the entailment principle, is entailed by the premise.

In general, an application of the entailment principle for the purpose of demonstrating the validity of an inference rule reduces the computation of a fuzzy quantifier to the solution of a variational problem or, in discrete cases, to the solution of a nonlinear program. As an illustration, we shall consider the following inference schema

$$\frac{Q_1 \ A\text{'s are } B\text{'s}}{?Q \ A\text{'s are } (\text{very } B)\text{'s}}, \tag{3.57}$$

where $?Q$ is the quantifier to be computed; the base set A is nonfuzzy and the modifier *very* is an intensifier whose effect is assumed to be defined by [85]

$$\text{very } B = {}^2B, \tag{3.58}$$

where the left exponent 2 signifies that the membership function of ${}^2B$ is the square of that of B.† Since A is nonfuzzy, we can assume, without loss of generality, that $A = U$.

With this assumption, the translation of the premise in (3.57) is given by

$$Q_1 \ U\text{'s are } B\text{'s} \rightarrow \Pi_{\Sigma\text{Count}(B/U)} = Q_1 \tag{3.59}$$

while that of the consequent is

$$Q \ U\text{'s are } {}^2B\text{'s} \rightarrow \Pi_{\Sigma\text{Count}({}^2B/U)} = Q. \tag{3.60}$$

Let $\mu_1, \ldots \mu_n$ be the grades of membership of the points $u_1, \ldots u_n$ in B. Then, (3.59) and (3.60) imply that the overall test scores for the premise and the consequent are, respectively,

$$\tau_1 = \mu_{Q_1}\left(\frac{1}{N}\Sigma_i\mu_i\right) \tag{3.61}$$

$$\tau_2 = \mu_Q\left(\frac{1}{N}\Sigma_i\mu_i^2\right), \tag{3.62}$$

where $N = \Sigma\text{Count}(U)$.

The problem we are faced with at this point is the following. The premise, $Q_1 \ U$'s *are* B's, defines via (3.61) a fuzzy set, P_1, in the unit cube $C^N = \{\mu_1, \ldots \mu_N\}$ such that the grade of membership of the point $\mu = (\mu_1, \ldots \mu_N)$ in P_1 is τ_1. The mapping $C^N \rightarrow [0,1]$ which is defined by the sigma-count

$$\Sigma\text{Count}(\text{very } B/U) = \frac{1}{N}\Sigma_1\mu_i^2, \tag{3.63}$$

induces the fuzzy set, Q, in $[0,1]$ whose membership function, μ_Q, is what we wish to determine. For this purpose, we can invoke the extension principle, which reduces the determination of μ_Q to the solution of the following nonlinear program:

$$\mu_Q(v) = \max_\mu\left(\mu_{Q_1}\left(\frac{1}{N}\Sigma_i\mu_i\right)\right), \quad v \in [0,1], \tag{3.64}$$

subject to the constraint

$$v = \frac{1}{N}\Sigma_i\mu_i^2.$$

†In earlier papers, the meanings of B^2 and ${}^2B$ were interchanged.

As shown in [90], this nonlinear program has an explicit solution given by

$$\mu_Q(v) = \mu_{Q_1}(\sqrt{v}), \quad v \in [0,1],$$

which implies that

$$Q = Q_1^2 = Q_1 \otimes Q_1. \tag{3.65}$$

We are thus led to the inference schema

$$\frac{Q_1 \ A\text{'s are } B\text{'s}}{Q_1^2 \ A\text{'s are } (very \ B)\text{'s}} \tag{3.66}$$

and, more generally, for any positive m and nonfuzzy A,

$$\frac{Q_1 \ A\text{'s are } B\text{'s}}{Q_1^m \ A\text{'s are } (^m B)\text{'s}}, \tag{3.67}$$

and

$$\frac{Q_1 \ A\text{'s are } ^m B\text{'s}}{Q_1^{1/m} \ A\text{'s are } B\text{'s}} \tag{3.68}$$

where

$$\mu_{Q_1^m}(v) = \mu_{Q_1}(v^{1/m}), \quad v \in [0,1] \tag{3.69}$$

$$\mu_{Q^{1/m}}(v) = \mu_{Q_1}(v^m), \tag{3.70}$$

and

$$\mu_{m_B}(u) = (\mu_B(u))^m, \quad u \in U. \tag{3.71}$$

As a simple example, assume that the premise in (3.66) is the proposition "Most men over sixty are bald." Then, the inference schema represented by (3.66) yields the syllogism:

$$\frac{most \ men \ over \ sixty \ are \ bald}{most^2 \ men \ over \ sixty \ are \ very \ bald}. \tag{3.72}$$

It should be noted that an inference schema may be formed by a composition of two or more other inference schemas. For example, by combining (3.46) and (3.68), we are led to the following schema:

$$\frac{Q_1 A\text{'s are } (not \ very \ B)\text{'s}}{(ant \ Q_1)^{0.5} \ A\text{'s are } B\text{'s}}, \tag{3.73}$$

in which the base set A is assumed to be nonfuzzy. Thus, the syllogism

$$\frac{most \ Frenchmen \ are \ not \ very \ tall}{(ant \ most)^{0.5} \ Frenchmen \ are \ tall} \tag{3.74}$$

may be viewed as an instance of this schema (see Fig. 5).

In the foregoing discussion, we have attempted to show how the treatment of fuzzy quantifiers as fuzzy numbers makes it possible to derive a wide variety of inference schemas for fuzzily-quantified propositions. These propositions were assumed to have a simple structure like "$Q \ A$'s are B's," which made it unnecessary to employ the full power of test-score

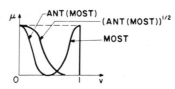

Fig. 5. The possibility distributions of the fuzzy quantifiers *most*, ant most and $(ant\ most)^{0.5}$.

semantics for representing their meaning. We shall turn our attention to more complex propositions in the following section and will illustrate by examples the application of test-score semantics to the representation of meaning of various types of fuzzily-quantified semantic entities.

4. MEANING REPRESENTATION BY TEST-SCORE SEMANTICS

As was stated in the Introduction, the process of meaning representation in test-score semantics involves three distinct phases: Phase I, in which an explanatory database frame, EDF, is constructed; Phase II, in which the constraints induced by the semantic entity are tested and scored; and Phase III, in which the partial test scores are aggregated into an overall test score which is a real number in the interval [0,1] or, more generally, a vector of such numbers.

In what follows, the process is illustrated by several examples in which Phase I and Phase II are merged into a single test which yields the overall test score. This test represents the meaning of the semantic entity and may be viewed as a description of the process by which the meaning of the semantic entity is composed from the meanings of the constituent relations in EDF.

In some cases, the test which represents the meaning of a given semantic entity may be expressed in a higher level language of logical forms. The use of such forms is illustrated in Examples 4 and 5.

When a semantic entity contains one or more fuzzy quantifiers, its meaning is generally easier to represent through the use of $\Sigma Counts$ than *FCounts*. However, there may be cases in which a $\Sigma Count$ may be a less appropriate representation of cardinality than an *FGCount* or an *FECount*. This is particularly true of cases in which the cardinality of a set is low, i.e. is a small fuzzy number like *several, few*, etc. Furthermore, what should be borne in mind is that $\Sigma Count$ is a summary of an *FGCount* and hence is intrinsically less informative.

In some of the following examples, we employ alternative counts for purposes of comparison: In others, only one type of count, usually the $\Sigma Count$, is used.

Example 1

$$SE \overset{\Delta}{=} several\ balls\ most\ of\ which\ are\ large.$$

For this semantic entity, we shall assume that *EDF* comprises the following relations:

$$EDF \overset{\Delta}{=} BALL\,[Identifier;\ Size] +$$

$$LARGE\,[Size;\ \mu] +$$

$$SEVERAL\,[Number;\ \mu] +$$

$$MOST\,[Proportion;\ \mu].$$

In this *EDF*, the first relation has n rows and is a list of the identifiers of balls and their respective sizes; in *LARGE*, μ is the degree to which a ball of size *Size* is large; in *SEVERAL*, μ is the degree to which *Number* fits the description *several*; and in *MOST*, μ is the degree to which *Proportion* fits the description *most*.

The test which yields the compatibility of *SE* with *ED* and thus defines the meaning of *SE* depends on the definition of fuzzy set cardinality. In particular, using the sigma-count, the test procedure may be stated as follows:

(1) Test the constraint induced by *SEVERAL*:

$$\tau_1 = {}_\mu SEVERAL[Number = n],$$

which means that the value of *Number* is set to *n* and the value of μ is read, yielding the test score τ_1 for the constraint in question.

(2) Find the size of each ball in *BALL*:

$$Size_i = {}_{Size}BALL[Identifier = Identifier_i],$$

$$i = 1, \ldots n.$$

(3) Test the constraint induced by *LARGE* for each ball in *BALL*:

$$\mu_{LB}(i) = {}_\mu LARGE[Size = Size_i].$$

(4) Find the sigma-count of large balls in *BALL*:

$$\Sigma Count(LB) = \Sigma_i \mu_{LB}(i).$$

(5) Find the proportion of large balls in *BALL*:

$$PLB = \frac{1}{n}\Sigma_i \mu_{LB}(i).$$

(6) Test the constraint induced by *MOST*:

$$\tau_2 = {}_\mu MOST[Proportion = PLB].$$

(7) Aggregate the partial test scores:

$$\tau = \tau_1 \wedge \tau_2,$$

where τ is the overall test score. The use of the min operator to aggregate τ_1 and τ_2 implies that we interpret the implicit conjunction in *SE* as the cartesian product of the conjuncts.

The use of fuzzy cardinality affects the way in which τ_2 is computed. Specifically, the employment of *FGCount* leads to:

$$\tau_2 = sup_i(FGCount(LB) \cap nMOST),$$

which expressed in terms of the membership functions of *FGCount* (*LB*) and *MOST* may be written as

$$\tau_2 = sup_i\left(\mu_{FGCount(LB)}(i) \wedge \mu_{MOST}\left(\frac{1}{n}\right)\right).$$

The rest of the test procedure is unchanged.

Example 2

$$SE \overset{\Delta}{=} several\ large\ balls.$$

In this case, we assume that the *EDF* is the same as in Example 1, with *MOST* deleted.

As is pointed out in [93], the semantic entity in question may be interpreted in different ways. In particular, using the so-called compartmentalized interpretation in which the constraints induced by *SMALL* and *SEVERAL* are tested separately, the test procedure employing the *FGCount* may be stated as follows:

(1) Test the constraint induced by *SEVERAL*:

$$\tau_1 \stackrel{\Delta}{=} {}_\mu SEVERAL[Number = n].$$

(2) Find the size of the smallest ball:

$$SSB \stackrel{\Delta}{=} {}_{Size}\min{}_{Size}(BALL),$$

in which the right-hand member signifies that the smallest entry in the column *Size* of the relation *BALL* is read and assigned to the variable *SSB* (Smallest Size Ball).

(3) Test the constraint induced by *LARGE* by finding the degree to which the smallest ball is large:

$$\tau_2 \stackrel{\Delta}{=} {}_\mu LARGE[Size = SSB].$$

(4) Aggregate the test scores:

$$\tau = \tau_1 \wedge \tau_2.$$

Example 3

$p \stackrel{\Delta}{=}$ *Hans has many acquaintances* and *a few close friends most of whom are highly intelligent.*

Assume that the *EDF* comprises the following relations:

$$ACQUAINTANCE\,[Name\,1;\,Name\,2;\,\mu] +$$

$$FRIEND\,[Name\,1;\,Name\,2;\,\mu] +$$

$$INTELLIGENT\,[Name;\,\mu] +$$

$$MANY\,[Number;\,\mu] +$$

$$FEW\,[Number;\,\mu] +$$

$$MOST\,[Proportion;\,\mu].$$

In *ACQUAINTANCE*, μ is the degree to which *Name* 1 is an acquaintance of *Name* 2; in *FRIEND*, μ is the degree to which *Name* 1 is a friend of *Name* 2; in *INTELLIGENT*, μ is the degree to which *Name* is intelligent; *MANY* and *FEW* are fuzzy quantifiers of the first kind, and *MOST* is a fuzzy quantifier of the second kind.

The test procedure may be stated as follows:
(1) Find the fuzzy set of Hans' acquaintances:

$$HA \stackrel{\Delta}{=} {}_{Name\,1\times\mu}ACQUAINTANCE[Name\,2 = Hans],$$

which means that in each row in which *Name* 2 is Hans, we read *Name* 1 and μ and form the fuzzy set *HA*.

(2) Count the number of Hans' acquaintances:

$$CHA \stackrel{\Delta}{=} \Sigma\, Count(HA).$$

(3) Find the test score for the constraint induced by *MANY*:

$$\tau_1 = {}_\mu MANY[Name\ 1 = CHA].$$

(4) Find the fuzzy set of friends of Hans:

$$FH \stackrel{\Delta}{=} {}_{Name\ 1 \times \mu}FRIEND[Name\ 2 = Hans].$$

(5) Intensify *FH* to account for *close* [89]:

$$CFH \stackrel{\Delta}{=} {}^2FH.$$

(6) Determine the count of close friends of Hans:

$$CCFH \stackrel{\Delta}{=} \Sigma Count({}^2FH).$$

(7) Find the test score for the constraint induced by *FEW*:

$$\tau_2 \stackrel{\Delta}{=} {}_\mu FEW[Number = CCFH].$$

(8) Intensify *INTELLIGENT* to account for *highly*. (We assume that this is accomplished by raising *INTELLIGENT* to the third power.)

$$HIGHLY.INTELLIGENT = {}^3INTELLIGENT.$$

(9) Find the fuzzy set of close friends of Hans who are highly intelligent:

$$CFH.HI \stackrel{\Delta}{=} CFH \cap {}^3INTELLIGENT.$$

(10) Determine the count of close friends of Hans who are highly intelligent:

$$CCFH.HI \stackrel{\Delta}{=} \Sigma Count(CFH \cap {}^3INTELLIGENT).$$

(11) Find the proportion of those who are highly intelligent among the close friends of Hans:

$$\gamma \stackrel{\Delta}{=} \frac{\Sigma Count(CFH \cap {}^3INTELLIGENT)}{\Sigma Count(CFH)}.$$

(12) Find the test score for the constraint induced by *MOST*:

$$\tau_3 \stackrel{\Delta}{=} {}_\mu MOST[Proportion = \gamma].$$

(13) Aggregate the partial test scores:

$$\tau = \tau_1 \wedge \tau_2 \wedge \tau_3.$$

The test described above may be expressed more concisely as a logical form which is semantically equivalent to *p*. The logical form may be expressed as follows:

$$p \leftrightarrow Count({}_{Name\ 1 \times \mu}ACQUAINTANCE[Name\ 2 = Hans])\ is\ MANY \wedge$$

$$Count({}_{Name\ 1 \times \mu}{}^2FRIEND[Name\ 2 = Hans])\ is\ FEW \wedge$$

$$Prop({}^3INTELLIGENT|_{Name\ 1 \times \mu}{}^2FRIEND[Name\ 2 = Hans])\ is\ MOST$$

where $\wedge$ denotes the conjunction.

Example 4

Consider the proposition

$$p \overset{\Delta}{=} \text{Over the past few years Nick earned far more than most of his close friends.}$$

In this case, we shall assume that *EDF* consists of the following relations:

$$EDF \overset{\Delta}{=} INCOME[Name; Amount; Year] +$$

$$FRIEND[Name; \mu] +$$

$$FEW[Number; \mu] +$$

$$FAR.MORE[Income\ 1; Income\ 2; \mu] +$$

$$MOST[Proportion; \mu].$$

Using the sigma-count, the test procedure may be described as follows:

(1) Find Nick's income in $Year_i$, $i = 1, 2, \ldots$ counting backward from present:

$$IN_i \overset{\Delta}{=} {}_{Amount}INCOME[Name = Nick; Year = Year_i].$$

(2) Test the constraint induced by *FEW*:

$$\mu_i \overset{\Delta}{=} {}_\mu FEW[Year = Year_i].$$

(3) Compute Nick's total income during the past few years:

$$TIN = \Sigma_i \mu_i IN_i,$$

in which the μ_i play the role of weighting coefficients.

(4) Compute the total income of each $Name_j$ (other than Nick) during the past several years:

$$TIName_j = \Sigma_i \mu_i IName_{ji},$$

where $IName_{ji}$ is the income of $Name_j$ in $Year_i$.

(5) Find the fuzzy set of individuals in relation to whom Nick earned far more. The grade of membership of $Name_j$ in this set is given by:

$$\mu_{FM}(Name_j) = {}_\mu FAR.MORE[Income\ 1 = TIN; Income\ 2 = TIName_j].$$

(6) Find the fuzzy set of close friends of Nick by intensifying the relation *FRIEND*:

$$CF = {}^2FRIEND,$$

which implies that

$$\mu_{CF}(Name_j) = ({}_\mu FRIEND[Name = Name_j])^2.$$

(7) Using the sigma-count, count the number of close friends of Nick:

$$\Sigma Count(CF) = \Sigma_j \mu_{FRIEND}^2(Name_j).$$

(8) Find the intersection of *FM* with *CF*. The grade of membership of $Name_j$ in the

intersection is given by

$$\mu_{FM \cap CF}(Name_j) = \mu_{FM}(Name_j) \wedge \mu_{CF}(Name_j).$$

(9) Compute the sigma-count of $FM \cap CF$:

$$\Sigma Count(FM \cap CF) = \Sigma_j \mu_{FM}(Name_j) \wedge \mu_{CF}(Name_j).$$

(10) Compute the proportion of individuals in FM who are in CF:

$$\rho \triangleq \frac{\Sigma Count(FM \cap CF)}{\Sigma Count(CF)}.$$

(11) Test the constraint induced by $MOST$:

$$\tau = {}_\mu MOST[Proportion = \rho],$$

which expresses the overall test score and thus represents the desired compatibility of ρ with the explanatory database.

For the proposition under consideration, the logical form has a more complex structure than in Example 3. Specifically, we have

$$Prop((\Sigma_j \mu_j / Name_j)/^2 FRIEND[Name\,2 = Nick]) \text{ is } MOST$$

where

$$\mu_j = {}_\mu FAR.MORE[Income\,1 = TIN; Income\,2 = TIName_j]$$

where $Name_j \neq Nick$ and

$$TIN = \Sigma_i \mu_{FEW}(i)_{Amount} INCOME[Name = Nick; Year = Year_i]$$

and

$$TIName_j = \Sigma_i \mu_{FEW}(i)_{Amount} INCOME[Name = Name_j; Year = Year_i].$$

Example 5

$$p \triangleq \text{They like each other.}$$

In this case there is an implicit fuzzy quantifier in p which reflects the understanding that not all members of the group referred to as *they* must necessarily like each other.

Since the fuzzy quantifier in p is implicit, it may be interpreted in many different ways. The test described below represents one such interpretation and involves, in effect, the use of an *FCount*.

Specifically, we associate with p the *EDF*

$$EDF \triangleq THEY[Name] +$$

$$LIKE[Name\,1; Name\,2; \mu] +$$

$$ALMOST.ALL[Proportion; \mu],$$

in which *THEY* is the list of names of members of the group to which p refers; *LIKE* is a fuzzy relation in which μ is the degree to which *Name* 1 likes *Name* 2; and *ALMOST.ALL* is a fuzzy quantifier in which μ is the degree to which a numerical value of *Proportion* fits a subjective perception of the meaning of *almost all*.

Let μ_{ij} be the degree to which $Name_i$ likes $Name_j$, $i \neq j$. If there are n names in *THEY*, then there are $(n^2 - n)\mu_{ij}$'s in *LIKE* with $i \neq j$. Denote the relation *LIKE* without its diagonal elements by *LIKE**.

The test procedure which yields the overall test score τ may be described as follows:

(1) Count the number of members in *THEY*:

$$n \overset{\Delta}{=} Count(THEY).$$

(2) Compute the *FGCount* of *LIKE**:

$$C \overset{\Delta}{=} FGCount(LIKE^*).$$

Note that in view of (2.6), C may be obtained by sorting the elements of *LIKE** in descending order, which yields $LIKE^* \downarrow$. Thus,

$$FGCount(LIKE^*) = NLIKE^* \downarrow.$$

(3) Compute the height (i.e. the maximum value) of the intersection of C and the fuzzy number $(n^2 - n)ALMOST.ALL$:

$$\tau = sup(FGCount(LIKE^*) \cap (n^2 - n)ALMOST.ALL).$$

The result, as shown in Fig. 6, is the overall test score.

The last two examples in this Section illustrate the application of test-score semantics to question-answering. The basic idea behind this application is the following.

Suppose that the answer to a question, q, is to be deduced from a knowledge base which consists of a collection of propositions:

$$KB = \{p_1, \ldots p_n\}. \tag{4.1}$$

Furthermore, assume that the p_i are noninteractive and that each p_i induces a possibility distribution, Π^i, which is characterized by its possibility distribution function, π^i, over a collection of base variables $X = \{X_1, \ldots X_m\}$. This implies (a) that p_i, $i = 1, \ldots, n$, translates into the possibility assignment equation

$$p_i \rightarrow \Pi^i_{(X_1, \ldots X_m)} = F_i,$$

where F_i is a fuzzy subset of U, the cartesian product of the domains of $X_1, \ldots X_m$, i.e.

$$U = U_1 \times \cdots \times U_m,$$

in which U_i is the domain of X_i; and (b) that the collection KB induces a combined possibility distribution Π whose possibility distribution function is given by

$$\pi_{(X_1, \ldots X_m)} = \pi^1_{(X_1, \ldots X_m)} \wedge \cdots \wedge \pi^n_{(X_1, \ldots X_m)}. \tag{4.2}$$

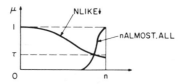

Fig. 6. Computation of the test score for "They like each other."

In test-score semantics, the translation of a question is a procedure which expresses the answer to the question as a function of the explanatory database. In terms of the framework described above, this means that the answer is expressed as a function of $(X_1, \ldots X_m)$, i.e.

$$ans(q) = f(X_1, \ldots X_m).$$

Thus, given the possibility distribution Π over U and the function f, we can obtain the possibility distribution of $ans(q)$ by using the extension principle. In more specific terms, this reduces to the solution of the nonlinear program:

$$\mu_{ans(q)}(v) = \max_{(u_1, \ldots u_m)} \pi_{(X_1, \ldots X_m)}(u_1, \ldots u_m) \tag{4.3}$$

subject to

$$v = f(u_1, \ldots, u_m),$$

where u_i denotes the generic value of X_i and $u_i \in U_i$, $i = 1, \ldots, m$. An example of such a program which we have encountered earlier is provided by (3.64).

In many cases, the nonlinear program (4.3) has special features which reduce it to a simpler problem which can be solved by elementary means. This is what happens in the following examples.

Example 6

$p_1 \overset{\Delta}{=}$ *There are about twenty graduate students in his class.*

$p_2 \overset{\Delta}{=}$ *There are a few more undergraduate students than graduate students in his class.*

$q \overset{\Delta}{=}$ *How many undergraduate students are there in his class?*

Let C_g, C_u and D denote, respectively, the number of graduate students, the number of undergraduate students, and the difference between the two counts, so that

$$C_u = C_g + D.$$

Applying the quantifier extension principle to this relation, we obtain

$$ans(q) = about\ 20 \oplus few,$$

where $ans(q)$, *about* 20 and *few* are fuzzy numbers which represent the possibility distributions of C_u, C_g and D, respectively. Using the addition rule for fuzzy numbers (see Appendix), the membership function of $ans(q)$ may be expressed more explicitly as

$$\mu_{ans(q)}(v) = sup_u(\mu_{ABOUT20}(u) \wedge \mu_{FEW}(v - u)).$$

Example 7

$p \overset{\Delta}{=}$ *Brian is much taller than most of his close friends*

$q \overset{\Delta}{=}$ *How tall is Brian?*

Following the approach described earlier, we shall (a) determine the possibility distribution induced by p through the use of test-score semantics; (b) express the answer to q as a function defined on the domain of the possibility distribution; and (c) compute the possibility distribution of the answer.

To represent the meaning of p, we assume, as in Examples 4 and 5, that the *EDF* comprises the following relations:

$$EDF \overset{\Delta}{=} POPULATION[Name;\ Height] +$$

$$MUCH.TALLER[Height\ 1;\ Height\ 2;\ \mu] +$$

$$MOST[Proportion;\ \mu].$$

For this *EDF*, the test procedure may be described as follows:
(1) Determine the height of each *Name*$_i$, $i = 1, \ldots, n$, in *POPULATION*:

$$HN_i = {}_{Height}POPULATION[Name = Name_i],$$

and, in particular,

$$HB \stackrel{\Delta}{=} {}_{Height}POPULATION[Name = Brian].$$

(2) Determine the degree to which Brian is much taller than *Name*$_i$:

$$\mu_{BMT}(Name_i) \stackrel{\Delta}{=} {}_{\mu}MUCH.TALLER[Height\ 1 = HB;\ Height\ 2 = HN_i].$$

(3) Form the fuzzy set of members of *POPULATION* in relation to whom Brian is much taller:

$$BMT \stackrel{\Delta}{=} \Sigma_i \mu_{BMT}(Name_i)/Name_i, \quad Name_i \neq Brian.$$

(4) Determine the fuzzy set of close friend of Brian by intensifying *FRIEND*:

$$CFB = {}^2({}_{\mu \times Name\ 1}FRIEND[Name\ 2 = Brian])$$

which implies that

$$\mu_{CFB}(Name_i) = ({}_{\mu}FRIEND[Name\ 1 = Name_i: Name\ 2 = Brian])^2, \quad Name_i \neq Brian.$$

(5) Find the proportion of *BMT*'s in *CFB*'s:

$$\Sigma Count(BMT/CFB) = \frac{\Sigma_i \mu_{BMT}(Name_i) \wedge \mu_{CFB}(Name_i)}{\Sigma_i \mu_{CFB}(Name_i)}.$$

(6) Find the test score for the constraint induced by the fuzzy quantifier *most*:

$$\tau = {}_{\mu}MOST[Proportion = \Sigma Count(BMT/CFB)].$$

This test score represents the overall test score for the test which represents the meaning of *p*. Expressed as a logical form, the test may be represented more compactly as:

$$Prop(BMT/^2({}_{\mu \times Name\ 1}FRIEND[Name\ 2 = Brian])\ is\ MOST,$$

where the fuzzy set *BMT* is defined in Steps 2 and 3.

To place in evidence the variables which are constrained by *p*, it is expedient to rewrite the expression for τ as follows:

$$\tau = \mu_{MOST}\left(\frac{\Sigma_i \mu_{MT}(h_B, h_i) \wedge \mu_{FB}{}^2(Name_i)}{\Sigma_i \mu_{FB}{}^2(Name_i)}\right),$$

in which h_B is the height of Brian; h_i is the height of *Name*$_i$; $\mu_{FB}(Name_i)$ is the degree to which *Name*$_i$ is Brian's friend; $\mu_{MT}(h_B, h_i)$ is the degree to which Brian is much taller than *Name*$_i$; and μ_{MOST} is the membership function of the quantifier *most*.

Now the variables $X_1, \ldots X_m$ are those entries in the relations in the explanatory database which are the arguments of τ, with the value of τ representing their joint possibility $\pi_{(X_1, \ldots X_m)}$.

In the example under consideration, these variables are the values of $h_i \stackrel{\Delta}{=} Height(Name_i)$,

$i = 1, \ldots n$; the values of $\mu_{MT}(h_B, h_i)$; the values of $\mu_{FB}(Name_i)$; and the values of $\mu_{MOST}(Pro$-$portion)$, where $Proportion$ is the value of the argument of μ_{MOST} in the expression for τ.

Since we are interested only in the height of Brian, it is convenient to let $X_1 \overset{\Delta}{=} h_B = Height(Brian)$. With this understanding, the possibility distribution function of $Height(Brian)$ given the values of $X_2, \ldots X_m$ may be expressed as

$$Poss\{Height(Brian) = u | X_2, \ldots X_m\} = \mu_{MOST} \left(\frac{\Sigma_i \mu_{MT}(u, h_i) \wedge \mu_{FB}^2(Name_i)}{\Sigma_i \mu_{FB}^2(Name_i)} \right),$$

where the range of the index i in Σ_i excludes $Name_i = Brian$. Correspondingly, the un-conditional possibility distribution function of $Height(Brian)$ is given by the projection of the possibility distribution $\Pi_{(X_1, \ldots X_m)}$ on the domain of X_1. The expression for the projection is given by the supremum of the possibility distribution function of $(X_1, \ldots X_m)$ over all variables other than X_1 [89, 90]. Thus

$$Poss\{Height(Brian) = u\} = sup_{(X_2, \ldots X_m)} \mu_{MOST} \left(\frac{\Sigma_i \mu_{MOST}(u, h_i) \wedge \mu_{FB}^2(Name_i)}{\Sigma_i \mu_{FB}^2(Name_i)} \right).$$

Example 8

$p_1 \overset{\Delta}{=} Most\ Frenchmen\ are\ not\ tall$

$p_2 \overset{\Delta}{=} Most\ Frenchmen\ are\ not\ short$

$q \overset{\Delta}{=} What\ is\ the\ average\ height\ of\ a\ Frenchman?$

Because of the simplicity of p_1 and p_2, the constraints induced by the premises may be found directly. Specifically, using (3.46), p_1 and p_2 may be replaced by the semantically equivalent premises

$p_i' \overset{\Delta}{=} ant\ most\ Frenchmen\ are\ tall$

$p_i' \overset{\Delta}{=} ant\ most\ Frenchmen\ are\ short.$

To formulate the constraints induced by these premises, let $h_1, \ldots h_n$ denote the heights of $Frenchman_1, \ldots, Frenchman_n$, respectively. Then, the test scores associated with the constraints in question may be expressed as

$$\tau_1 = \mu_{ANT\ MOST} \left(\frac{1}{n} \Sigma_i \mu_{TALL}(h_i) \right)$$

and

$$\tau_2 = \mu_{ANT\ MOST} \left(\frac{1}{n} \Sigma_i \mu_{SHORT}(h_i) \right),$$

where

$$\mu_{ANT\ MOST}(u) = \mu_{MOST}(1 - u), \quad u \in [0,1],$$

and μ_{TALL} and μ_{SHORT} are the membership functions of $TALL$ and $SHORT$, respectively. Correspondingly, the overall test score may be expressed as

$$\tau = \tau_1 \wedge \tau_2.$$

Now, the average height of a Frenchman and hence the answer to the question is given by

$$ans(q) = \frac{1}{n} \Sigma_i h_i.$$

Consequently, the possibility distribution of $ans(q)$ is given by the solution of the nonlinear program

$$\mu_{ans(q)}(h) = \max_{h_1, \ldots h_n} (\tau)$$

subject to

$$h = \frac{1}{n} \Sigma_i h_i.$$

Alternatively, a simpler but less informative answer may be formulated by forming the intersection of the possibility distributions of $ans(q)$ which are induced separately by p_1' and p_2'. More specifically, let $\Pi_{ans(q)|p_1'}$, $\Pi_{ans(q)|p_2'}$, $\Pi_{ans(q)|p_1' \wedge p_2'}$ be the possibility distributions of $ans(q)$ which are induced by p_1', p_2', and the conjunction of p_1' and p_2', respectively. Then, by using the minimax inequality[84], it can readily be shown that

$$\Pi_{ans(q)|p_1'} \cap \Pi_{ans(q)|p_2'} \supset \Pi_{ans(q)|p_1' \wedge p_2'}$$

and hence we can invoke the entailment principle to validate the intersection in question as the possibility distribution of $ans(q)$. For the example under consideration, the possibility distribution is readily found to be given by

$$Poss\{ans(q) = h\} = \mu_{ANT\,MOST}(\mu_{TALL}(h)) \wedge \mu_{ANT\,MOST}(\mu_{SHORT}(h)).$$

CONCLUDING REMARK

As was stated in the Introduction, the basic idea underlying our approach to fuzzy quantifiers is that such quantifiers may be interpreted as fuzzy numbers—a viewpoint which makes it possible to manipulate them through the use of fuzzy arithmetic and, more generally, fuzzy logic.

By applying test-score semantics to the translation of fuzzily-quantified possibilities, a method is provided for inference from knowledge bases which contain such propositions—as most real-world knowledge bases do. The examples presented in this section are intended to illustrate the translation and inference techniques which form the central part of our approach. There are many computational issues, however, which are not addressed by these examples. One such issue is the solution of nonlinear programs to which the problem of inference is reduced by the application of the extension principle. What is needed for this purpose are computationally efficient techniques which are capable of taking advantage of the tolerance for imprecision which is intrinsic in inference from natural language knowledge bases.

REFERENCES

1. E. W. Adams, The logic of "almost all." *J. Philos. Logic* 3, 3–17 (1974).
2. E. W. Adams and H. F. Levine, On the uncertainties transmitted from premises to conclusions in deductive inferences. *Synthese* 30, 429–460 (1975).
3. E. W. Adams and I. F. Carlstrom, Representing approximate ordering and equivalence relations. *J. Math. Psych.* 19, 182–207 (1979).
4. E. W. Adams, Improbability transmissibility and marginal essentialness of premises in inferences involving indicative conditionals. *J. Philos. Logic* 10, 149–177 (1981).
5. A. Barr and E. W. Feigenbaum, *The Handbook of Artificial Intelligence*, Vols. 1–3. Kaufmann, Los Altos (1982).
6. R. Bartsch and T. Vennemann, *Semantic Structures*. Attenaum Verlag, Frankfurt (1972).
7. J. Barwise and R. Cooper, Generalized quantifiers and natural language. *Linguistics and Philos.* 4, 159–219 (1981).
8. R. E. Bellmann and L. A. Zadeh, Local and fuzzy logics. In *Modern Uses of Multiple-Valued Logic* (Edited by G. Epstein), pp. 103–165. Reidel, Dordrecht (1977).
9. N. Blanchard, Theories cardinales et ordinales des ensembles flou: les multiensembles. Thesis, University of Claude Bernard, Lyon (1981).
10. I. F. Carlstrom, Truth and entailment for a vague quantifier. *Synthese* 30, 461–495 (1975).
11. R. Carnap, *Meaning and Necessity*. University of Chicago Press (1952).
12. W. S. Cooper, *Logical Linguistics*. Reidel, Dordrecht (1978).
13. M. J. Cresswell, *Logic and Languages*. Methuen, London (1973).
14. S. Cushing, The formal semantics of quantification. In *Indiana Univ. Linguistics Club* (1977).
15. S. Cushing, *Quantifier Meanings—A Study in the Dimensions of Semantic Competence*. North-Holland, Amsterdam (1982).

16. F. J. Damerau, On fuzzy adjectives. *Memo. RC* 5340, *IBM Research Laboratory*, Yorktown Heights, New York (1975).
17. A. DeLuca and S. Termini, A definition of non-probabilistic entropy in the setting of fuzzy sets theory. *Inform. Control* **20**, 301–312 (1972).
18. D. R. Dowty *et al.*, *Introduction to Montague Semantics*. Reidel, Dordrecht (1981).
19. D. Dubois, A new definition of fuzzy cardinality of finite fuzzy sets. *BUSEFAL* **8**, 65–67 (1981).
20. D. Dubois and H. Prade, *Fuzzy Sets and Systems: Theory and Applications*. Academic Press, New York (1980).
21. D. Dubois and H. Prade, Operations on fuzzy numbers. *Int. J. Systems Sci.* **9**, 613–626 (1978).
22. D. Dubois and H. Prade, Addition of interactive fuzzy numbers. *IEEE Trans. on Automatic Control* **26**, 926–936 (1981).
23. D. Dubois, Proprietes de la cardinalite floue d'un ensemble flou fini. *BUSEFAL* **8**, 11–12 (1981).
24. R. O. Duda, J. Gaschnig and P. E. Hart, Model design in the PROSPECTOR consultation system for mineral exploration. In *Expert Systems in the Micro-Electronic Age* (Edited by D. Michie), pp. 153–167. Edinburgh University Press, Edinburgh (1979).
25. H.-D. Ebbinghaus, Uber fur-fast-alle quantoren. *Archiv fur Math. Logik und Grundlageusforschung* **12**, 39–53 (1969).
26. B. R. Gaines and L. J. Kohout, The fuzzy decade: a bibliography of fuzzy systems and closely related topics. *Int. J. Man-Machine Studies* **9**, 1–68 (1977).
27. B. R. Gaines, Logical foundations for database systems. *Int. J. Man-Machine Studies* **11**, 481–500 (1979).
28. J. A. Goguen, The logic of inexact concepts. *Synthese* **19**, 325–373 (1969).
29. H. M. Hersh and A. Caramazza, A fuzzy set approach to modifiers and vagueness in natural language. *J. Exper. Psych.* **105**, 254–276 (1976).
30. R. Hilpinen, Approximate truth and truthlikeness. In *Proc. Conf. Formal Methods in the Methodology of the Empirical Sciences, Warsaw, 1974* (Edited by M. Przelecki and R. Wojcicki). Reidel, Dordrecht (1976).
31. J. K. Hintikka, *Logic, Language-Games, and Information: Kantian Themes in the Philosophy of Logic*. Oxford University Press, Oxford (1973).
33. J. Hobbs, Making computational sense of Montague's intensional logic. *Artificial Intell.* **9**, 287–306 (1978).
34. T. R. Hofmann, Qualitative terms for quantity, In *Proc. 6th European Meeting on Cybernetics and Systems Research* (Edited by R. Trappl). North-Holland, Amsterdam (1982).
35. D. N. Hoover, Probability logic. *Annals Math. Logic* **14**, 287–313 (1978).
36. M. Ishizuka, K. S. Fu and J. T. P. Yao, A rule-based inference with fuzzy set for structural damage assessment. In *Fuzzy Information and Decision Processes* (Edited by M. Gupta and E. Sanchez). North-Holland, Amsterdam (1982).
37. P. N. Johnson-Laird, Procedural semantics. *Cognition* **5**, 189–214 (1977).
38. A. Kaufmann, La theorie des numbres hybrides. *BUSEFAL* **8**, 105–113 (1981).
39. E. L. Keenan, Quantifier structures in English. *Foundations of Language* **7**, 255–336 (1971).
40. E. P. Klement, W. Schwyhla and R. Lowen, Fuzzy probability measures. *Fuzzy Sets and Systems* **5**, 83–108 (1981).
41. E. P. Klement, Operations on fuzzy sets and fuzzy numbers related to triangular norms. *Proc. 11th Conf. Multiple-Valued Logic*, Univ. of Oklahoma, Norman, pp. 218–225, 1981.
42. E. P. Klement, An axiomatic theory of operations on fuzzy sets. Institut fur Mathematik, Johannes Kepler Universitat Linz, Institutsbericht 159 (1981).
43. G. Lakoff, Hedges: A study in meaning criteria and the logic of fuzzy concepts. *J. Phil. Logic* **2**, 458–508 (1973) Also in *Contemporary Research in Philosophical Logic and Linguistic Semantics* (Edited by D. Jockney, W. Harper and R. Freed), pp. 221–271. Reidel, Dordrecht (1973).
44. K. Lambert and B. C. van Fraassen, Meaning relations, possible objects and possible worlds. *Philos. Problems in Logic* 1–19 (1970).
45. E. H. Mamdani and B. R. Gaines, *Fuzzy Reasoning and its Applications*. Academic Press, London (1981).
46. J. McCarthy, Circumscription: A non-monotonic inference rule. *Artificial Intell.* **13**, 27–40 (1980).
47. J. D. McCawley, *Everything that Linguists have Always Wanted to Know about Logic*. University of Chicago Press, Chicago (1981).
48. D. V. McDermott and J. Doyle, Non-monotonic logic. I. *Artificial Intell.* **13**, 41–72 (1980).
49. D. V. McDermott, Non-monotonic logic II: non-monotonic modal theories. *J. Assoc. Comp. Mach.* **29**, 33–57 (1982).
50. J. S. Mill, *A System of Logic*. Harper, New York (1895).
51. D. Miller, Popper's qualitative theory of verisimilitude. *Brit. J. Philos. Sci.* **25**, 166–177 (1974).
52. G. A. Miller and P. N. Johnson-Laird, *Language and Perception*. Harvard University Press, Cambridge (1976).
53. M. Mizumoto, S. Fukame and K. Tanaka, Fuzzy reasoning Methods by Zadeh and Mamdani, and improved methods. *Proc. 3rd Workshop on Fuzzy Reasoning*, Queen Mary College, London, 1978.
54. M. Mizumoto and K. Tanaka, Some properties of fuzzy numbers. In *Advances in Fuzzy Set Theory and Applications* (Edited by M. M. Gupta, R. K. Ragade and R. R. Yager), pp. 153–164. North-Holland, Amsterdam (1979).
55. M. Mizumoto, M. Umano and K. Tanaka, Implementation of a fuzzy-set-theoretic data structure system. *3rd Int. Conf. Very Large Data Bases*, Tokyo, 1977.
56. G. C. Moisil, *Lectures on the Logic of Fuzzy Reasoning*. Scientific Editions, Bucarest (1975).
57. R. Montague, *Formal Philosophy*. In: *Selected Papers* (Edited by R. Thomason). Yale University Press, New Haven (1974).
58. R. E. Moore, *Interval Analysis*. Prentice-Hall, Englewood Cliffs (1966).
59. C. F. Morgenstern, The measure quantifier. *J. Symbolic Logic* **44**, 103–108 (1979).
60. A. Mostowski, On a generalization of quantifiers. *Fund. Math.* **44**, 17–36 (1957).
61. A. S. Naranyani, Methods of modeling incompleteness of data in knowledge bases. In *Knowledge Representation and Modeling of Processes of Understanding*, pp. 153–162. Academy of Sciences of U.S.S.R., Novosibirsk (1980).
62. H. T. Nguyen, Toward a calculus of the mathematical notion of possibility. In *Advances in Fuzzy Set Theory and Applications* (Edited by M. M. Gupta, R. K. Ragade and R. R. Yager), pp. 235–246. North-Holland, Amsterdam (1979).
63. I. Niiniluoto and R. Tuomela, *Theoretical Concepts and Hypothetico-inductive Inference*. Reidel, Dordrecht (1973).
64. I. Niiniluoto, On the truthlikeness of generalizations. In *Basic Problems in Methodology and Linguistics* (Edited by J. Hintikka and R. Butts), pp. 121–147. Reidel, Dordrecht (1977).
65. K. Noguchi, M. Umano, M. Mizumoto and K. Tanaka, Implementation of fuzzy artificial intelligence language FLOU. *Tech. Rep.*, Automation and Language of IECE (1976).
66. A. I. Orlov, *Problems of Optimization and Fuzzy Variables*. Znaniye, Moscow (1980).

67. B. Partee, *Montague Grammar*. Academic Press, New York (1976).
68. P. Peterson, On the logic of *few, many* and *most. Notre Dame. J. Formal Logic* **20**, 155–179 (1979).
69. R. Reiter, A logic for default reasoning. *Artificial Intell.* **13**, 81–132 (1980).
70. N. Rescher, *Plausible Reasoning.* Van Gorcum, Amsterdam (1976).
71. L. K. Schubert, R. G. Goebel and N. Cercone, The structure and organization of a semantic net for comprehension and inference. In *Associative Networks* (Edited by N. V. Findler), pp. 122–178. Academic Press, New York (1979).
72. J. Searle (Ed.) *The Philosophy of Language.* Oxford University Press, Oxford (1971).
73. E. H. Shortliffe, *Computer-based Medical Consultations: MYCIN.* American Elsevier, New York (1976).
74. A. B. Slomson, Some problems in mathematical logic. Thesis, Oxford University (1967).
75. M. Sugeno, Fuzzy measures and fuzzy integrals: a survey, In: *Fuzzy Automata and Decision Processes* (Edited by M. M. Gupta, G. N. Saridis and B. R. Gaines), pp. 89–102. North-Holland, Amsterdam (1977).
76. P. Suppes, Elimination of quantifiers in the semantics of natural languages by use of extended relation algebras. *Revue Int. Philosphie*, 117–118, 243–259 (1976).
77. T. Terano and M. Sugeno, Conditional fuzzy measures and their applications. *Fuzzy Sets and Their Applications to Cognitive and Decision Processes* (Edited by L. A. Zadeh, K. S. Fu, K. Tanaka and M. Shimura), pp. 151–170. Academic Press, New York (1975).
78. K. Van Lehn, Determining the scope of English quantifiers, *Tech. Rep.* 483, AI Laboratory, M.I.T. (1978).
79. Y. Wilks, Philosophy of language. In *Computational Linguistics* (Edited by E. Charniak and Y. Wilks), pp. 205–233. North-Holland, Amsterdam (1976).
80. R. R. Yager, A note on probabilities of fuzzy events. *Inform. Sci.* **18**, 113–129 (1974).
81. R. R. Yager, Quantified propositions in a linguistic logic. In *Proc. 2nd Int. Seminar on Fuzzy Set Theory* (Edited by E. P. Klement). Johannes Kepler University, Linz, Austria (1980).
82. R. R. Yager, A foundation for a theory of possibility. *J. Cybernetics* **10**, 177–204 (1980).
83. L. A. Zadeh, Probability measures of fuzzy events. *J. Math. Anal. Appl.* **23**, 421–427 (1968).
84. L. A. Zadeh, Similarity relations and fuzzy orderings. *Inform. Sci.* **3**, 177–200 (1971).
85. L. A. Zadeh, Fuzzy languages and their relation to human and machine intelligence. *Proc. Int. Conf. on Man and Computer*, Bordeaux, France, pp. 130–165. Karger, Basel (1972).
86. L. A. Zadeh, Fuzzy logic and approximate reasoning (in memory of Grigore Moisil). *Synthese* **30**, 407–428 (1975).
87. L. A. Zadeh, The concept of a linguistic variable and its application to approximate reasoning. *Inform. Sci.* **8**, 199–249, 301–357, **9**, 43–80 (1975).
88. L. A. Zadeh, Fuzzy sets as a basis for a theory of possibility. *Fuzzy Sets and Systems* 3–28 (1978).
89. L. A. Zadeh, PRUF—a meaning representation language for natural languages. *Int. J. Man-Machine Studies* **10**, 395–460 (1978).
90. L. A. Zadeh, A theory of approximate reasoning. *Electronics Research Laboratory Mem. M77/58* University of California, Berkeley (1977); also in *Machine Intelligence* 9 (Edited by J. E. Hayes, D. Michie and L. I. Kulich), pp. 149–194. Wiley, New York (1979).
91. L. A. Zadeh, Inference in fuzzy logic. *Proc. 10th Inter. Symp. on Multiple-valued Logic*, Northwestern University, pp. 124–131, 1980.
92. L. A. Zadeh, Possibility theory and soft data analysis. *Electronics Res. Laboratory Mem. M79/59*, University of California, Berkeley (1979); also in *Mathematical Frontiers of the Social and Policy Sciences* (Edited by L. Cobb and R. M. Thrall), pp. 69–129. Westview Press, Boulder (1981).
93. L. A. Zadeh, Test-score semantics for natural languages and meaning-representation via PRUF. *Tech. Note* 247, AI Center, SRI International, Menlo Park, Calif. (1981); also in *Empirical Semantics* (Edited by B. B. Rieger), pp. 281–349. Brockmeyer, Bochum (1981).
94. L. A. Zadeh, Fuzzy probabilities and their role in decision analysis. *Proc. 4th MIT/ONR Workshop on Command, Control and Communications*, M.I.T. pp. 159–179, 1981.
95. A. Zimmer, Some experiments concerning the fuzzy meaning of logical quantifiers. In *General Surveys of Systems Methodology* (Edited by L. Troncoli), pp. 435–441. Society for General Systems Research, Louisville (1982).
96. H.-J. Zimmermann and P. Zysno, Latent connectives in human decision making. *Fuzzy Sets and Systems* **4**, 37–52 (1980).

APPENDIX

The extension principle

Let f be a function from U to V. The extension principle—as its name implies—serves to extend the domain of definition of f from U to the set of fuzzy subsets of U. In particular, if F is a finite fuzzy subset of U expressed as

$$F = \mu_1/u_1 + \cdots + \mu_n/u_n$$

then $f(F)$ is a finite fuzzy subset of V defined as

$$f(F) = f(\mu_1/u_1 + \cdots + \mu_n/u_n) \tag{A1}$$

$$= \mu_1/f(u_1) + \cdots + \mu_n/f(u_n).$$

Furthermore, if U is the cartesian product of $U_1, \ldots U_N$, so that $u = (u^1, \ldots u^N)$, $u^i \in U_i$, and we know only the projections of F on $U_1, \ldots U_N$, whose membership functions are, respectively, $\mu_{F1}, \ldots \mu_{FN}$, then

$$f(F) = \Sigma_u \mu_{F1}(u^1) \wedge \cdots \wedge \mu_{FN}(u^N)/f(u^1, \ldots u^N), \tag{A2}$$

with the understanding that, in replacing $\mu_F(u^1, \ldots u^N)$ with $\mu_F(u^1) \wedge \cdots \wedge \mu_{FN}(u^N)$, we are tacitly invoking the *principle of maximal possibility*[87]. This principle asserts that in the absence of complete information about a possibility distribution Π, we should equate Π to the maximal (i.e. least restrictive) possibility distribution which is consistent with the partial information about Π.

As a simple illustration of the extension principle, assume that $U = \{1, 2, \ldots 10\}$; f is the operation of squaring; and

SMALL is a fuzzy subset of U defined by

$$SMALL = 1/1 + 1/2 + 0.8/3 + 0.6/4 + 0.4/5.$$

Then, it follows from (A2) that the *right square* of *SMALL* is given by

$$SMALL^2 \overset{\Delta}{=} 1/1 + 1/4 + 0.8/9 + 0.6/16 + 0.4/25.$$

On the other hand, the *left square* of *SMALL* is defined by

$$^2SMALL \overset{\Delta}{=} 1/1 + 1/2 + 0.64/3 + 0.36/4 + 0.16/5$$

and, more generally, for a subset F of U and any real m, we have

$$\mu_{m_F}(u) \overset{\Delta}{=} (\mu_F(u))^m, \quad u \in U. \tag{A3}$$

Fuzzy numbers†

By a fuzzy number, we mean a number which is characterized by a possibility distribution or is a fuzzy subset of real numbers. Simple examples of fuzzy numbers are fuzzy subsets of the real line labeled *small, approximately* 8, *very close to* 5, *more or less large, much larger than* 6, *several*, etc. In general, a fuzzy number is either a convex or a concave fuzzy subset of the real line. A special case of a fuzzy number is an interval. Viewed in this perspective, fuzzy arithmetic may be viewed as a generalization of interval arithmetic[58].

Fuzzy arithmetic is not intended to be used in situations in which a high degree of precision is required. To take advantage of this assumption, it is expedient to represent the possibility distribution associated with a fuzzy number in a standardized form which involves a small number of parameters—usually two—which can be adjusted to fit the given distribution. A system of standardized possibility distributions which suits this purpose in most cases of practical interest is the following[87].

(1) *π-numbers*. The possibility distribution of such numbers is bell-shaped and piecewise-quadratic. The distribution is characterized by two parameters: (a) the peak-point, i.e. the point at which $\pi = 1$, and (b) the bandwidth, β, which is defined as the distance between the cross-over points, i.e. the points at which $\pi = 0.5$. Thus, a fuzzy π-number, x, is expressed as (p, β), where p is the peak-point and β is the bandwidth; or, alternatively, as (p, β'), where β' is the normalized bandwidth, i.e. $\beta' = \beta/p$. As a function of u, $u \in (-\infty, \infty)$, the values of $\pi_x(u)$ are defined by the equations

$$\pi_x(u) = 0 \text{ for } u \le p - \beta \text{ and } u \ge p + \beta \tag{A4}$$

$$= \frac{2}{\beta^2}(u - p + \beta)^2 \text{ for } p - \beta \le u \le p - \frac{\beta}{2}$$

$$= 1 - \frac{2}{\beta^2}(u - p)^2 \text{ for } p - \frac{\beta}{2} \le u \le p + \frac{\beta}{2}$$

$$= \frac{2}{\beta^2}(u - p - \beta)^2 \text{ for } p + \frac{\beta}{2} \le u \le p + \beta.$$

(2) *s-numbers*. As its name implies, the possibility distribution of an s-number has the shape of an s. Thus, the equations defining an s-number, expressed as (p/β), are:

$$\pi_x(u) = 0 \text{ for } u \le p - \beta \tag{A5}$$

$$= \frac{2}{\beta^2}(u - p + \beta)^2 \text{ for } p - \beta \le u \le p - \frac{\beta}{2}$$

$$= 1 - \frac{2}{\beta^2}(u - p)^2 \text{ for } p - \frac{\beta}{2} \le u \le p$$

$$= 1 \text{ for } u \ge p,$$

where β (the bandwidth) is the length of the transition interval from $\pi_x = 0$ to $\pi_x = 1$ and p is the left peak-point, i.e. the right end-point of the transition interval.

(3) *z-numbers*. A z-number is a mirror image of an s-number. Thus, the defining equations for a z-number, expressed as $(p \setminus \beta)$, are:

$$\pi_x(u) = 0 \text{ for } u \le p - \beta \tag{A6}$$

$$= \frac{2}{\beta^2}(u - p + \beta)^2 \text{ for } p - \beta \le u \le p - \frac{\beta}{2}$$

$$= 1 - \frac{2}{\beta^2}(u - p)^2 \text{ for } p - \frac{\beta}{2} \le u \le p + \beta$$

$$= 0 \text{ for } u \ge p + \beta,$$

where p is the right peak-point and β is the bandwidth.

†A more detailed exposition of the properties of fuzzy numbers may be found in Dubois and Prade (1980).

(4) s/z-*numbers*. An s/z-number has a flat-top possibility distribution which may be regarded as the intersection of the possibility distributions of an s-number and a z-number, with the understanding that the left peak-point of the s-number lies to the left of the right peak-point of the z-number. In some cases, however, it is expedient to disregard the latter restrictions and allow an s/z-number to have a sharp peak rather than a flat top. An s/z-number is represented as an ordered pair $(p_1/\beta_1; p_2\setminus\beta_2)$ in which the first element is an s-number and the second element is a z-number.

(5) $z\setminus s$-*numbers*. The possibility distribution of a $z\setminus s$ number is the complement of that of an s/z-number. Thus, whereas an s/z-number is a convex fuzzy subset of the real line, a $z\setminus s$-number is a concave fuzzy subset. Equivalently, the possibility distribution of a $z\setminus s$-number may be regarded as the union of the possibility distributions of a z-number and an s-number. A $z\setminus s$-number is represented as $(p_1\setminus\beta_1; p_2/\beta_2)$.

Arithmetic operations on fuzzy numbers

Let * denote an arithmetic operation such as addition, subtraction, multiplication or division, and let $x*y$ be the result of applying * to the fuzzy numbers x and y.

By the use of the extension principle, it can readily be established that the possibility distribution function of $x*y$ may be expressed in terms of those of x and y by the relation

$$\pi_{x*y}(w) = \vee_{u,v}(\pi_x(u) \wedge \pi_y(v)), \tag{A7}$$

subject to the constraint

$$w = u*v, \quad u, v, w \in (-\infty, \infty)$$

where $\vee_{u,v}$ denotes the supremum over u, v, and $\wedge \overset{\Delta}{=}$ min.

As a special case of a general result established by Dubois and Prade[20] for so-called L-R numbers, it can readily be deduced from (A7) that if x and y are numbers of the same type (e.g. π-numbers), then so are $x + y$ and $x - y$. Furthermore, the characterizing parameters of $x + y$ and $x - y$ depend in a very simple and natural way on those of x and y. More specifically, if $x = (p, \beta)$ and $y = (q, \gamma)$, then

$$(p,\beta) + (q,\gamma) = (p + q, \beta + \gamma)$$

$$(p/\beta) + (q/\gamma) = (p + q/\beta + \gamma)$$

$$(p\setminus\beta) + (q\setminus\gamma) = (p + q\setminus\beta + \gamma)$$

$$(p_1/\beta_1; p_2\setminus\beta_2 + (q_1/\gamma_1; q_2\setminus\gamma_2)$$

$$= (p_1 + q_1/\beta_1 + \beta_2; p_2 + q_2\setminus\gamma_1 + \gamma_2)$$

$$(p,\beta) - (q,\gamma) = (p - q, \beta + \gamma)$$

and similarly for other types of numbers.

In the case of multiplication, it is true only as an approximation that if x and y are π-numbers then so is $x \times y$. However, the relation between the peak-points and normalized bandwidths which is stated below is exact:

$$(p,\beta') \times (q,\gamma') = (p \times q, \beta' + \gamma'). \tag{A8}$$

The operation of division, x/y, may be regarded as the composition of (a) forming the reciprocal of y, and (b) multiplying the result by x. In general, the operation $1/y$ does not preserve the type of y and hence the same applies to x/y. However, if y is a π-number whose peak point is much larger than 1 and whose normalized bandwidth is small, then $1/y$ is approximately a π-number defined by

$$1/(p, \beta') \cong (1/p, \beta') \tag{A9}$$

and consequently

$$(p, \beta')/(q, \gamma') \cong (p/q, \beta' + \gamma') \tag{A10}$$

As a simple example of operations on fuzzy numbers, suppose that x is a π-number (p,β) and y is a number which is much larger than x. The question is: What is the possibility distribution of y?

Assume that the relation $y \gg x$ is characterized by a conditional possibility distribution $\Pi_{(y|x)}$ (i.e. the conditional possibility distribution of y given x) which for real values of x is expressed as an s-number

$$\Pi_{(y|x)} = (q(x)/\gamma(x)) \tag{A11}$$

whose peak-point and bandwidth depend on x.

On applying the extension principle to the composition of the binary relation $\gg$ as defined by (A11) with the unary relation x, it is readily found that y is an s-number which is approximately characterized by

$$y = (q(p)/[q(p) - q(p - \beta)]). \tag{A12}$$

In this way, then, the possibility distribution of y may be expressed in terms of the possibility distribution of x and the conditional possibility distribution of y given x.

Because of the reproducibility property of possibility distributions, the computational effort involved in the manipulation of fuzzy numbers is generally not much greater than that required in interval arithmetic. The bounds on the results, however, are usually appreciably tighter because in the case of fuzzy numbers the possibility distribution functions are allowed to take intermediate values in the interval [0,1], and not just 0 or 1, as in the case of intervals.

Comp. & Maths. with Appls. Vol. 9, No. 1, pp. 185–199, 1983
Printed in Great Britain.

0097–4943/83/010185–15$03.00/0
Pergamon Press Ltd.

RECOGNITION MECHANISMS FOR SCHEMA-BASED KNOWLEDGE REPRESENTATIONS

William S. Havens

Department of Computer Science, University of British Columbia, Vancouver, Canada V6T 1W5

Abstract—This paper is concerned with generalizing formal recognition methods from parsing theory to schemata knowledge representations. Within Artificial Intelligence, recognition tasks include aspects of natural language understanding, computer vision, episode understanding, speech recognition, and others. The notion of schemata as a suitable knowledge representation for these tasks is discussed. A number of problems with current schemata-based recognition systems are presented. To gain insight into alternative approaches, the formal context-free parsing method of Earley is examined. It is shown to suggest a useful control structure model for integrating top-down and botton-up search in schemata representations.

1. INTRODUCTION

Recognition tasks are a general class of problems in Artificial Intelligence (A.I.). Such tasks include aspects of natural language understanding, computer vision, speech recognition, and episode understanding. This paper is concerned with presenting new computational mechanisms for their efficient implementation. In particular, we will explore the possibility of generalizing ideas developed in formal parsing theory to controlling search in schema knowledge representations.

Recognition tasks are characterized by the use of a finite knowledge base to classify or *recognize* an arbitrarily large number of inputs. The knowledge base provides *models* of the objects that can legitimately be input to the system. These models are sufficiently powerful to decide class membership for any input. The output of the recognizer is a (perhaps unique) symbolic structural description of the input. The description makes explicit the objects and their relationships that were found in the input.

The knowledge base must be expressed in a formalism appropriate to the task. In the past few years, an apparent convergence of ideas towards the notion of *schemata*[4] as a suitable knowledge representation has occurred[5]. The theoretical properties of schemata are still emerging and have been discussed at length under various names in the literature (*frames*[2, 6, 7], *scripts*[8], *plans*[9], *schemata*[10]). Related work in *semantic network* representations has also seen keen research interest[11–14]. Most of this research has been concerned with the descriptive adequacy of schemata. Issues of search and control in schema representations are still poorly understood. We argue that knowledge representation cannot be studied independently of a theory of recognition encompassing both description and the methods that interpret the knowledge structures. The focus of this paper is this procedural aspect of recognition in schema-based systems.

In the next section, we will review current schema methodology. In Section 3, search mechanisms for this representation will be characterized and some fundamental difficulties will be presented. To gain insight into alternative techniques, the formal recognition methods employed in the parsing of context-free languages will then be examined. In particular, in Section 4, we will focus on the elegant parsing algorithm of Earley[3] for its application in unrestricted domains. In Section 5, we will present a model for recognition in schema-based systems that incorporates these ideas. Finally, in the concluding section, the advantages of this model and its relationships to other recognition paradigms will be discussed.

This methodology has recently been used in an experimental computer program called *Mapsee2*[34]. The program is a sequel to an earlier program, Mapsee[35], that employed a network consistency representation and a uniform constraint propagation control structure[39]. Both programs interpret hand-drawn sketch maps of cartographic scenes which may contain conventional symbols for roads, rivers, mountains, towns, bridges, islands and lakes. A typical input map for Mapsee2 is shown in Fig. 1. This sketch map is a liberal rendition of the Madison, Wisconsin metropolitan area.

MADISON

Fig. 1. A sketch map of Madison, Wisconsin.

The sketch map domain was chosen for the following reasons:

(1) Sketch maps capture in a simple form fundamental problems in representing and applying knowledge in model-driven visual recognition.

(2) Techniques for understanding maps have application in interpreting real imagery. In particular, sketch maps are being used to guide the automatic interpretation of aerial photography [40].

(3) By employing the same task domain, the capabilities of schema-based systems can be compared with the well understood network consistency methodology.

2. SCHEMATA

Although Artificial Intelligence encompasses a multitude of diverse research domains, issues in the representation and efficient application of knowledge are central to the entire field. It is not possible in this paper to discuss the theoretical properties of schemata in detail. Instead, the reader is referred to the reference given above. However, aspects of the representation that support recognition do need to be outlined.

2.1 Composition and specialization

Schemata are structural models for representing objects, events, actions, situations, and their sequences [5]. The representation is modular and object-centered, implying that each schema represents a single concept. Schemata contain relations with other schemata, forming *schema networks*.

In recognition systems, two types of relations are of particular importance: *composition* and *specialization*. Complex concepts are represented as specific compositions of simpler schemata, resulting in *composition hierarchies*. The recognition of a complex schema proceeds by the recursive recognition of its component parts such that the internal constraints of the schema remain satisfied. Illustrated in Fig. 2 is the schema composition hierarchy for the Mapsee2 sketch understanding system.

In this hierarchy, each node is a schema and the arcs between nodes represent relations between schemata. Looking downward, these arcs represent "composition" whereas in the upward direction, they represent its inverse relation, "part-of". The intuitive interpretation of the hierarchy is that a cartographic *World* is composed of some number of geographic systems, called *Geo-Systems*, which are in turn composed of combinations of *River-Systems, Road-Systems, Mountain-Ranges, Shorelines* and *Towns*. Each of these are, in turn, composed of simpler sub-schemata finally terminating in the primitive input sketch lines, called *chains*, and the "white space" *regions* bounded by the chains. Conversely, the hierarchy can be viewed as a *part-of hierarchy* representing, for example, that Town schemata are component parts of both Geo-Systems and Road-Systems.

Schemata form a second type of hierarchy important for recognition systems called a *specialization hierarchy* or historically, the *ISA hierarchy* [41]. The top node of this hierarchy is a schema which represents a generic class of objects. Each descendent node in the hierarchy represents a specialization of the class of its parent. For example, the specialization hierarchy for Geo-Systems in Mapsee2 is given in Fig. 3. A Geo-System is initially a set of undifferentiated regions and embedded chains in a sketch map. As additional constraints on a Geo-System are found

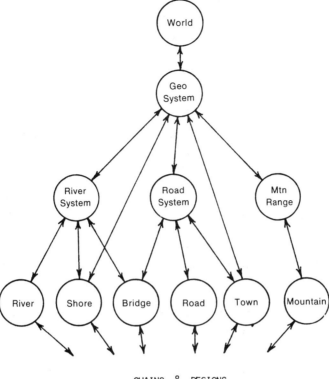

Fig. 2. Mapsee2 composition hierarchy.

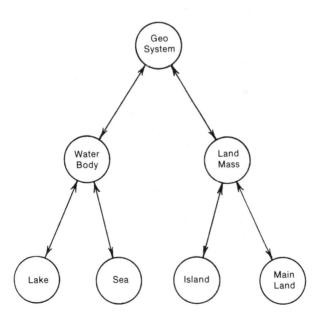

Fig. 3. Geo-System specialization hierarchy.

during recognition, its interpretation can be refined first to either a Landmass or a Waterbody and finally to one of Island, Mainland, Lake, or Sea. Each of these specializations can be a distinct type of schema in the hierarchy.

2.2 Classes and instances

Schemata are used to represent both stereotypical knowledge about *classes* of objects and specific information about particular *instances* of some class[24]. Every class contains a set of variables, $V = \{v_i, i = 1, \ldots k\}$, often called *slots* [6]. Each variable, v_i, may be typed, its domain, $D(v_i)$, restricted, for example, to a range of integer values or to instances of a specified class. Each class also contains a set on *n*-ary relations over V,

$$R = \{R_j(v_1, v_2, \ldots v_{n_j}), \; j = 1, \ldots m\},$$

which are constraints on the legitimate combinations of values that the variables may assume. Some of the variables in V are initially bound thereby defining the static properties of the class.

During recognition, classes are copied to form instances to represent each occurrence of an object known or hypothesized to exist in the input. Instances inherit all the relations and variables of their class. In particular, instances inherit the composition and specialization hierarchies. A new instance, S, of some class is created when the object represented by the class is first hypothesized. S records the state of the recognition of the object until it is successful or has failed. The recognition of S proceeds by binding each variable in V such that every relation in R remains satisfied. S has *completed* when every variable in V has been consistently bound.† The recognition of S fails if some variable, v_i, $1 \le i \le n_j$, is forced by the network to have a particular value but a relation,

$$R_j(v_1, \ldots, v_i, \ldots, v_{n_j}), \; 1 \le j \le m,$$

in S is not defined for that value.

For example, consider the simple map of Fig. 4(a). This sketch map depicts an island having

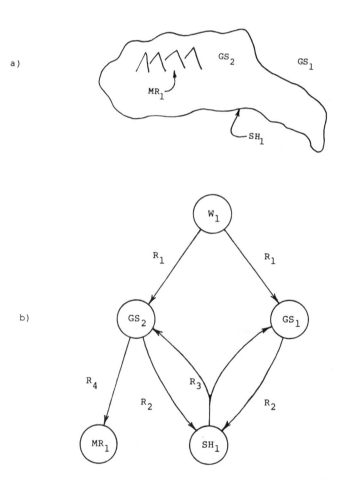

Fig. 4. A simple sketch map example.

---

†Some applications allow specific variables to assume default values if not explicitly bound [6].

an interior mountain range surrounded by a waterbody. The map is represented by the schema network of Fig. 4(b) which is an instance, W_1, of the World having two composition relations, R_1, with Geo-System instances, GS_1 and GS_2, which are separated by a Shoreline, SH_1. Both Geo-Systems contain a relation, $R_2(SH_1)$, that holds if the interpretation of the instance is consistent with the interpretation of SH_1. Likewise, SH_1 has a relation, $R_3(GS_1, GS_2)$, which is consistent if either GS_1 has an interpretation as a Landmass (or its specializations Island and Mainland) while GS_2 has an interpretation as a Waterbody (or its specializations Lake and Sea) or vice-versa.

   GS_2 also has a composition relation, $R_4(MR_1)$, with Mountain-Range, MR_1. If MR_1 is temporarily excluded from the sketch map, then the interpretations for both Geo-Systems are ambiguous. Including MR_1 forces a final interpretation. $R_4(MR_1)$ specializes the interpretation of GS_2 to be a Landmass (Mountains are necessarily land features). As well, $R_2(SH_1)$ in GS_2 further refines GS_2 to be an Island (a landmass surrounded by a shoreline is an island). These constraints can now propagate through the network. $R_3(GS_1, GS_2)$ in SH_1 forces the interpretation of SH_1 to be the Coastline of an Island. This refinement, in turn, forces $R_2(SH_1)$ in GS_1 to specialize GS_1 to a surrounding Waterbody. The interpretation of the network is now complete.

3. SEARCH IN SCHEMA NETWORKS

Unfortunately, recognition usually requires search. In schema representations, the purpose of the search is to construct a network of schema instances from the composition and specialization hierarchies to correctly represent the input data. The search is a non-deterministic and therefore inefficient process for two reasons. First, input symbols can be highly ambiguous in their immediate or local interpretation. Second, the knowledge base may have inadequate descriptive power to disambiguate the interpretation of the individual symbols.

3.1 *Top-down mechanisms*

In general, search in schema networks can be characterized as either *top-down* or *bottom-up*. Top-down search is well understood. Minsky, in his original frame systems paper [6], proposed a purely top-down, goal-driven scheme. Schank[8], Abelson[7], Charniak[9] and others have relied on similar mechanisms for episode understanding. Unfortunately, a number of acknowledged deficiencies exist with this approach:

(1) A schema must explicitly be hypothesized as a likely *subgoal* (by some higher schema) before its knowledge can be employed to recognize an instance of its class from the input data.
   An essential property of the schema representation is modularity. Knowledge particular to the recognition of a schema is wholly contained within it. Therefore, before its expertise can be made available to constrain and guide the search process, the schema must first be made an active hypothesis. For example, consider a Geo-System instance. For a given input sketch map, it should contain a variety of River-Systems, Road-Systems, Mountain-Ranges, Shorelines, and Towns. Unfortunately a commitment must be made to a correct subschema as a subgoal before evidence can be discovered confirming that decision. The choice must be made on "blind expectation" alone.

(2) The pursuit of alternate subgoals is failure driven.
   A schema instance can contain a number of possible combinations of its subschemata. Since alternate compositions of subschemata form mutually exclusive interpretations, top-down search forces the independent pursuit of their subgoals. Two different implementation techniques are widely employed.
   In *depth-first search*, the alternate subgoals are ordered and explored in sequence. Unfortunately, the mechanism for activating alternatives, called *automatic backtracking*, is completely failure driven. Each untried subgoal must wait its turn until the failure of every predecessor in the sequence permits it to be the current hypothesis. Depth-first search requires exponential computing time for both its worst case and, frequently, its average case behaviour. In the Geo-System example, every chain in the input sketch must be interpreted as a component of some Geo-System. Yet, a particular chain meandering in the interior of the

Geo-System might be either a Road-System or a River-System. In top-down, depth-first search, a choice must be made to, say, the Road-System as a subgoal. Likewise, this schema must order and attempt its own subgoals. Only if the chain eventually cannot be interpreted as a Road-System, will the River-System subgoal be explored.

Breadth-first search, on the other hand, often exhibits better performance. Alternate subgoals are explored in pseudo-parallel. Each subgoal is called to return a value but the internal state of the subgoal (and the state of its own subgoals) is retained. If the value it returned is later found to be inappropriate, then the subgoal can be recalled to attempt a new value. Unfortunately, breadth-first search is very inefficient in its use of memory space and its worst case time requirements are also exponential.

Many embellishments have been added to improve top-down search especially in game playing programs[43]. Kaplan[22] has implemented a natural language parser which allows pursuit of individual subgoals in either depth or breadth-first order.

(3) Identical subgoals must be explored independently.

In top-down search, a schema may be successful at achieving a number of its subgoals. If, however, a subsequent and necessary subgoal should fail, the schema must itself return a failure to its caller. Later, the system may re-compute some of those identical subgoals. This pathological behaviour has been called *thrashing*[16].

To avoid thrashing, a number of techniques have been advanced. Woods[42] employed a "well-formed substring table" in his parser to retain partial results in the event of failure. Likewise, a *similarity network*[6], first used by Winston[17] in his learning system, can be employed to associate a set of replacement schemata with each schema. If the schema fails to satisfy one of its subgoals, it can consult the similarity network to recommend a replacement based on its mismatch to the observed input. The failing schema then attempts to map its correctly bound variables into the variables of the new schema and then passes control to it. Unfortunately, this mechanism assumes both that a mapping exists from the failing schema to each next candidate and that the similarity network is sufficiently complete that relatively few inexplicable failures occur. Such surprises force the system to rely on automatic backtracking to continue the search.

The three deficiencies in top-down search noted above require the system to hypothesize the correct interpretation before it can be found. Otherwise, the system must laboriously try hypothesis after hypothesis until a correct schema or at least a "near miss"[17] is found. Such a paradox has been identified in computer vision research as the "chicken and egg problem"[19, 20]. The difficulty stems from the fact that a particular schema must be chosen as a plausible hypothesis and attempted before any of its expertise becomes available to guide the search. Its knowledge comes too late! More flexible mechanisms are needed.

3.2 *Bottom-up mechanisms*

At the other extreme, bottom-up search can avoid some of the pitfalls of top-down search. An instance need only be recognized once. When complete, it is used as a component in every schema higher in the composition hierarchy of which it can be part. Each such higher schema becomes a *supergoal* of the completed instance and is invoked to look for its remaining components. The result is concurrently active hypotheses thereby directly eliminating the chicken and egg problem. However, no particular schema is in control to guide the recognition process. Again recognition is blind. What is needed are mechanisms which allow top-down search to give overall guidance, yet permit bottom-up techniques to circumvent the inefficiencies of purely top-down schemes.

3.3 *Procedural methods*

A promising approach is the use of procedures within schemata to control search. Schemata can contain both declarative and procedural knowledge, an advantage over other purely declarative knowledge representations[2]. The purpose of a procedure local to a schema class is to heuristically guide the search process for instances of that class by augmenting global uniform search techniques.

A *method*[44] is a procedure attached to a variable slot, v_i, in a class. Following the terminology of [2], methods are of two basic types: *servants* and *demons*. A servant is a method that, when associated with an unbound variable, v_i, in some instance, S, can be invoked to search for a value for v_i that is consistent with the relations in S. Demons have a complementary purpose. When a variable, v_i, is bound to a value, the associated demon can be invoked to use the newly acquired information to guide the search for the remaining unbound variables in S.

A number of investigators have studied the interaction of top-down and bottom-up search[22, 23, 45, 46]. For example, Freuder[24] developed a system to recognize common hammers from digital photographs by using features computed in the image as cues to invoke goals. When a goal has been satisfied, it may result in the creation of additional higher goals. A priority queue is used to schedule goals. Unfortunately, priority queues attempt to encode complex control interactions as simple scalar quantities. Instead, Rumelhart and Ortony[5] have argued for:

> ... the activation of a schema as being like the invocation of a procedure. ... However, unlike ordinary procedure calls, in which the flow of control is only from procedure to subroutine, the flow of control in a schema system operates both ways. It is as though a given procedure not only could invoke its own subroutines (conceptually driven processing) but also could invoke those procedures in which it was itself a subroutine (data-driven processing). Finally, one must image these procedures as all operating simultaneously (p. 46).

What remains to be defined, and the essence of the problem, is the definition of a suitable control regime to coordinate the efforts of the multiple active schemata.

4. FORMAL PARSING ALGORITHMS

As a step towards defining an effective control regime, we examine the types of formal recognition algorithms developed for parsing context-free languages. In particular, the bottom-up parser of Earley[3] will be discussed in some detail.

4.1 Context-free parsing

Context-free parsing can be viewed as a restricted recognition domain. In parsing, the knowledge base is a *phrase structure grammar*[25]. The input is a string of symbols in the alphabet of the language, and if the input belongs to the language described by the grammar, the output is a structural description of the input, called a *parse tree*, and failure otherwise. Formally, a context-free grammar, CFG, is:

$$G = (Vn, Vt, P, S),$$

where Vn is an alphabet of *non-terminal symbols*, Vt is the alphabet of *terminal symbols*, P is a set of *production rules*, and S is a distinguished member of Vn called the *start symbol*.

Each rule in P is a pair of the form:

$$A \rightarrow \alpha$$

where A is in an element of Vn and is called the *left-hand-side* (LHS) of the rule and α is a string of symbols from $\{Vn \cup Vt\}$ and is called the *right-hand-side* (RHS).† Since α may contain symbols in Vn which necessarily appear as the LHS of some rule in P, G represents an hierarchical knowledge base. Parsing context-free languages is inherently a search of this hierarchy.

Both top-down and bottom-up parsing algorithms have been developed exhibiting well understood properties[26]. In general, such algorithms are straightforward but inefficient for non-deterministic CFGs. At each point in the parse where more than a single rule could be used to generate part of the sentence, the parser must allow for every possibility. This non-determinism can be simulated by employing automatic backtrack control. Performance for these parsers, in worst case, requires order C^n time for some constant C and an input sentence

---

†We will use the Greek alphabet to represent strings from $\{Vn \cup Vt\}$, capital Roman to represent symbols in Vn, and lower Roman for symbols in Vt.

of length n-symbols. By heuristically ordering the productions of P which share the same LHS, some constant improvements in performance can be achieved. But for ill-formed inputs, all productions still must be tried. More typically, by suitably restricting the language of G, which is an acceptable compromise for programming languages, parsers having performance linear with length n-symbols can be constructed. Neither of these enhancements make parsing an appealing model for A.I. recognition.

4.2 Earley's parsing algorithm

There are, however, algorithms for parsing arbitrary context-free languages which are much more efficient than the exponential behaviour described above[27]. In particular, the method of Earley[3] operates in polynomial times, Cn^3 in worst case, and better in most cases.

The algorithm is an efficient bottom-up recognizer that can operate directly from any CFG that is not left-recursive. Moreover, it does not require automatic backtracking to handle non-determinism but instead dynamically inverts portions of the grammar as required to interpret the input sentence. Conceptually, the algorithm creates a process for some rule, $A \rightarrow \alpha$, in P whenever (and not until) A could be part of some global interpretation beginning at the current symbol in the input. This is called the *left-context mechanism*. Each process attempts to recognize an instance of its rule's LHS, A, by finding a sentential form in the input satisfying each symbol in its RHS, α. The result is a control tree of competing and cooperating processes. Cooperating processes occur when $\alpha = \gamma B \delta$ for B an element of Vn. At least one subprocess is created for B when it could appear next in the input, that is, when γ has just been recognized. Competing processes occur when more than a single rule in P has the same LHS, A. A subprocess is created for each such rule. The goal of each process is the same and their successes are mutually exclusive.

The essential problem for the algorithm is the efficient coordination of these processes. The algorithm can be viewed as a "bookkeeping" scheme for the simulation of multiple bottom-up processes operating on the same input. As well, it provides a process scheduling mechanism that invokes processes only when they are currently appropriate to recognition.

The algorithm is defined as follows. We are given a *CFG*, G, as above and an input sentence:

$$w = a_1 a_2 a_3 \ldots a_n$$

with every a_i in V_t, $1 \le i \le n$. We define a parse *item* to be:

$$[A \rightarrow \alpha \cdot \beta, i]$$

for rule $A \rightarrow \alpha \beta$ and $0 \le i \le n$. An item represents the internal state of a process charged with the recognition of a non-terminal symbol A starting at position i in w. The *parse dot*, " $\cdot$ ", between α and β marks what portion, α, of the RHS has already been recognized and what part, β, yet needs to be found.

For steps j, $0 \le j \le n$, the algorithm constructs *parse lists*, Q_j, of items. An item, $[A \rightarrow \alpha \cdot \beta, i]$, $0 \le i \le j$, is an element of the parse list, Q_j, if and only if a sentential form, $\gamma A \delta$, with $\gamma = a_1 a_2 \ldots a_i$ can be derived from the start symbol, S, and $\alpha = a_{i+1} \ldots a_j$. That is, i through j bracket the portion of w derivable from α and the rule, $A \rightarrow \alpha \beta$, can be used in a valid derivation of w upto position j. In other words, all items in Q_j represents derivations that agree with w at least to position j.

The algorithm is initialized by forming a parse list, Q_0, containing the items $[S \rightarrow .\alpha, 0]$ for each rule $S \rightarrow \alpha$ in P. As each new symbol a_{j+1} of w is processed, the algorithm generates a new parse list, Q_{j+1}. The cycle is continued until the last symbol a_n is read and Q_n generated. However, the algorithm is halted if some new Q_{j+1} is empty indicating w is not a valid sentence in the language of G. If at the end of the sentence, any item, $[S \rightarrow \alpha., 0]$, is contained in Q_n, then the algorithm succeeds accepting w.

The algorithm proceeds by the repeated application of three functions called the *predictor*, *scanner*, and *completer*. First, the predictor computes from the rules in P and the current valid left-context what rules may be involved in derivations to follow. Conceptually, it spawns new processes to look for the applications of these rules. If the item, $[A \rightarrow \alpha.B\beta, i]$, is an element of

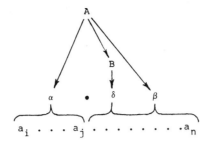

Fig. 5. Predictor.

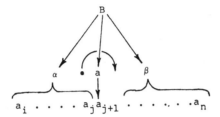

Fig. 6. Scanner.

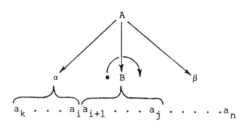

Fig. 7. Completer.

parse list, Q_j, and $B \rightarrow \delta$ is a rule in P, then a new item, $[B \rightarrow .\delta, j]$ is added to Q_j. The index, j, in the new item indicates at position in w, a new process was created to look for the RHS of rule, $B \rightarrow \delta$. Figure 5 illustrates the portion to the left of the parsing dot already recognized and the part predicted to be recognized to the right of the dot by the application of the rule for B.

Next, the scanner function, by reading the input symbol, a_{j+1}, generates seed items for the next parse list, Q_{j+1}. For each item, $[B \rightarrow \alpha. \, a\beta, i]$, that is contained in Q_j, such that $a = a_{j+1}$, the item, $[B \rightarrow \alpha a.\beta, i]$, is added to Q_{j+1}. The scanner propagates all processes in Q_j to the next parse list that were expecting the symbol, a_{j+1}, to appear next in w. As is shown in Fig. 6, the scanner increments the internal state of a process by moving the parsing dot one terminal symbol to the right in the item.

The completer function performs bottom-up reductions of sentential forms that appear as the RHS of production rules in P to their corresponding LHS. If $[B \rightarrow \delta, i]$ is an element of Q_j, then the non-terminal, B, has been recognized in w. The rule $B \rightarrow \delta$ has provided a valid derivation of the substring, $a_{i+1} \ldots a_j$, of w. From Q_i, the originating item, $[A \rightarrow \alpha.B\beta, k]$ is retrieved and propagated as $[A \rightarrow \alpha B.\beta, k]$ into Q_{j+1}. The completer acts as a scanner for non-terminal symbols, as is shown in Fig. 7. For examples of the parser's behaviour on sample context-free grammars, see [26].

5. RECOGNITION MECHANISMS FOR SCHEMATA

In this section, we present an overview of a control regime for schema-based recognition based on the formal recognition techniques developed above. The elegance of the parsing method of Earley makes it tempting as a metaphor for control in schemata. Recognition in A.I. domains endures similar constraints as formal recognition. In fact, others have considered applying Earley's algorithm in A.I.[28, 29]. Unfortunately, for our purposes, it exhibits a number of limitations:

(1) The algorithm is defined only for context-free grammars. Artificial Intelligence tasks (natural language understanding in particular) are believed to be at least context-sensitive. As well, large knowledge bases are too complex and diverse to be expressed as phrase structure grammars[38].

(2) Parsing assumes an intrinsically ordered input. Unfortunately, many A. I. recognition tasks do not have an ordered input. For example, the input to computer vision systems is typically a two-dimensional array containing perhaps 10^5 picture elements (pixels) from which an unordered set of features may be extracted and employed as the actual input data.

(3) Earley's algorithm supports only bottom-up recognition. There is no integration of top-down and bottom-up search, as has been argued is necessary.

(4) Parsing algorithms employ a uniform interpreter. The notion of procedural methods to heuristically guide recognition is not defined.

(5) Technically, the predictor function of Earley's algorithm would be prohibitively expensive for large knowledge-bases. By exploiting the sequential nature of the input and by keeping the size of the grammar small, prediction does not proliferate in parsing. This is not possible for unrestricted A. I. tasks.

To overcome these shortcomings, we will consider Earley's algorithm only to be a multi-process bookkeeping scheme for coordinating simultaneous competing and cooperating goals, as mentioned earlier. We define three recognition phases called *expectation*, *matching* and *completion* which are analogues of the three parsing functions: the predictor, scanner, and completer, respectively.

5.1 *Expectation*

An *expectation* for a variable, v_i, in an instance, S, is the projection onto the domain of v_i of all its values that remain consistent with the relations defined in S. More precisely, for variables, $v_1, \ldots v_{i-1}$, $i \le n_j$, in V which are already bound, the expectation, $E_i(v_i)$, for v_i is the subset of the domain, $D(v_i)$, for which there exists legitimate values for the remaining unbound variables, $v_{i+1}, \ldots v_{n_j}$, such that

$$R_j(v_1, \ldots v_{i-1}, v_i, v_{i+1}, \ldots v_{n_j}), \; j = 1, \ldots m.$$

The set of expectations, $E = \{E_i(v_i), 1 \le i \le k\}$, for all the variables, V, in S represents what information to search for in order to complete the recognition of S. From a control perspective, expectations serve two purposes. In top-down search, a schema's expectations provide parameters to guide subschemata as subgoals. A subgoal for v_i can succeed only if returns a value in $E_i(v_i)$.[†] In bottom-up search, the expectations of S restrict which subschemata of S can invoke it as a supergoal. A subschema instance can only bind to v_i if it is in $E_i(v_i)$.[†]

We draw an analogy between a schema, A, and a context-free production rule, $A \rightarrow \alpha\beta$, where α and β represent collections of variables of the schema. The domains of these variables may be either primitive values from the input (terminal symbols) or subschemata (non-terminal symbols). It is assumed that the variables in α have already been bound and the variables for β remain to be filled. The state of this schema instance can be represented by the parse item,

$$[A \rightarrow \alpha, \beta, i]$$

where the dot separates bound and unbound variables and the index, i, references the instance which created A. So far in this parsing analogy, the recognition of β is context-free and does not depend on any constraints established by α. Furthermore, the sequential nature of parsing ensures that β need not be predicted until α has been found.

In schema-based recognition, neither assumption may be valid. First, the expectations computed for β depend on the particular instantiation for α. For example, consider a Geo-System instance from Mapsee2. Geo-Systems are specific compositions of their component

---

[†]$E_i(v_i)$ is a necessary but not sufficient constraint on any final value for v_i in S.

parts. If a Shoreline for the Geo-System is found, then the boundary of that component (α) constrains the possible location, size, and interpretation of every other component (β) of the Geo-System.

Second, expectations cannot depend on a sequential ordering of the input. Components α and β may be presented to the system in specific order (e.g. episode understanding) or they may be discovered in arbitrary order (e.g. computer vision). Considering the Geo-System example further, an instance of this schema must be recognizable regardless of the order in which its component Road-Systems, River-Systems, and Mountain-Ranges are found.

Unfortunately, relaxing the ordering constraint plus allowing schemata to be arbitrarily rich compositions of other schemata can make expectation an expensive process. In general the expectations for an instance must be recomputed whenever the state of the instance changes perhaps entailing an encyclopaedic tour of the knowledge base. To alleviate this problem, expectations can be separated into two categories: *dynamic* and *static*.

Dynamic expectations follow faithfully the algorithm developed by Earley. They retain the left-context mechanism at the expense of prediction. No expectations are made for any variable in α or β of A until A can legitimately be part of some global interpretation of the input. Consequently, no anomalous appearance of A in the input is allowed to be recognized.

On the other hand, static expectations can avoid the expense of prediction by sacrificing the left-context. Initial context-free expectations are pre-compiled for every variable in A as static properties of the class. The use of static expectations are implicit in most discussions of schemata[2, 6, 8, 18, 21]. Static expectations, besides avoiding the potential prediction explosion, are able to handle unpredicted appearances of objects and partially well-formed inputs. Their major disadvantage is the loss of the left-context mechanism which postpones detection of errors, or worse, allows erroneous compositions.

5.2 *Matching*

Recognition in schemata representations has been described as a semantic pattern match of the knowledge base to the input data[21]. This process has two parts: The use of features, or *cues*, computed from the input data to find candidate schemata in the knowledge base, followed by an attempt to match the expectations of each candidate to the data. In natural language understanding, cues can be words or parts of speech suggesting a particular schema. In computer vision, cues are often derived features such as edges, regions, and shapes. First, we consider the problems involved in matching and leave until Section 5.3 the problem of finding likely candidates.

The matching phase can be compared to the scanner function. We assume an active instance, B, analogous to some parse rule, $B \rightarrow \alpha a \beta$, for collections of variables, α and β, and a single variable, "a". Associated with each variable is a method (a "demon") which knows how to guide the recognition of B based on the satisfaction of its expectation.

We assume for convenience that all the components of B are ordered. If the current state of B is such that every variable in α is bound, then the parse item

$$[B \rightarrow \alpha . a \beta]$$

represents that state where "a" is an unbound variable in B containing a current expectation. If data satisfying the expectation for "a" is subsequently found in the input, then the variable's method is invoked. Once invoked, the method can employ the newly acquired information to guide the search for the remaining variables, β.

However, the method is not restricted to continuing the search using only bottom-up techniques. By considering each method, once invoked, to be an independent process whose purpose is to guide the recognition of the instance to which it is attached, an integration of top-down and bottom-up search can be realized. In particular, three distinct modes of search are possible: top-down, bottom-up, and a hybrid combination of the two.

If the success of finding α and "a" indicates a high probability of finding β and the relations in B, given α and "a", can sufficiently restrict the expectations of β, then top-down search for β is warranted. Top-down search is best viewed as useful for confirming the last details of an instance after sufficient evidence has been collected to be confident of success. A subgoal is then attempted for each variable in β.

On the other hand, if little or no evidence has been found for an instance, B, then bottom-up search is appropriate for inferring that B should be an active hypothesis. When the expectation for "a" is matched and its method invoked, the method recomputes the expectations for the remaining variables in β from the new constraints implied by "a" and halts. When some expection for β is subsequently matched, another method of β will be invoked to continue the recognition of B.

It is clear that a schema can heuristically switch back and forth between top-down and bottom-up modes as is advantageous. However, it is also possible to blend the desirable properties of both methods into a hydrid mode. In the above discussion, after the method for "a" had recomputed the expectations remaining for β, its task was over. Some other method associated with a variable in β, if invoked, would continue the recognition for B. Instead of halting, however, after a method recomputes the expectations for the remaining unbound variables in its instance, it can retain control to direct the bottom-up search for components which will match those expectations. If it is successful, then other methods in the same instance, B, will be invoked to continue the search.

On the other hand, if it fails or finds components which match the expectations of other instances, then the methods of those instances will be invoked. The advantage is that the schema can employ its methods to look for evidence matching its own expectations without a commitment to top-down search. As long as those expectations are matched, the schema retains control. However, as soon as evidence is recognized supporting the expectations of a different schema, control is appropriately transferred to that schema.

Since an instance may have an arbitrary number of variables, the process of matching an expectation, refining the expectations for the remaining variables, and directing observation for new cues forms an *expectation/matching cycle*, which is illustrated in Fig. 8. Each active instance has its own cycle which may exist concurrently with those of every other instance in the network.

5.3 *Completion*

The paradigm of invoking models (schemata) via cues is dominant in computer vision[32]. The complexity of vision tasks has necessitated a bottom-up, yet model-driven approach. A major problem in vision systems has been the reliance on low-level cues computed directly from the input data to invoke high-level models[31]. Such cues are highly ambiguous, matching the expectations of too many models. Indeed this deficiency is the problem of selecting appropriate candidate schemata from the knowledge base. What is needed is a high-level retrieval mechanism that fetches appropriate candidates by employing high-level abstract cues.

Such a mechanism is the *cue/model hierarchy*[30]. A schema can function both as a model and a cue. When an instance, S, of some class has been recognized, S becomes an abstract cue for other schemata higher in the composition hierarchy. In top-down search, S was necessarily called as a subgoal and must return its success (or failure) to its caller. However, in bottom-up search, S has no explicit caller. Instead, it must return its success to every higher schema of which it may be part as a supergoal.

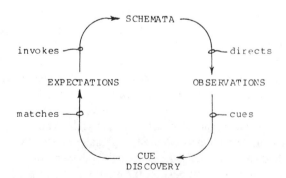

Fig. 8. Expectation/Matching cycle.

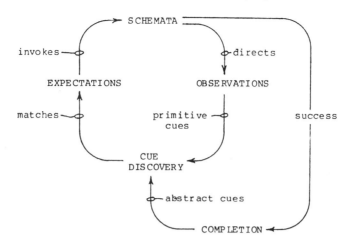

Fig. 9. Recursive recognition cycle.

Completion for schemata is comparable to the parsing completer function. We are given one or more instances, A, analogous to the rule, $A \rightarrow \alpha B\beta$, such that the state of A is represented by

$$[A \rightarrow \alpha.B\beta, i]$$

and another instance, B, from the rule, $B \rightarrow \gamma$. B is currently a non-primitive expectation of A, that is, B is predicted to be a subschema component of A. If B succeeds in recognizing all of its components in γ, then B is a cue for the invocation of every schema, A, which has an expectation for B. Each A successfully matched by B is invoked and its state advanced to

$$[A \rightarrow \alpha B.\beta, i].$$

Completion provides a high-level retrieval mechanism which is itself recognition. Low-level schemata are invoked by low-level cues computed directly from the input. High-level schemata are invoked by abstract cues computed recursively as the result of recognition. Figure 9 illustrates this recursive recognition cycle.

6. CONCLUSION

In this paper, we have attempted to examine schema-based recognition. By comparing current methodology in Artificial Intelligence to better understood techniques in parsing theory, A different perspective on issues of control and search in schemata representations is obtained. We argued that integrated top-down and bottom-up search guided by procedural methods local to each schema is necessary to avoid the inefficiency of uniform search techniques.

A control structure model for schemata was presented that has the desired capabilities. The model handles non-determinism efficiently by using a hierarchy of cues to invoke appropriate schemata. Only those higher schemata for which the completed instance is a plausible cue need be attempted removing the need for priority queues and a separate schema retrieval mechanism.

Finally, since methods attached to schemata are independent processes, both top-down and bottom-up search can be employed. The choice is made by the schema itself based on its estimation of the likelihood of success. If success is not forthcoming, a method can re-compute expectations for its schema and either wait for further collaborative evidence to be found or direct the bottom-up search for that evidence.

6.1 *Related models*

A number of other control models have been proposed recently for recognition [30, 33, 37]. For example, Mackworth[30] has suggested a *cycle of perception* model as shown in Fig. 10 which he attributes to the early computer vision research of Roberts[36]. In this model,

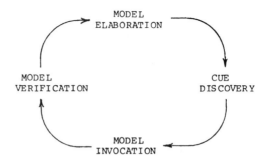

Fig. 10. Mackworth's cycle of perception.

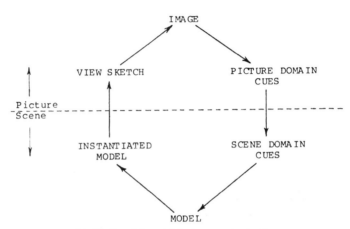

Fig. 11. Kanade's model for image understanding.

recognition is seen as an iterative process. Cues are used to invoke appropriate models (schemata) which attempt to verify their hypotheses by observation. Successful models cause the elaboration of the consequences of their hypotheses resulting in the discovery of new cues.

Although the necessity of a theory of control in schema-based recognition is generally accepted, it has not been sufficiently characterized. To this end, we offer the methodology presented in this paper.

REFERENCES

1. C. Hewitt, P. Bishop and R. Steiger, A universal modulactor formalism for artificial intelligence. *Proc. 3-IJCAI*, (Edited by D. G. Bobrow and A. Collins), pp. 185–210. academic Press, New York (1975).
2. T. Winograd, Frame representations and the procedural-declarative contraversy. In *Representation and Understanding* (Edited by D. G. Bobrow and A. Collins), pp. 185–210. Academic Press, New York (1975).
3. J. Earley, An efficient context-free parsing algorithm. *CACM* **13**(2), 94–102 (1970).
4. F. C. Barlett, *Remembering*. Cambridge Univ. Press, Cambridge (1932).
5. D. E. Rumelhart and A. Ortony, The representation of knowledge in memory. *TR* (55), Center for Human Information Processing, Dept. of Psych., University of california at San Diego, La Jolla, Calif. (1976)
6. M. Minsky, A framework for representing knowledge. In *The Psychology of Computer Vision* (Edited by P. Winston). McGraw-Hill, New York (1975).
7. E. Charniak, Organization and inference in a frame-like system of knowledge. *Proc. Theoretical Issues in Natural Lang. Processing*, Cambridge, Mass., June 1975.
8. R. C. Schank, The structure of episodes in memory. In *Representation and Understanding* (Edited by D. G. Bobrow and A. Collins), pp. 237–272. Academic Press, New York (1975).
9. R. P. Abelson, Concepts for representing mundane reality in plans. In *Representation and Understanding* (Edited by D. G. Bobrow and A. Collins), pp. 273–309. Academic Press, New York (1975).
10. D. E. Rumelhart and D. Norman, Active Semantic Networks as a model of human memory. *Proc. 3-IJCAI*, Stanford Univ., Stanford, Calif., p. 450, August 1973.
11. W. A. Woods, What's in a Link. In *Representation and Understanding* (Edited by D. G. Bobrow and A. Collins) pp. 35–82. Academic Press, New York (1975).
12. L. Schubert, Extending the expressive power of semantic networks. *Proc. 4-IJCAI*, tbilisi, USSR p. 158, Sept. 1975.
13. G. Hendrix, Expanding the utility of semantic networks through partitioning. *Proc. 4-IJCAI*, tbilisi, U.S.S.R., pp. 115–121, Sept. 1975.

14. N. Cercone and L. Schubert, Towards a state-based conceptual representation. *Proc. 4-IJCAI*, Tbilisi, U.S.S.R., pp 83–90, Sept. 1975.
15. W. S. Havens, A procedural model of recognition for machine perception. *TR*-78-3, Dept. of Comp. Science, Univ. of British Columbia, Vancover, Canada (1978).
16. D. G. Bobrow and B. Raphael, New programming Languages for artificial intelligence research. *Comp. Surveys* **6**, 153–174 (1974).
17. P. H. Winston, Learning structural descriptions from examples. In *The Psychology of Computer Vision*. (Edited by P. H. Winston). McGraw-Hill, New York (1975).
18. B. J. Kuipers, A frame for frames: representing knowledge for recognition. In *Representation and Understanding* (Edited by D. G. Bobrow and A. Collins), pp. 151–184. Academic Press, New York (1975).
19. W. S. Havens, Can frames solve the chicken and egg problem?. *Proc. 1st CSCSI Nat. Conf.*, Univ. of B. C., Vancouver, Canada, August 1976.
20. A. K. Mackworth, How to see a simple world. In *Machine Intelligence 8* (Edited by E. W. Elcock and D. Michie). Halstead Press, New York (1977).21. D. G. Bobrow and T. Winograd, An overview of KRL: a knowledge representation language. *Cognitive Sci.* **1** (1) (1977).
21. D. G. Bobrow and T. Winograd, An Overview of KRL: A Knowledge Representation Language, *Cognitive Science* 1, #1 (1977).
22. R. Kaplan, A general syntactic processor. In *Natural Language Processing* (Edited by R. Rustin). Algorithmic Press, New York (1973).
23. L. D. Erman *et al.*, The Hearsay—II speech understanding system: integrating knowledge to resolve uncertainty. *Comp. Surveys* **12** (2), 213–254 (1980).
24. E. C. Freudler, A computer system for visual recognition using active knowledge. Ph.D. Thesis, *AI-TR*-345, MIT AI Laboratory, Cambridge, Mass. (1976).
25. N. Chomsky, *Syntactic Structures*. Mouton, The Hague (1957).
26. A. V. Aho and J. D. Ullman, *The Theory of Parsing, Translation, and Compiling*, Vol. 1. Prentice-Hall, Englewood Cliffs, New York (1972).
27. D. G. Hays, *Introduction to Computational Linguistics*. American Elsevier, New York (1967).
28. W. A. Woods, Augmented transition networks for natural language analysis. *Report CS*-1, Computation Lab, Harvard Univ., Cambridge, Mass. (1969).
29. J. Minker and G. J. Vandenbrug, The Earley Algorithm as a Problem Representation, TR-247, Comp. Science Center, Univ. of Md., College Park, Md. (1973).
30. A. K. Mackworth, Vision research strategy: black magic, metaphors, mechanisms, miniworlds, and Maps. In *Computer Vision Systems* (Edited by A. R. Hanson and E. M. Riseman). Academic Press, New York (1978).
31. H. G. Barrow and J. M. Tenenbaum, Representation and use of knowledge in vision. *Tech. Note* 108, Artificial Intelligence Center, SRI International, Menlo Park, Calif. (1975).
32. A. K. Mackworth, Model driven interpretation in intelligent vision systems. *Perception* **5**, 349–370 (1976).
33. T. Kanade, Region segmentation: signal vs semantics. *Proc. 3-IJCPR* (1977).
34. A. K. Mackworth and W. S. Havens, Structuring domain knowledge for visual perception. *Proc. 7-IJCAI*, Univ., of British Columbia, Vancouver, Canada, p. 625, August 1981.
35. A. K. Mackworth, On reading sketch maps. *Proc. 5-IJCAI*, MIT, Cambridge, Mass., pp. 598–606, August 1977.
36. L. G. Roberts, Machine Perception of Three-Dimensional Objects. In *Optical and Electro-optical Information Processing* (Edited by J. T. Tippet *et al.*) pp.159–197. MIT Press, Cambridge, Mass. (1965).
37. U. Neisser, *Cognition and Reality*. Freeman, San Francisco (1976).
38. R. B. Stanton, The Interpretation of Graphics and Graphic Languages. *Graphic Languages* (Edited by F. Nake and A. Rosenfeld), pp. 144–159. North Holland, Amsterdam (1972).
39. A. K. Mackworth, Consistency in networks of relations. *Artificial Intelligence* **8** (1), 99–118.
40. J. Glicksman, A schemata-based system for utilizing cooperating knowledge sources in computer vision. *Proc. 4th Biennial Conf. of Can. Society for the Comp. Studies of Intelligence*, Univ. of Sask., Saskatoon, Canada, pp. 33–39. May (1982).
41. R. J. Brachman, What ISA is and isn't. *Proc. 4th Biennial Conf. Can. Society for the Comp. Studies of Intelligence*, Univ. of Saskatoon, Saskatoon, Canada, pp. 212–221, May 1982.
42. W. A. Woods, An experimental parsing System for Transition Network Grammars. In *Natural Language Processing* (Edited by R. Rustin). Algorithmics Press, New York (1973).
43. N. J. Nilsson, *Problem-solving Methods in Artificial Intelligence*. McGraw-Hill, New York (1971).
44. D. V. McDermott and G. Sussman, *Son of Conniver: The Conniver Reference Manual, MIT AI Lab*. Cambridge, Mass. (1973).
45. A. R. Hanson and E. M. Riseman, Visions: A Computer System for Interpreting Scenes. In *Computer Vision Systems*, (Edited by A. R. Hanson and E. M. Riseman), pp. 303–333. Academic Press, New York (1978).
46. D. H. Ballard, *Hierarchic Recognition of Tumors in Chest Radiographs*, (*ISR*-16). Birkhauser-Verlag (1976).

Comp. & Maths. with Appls. Vol. 9, No. 1, pp. 201–214, 1983
Printed in Great Britain.

0097–4943/83/010201–14$03.00/0
Pergamon Press Ltd.

AN APPROACH TO THE ORGANIZATION OF KNOWLEDGE AND ITS USE IN NATURAL LANGUAGE RECALL TASKS

GORDON I. McCALLA

Department of Computational Science, University of Saskatchewan, Saskatoon, Saskatchewan, Canada S7N 0W0

Abstract—The viewpoint espoused in this paper is that natural language understanding and production is the action of a number of highly integrated domain-specific specialists. Described first is an object oriented representation scheme which allows these specialists to be built. Discussed next is the organization of these specialists into a four-level goal hierarchy that enables the modelling of natural language conversation. It is shown how the representation and natural language structures can be used to facilitate the recall of earlier natural language conversations. Six specific kinds of recall tasks are outlined in terms of these structures and their occurrence in several legal dialogues is examined. Finally, the need for intelligent garbage collection of old episodic information is pointed out.

1. INTRODUCTION

As with much current work on connected discourse, the viewpoint of this research is that it is oversimplified to view natural language comprehension and production as the action of domain-independent and basically sequential syntactic, semantic, and pragmatic processes. It is instead more appropriate to build domain specific specialists which do whatever needs to be done (be it syntactic, semantic, or pragmatic) whenever it needs to be done. This is not to say there is no structure whatsoever on natural language processing. In fact, it is very useful to break down natural language processing into four levels according to the goals of the language user. At the top level are non-linguistic goals which call in scripts (like those in [1], for example) to direct any linguistic processing. Scripts call in speech act level goals (a linguistic construct first proposed by Austin[2]) to interpret or produce individual utterances, and these, in turn, can call in language level specialists that handle much of the traditional parsing and other "linguistic" activity.

This domain-specific approach also leads to a basic concern for techniques to represent these specialists in order to reduce the complexity of the task of putting together a large knowledge base of them. An approach to representing knowledge is proposed which combines aspects of semantic network representation formalisms (surveyed in [3]) and frame-based knowledge representation schemes (see [4], [5] and many articles in [6]). As in many of these schemes, knowledge is represented in frame-like objects each of which can be considered as a node in an "extended" semantic network (extended in the sense that the relations are not necessarily binary). ISA and PART-OF hierarchies also exist and have the usual use in abstracting information.

At this point the scheme proposed here begins to differ from frame or network representation schemes. First, a context mechanism is proposed which not only allows dynamic focussing on relevent information to be achieved, but also forms the basis of an easily acquired "episodic memory". Second, the basic frame-like objects have much more in the way of procedural capabilities than is usual. In particular they send messages to one another in order to achieve sub-goals or glean information (much as in the SMALLTALK[7] or ACTOR[8] formalisms). If an object is not able to directly achieve some sub-goal or provide the required information, inheritance and other inferencing capabilities can be used as a consequence of the initial failure of this message passing.

In order to display the usefulness of the representation scheme proposed here, a natural language application has been selected: the *recall task*. In this particular type of natural language understanding an individual is asked to remember conversations which occurred sometime in the past. Real life examples of this task are legion—earlier linguistic performance must be recalled in debates, on the witness stand, in reading tests, in lectures, and frequently during ordinary conversation. This task turns out to be particularly well suited for the representation scheme, especially the scheme's dynamic focussing and episodic memory capabilities.

The paper is organized as follows. In Section 2 the representation scheme is described. Next, a particular conversation (a conversation to buy a ticket to a concert) is modelled in terms of the representation scheme. In Section 4 various recall tasks are categorized and the representation scheme's capabilities in handling these tasks are illustrated. Examples are given using recollections of the ticket buying conversation and using a number of legal dialogues. Finally, conclusions are drawn and open questions are discussed.

2. THE REPRESENTION SCHEME

The primitive units of the representation scheme proposed here are frame-like (in the Minsky[5] sense) objects called *pattern expressions* which can pass *messages* to each other and receive *responses*. All messages and responses are coordinated by an *interpreter* which reads messages from source objects, steers them to the proper target objects, and later directs the responses back to the appropriate source objects.

The representation scheme is implemented as a set of programs collectively called |LISP (pronounced "bar-lisp"). System notation is based as closely as possible on LISP, and, in fact most of LISP can be invoked directly from |LISP. The version of |LISP described here has not been fully implemented, although it differs only slightly from previous versions which have. For a complete description of the representation scheme and its notation see[9].

Looking in more detail at the representation scheme, a *pattern expression* (|PEXPR) is an object whose structure (body) is a list of (possibly labelled) patterns. A *pattern* is a list whose first element is the name of a pattern expression, and the rest of whose elements are either the names of pattern expressions or are further sub-patterns. *Messages* to |PEXPRs are also patterns, handled by *matching* them against patterns in the |PEXPR and returning as response the first matching pattern. As in many AI programming languages (e.g. CONNIVER[10]) the matching is complicated by the possible presence of single macro characters ("?", "!", "=", " ↓ ", "/") which may precede any element of either a message pattern or a |PEXPR pattern. These macros act as instructions to the matcher to perform special processing of various sorts when trying to achieve a match. As a knowledge base designer understands the domain being modelled, it is possible to gradually simplify or even eliminate many of these macros and achieve a smooth "procedural to declarative" evolution of the knowledge base.

Here is a simple pattern expression:

```
< |PDEF WIDGET-PEDDLER
      S1: (SUPERSET WIDGET-PEDDLER SELLER)
      S2: (SUPERSET WIDGET-PEDDLER PERSON)
      S3: (SELL ↓WIDGET-PEDDLER ↓WIDGET)
      S4: (TRADE ↓WIDGET-PEDDLER ↓BUYER ?GOODS
              !(COND ((SUB-INSTANCE-OF GOODS WIDGET)
                              (CREATE-NEW 'MONEY))
                          (T (CREATE-NEW 'SERVICES))))
      S5: (CORE WIDGET-PEDDLER (/S3 /S4))
      S6: (INSTANCE WIDGET-PEDDLER PETER)
      S7: (INSTANCE WIDGET-PEDDLER MARTHA) >
```

This is a simplified version of a knowledge base's explicit knowledge about widget peddlers. It can be interpreted as follows:

(i) the name of the |PEXPR is WIDGET-PEDDLER;

(ii) the body of the |PEXPR is the collection of patterns S1–S7;

(iii) each pattern in the body is designated with an (optional) label Si;

(iv) patterns S1 and S2 define two supersets of WIDGET-PEDDLER, SELLER and PERSON;

(v) pattern S3 says that an arbitrary instance of WIDGET-PEDDLER sells an arbitrary instance of WIDGETs (the " ↓ " macro indicates that instances of the classes, not the classes themselves, are required);

(vi) pattern S4 says that an arbitrary instance of WIDGET-PEDDLER trades with an arbitrary instance of BUYER as follows: the widget peddler exchanges "goods" for either money or services depending on whether the goods are widgets or not (the "!" macro indicates that the form following the macro should be executed (|EVALed) not taken as is; the "?" macro is explained below);

(vii) pattern S5 says that patterns S3 and S4 are the core patterns of the |PEXPR; i.e. they are more central to its meaning than are other patterns;

(viii) patterns S6 and S7 "point to" a couple of instances of the widget peddler, PETER and MARTHA (PETER and MARTHA will have reverse INSTANCE-OF "pointers"—together with EX-INSTANCE-OF pointers described below, INSTANCE-OF and SUPERSET define a standard generalization hierarchy, or as it is now usually designated (see [11]) an *ISA hierarchy* of pattern expressions).

To see how WIDGET-PEDDLER might respond to a message sent to it, assume another pattern expression, say BUY-WIDGET, formulates the message (WIDGET-PEDDLER (TRADE PETER SELF SQUIGGLY-WIDGET ?COST)) Thus, BUY-WIDGET is interested in seeing what (according to WIDGET-PEDDLER) SELF might give to PETER in return for the SQUIGGLY-WIDGET. Here is a simplified outline of what happens to the message.

The interpreter reads the message form and determines that the target pattern expression is WIDGET-PEDDLER. It thus creates a new, initially empty, pattern expression to serve as a working-storage area for WIDGET-PEDDLER as it answers the message. The new |PEXPR is given an internal name (WIDGET-PEDDLER-1, say) and is called an *execution instance* of WIDGET-PEDDLER. Next, three patterns are asserted in WIDGET-PEDDLER-1:

(EX-INSTANCE-OF WIDGET-PEDDLER-1 WIDGET-PEDDLER)
(EX-ENVIRON WIDGET-PEDDLER-1 BUY-WIDGET-1)
(|STACK WIDGET-PEDDLER-1 NIL)

The EX-INSTANCE-OF pattern points to WIDGET-PEDDLER, the object which has been sent the message; via this pointer all of the ISA environemt can be accessed. The EX-ENVIRON pattern points to the execution instance of the sending |PEXPR (BUY-WIDGET-1, say) in the *execution environment* or dynamic context of WIDGET-PEDDLER-1. |STACK indicates the local pattern expression stack, initially empty, that will contain any name/value bindings assigned during processing within WIDGET-PEDDLER-1. Finally, the message pattern itself is recorded in WIDGET-PEDDLER-1 for use when the interpreter decides to activate the |PEXPR. (WIDGET-PEDDLER-1 is not immediately executed, but is instead scheduled for future execution. This allows, among other things, pseudo-parallelism and multiprocessing to be simulated and is similar to KRL's[12] use of an agenda.)

When WIDGET-PEDDLER-1 becomes the current pattern expression, the message pattern is retrieved and matched against target patterns in the body of WIDGET-PEDDLER. If a pattern that matches the message pattern is found, it is returned to BUY-WIDGET-1 as the answer to the message. It is also asserted in the body of WIDGET-PEDDLER-1 as sort of a declarative residue of procedural activity and can later be accessed if desired.

In this example the pattern S4 is discovered and is found to match under the assumption that PETER is a particular WIDGET-PEDDLER (a fact discoverable by looking at the |PEXPR to see if it has a pattern

(INSTANCE-OF PETER WIDGET-PEDDLER),

and SELF is a particular BUYER. Assuming that SQUIGGLY-WIDGET is a particular WIDGET, the |EVALuation of the pattern's last element will result in the creation of a new |PEXPR (called MONEY1) representing an individual price appropriate to the widget. Thus, the pattern to be returned in answer to the TRADE message is

(TRADE PETER SELF SQUIGGLY-WIDGET MONEY1).

This pattern will be asserted in both WIDGET-PEDDLER-1 and BUY-WIDGET-1. In addition

MONEY1 will be bound as the value of COST on the BUY-WIDGET-1 stack (due to the "?" macro which says to bind a value on the stack of the execution instance containing the pattern with the macro). Such bindings may be useful to procedures executing in BUY-WIDGET-1.

The question arises: what would have happened if no match had been discovered in WIDGET-PEDDLER? In cases such as this, the matcher does not give up. Instead, it looks at the first element of the pattern to be matched and seeks the aid of the pattern expression corresponding to that element (i.e. TRADE here). The rationale for consulting TRADE is that the first element of a pattern usually acts as the relation connecting all the other elements, and is thus the most crucial part of the pattern. The hope is that TRADE will have associated with it a *failure to match* pattern (such as, for example.

(FAILURE-TO-MATCH TRADE ?PAT ?OBJ !(SEARCH-ISA PAT OBJ)))

that tells the matcher what to do if at any time a pattern headed by TRADE is unmatched. The builder of the knowledge base can specify various possibilities: e.g. look into the ISA environment of WIDGET-PEDDLER-1, look into the execution environment of WIDGET-PEDDLER-1, perform an inference, return final failure, and so on. This puts into the hands of the designer the power to use local knowledge and context to determine what to do for a particular failure, although s/he must be very careful to take into account the subtleties involved in such inference, particularly inheritance (see[13] for a thorough analysis of these subtleties). In any event this is one of the strong points of this representation scheme and contrasts with more uniform inferencing and procedural attachment mechanisms (e.g. KRL[12] or FRL[14]).

Once the message has been answered, the |PEXPR which sent the message (BUY-WIDGET-1, discovered by looking at the EX-ENVIRON pointer) is rescheduled. When it again becomes active, BUY-WIDGET-1 can pick up the answer to the message and proceed with its computations.

Of particular importance is the fact that WIDGET-PEDDLER-1 has not disappeared. Execution instances are kept to maintain a record of the events taking place when they were executed, a crucial ability for the recall tasks discussed in Section 4. These execution instances not only still maintain their EX-ENVIRON and EX-INSTANCE-OF patterns, but they also still contain all other relevent patterns that were asserted during their execution. To retrieve knowledge in such an execution instance requires the sending of a message to the instance, with the consequent creation of an execution instance of an execution instance. The old execution instance has access to the old execution environment in which it was run; the newly created execution instance has access to the current execution environment. This gives a facility similar to that provided by the ALINK/CLINK distinction of [15] in that it allows information to be accessed in one context and returned to another. Moreover, it is possible in |LISP to have multiple levels of execution instances and hence to have the equivalent of many ALINKs.

Eventually, of course, some sort of pruning or garbage collection of all this information must take place. Furthermore, given the potential importance of some execution instances, it seems crucial to do such garbage collection intelligently. This is further discussed in Section 6.

Before proceeding to a discussion of how |LISP can be used in a natural language domain, some comment on its potential efficiency should be made. Since typically there are only relatively few patterns within a pattern expression, matching a pattern becomes computationally expensive only when failure-to-match inferences must be undertaken or when macro elements require further processing. Although in theory failure-to-match inferences can be arbitrary, in practice they usually involve non-explosive searches along converging and not very deep hierarchies. The presence of macro elements usually implies some sort of message passing is going on and this will be efficient if the knowledge in the system imposes strong constraints on the choice of target objects. Work on expert systems (e.g.[16]) seems to indicate that for many domains enough such knowledge can be accumulated. The big question is whether for a really large and diverse domain this is possible and in particular whether the sheer size and complexity of the task will be overwhelming. It is an article of faith of this and other frame theories that knowledge can be divided elegantly into large, nearly decomposable "chunks"[17] and that these chunks (frames) can be incrementally added to a knowledge base without undue complexity ever arising. The relatively small number of examples developed so far in the literature does not provide definitive evidence one way or the other of this contention, but the very existence of so much frame research activity seems to indicate a widespread optimism.

3. USING |LISP IN A NATURAL LANGUAGE DOMAIN

|LISP can be used to represent the various data and procedures necessary for appropriate natural language processing. To illustrate, assume the following typical task-oriented (in the sense of [18]) conversation occurs between a computer "model" and a ticket seller when the model "wants" to go to a symphony concert:

Ticket-seller: "Yes?"
Model: "I'd like a ticket to the concert."
Ticket-seller: "How about K–5? It is right centre about 10 rows back."
Model: "Fine. How much is that?"
Ticket-seller: "10 dollars."
Model: "O.K. (pays the money)
Ticket-seller: (produces the ticket)
Model: "Thanks."
Ticket-seller: "Thank you sir."

First, much information about tickets, concerts, costs, ticket sellers, etc. must be represented. This can be done rather straightforwardly by building appropriate pattern expressions and connecting them together using appropriate links. These pattern expressions will contain largely declarative patterns, e.g.

```
< |PDEF LOWER-BALCONY-SEAT
   (SUPERSET LOWER-BALCONY-SEAT AUDITORIUM-SEAT)
   (COST ↓ LOWER-BALCONY-SEAT ↓ 10-DOLLARS)
   (VIEW ↓LOWER-BALCONY-SEAT EXCELLENT)
   (HEARING ↓LOWER-BALCONY-SEAT AVERAGE)>
```

Note that the ticket seller |PEXPR will constitute a model of the conversant, a crucial need as Cohen[19] and Allen[20] have discussed at length.

But, these pattern expressions are secondary to the primary pattern expressions which actually carry out the goals of the model (both linguistic and non-linguistic). There are several major types of goals ranging from non-linguistic goals through scripts (akin to the scripts of [1] or [21]), and speech acts (computational analogues of the speech acts of [2] and [22] and similar to those proposed in, for example, [19]) down to low level language goals. Non-linguistic goals tend to be "high level" goals which invoke scripts when a conversation is necessary to achieve the purposes of the high level goal. Scripts, in turn, direct a conversation, calling in speech act subgoals to understand or produce individual utterances of the conversants. Speech acts will usually (although not always) need to call on the expertise of still more specific language level goals to actually generate or interpret appropriate surface language.

For example, in the ticket buying situation, the non-linguistic goal of buying the ticket may necessitate the invocation of a script to direct a conversation with the ticket seller. This script will need to both understand particular speech acts (e.g. requests by the ticket seller for money, inquiries into types of tickets desired) and produce certain speech acts (e.g. to inform the ticket seller of the type of ticket desired). Finally, surface utterances such as "Yes", "How much is that?", etc. will have to be handled at the language level.

Of course, the strict top-down processing suggested here will not always work completely satisfactorily. Sometimes an invoked subgoal will fail, in which case the supergoal must explain what went wrong and invoke a more appropriate subgoal, perhaps trying to preserve partial results already provided in the failed subgoal's execution instance. Recovery from error and making use of partial information are very hard problems as Minsky's work [5] and much subsequent work on frames has pointed out, and, although McCalla[9] discusses these problems, this research provides no definitive solutions.

An alternative to top-down processing with error recovery is a judicious mixture of top-down and bottom-up processing. Bottom-up processes identify potentially relevent information and top-down processes then pick and choose the most relevant such information to integrate into the evolving context. Again, an example in [9] is given where bottom-up processing of this ilk proves useful, but no general solutions are provided. The definitive research into this problem has been done by Havens[23] and many of his insights for the vision area would likely carry over to natural language processing. For the rest of this paper the problems of error recovery and bottom-up processing will be downplayed in order to allow a more extensive discussion of recall issues.

Returning to the ticket buying example, it is important to realize that the various goals can be represented by pattern expressions, ones with more procedurally oriented patterns (i.e. patterns containing "!" and similar macros) than the secondary pattern expressions. For example, a simplified version of the script that directs a ticket buying conversation would look something like

```
<|PDEF BUY-CONVERSATION
      SUPERSET BUY-CONVERSATION CONVERSATION)
      (EXECUTE BUY-CONVERSATION ?BUYER ?SELLER ?ITEM
        !(EVENT-SEQUENCE
          ;start up conversation
          (WHAT-DO-YOU-WANT
            (EXECUTE WHAT-DO-YOU-WANT !SELLER !BUYER
                                        ?WHAT-WANT-CONV))
          ;bargain over what buyer wants
          ;first get bargaining positions
          ;from conversant models
          (!BUYER (WANT !BUYER
                    (EXCHANGE ?BUYER-HAS ?SELLER-WANTS)))
          (!SELLER (WANT !SELLER
                    (EXCHANGE ?SELLER-HAS ?SELLER-WANTS)))
          ;next enter into actual bargaining
          (BARGAIN
            (EXECUTE BARGAIN !SELLER !BUYER !SELLER-HAS
                !BUYER-WANTS !ITEM ?BARGAIN-1-CONV))
          ;bargain over what seller wants
          (BARGAIN
            (EXECUTE BARGAIN !BUYER !SELLER !BUYER-HAS
                !SELLER-WANTS !ITEM ?BARGAIN-2-CONV))
          ;exchange cost of item for item
          (EXCHANGE
            (EXECUTE EXCHANGE !BUYER !SELLER
                !(|POINTER COST ITEM) !ITEM ?CONV-EXCHANGE))
          ;close out the conversation
          (FAREWELL
            (EXECUTE FAREWELL !BUYER !SELLER ?BYE)),>
```

The pattern expressions representing these goals invoke one another by passing messages, resulting in a dynamic subgoal hierarchy (the execution environment) containing non-linguistic goals at the top and low level language goals at the bottom. Any goal knows and can access knowledge in the goal which invoked it, and also in all supergoals. This is useful not only to avoid redundancy of information, but also to enable subgoals to execute in the context of their supergoals. Thus, the ticket-buying script (and all its subgoals) can know that the conversant is a ticket seller because this is knowledge "discovered" by the non-linguistic supergoal which wants the ticket to be bought. Just being able to diagnose the existence of a particular supergoal can be crucial in understanding such utterances as "Yes?", "What are you doing here?", etc. which are questions specifically asking for the goals of a language user.

The subgoal hierarchy is the basic context feature of this approach to language. It provides a natural focussing mechanism by suggesting an ever narrower set of goals of interest to a particular situation. The goals in this "context" are not static and predetermined as is information in the context mechanism in, say, [24]; instead, goals are always changing as certain subgoals get accomplished (and hence become irrelevant) while others then become important. Moreover, these changes are nicely structured in terms of "level of detail"—lower goals change rapidly as minor changes occur in a situation; upper goals change more gradually (usually only after a succession of lower goals have been accomplished) as entire situations evolve into other situations.

The subgoal hierarchy also acts as a starting point for searches of the knowledge base. The ISA hierarchy above a goal pattern expression can be accessed along SUPERSET, IN-STANCE-OF, or EX-INSTANCE-OF pointers. Similarly it is possible to access the PART-OF (or aggregation) hierarchy (see, e.g. [23]), as well as many "one-shot" pointers (forming no coherent organizational principle) to relevant information such as the current conversant, the kind of ticket currently wanted, the discovered location of a ticket outlet, etc.

Since the execution instances in the subgoal hierarchy do not disappear, whole trees of old subgoal instantiations are available to provide "episodic" information (in the sense of [25]). At a given level of such an episodic tree are episodes which followed one another in sequence; going down a level gives a more detailed view of a particular sub-episode. This combination of both sequence information and subgoal information is different from the usual basically sequential view of episodic memory. Moreover, from each execution instance in this episodic memory the ISA hierarchy above the execution instance can be accessed so the episodic and semantic memories are perfectly compatible.

4. THE RECALL TASK

As mentioned in the introduction, a common kind of natural language understanding involves recalling earlier conversations. The |LISP representation scheme turns out to be very useful for handling this kind of natural language task. The major useful feature is the episodic capability mentioned at the end of the last section.

There has been work on the recall task from the perspective of "story trees" [26, 27] which are hierarchical, like execution instance trees, but not in terms of the goals of the language understander, rather in terms of the story structure itself. Kintsch and van Dijk [26] do suggest that the story trees are created as the text is being processed, which corresponds to the automatic creation of execution instance trees as a by-product of the original linguistic processing. Wilensky [28] also structures story memory hierarchically according to its "point" content (at various levels of abstraction) rather than the language understander's goals.

For the purposes of illustration, assume the ticket-buying conversation of Section 3 has been recorded as in Fig. 1. (Note that the execution instances of many secondary pattern expressions invoked during the conversation have been trimmed by the intelligent garbage collector as have lower language level goals. More of this in Section 6.)

Before the model can recall details of this conversation, the appropriate execution instance goal hierarchy must be restored from memory. Although this paper doesn't propose a complete solution to this problem, it appears from the court room recall dialogues discussed in Section 5 that the recall request usually contains the information necessary in order for the hearer to associate to the episode in question. Things like dates, times, conversant names, places, etc. seem to work fairly well for people. It would be possible to structure a |LISP knowledge base with similar associative links in order to allow the appropriate retrieval. This has not been done—instead, the appropriate hierarchy is assumed to be readily available.

Once the particular episode is retrieved from memory, many types of requests can be made. One such request is

(1a) "How much did the ticket seller claim the ticket cost?"

To answer this request, the various execution instances in the hierarchy can be examined and the fact (stored in this case in INFORM-3) can be retrieved. This illustrates a *fact retrieval*

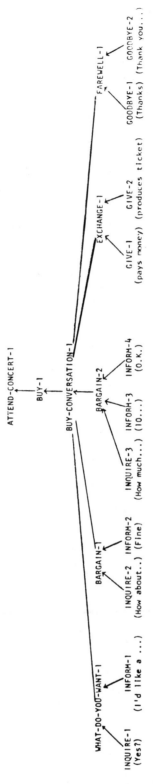

Fig. 1. An execution instance goal tree for the ticket buying conversation. (Note: all arcs are EX-ENVIRON pointers).

recall request, i.e. a task requiring access to a specific fact from a particular execution instance. There are many such examples:

(1b) "Who sold the ticket?"
(1c) "Where was the ticket located in the auditorium?"
(1d) "How much was paid for the ticket?"

In fact retrieval requests, the execution instance goal hierarchy often acts as a context mechanism in that it provides a starting point for memory searches for the required information rather than necessarily acting as the direct container of the information itself. Thus, if asked

(1e) "What were the various possible ticket prices?"

the pattern expression containing information about the ticket actually bought could be retrieved from INFORM-1, but it wouldn't contain the answer directly. Instead, inheritance from its superset (the pattern expression representing general ticket knowledge) of the various prices would be necessary. Thus, not only has the episodic memory constrained the search for the required ticket knowledge, but the failure-to-match processing that was useful in handling the original episode would also be useful in the recall domain.

The biggest problem in handling fact retrieval recall is identifying the particular execution instance containing the fact. An associative activation style search (as discussed in [29], say) from various key concepts (e.g. TICKET, COST,...) mentioned in the recall sentence will fairly quickly intersect appropriate execution instances from the episode under consideration and hence provide a small number of execution instances to search. Examining the structure of the script-level execution instances (or the corresponding generic scripts themselves) may also prove useful in identifying likely steps which might contain the desired information. Finally, there is frequently an implicit structure to the recall dialogue that focusses attention on a particular execution instance in one utterance before requesting a fact from that instance in the next utterance. Such focussing is not only obvious in the legal dialogues that have been examined (see Section 5), but has also been the subject of much study recently (e.g. [30, 31]).

Another common kind of recall task is the *motivation* recall request where the various goals, desires, and motivations of the speakers are requested. For example, the following questions

(2a) "Why did the ticket seller give the ticket to the ticket buyer?"
(2b) "Why did the ticket buyer say "thanks"?"
(2c) "What was the ticket buyer attempting to do in this episode?"

all require implicit or explicit motivations to be retrieved. If the speaker who made the original utterances is later queried as to motivation it usually suffices to look at the pattern expressions in the goal hierarchy themselves to answer such a query. Thus, from the later perspective of the ticket buyer, query (2c) above can be answered by looking at the top level pattern expressions in the goal tree; i.e. the purpose of the ticket buyer is to ATTEND-CONCERT (discovered as the generic associated with the top level ATTEND-CONCERT-1 pattern expression) or more specifically to BUY a ticket to the concert or yet more specifically to take part in a BUY-CONVERSATION to get a ticket to the concert.

But if the motivation requested is not that of the model, then these goals must be inferred. This is a complicated task, as [20], [32], [33] and [34] and much other research has shown. From the structural point of view taken in this paper, however, the episodic tree at least provides a starting point. Patterns will have been left in the execution instances themselves recording the presumed goals or motivations of the other party. Thus, a pattern or patterns indicating that the purpose of the ticket seller is to sell tickets can be explicitly left in the BUY-CON-VERSATION-1 execution instance and later retrieved. If this hasn't been done, failure-to-match processing can search the pattern expression representing the particular ticket seller (which *is* recorded in BUY-CONVERSATION-1) and its ISA parents for general motivations of ticket sellers. This kind of other party motivation request thus boils down to a special case of fact retrieval recalls.

Closely related to motivation recall requests are requests that ask for summaries of what happened, e.g.

(3a) "What, overall, was she getting at when she said that?"
(3b) "What was the conversation about?"
(3c) "What were you trying to do?"

These *summary* requests can be answered by looking at the execution instances in the upper levels of the goal hierarchy rather than at specific speech act or language level execution instances. The request can be an explicit one asking for a summary (as in (3b) where the BUY-CONVERSATION-1 execution instance would be at the appropriate level of detail) or can be a relative request to go to a higher level of detail than the one currently being recalled (as in (3a) if it were issued after the person had been recounting a specific series of speech acts, say, and was being asked to move up to a script level). The ability to summarize, as Correira[27] suggests, is a very important attribute of any text understanding task.

The opposite kind of request is one requiring the recaller to specify things to a lower level of detail as in

(4b) "Exactly what did he say at this point?"
(4b) "Be more specific."
(4c) "Recall the exact words that were used if you can."

Such *specify* requests will usually be issued after a definite level has been established from which to plunge downwards into more detail. Sometimes specify requests can even require language level execution instances, as in (4c), although it seems reasonable to assume that most actual wordings will have been garbage collected.

The fifth kind of recall task requires a specific sequence of events to be scanned. Examples of such *event sequence* recall requests include

(5a) "Tell me what the ticket seller said next."
(5b) "Tell the court what happened after the ticket buyer and the ticket seller exchanged the money for the ticket."
(5c) "Recount in your own words the sequence of events leading up to the ticket buyer getting the ticket."

Answering these requests requires a horizontal scan at a particular level of detail rather than the vertical movements required in motivation, summary, or specify requests. Sometimes the focus is already established (as in 5a) and the next event is all that is required. Other times, the amount of specificity indicated in the recall request determines the level chosen. For example, the event referred to in (5b) above corresponds to the script level execution instance EXCHANGE-1. Thus, the next required event corresponds to the script level execution instance FAREWELL-1 (i.e. the answer to (5b) would be something like "The two parties said farewell.").

In (5c), however, the event referred to is GIVE-2, a speech act (actually in this case a motor act!) The required events would thus be the immediately preceding speech act level events at least within the same sub-script. Of course, earlier events might be somewhat summarized (i.e. a possible answer could be something like "The seller and buyer greeted one another and bargained over cost and location of the ticket. The buyer than handed over $10 at which point he got the ticket."). The episodic goal tree thus not only provides the basic event sequence, but also provides at least some structure as to the right level of response. Of course, specific heuristics must be worked out as to when to summarize and when not.

The sixth type of request is a *meta* request in the sense that the structure of the goal hierarchy itself is being queried rather than its contents. Thus,

(6a) "How long did you talk?"
(6b) "Was the discussion uninterrupted?"
(6c) "So you remember nothing after that?"

force an examination of the structure itself; i.e. to look, respectively, for length of conversation, large numbers of non-linguistic execution instances in the tree, or the boundaries of the tree.

No doubt there are many other types of recall possible besides these six (for example, since it is possible to have execution instances of execution instances, recalls of recall dialogues could be undertaken in order to answer queries like "What did you do after you told her how I had been buying a ticket?"). The important point is that the structure of episodic memory provides a basis for categorizing the various kinds of recall requests and for answering them in an appropriate way. This provides for the recall domain a similar insight to the use in [18] of task structure to determine focus in task oriented dialogues.

5. SOME LEGAL EXAMPLES

In this section five stereotypical legal dialogues (taken from the series of volumes American Jurisprudence Proof of Facts [35]) are examined for evidence of both hierarchically structured episodes and the various types of recall requests. In each of these dialogues a witness is being queried by a lawyer about some conversation he or she had in the past with (usually) a defendent who is being sued. Each dialogue starts with the lawyer evoking in the mind of the witness the conversation to be recalled by specifying dates, times, etc.

Once this has been accomplished, details of the conversation are elicited by specify requests such as "What exactly was said?" Then, frequently, the lawyer issues a series of event sequence requests such as "What was said next?" to force the witness to march through the previous conversation. Information as to what was said is usually provided at the speech act level, but occasionally the witness is asked to abstract a summary at an obviously higher level ("Was there a discussion between you and the defendant about this asking price?") or the witness crawls up and down levels summarizing and specifying. Fact retrieval requests frequently occur ("How much of a down payment did the defendant want?") Sometimes something like ISA inheritance seems to have taken place to retrieve a fact (as in the italicized parts of "... to finance a mortgage on $40,000, *the amount of the purchase price minus the down payment...*") There are several occasions where meta responses are given by the witness ("I thought to myself for a couple of minutes...", "...a few minutes later...", "I don't recall anything else") although such responses are not directly requested. There is even an occasion where exact wording is requested (i.e. language level goals). There are no motivation requests, probably because they are inappropriate in a legal setting.

It seems clear from the examples that the methodology proposed here is quite useful. However, this usefulness will rapidly diminish in any realistic setting unless the many episodic memory structures can be intelligently garbage collected.

6. INTELLIGENT GARBAGE COLLECTION

It is crucial to wisely clean up the incredible amount of information that accumulates during natural language processing. This is the function of the intelligent garbage collection routines. First and foremost, these routines must delete many of the execution instances which have been accumulated. In most of the legal dialogues, only speech act level paraphrases of prior discussions are given. This suggests that a useful heuristic is to delete all execution instances at or below the language level. Of course, this doesn't always work. In certain situations (e.g. very embarrassing situations, important discussions, the occurrence of a shocking event such as an assassination, etc.) execution instances might stay around in much more detail. In any event if this deletion by level is done poorly, later recollections will be overgeneralized.

As well as removing execution instances by taking a horizontal cut at the hierarchy, many must also be pruned by chopping vertically. During any processing many secondary pattern expressions will be contacted, many irrelevant pattern expressions will be tried and rejected, and many low-level "housekeeping" duties will need to be undertaken. The execution instances associated with these can be removed. Of course, too much pruning of this sort would result in a *selective memory* where certain steps are forgotten. A useful heuristic here is to keep only execution instances of scripts and speech acts and not keep execution instances of the conversant models and the like since they aren't major plan steps.

In task oriented dialogues with lots of packaged scripts already in existence, the examinable nature of the scripts allows perusal of the script itself to get most of the required information during a recall. All that needs to be kept for each script is a skeletal execution instance. Messages can still be sent to the execution instance as before; failure to match processing would automatically initiate inheritance from the script level without the rest of the knowledge base needing to know the execution instance is a mere skeleton. Of course, certain data such as speakers, locales, etc. which change each time the script is invoked, also need to be kept, but these data would be relatively fewer in number.

In non-task-oriented dialogues execution instances take on added importance and hence shouldn't be as readily removed. Here, the script level must be abstracted somehow "on the fly" since specific preordained scripts will not be available. Some of these higher level pattern expressions will arise as plans created by general purpose conversation scripts to handle specific situations as they arise in conversation. Such planning takes place frequently as [1], [19], [36] and other research has shown. Since a plan is not as permanent nor as tested as a script, it seems appropriate to keep the execution instances around to record how the plan actually worked out. Moreover, there would usually be in absolute number more execution instances in a planned conversation than in a scripted one as various interpretation and generation strategies were tried, further enhancing the likelihood of at least some execution instances surviving. Evidence for this can be seen in Bartlett's[4] experimental results that subjects recalled things they had found difficult to understand (i.e. things that in |LISP would require more processing to comprehend, and hence more execution instances) more readily than easy to understand things.

Another role for execution instances (especially in non-task-oriented dialogues) is to act as origins for the ISA generalization of information from low level sequences of speech acts. Such generalization (by the intelligent garbage collector) may be a way (other than planning) of creating script level pattern expressions. Both plans and the generalized pattern expressions may eventually become scripts as use proves their worth.

The intelligent garbage collector also needs to integrate newly acquired episodes into the overall knowledge base. Many links are already there since an episode's execution instances are laden with patterns that connect the episode to other pattern expressions. But the legal dialogues of Section 5 illustrate that these must be better organized and new ones added. The legal dialogues start off with a number of facts (e.g. "Do you know the price which the defendant, Mr. Smith, was asking for the property on Oak Street at the time you noticed it was for sale?") which obviously uniquely pinpoint the episode in memory. During the dialogues, the witnesses often are able to skip through several different episodes which all relate to the same topic even if they happened at widely different times ("[then] the agent came back to my service station about two weeks later..."). The witnesses seem to be able to organize their memories around certain topic designations, maybe not at first, but certainly later when rehearsing for a courtroom appearance. Somehow, the intelligent garbage collector will have to do this kind of topic organization and will have to add the various links into the episode from other relevent pattern expressions. Perhaps Reichman's work [37] on topic delineated context spaces may be useful here.

Such "learning" capabilities are an interesting aspects of the intelligent garbage collector's duties and need to be explored in much more detail. At least in |LISP the raw materials for appropriate learning are provided in the form of the execution instances themselves and the various hierarchies to which they are attached.

7. CONCLUSIONS

The most important lesson to be drawn from this research is the value of taking an integrated view of the whole linguistic endeavour. This broad view has led to a recognition of the versatility of many of the language and representation features. Thus, pattern expressions can represent both static and dynamic information. They have aspects of both frame and network approaches. Execution instances are needed purely from a computational point of view, but also turn out to be helpful both during conversation and during recall. The execution environment is a useful context mechanism; it also forms the basis for episodic memory. The goal hierarchy is important for handling the original conversation and also is crucial in allowing recall at varying levels of detail.

The most interesting single feature of this approach is the use of execution instances in recalling earlier behaviour. Making the execution instances pattern expressions has allowed them to be useful later. It means that episodic memory is built up automatically as a by-product of message passing behaviour. It also means that the structure of episodic memory closely parallels the original structure of the episode being modelled and isn't something artificially reconstructed later. This structure allows the delineation, in structural terms, of several different types of recall (fact retrieval, motivation, summary, specify, event sequence and meta) and a couple of types of memory failure (overgeneralization and selective memory).

There are a host of open computational issues regarding how to access an episode, how to best peruse it under different circumstances, etc. There are also many unresolved linguistic and representation subtleties. But, the most interesting and crucial task is to discover a lot more about the intelligent garbage collection process. To paraphrase Schank and Abelson[38]—forgetting promises to be a major endeavour in computational linguistics research.

Acknowledgements—I would like to thank Richard Rosenberg, especially, for his help in the elaboration of many of the ideas presented here. Hector Levesque, Nick Cercone, and Alan Mackworth also provided much in the way of useful input to this research. I would like to express my gratitude to Peta Bates both for her encouragement and for wading through much verbiage to extract the legal dialogues of Section 5. Finally, the financial support of the National Sciences and Engineering Research Council of Canada and the University of Saskatchewan are acknowledged.

REFERENCES

1. R. C. Schank and R. P. Abelson, *Scripts, Plans, Goals and Understanding*. Lawrence Erlbaum Press, Hillsdale, N.J. (1977).
2. J. L. Austin, *How to do Things with Words*. Oxford University Press, Oxford (1962).
3. N. Findler (Ed.), *Associative Networks*. Academic Press, New York (1979).
4. Sir F. Bartlett, *Remembering*. Cambridge University Press, Cambridge (1932).
5. M. Minsky, A framework for representing knowledge. *MIT Al Memo* 306, Cambridge, Mass. (1974).
6. R. C. Schank and B. L. Nash-Webber (Eds.), *Theoretical Issues in Natural Language Processing. Workshop Proc.* (1975).
7. A. Goldberg *et al.* Introducing the SMALLTALK-80 system, and other SMALLTALK papers. *Byte* **6**, 8 (1980).
8. C. Hewitt, Viewing control structures as patterns of passing messages. *Artificial Intell.* **8**(3), 324–364 (1977).
9. G. I. McCalla, An approach to the organization of knowledge for the modelling of conversation. *Tech. Rep.* 78–4 (Ph.D. Thesis), Dept. of Computer Science, U. of British Columbia, Vancouver, B.C. (1978).
10. D. V. McDermott and G. J. Sussman, The CONNIVER reference manual. *MIT AI Memo* 259a, Cambridge, Mass. (1974).
11. R. J. Brachman, What ISA is and isn't. *Proc. 4th Conf. Canadian Society for Computational Studies of Intelligence*, 212–221, Saskatoon, Saskatchewan (1982).
12. D. G. Bobrow, T. Winograd and KRL Research Group. Experience with KRL-0: one cycle of a knowledge representation language. *Proc. 5th Int. Joint Conf. Artificial Intelligence*. pp. 213–222, Cambridge, Mass. (1977).
13. H. J. Levesque and J. Mylopoulos, A procedural approach to semantic networks. In *Associative Networks* (Edited by N. Findler). Academic Press, New York (1979).
14. B. P. Roberts and I. Goldstein, The FRL primer. *MIT AI Memo* 408, Cambridge, Mass. (1977).
15. D. G. Bobrow and B. Wegbreit, A model and stack implementation of multiple environments. *Commun. ACM* **16**(10), 591–602 (1973).
16. D. Michie (Ed.), *Expert systems in the Micro Electronic Age*. Edinburgh University Press, Edinburgh (1979).
17. H. A. Simon, The architecture of complexity. In *The Sciences of the Artificial* (Edited by H. A. Simon). MIT Press, Cambridge, Mass. (1969).
18. B. J. Deutsch (Grosz), The structure of task oriented dialogues. *IEEE Symp. Speech Recognition*, Carnegie-Mellon Univ. (April 1974).
19. P. R. Cohen, On knowing what to say: planning speech acts. *Tech. Rep.* 118 (Ph.D. Thesis), Dept. Computer Science, Univ. of Toronto (1978).
20. J. Allen, A plan based theory of speech act recognition. *Tech. Rep.* 131 (Ph.D. Thesis). Dept. of Computer Science, Univ. of Toronto (1979).
21. R. E. Cullingford, Organizing world knowledge for story understanding by computer. *Res. Rep.* 116 (Ph.D. Thesis), Dept. of Computer Science, Yale Univ. (1978).
22. J. Searle, *Speech Acts*. Cambridge University Press, Cambridge (1969).
23. W. S. Havens, A procedural model of recognition for machine perception. *Tech. Rep.* 78–3 (Ph.D. Thesis), Dept. of Computer Science, Univ. of British Columbia, Vancouver, B.C. (1978).
24. G. Hendrix, Expanding the utility of semantic networks through partitioning. *Proc. 4th Int. Conf. Artificial Intelligence*, pp. 115–121, Tbilisi, USSR (1975).
25. E. Tulving, Episodic and semantic memory. In *Organization of Memory*. (Edited by E. Tulving and W. Donaldson). Academic Press, New York (1972).
26. W. Kintsch and T. van Dijk, Recalling and summarizing stories. In *Current Trends in Textlinguistics* (Edited by W Dressler). de Gruyter Hawthorne, New York (1978).
27. A. Correira, Computing story trees. *Am. J. Computat. Linguistics* **6**(3–4). 135–149 (1980).

28. R. Wilensky. What's the point? *Proc. 3rd Conf. Canadian Society for Computational Studies of Intelligence.* pp. 156–262, Victoria, B.C. (1980).
29. S. Fahlman, Three flavors of parallelism, *Proc. 4th Conf. Canadian Society for Computational Studies of Intelligence,* pp. 230–235, Saskatoon, Saskatchewan (1982).
30. B. J. Grosz, The representation and use of focus in a system for understanding dialogues. *Proc. 5th Int. Joint Conf. Artificial Intelligence,* pp. 67–76, Cambridge, Mass. (1977).
31. S. L. Sidner, Focussing for interpretation of pronouns. *Am. J. Computational Linguistics* 7(4), 217–231 (1981).
32. B. Bruce and C. F. Schmidt, Episode understanding and belief guided parsing. *Assoc. Computational Linguistics Conf.,* Amherst, Mass. (1974).
33. J. Carbonell, POLITICS: automated ideological reasoning. *Cognitive Sci.* 2(1), 27–51 (1978).
34. R. Cohen, Understanding arguments. *Proc. 3rd Conf. Canadian Society for Computational Studies of Intelligence,* pp. 272–279, Victoria, B.C. (1980).
35. *American Jurisprudence Proof of Facts: Text and Sample Testimony...,* Vols. I–VI, Second Series. Lawyers Co-operative, Rochester, New York (1974).
36. R. Wilensky, Understanding goal based stories. *Res. Rep.* 140 (Ph.D. Thesis), Dept. of Computer Science, Yale (1978).
37. R. Reichman, Conversational coherency. *Cognitive Sci.* 2(4) 283–327 (1978).
38. R. C. Schank and R. P. Abelson, Scripts, plans, and knowledge. *Proc. 4th Int. Joint Conf. Artificial Intelligence,* pp. 151–158, Tbilisi, U.S.S.R. (1975).

Comp. & Maths. with Appls. Vol. 9, No. 1, pp. 215–231, 1983
Printed in Great Britain.

0097–4943/83/010215–17$03.00/0
Pergamon Press Ltd.

MINIMAL AND ALMOST MINIMAL PERFECT HASH FUNCTION SEARCH WITH APPLICATION TO NATURAL LANGUAGE LEXICON DESIGN

Nick Cercone, Max Krause and John Boates

Computing Science Department, Simon Fraser University, Burnaby, British Columbia, Canada

Abstract—New methods for computing perfect hash functions and applications of such functions to the problems of lexicon design are reported in this paper. After stating the problem and briefly discussing previous solutions, we present Cichelli's algorithm, which introduced the form of the solutions we have pursued in this research. An informal analysis of the problem is given, followed by a presentation of three algorithms which refine and generalise Cichelli's method in different ways. We next report the results of applying programmed versions of these algorithms to problem sets drawn from natural and artificial languages. A discussion of conceptual designs for the application of perfect hash functions to small and large computer lexicons is followed by a summary of our research and suggestions for further work.

1. INTRODUCTION

Skilful lexical design can engender good results in automated natural language understanding endeavours. Lexicons are an integral part of natural language systems (as well as many other systems, e.g. compilers). Although different authors writing about implementations of such systems have had different criteria for using particular lexicons, nevertheless similarities become evident in both the use and function of the lexical component of their systems. In particular, one manifest similarity ensues since lexical items serve as access to (corresponding) meaning representations. The experimental program reported in Cercone[4] explores the nature and computational use of meaning representations for word concepts in the context of a natural language understanding system. Word meanings are represented as extended semantic networks and are accessed via a tiny (approximately 200 words) lexicon.

It is interesting to note that many natural language system designers make extensive use of morphological analysis to avoid explicit storage of regularly inflected words and some irregular forms. Most systems rely on LISP (Allen[1]) to access word meanings through the word's property list. Small dictionaries with few syntactic features and simple semantic features are not penalised with this use of LISP. However, when the size of the dictionary and especially the complexity of lexical entries becomes great, more explicit control over the dictionary is desirable.

Advantages accrue when processing natural or artificial languages with fixed vocabularies of f frequently used words by direct random access to items in the database. Perfect hash functions, a deterministic refinement of key-to-address transformation techniques, provide this single probe retrieval of keys from a static table. Given a set of N keys and a hash table of size $r \geq N$, a perfect hash function maps the keys into the hash table with no collisions since the function locates each key at a unique table address. The loading factor (LF) of a hash table is the ratio of the number of keys to the table size N/r. A "minimal" perfect hash function maps N keys into N contiguous locations for a LF of one. A perfect hash function with LF ≥ 0.8 is called an "almost minimal" perfect hash function.

Criteria for a good hash function include: (1) the hash address is easily calculated; (2) the loading factor of the hash table is high for a given set of keys; and (3) the hash addresses of a given set of keys are distributed uniformly in the hash table. A perfect hash function is optimal with respect to the uniform distribution of hash addresses in the hash table; adding minimality to the perfect hash function makes it also optimal with respect to the LF.

Perfect hash functions are difficult to find, even when almost minimal solutions are accepted. Knurth[16] estimates that only one in 10 million functions is a perfect hash function for mapping the 31 most frequently used English words into 41 addresses.

Greniewski and Turski[12] used a non-algorithmic method for finding a perfect hash function to map the operation codes of the KLIPA assembler into an almost minimal hash table. Their hash function took the form:

$$H(k_i) = A \times k_i + B$$

where k_i is the ith key in the set of N keys and A, B are constants.

Sprugnoli[26] fashioned algorithmic methods to produce perfect hash functions of the form:

$$H_q(k_i) = \text{floor } [(k_i + A)/B] \qquad \qquad \text{\{Quotient Reduction Method\}}$$
$$H_r(k_i) = \text{floor } \{[(A + k_i \times B) \bmod C]/D]\} \qquad \text{\{Remainder Reduction Method\}}$$

where k_i is the ith key in the set of N keys and A, B, C, D are constants.

Jaeschke[15] devised Reciprocal Hashing to generate perfect hash functions of the form:

$$H_j(k_i) = \text{floor}(A/B \times k_i + C) \bmod D$$

where k_i is the ith in the set of N keys and A, B, C, D are constants.

Sprugnoli's and Jaeschke's methods will only produce minimal perfect hash functions for limited sets of keys. Keysets larger than 15 keys must be partitioned into smaller segments for each of which a perfect hash function is computed. Both Sprugnoli's and Jaeschke's solutions are machine dependent since the number-theoretic properties of the machine character code representations of keys are used to guide the search for appropriate values of the hash addresses.

Cichelli[6] devised an algorithm (Algorithm 0) for computing machine independent, minimal perfect hash functions of the form:

hash value = hash key length
                    + associated value of the key's first letter
                    + associated value of the key's last letter.

Cichelli's hash function is machine independent because the character code used by a particular machine never enters into the hash calculation. The algorithm incorporates a two stage ordering procedure for keys which effectively reduces the size of the search for associated values but excessive computation is still required to find hash functions for sets of more than 40 keys. Cichelli's method is also limited since two keys with the same first and last letters and the same length are not permitted.

The objective of this research was to develop faster and more general algorithms for finding perfect hash functions of the general form of Cichelli. The cost of the combinatorial search for acceptable integer assignments to letters dictates the maximum size of key sets which Cichelli's method can process. Several heuristic search methods were investigated to accelerate the search, yet produce nearly optimal hash tables. Faster and more general algorithms of the form of Cichelli's could be used to find perfect hash functions to organise large dictionaries (50–70,000 items). Such lexicons would be useful in computational studies of natural language, and artificial languages for programming and conversational terminal interactions.

Three algorithms for finding perfect hash functions were developed (Algorithms 1, 2 and 3). The data objects utilised in the algorithms were strings of characters of length P drawn from alphabet A, the 26 lower-case English letters. The alphabetic ordering of A was accepted as the basis for lexicographic ordering of sets of keys. The algorithms were implemented in APL and Pascal, which store the keys as character arrays. The performance of each algorithm was evaluated.

2. DEVELOPMENT OF THE PERFECT HASH ALGORITHMS

The problem of finding faster and more general algorithms derived from the method of Cichelli was divided into three subproblems: (1) choosing a hash identifier which will uniquely identify members of a lexical key; (2) efficiently finding an assignment of integer values to letters which will map keys into a hash table without collisions; and (3) finding ways of enforcing or attaining a reasonable degree of the minimality of the solution.

2.1 Choosing a hash identifier

Optimally a hash identifier uniquely identifies each key so that each may be placed in a unique hash table location. The set of formal properties of lexical keys which could be used in a hash identifier include: the letters of the alphabet, their position of occurrence in the key, and key length. A given maximum key length P and alphabet A determine a space T of possible keys. If $T' = card(T)$ and $A' = card(A)$, then we can express the cardinality of the set of all possible keys as the sum of the number of keys of length P plus the number of keys of length $P - 1$ plus the number of keys of each of the lengths $P - 2, P - 3, \ldots, 1$.

$$T' = A'^P + A'^{P-1} + \ldots + A'$$
$$= \sum_{i=1}^{P} A'^i$$
$$= A' \times (A'^P - 1)/(A' - 1)$$
$$= \theta(A'^P)$$

When A' becomes arbitrarily large, the limit of $A'/(A' - 1)$ approaches 1. The resultant factor, $(A'^P) - 1$, reduces to (A'^P). Thus the key space grows at a rate polynomial in A' and exponential in P.

When the occurrence of an alphabetic symbol, a_{ij}, in one position, a_{i1}, is treated differently from the occurrence in a different position, a_{i2}, of the same symbol, the number of keys which can be distinguished is exactly the number of keys, T', in the space of keys, T. When the hash function assigns the same value to a letter independent of the letter's position in the key, the number of keys which can be distinguished is given by the expression:

$$CH(A' + i - 1, i), 1 \leqslant i \leqslant P$$

where $CH(m, m)$ is the familiar "choose" function, defined as $CH(n, m) = n!/(m! * (n - m)!)$. If $A' = 26$, $P = 6$, then the size of the key space is:

"Letter value dependent on position"
$$\sum_{i=1}^{6} 26^i, 1 \leqslant i \leqslant 6$$
$$= \text{approx } 3.2 \times 10^8$$
distinguishable keys

"Letter value independent of position"
$$CH(26,1) + CH(27,2) + \ldots + CH(31,6)$$
$$= \text{approx } 9 \times 10^5$$
distinguishable keys

Including a consideration for letter position in the hash identifier improves its representational power. There is no lexical key which cannot be uniquely represented by such a hash identifier.

Three procedures for specifying the hash identifier were implemented, including: (1) a previously defined hash identifier (Algorithms 0 and 2); (2) a hash identifier determined by an automatic procedure in the algorithm (Algorithm 1); and (3) a hash identifier specified by the user interactively (Algorithm 3).

2.2 Assigning associated letter values

Once a hash identifier has been defined, an efficient search must be organised to find an assignment of integer values to the letters which will map the keys into the hash table with no collisions.

A series of integer values must be chosen for assignment to the letters of the lexical keys. An easily generated integer series which guarantees distinct sums would have advantages but assignment of such values tends to decrease the hash table loading factor. An integer series which grows slowly and produces distinct addresses would map the hashkeys into a compact address space. Since no naturally occurring integer series investigated, e.g. powers of two or modified Fibanocci series, satisfies the requirements for assignment values, procedures for searching for an acceptable assignment of integers were developed.

In a search space viewed as a tree with three keys ($N = 3$), two letter positions included in the hash identifier ($S = 2$) and a maximum associated value of two ($m = 3$, $M = [0, 1, 2]$), the number of different assignments of integers to letters is (m^S), the number of leaf nodes in the tree (Fig. 1).

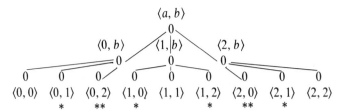

keyset = {aa, ab, bb}, letters are ordered $\langle a, b \rangle$.
Minimal solutions are marked *,
non-minimal ones are marked **.

Figure 1.

The number of integer values which is tested as an acceptable integer assignment during the search, m, is the branching factor of the tree. It controls the extent of the search and whether or not a solution is possible. Procedures used to determine the upper bound of the search variable include: the user deciding on an upper bound, the algorithm deciding on a upper bound, and no upper bound being placed on the search variable.

An efficient search will lead to an acceptable assignment of associated values while generating as little as possible of the search tree. Backtracking (Algorithms 0, 1 and sometimes 3) and non-backtracking (Algorithms 2 and sometimes 3) search methods were used to find an acceptable assignment of integer values to letters in lexical keys. A non-backtrack search is preferable if the integer assignment made at any stage in the search is certain to not ultimately cause collisions. During a backtrack search the validity of all partial solutions is tested against the search predicate. If a partial solution $\langle x_1, x_2, \ldots, x_i \rangle$, $1 \leq i \leq N$, fails to satisfy the predicate, the subtree with this value of x_i as its root can be pruned. This pruning processes, called preclusion, avoids generating, for a value rejected at level i in the search tree, $\sum_{j=1}^{s-i} m^j$, $1 \leq j \leq s - i$ full and partial solutions which have $\langle x_1, x_2, \ldots, x_i \rangle$ as an initial segment, where m is the branching factor of the search tree and s is the depth.

For each potential value eliminated, an exponentially growing subtree will be pruned. This justifies application of any polynomial-cost analysis that can be performed dynamically in the depth-first search which excludes values in the domain of the search variable from consideration. Preclusion is most effective when failure to satisfy the search predicate is discovered at a minimal tree depth. Fortunately, the frequency of occurrence of letter a_i is an excellent heuristic for predicting how likely it is that a_i occurs in a key which may collide with other keys. The sum (or product) of letter occurrences for one key is likewise an excellent predictor of how likely it is that a key will collide with other keys.

An ideal heuristic ordering strategy for the letters would order the letters by frequency in non-increasing order, so that a_1 would have the highest frequency of occurrence and a_s would have the lowest. This arrangement tends to occur when the keys are first ordered by sum of letter frequencies, then for each key the letters which have not occurred before are chosen in decreasing order of the frequency of occurrence. However, ordering the keys by sum of letter frequencies does not in general produce a strict ordering of letters to be assigned values, so between when an integer is assigned to a letter and when the hash address is tested, other hash addresses may have been added to the table. When collisions do occur, the program may have to backup and find new addresses for several keys. For example: the set of keys $K = \{aa, ab,$ $ac, ad, ae, af, ag, bd, cd, ce, de, fg\}$ after first ordering yields $\{aa, ad, ac, ae, ab, af, ag, cd, de,$ $bd, ce, fg\}$. The letter frequencies for K can be ordered into decreasing frequency of occurrence as $\langle a, d, c, e, b, f, g \rangle$. Although the key "$cd$" is determined as soon as key "ac" is placed in the hash table, the placement of "cd" is not tested until four intervening keys, ("ae", "ab", "af", "ag"), have been assigned hash addresses.

Given a permutation $B = \langle a_1, \ldots a_s \rangle$ of the search variables, $D\langle B \rangle$ represents the number of keys, d_i, whose hash addresses are newly determined when a_i is assigned a value. $C(B)$ [essentially $D(B)$ with $c_i = d_i + 1$, $0 \leq i \leq s$, so that c_i is the cost of visiting any node at level i] is a vector of coefficients, $\langle c_1, \ldots, c_s \rangle$, for the series of terms (m^i, $0 \leq i \leq s$, which constitute the weighted tree cost [WTC]:

$$WTC = \sum_{i=1}^{s-1} c_i \times m^i, 0 \leqslant i \leqslant s$$

$$= c_0 + c_1 \times m^1 + \ldots + c_s \times m^s)$$

where the c_i's are the associated costs at level i.

The m factor in each of the terms in the total cost grows exponentially from the root. Cost will be minimised when the smallest possible values are assigned to the coefficients in the order c_s, $c_{s-1}, \ldots, c_2$, c_1, where c_s is as small as possible and c_1 is as large as possible. The smallest possible c_s is a value of two, which would derive from a letter, a_s, having a frequency count of one so that it determines the value of only one key.

In the polynomial describing the size of the search tree, (m^s) is larger than the sum of the remaining terms:

(1) $\sum_{i=1}^{s-1} m^i = m \times (m^{s-1} - 1)/(m - 1), \ 1 \leqslant i \leqslant s - 1$;

(2) $m^s = m \times (m^{s-1})$

(3) $m \times (m^{s-1}) > m \times (m^{s-1} - 1)/(m - 1)$; and

(4) $m^{s-1} > (m^{s-1} - 1)/(m - 1)$.

Since (m^s) will contribute most of the cost of generating the search tree, its coefficient (in the tree of minimal cost) MUST be the smallest which occurs in any of the $s!$ possible permutations of the variables. A key is therefore sought which has at least one unique letter occurrence since only such a letter will come last in the ordering and still place a single key in the hash table. As a consequence, following from the necessity of placing letters which have a unique occurrence at the end of the ordering of letters, the optimal ordering will have all the keys which contain a unique letter occurrence at the end of the key ordering.

After the keys are ordered by the sum of the chosen letter frequencies, a second ordering, which rearranges the yet to be determined keys in the keyset depending on the partial assignment of integers to letters to this point, has the effect of making the coefficients of the m factors of the cost equation increase for smaller factors and decrease for the larger m factors. This process of moving the key forward in the ordering may be visualised as shifting the key's "weight" toward the root of the search tree, reducing the WTC for that tree if the order of letters induced by the new key order has larger weights nearer the root. [Recall that the sum of these coefficients along any root-to-leaf path in the search tree is the sum of the number of keys and the number of letters which occur in chosen positions, $N + s$; this is a constant for a given problem instance.]

The optimal ordering of the search variables, $B_{\min} = \langle a_1, a_2, \ldots, a_s \rangle$, is that for which WTC is a minimum. Generating all $s!$ permutations of the letters would demonstrate that the optimal ordering is that for which $D(B)$, and therefore $C(B)$, has the largest lexicographic sort value.

Refining the second ordering (Slingerland and Waugh [25]) permits examination of fewer than the $s!$ permutations, speeding the computation of solutions. The key reordering process, and ultimately the ordering of the s letters which occur in chosen positions is modified such that "each sublist of words which have equal frequency counts be ordered such that the words that will all have the greatest second ordering effect, that is, words that will 'expose' the most words from the rest of the list, occur first".

Ordering procedures were used which arranged the keys by sum of letter frequencies, then reordered the keys so that any key whose hash value is determined by assigning the associated letter values already determined by previous keys is placed next (Algorithms 0, 1 and 2). In the example, the key "cd" would be placed next after "c" is assigned a value so it would follow the key "ac". The ordering procedures were further refined to include ordering by product frequencies, key grouping, and unique letter appearance within key groups. These procedures are embodied in Algorithm 3 and details will be explained in the discussion of Algorithm 3.

2.3 *Ensuring minimality of hash tables*

Various methods were used to ensure a minimum loading factor 0.8. One heuristic which is applied in Algorithms 0, 1, 2 and 3 assigns the smallest associated values to those letters which occur most frequently in chosen letter positions, promoting small hash addresses for many keys. All hash addresses fall within the range [least ... least + (N/0.8)]; keys can always be mapped into addresses [0 ... N/0.8].

When backtrack search is used to assign associated values, as in Algorithms 0 and 1, a LF of at least L can be achieved by simply limiting the size of the hash table to $r = N/L$. The search procedure will then be forced to backtrack upon encountering any combination of letter values $(x_1, x_2, \ldots, x_i)$ such that for some k_j in $K: H(k_i) > N/L$. All values smaller than x_i in the domain of a_i have been excluded and any larger values of x_i will surely make $H(k_j)$ greater than N/L.

When backtracking is not used in the search, as in Algorithms 2 and 3, the LF is maximised by careful ordering of search variables and selection and testing of assigned integer values. Through non-backtracking algorithms produce solutions quickly, as the number of keys increases the LF tends to diminish. Algorithm 3 uses backtracking whenever the hash table is becoming too sparsely populated with keys.

3. DESCRIPTION OF THE ALGORITHMS

Cichelli's algorithm (Algorithm 0) uses key length and the first and last letters without regard to letter position as the hash identifier. The number of keys which can be distinguished is restricted to $P \times CH(A', 2)$ where P is the maximum key length, CH is the familiar "choose" function, and A' is the cardinality of the alphabet.

Integer assignment values are found using a simple backtracking process. Cichelli proposes no method of choosing a value of m, the size of associated latter values.

Algorithm 0 employs a two-step ordering heuristic which first arranges the keys in decreasing order of the sum of frequencies of occurrence of the first and last letters. This ordering simply sorts the letters so that letters which occur most frequently are assigned integer values first. During the second step of the ordering any key whose hash value has already been determined, because its first and last letters have both occurred in keys previous to the current one is placed next in the list. This double ordering strategy arranges the static set of keys in such a way that hash value collisions will occur and be resolved as early as possible during the backtracking process.

Algorithm 0 produces perfect minimal hash functions.

Step 1. Compare each key against the rest. If two keys have the same first and last letters and the same length then report conflict and stop, otherwise continue.

Step 2. Reorder the keys by decreasing sum of frequencies of occurrence of first and last letters.

Step 3. Reorder the keys from the beginning of the list so that if a key has first and last letters which have appeared previously in the list, then that key is placed next in the list.

Step 4. Add one word at a time to the solution, checking for hash value conflicts at each step. If a conflict occurs, go back to the previous word and vary its associated values until it is placed in the hash table successfully, then add the next word.

Algorithm 1, the first of the three new algorithms we developed, partitions the original set of keys into subsets according to their length, calculates perfect hash functions for each subset, then combines them to form one perfect hash function for the entire set. The complexity of each subproblem is at least linearly and often exponentially smaller than that of the overall problem, while the increase in the number of problem sets is linear, resulting in a marked reduction in computation. Which letter positions are chosen to identify each subset is recorded in a vector of Boolean values and a table is constructed which associates an integer value with each letter which occurs in a chosen position. For each subset an offset is maintained which keeps the subsets' hash addresses separate from those of any of the other hash functions, so that the subset hash functions can be fitted into a single hash table.

A procedure in Algorithm 1 automatically chooses, for each subset of keys of the same length, the smallest set of letter positions which will distinguish each key without regard for the order of occurrence of letters within a key. The number of different subsets of letters is much smaller than the key space with the same maximum length. The algorithm which makes the choice of letter positions generates trial combinations of one position, then two positions, up to all P positions. When each trial combination is generated, it is tested for its ability to discriminate members of the set of keys. If no two keys have the same letter occurrences in the p selected positions, then the algorithm returns this trial combination as the solution and terminates; otherwise, the next combination is generated. The use of the cardinality of a subset as the upper bound on the range of associated values for the letters in chosen positions is a refinement of the choice of m in Algorithm 0.

Algorithm 1 order the keys in the same manner as Algorithm 0, but ties between keys with equal sums of letter frequencies are broken using Slingerland and Waugh's refinement of the second ordering.

Algorithm 1 incorporates a method a method of precluding the generation and testing of inadmissible combinations of associated values during the backtrack search process.

Algorithm 1 dosen't guarantee minimality, but a high loading factor is obtained by using a good heuristic choice of domain size for the associated letter values and by allowing the ranges of hash addresses for the subsets to overlap slightly.

Step 1. Sort the keys into order of increasing length and partition the keyset into subsets of keys which share the same length. Upon each of these subsets, perform the following steps.

Step 2. Choose the smallest set of letter positions such that no two keys of a subset have the same set of letters in the chosen positions.

Step 3. Order the keys in each subset using Cichelli's two ordering strategies with Slingerland and Waugh's refinement, to produce an approximately optimal ordering of the keys and of the letters which occur in the chosen positions.

Step 4. For each subset define the range of values associated with letters in the chosen positions using zero as the lower bound and the cardinality of the subset as the upper bound.

Step 5. Using a modified Cichelli backtrack search assign integer values to letters such that each key is mapped into a unique hash address in the subrange of the hash table defined by [offset...$(p \times m)$], where offset is the integer offset for the current subset of keys, p is the number of chosen positions, and m is the upper bound of the range of associated letter values.

Step 6. Add remaining unprocessed subsets sequentially to the hash table, allowing the different subsets to overlap somewhat by initialising the next offset by the number of keys which have been placed in the hash table (n), then finding the first open position (r, $r \geq n$).

Step 7. If any unprocessed subsets remain, return to Step 2; otherwise all keys have been placed in the hash table.

Step 8. Combine the subset perfect hash functions to make one perfect hash function for the entire keyset.

Algorithm 2 uses the key length and the first and last letters for the hash identifier, and the value of each letter is independent of position. If any two keys have all characteristics in common, this algorithm cannot be applied to the keyset. If the maximum key length is P, then $P \times CH(A', 2)$ keys can be distinguished using Algorithm 2.

Algorithm 2 chooses an upper bound for each search variable from a naturally occurring integer series which has no pairwise sums among its elements. The upper bound is a solution, though not necessarily the best solution overall, and all lower potential associated values are tested in hopes of finding a better assignment of integer values. This method of assigning integer values avoids all backtracking yielding a rapid search algorithm. Algorithm 2 is not a backtracking algorithm in the classical sense, but an intelligently controlled enumerative one. Unlike backtracking search, this method never "undoes" partial results. Once a key is placed in the table, its address never changes.

Using the upper bounds for the associated values ensures that a solution will be found, but makes no guarantee that the loading factor of the resulting hash table will be acceptable (though it usually is for sets of a small number of keys). the search relies entirely on the good effects of the ordering of search variables to achieve a compact solution.

Step 1. Count the frequency of occurrence of each letter which appears in the first and last positions in the set of keys. Order the letters by decreasing frequency of occurrences.

Step 2. To each a_i in the ordered set of letters assign the upper bound $F(i)$, where $F(n)$ is a series like a modified Fabanocci or powers of two. This assigns the smallest limiting values of the most frequently occurring letters, promoting the minimality of the resulting hash table.

Step 3. For each key k_i, $0 < i \leq N$, calculate tval[i], the sum of the temporary values of the first and last letters plus the length of the key. Sort the keys on the sum, producing a list of keys ordered by the sum of the frequencies of their first and last letters; keys with the same combination of letters in these positions will be ordered by increasing length. During this ordering, Algorithm 2 ceases to function if any two keys have all characteristics in common;

Step 4. For each key k_i, $0 < i \leq N$, do the following: (a) if both the first and last letters in k_i have been assigned values, continue with the next key: k_i has been placed in the hash table previously; (b) if neither letter has been assigned a value, set the most frequent of them to zero; and (c) if only one letter a_j has no assigned value, vary its associated value from zero to the upper bound until all the keys whose hash addresses are determined by this letter have been placed in open hash table locations. Each time the associated value is incremented, the function "check" is called which first changes all hash values which are affected by the current letter, then makes an $O(N^2)$ pass through the set of keys to determine whether any pair of keys have the same hash address; and

Step 5. Mark the current letter "tried" and continue at step 4 with the next key in the ordering. If there is none, we have a solution and the algorithm terminates.

The user interactively specifies a set of letter positions and whether or not to include the key length in the hash identifier when using Algorithm 3. The program then tests the user's selection for key discrimination, inviting the user to try again if any two keys cannot be distinguished. Algorithm 3 takes into account the position of occurrence of letters and therefore has the greatest possible discriminatory power of the three algorithms developed. There is no set of distinct lexical keys which cannot be distinguished by Algorithm 3.

No upper bound is placed on the size of associated letter values.

Algorithm 3 incorporates a development and refinement of the non-backtracking ennumerative search procedure of Algorithm 2. An improved version of search which performs a limited amount of backtracking when a solution has a low loading factor has been implemented, This promises to retain much of the speed of the current version while reducing the size of the hash tables. By analysing the occurrence of letters shared amongst the keys, Algorithm 3 eliminates many doomed choices of associated values, streamlining the search process.

Step 1. The user is prompted to supply two specifications: (i) the set of letter positions to be used in the hashing, and (ii) whether or not the key length is to be a part of the hash identifier.

Step 2. If any two words cannot be distinguished with the hash function as specified by the user, then report conflicting keys and return to step 1; if the hash identifier is acceptable, then continue with step 3.

Step 3. Count the number of occurrences of each letter in each position, then subtract one from each total. For each key, assign a value which is the product of the occurrence counts for the selected letters in this key. Those keys whose assigned values are zero must have at least one unique occurrence of a letter in some chosen position. Place these keys at the head of a list of keys with unique occurrences. Repeat step 3 for the non-zero keys until no more keys with unique letter occurrences are found. Keys selected in this process will follow all keys with no unique letter occurrences in the final ordering.

Step 4. Order the remaining keys, those with no unique letter occurrences, by decreasing product of their letter frequency counts.

Step 5. Form a group by first choosing the key nearest the head of the list which has the fewest letters with no assigned value ("new" letters); next, find all the keys whose hash addresses will be determined when the chosen key's new letters are assigned integer values. Repeat step 5 until all keys have been chosen.

Step 6. Order the keys within each group so that for any two keys k_i and k_j, if we calculate the set differences between the letters from chosen positions in each key [$D_{ij} := L(k_i) - L(k_j)$; $D_{ji} := L(k_j) - L(k_i)$, where $L(k_m)$ is the set of letters in chosen positions for k_m], then if k_i preceeds k_j in the ordering, all letters in D_{ij} will be assigned values before the last letter in D_{ji} is assigned a value.

Step 7. For each key, determine which of its chosen letters will be the last to be assigned a value in the search. This letter's value can be manipulated to place the key into an open hash address. In cases where length is the only difference between neighboring keys, the distance back to a key which differs in letters is noted.

Step 8. Taking these noted letters in order, determine for the next letter which of its possible values are precluded by conflict with the hash addresses assigned to previous keys.

Step 9. Assign letter values. If a single key is being placed, its determining letter value is just the one which places it in the lowest possible open hash address. If the key is part of a group whose hash addresses are determined by assigning the current key's hash address, then choose the smallest possible value that maps all the keys into open hash addresses.

Step 10. If no two letters (and therefore no keys) remain, then the algorithm terminates. Otherwise, continue at step 8.

A second version of this algorithm has been written which allows backtracking whenever it is discovered, at step 10, that the hash table has become too sparse. In that case, step 10 is replaced by the following two steps.

Step 10. The loading factor [LF] of the partial solution generated to this point is calculated. If LF is too small and the number of allowable backtracks (set by the user in step 1 in response to a prompt) is not exceeded, then proceed to step 11; otherwise continue with step 8; and

Step 11. For the latest group added to the table, determine which keys have the highest and lowest hash address; call them k_{max} and k_{min}. Choose a letter from k_{min}, say a_i, which does not affect the hash address of k_{max} and increment the associated value of a_i by one. Reset to zero the associated values of all letters which were assigned after a_i. Remove from the table all keys which were placed after the value of a_i was assigned, and adjust the sum of assigned letter values of each affected key. Place these keys and the head of the list of keys which have not yet been assigned a hash address. Adjust the order of letters which determine the hash addresses of groups of keys and return to step 8.

4. PERFORMANCE OF THE ALGORITHMS

Analytic comparison of the relative performance of backtracking algorithms is difficult (Knuth[17]). The execution time, maximum number of keys which can be processed in a reasonable time, and the loading factor of the hash tables produced by Algorithms 0, 1, 2 and 3 were compared. The number of basic operations of the algorithm and the memory requirements should be considered in algorithm expense. Krause[18] reports the number of times basic operations are performed by Algorithms 0, 1, 2 and 3.

The effective loading factor [ELF] of a perfect hash function is defined as:

$$ELF = N/(r + t)$$

where N is the number of keys, r is the range of calculated hash addresses and t is the number of associated letter values stored. ELF is a realistic measure of the amount of memory needed for implementing each algorithm since associated value tables are an essential part of each algorithm and they differ in each algorithm. Utility [U] is proposed as a further measure of relative performance

$$U = N \times LF/T$$

where N represents the number of keys to be hashed, LF is the loading factor and T is the search time in milliseconds. Larger values of U imply a greater degree of utility. This is an arbitrary measure; it does, however, reward compact solutions to large problem sets and penalises algorithms using excessive execution time.

Algorithms 0, 1 and 2 were implemented as Pascal programs [Pascal/UBC]; Algorithm 3 was written in APL. All programs were run on an IBM 4341 computer under the Michigan Terminal System [MTS] time-sharing operating environment. Timing comparisons were gathered via MTS system subroutines which return *cpu* time, in milliseconds. Time-sharing overhead, such as swapping, was excluded from totals so that time is time actually used to execute the algorithms.

Cichelli[6] reported the results of applying his algorithm (Algorithm 0) to five sets of keys: (1) the 12 three-letter month abbreviations; (2) the 31 most frequently occurring English words;

(3) the 34 ASCII control codes; (4) the 36 Pascal reserved words (including 'OTHERWISE'); and (5) the 39 Pascal predefined identifiers (excluding 'ODD'). The three recently developed algorithms were also tested on: (6) the 33 Basic keywords; (7) the 42 Algol-*W* reserved words; (8) the 64 most frequently occurring English words; (9) the 76 Pascal reserved words plus predefined identifiers; and (10)–(12) the 100, 200 and 500 most frequently occurring English words.

Table 1. presents the search times and loading factors obtained by running each algorithm on the test problem sets.

For Algorithm 1 the worst case computation of the procedure for choosing a set of letter positions which produce unique hash identifiers requires calculation exponential in key length. In the tested examples the execution time for this procedure was linear with respect to N, the number of keys in the keyset. The worst case analytic estimate for the ordering of keys to produce a beneficial ordering of the letters which appear in the chosen positions for Algorithm 1 was $O(N^3)$. For the small problem sets tested the times required for this ordering fell between $5 + 2 \times N$ and $3 \times N$. Surprisingly, 30, 735 milliseconds were required to order 42 keys of length 3 in the 200 most frequently occurring English words [MFEW] compared to 42 milliseconds required to order 61 keys of length 4 in the same example. We hypothesize that the complexity of these problems is dependent on the way in which letters are shared among the keys.

Although Algorithm 1 does not guarantee minimal hash tables, it almost always produces minimal results for the set of keys as a whole. Allowing the ranges of the subsets to overlap promotes minimality even though the combined subsets are non-minimal. The most demanding test, the 200 MFEW produced a hash table with an LF = 0.97.

Algorithm 1 performs well as long as the largest subset contains approximately 50 or fewer keys. At this point the pattern of sharing letters among the keys of the subsets starts to affect the number of nodes in the backtrack search tree which must be examined. We conclude that the procedure for choosing a set of letter positions which produce unique hash identifiers is of marginal utility.

Algorithm 2 gives acceptable results for sets of up to 100 keys. Two major problems with Algorithm 2 are: (i) the loading factors of the solutions produced degenerate quickly for keysets

Table 1. Comparison of time [T] (in milliseconds) and loading factor [LF] for all four algorithms on some representative key sets

Key Set	Algorithm 0	Algorithm 1	Algorithm 2	Algorithm 3
12 Three Letter Month Abbrev.	T=69 LF=1.0	T=45 LF=1.0	T=872 LF=1.0	T=84 LF=1.0
31 Most Frequent English Words	T=290 LF=0.97	T=23 LF=1.0	T=2466 LF=0.94	T=1763 LF=1.0
33 Basic Keywords	no results	T=0.016 LF=1.0	no results	T=0.669 LF=1.0
34 ASCII Control Codes	T=1833 LF=1.0	T=41 LF=1.0	T=6916 LF=1.0	T=1993 LF=1.0
36 Pascal Reserved Words	T=579 LF=1.0	T=29 LF=1.0	T=5712 LF=0.88	T=2609 LF=1.0
40 Pascal Predefined IDs	T=360641 LF=1.0	T=30 LF=1.0	T=6242 LF=0.89	T=3060 LF=1.0
42 Algol-W Reserved Words	no results	T=0.018 LF=1.0	T=6.046 LF=0.913	T=0.616 LF=1.0
64 Most Frequent English Words	T>>1 hr	T=383 LF=1.0	T=26619 LF=0.69	T=2933 LF=1.0
76 Pascal Reserved + Predefined IDs	no results	T=68 LF=1.0	no results	T=3414 LF=0.98
100 Most Frequent English Words	no results	T=10062 LF=1.0	T=125973 LF=0.70	T=5190 LF=0.96
200 Most Frequent English Words	no results	T=62035 LF=0.97	T=1505328 LF=0.42	T=8986 LF=0.70
500 Most Frequent English Words	no results	no results	no results	T=33505 LF=0.68

of more than 60 keys; and (ii) the mechanism used for distinguishing keys, like Cichelli's (Algorithm 0), is not adequate for many problem sets.

The refinements to Algorithm 2, which led to the development of a substantially different Algorithm 3, addressed these problems directly with moderate success with respect to problem (i) and complete success with problem (ii). Algorithm 3 outperforms the other algorithms generally and shows the greatest promise for further development. Algorithm 3 does require additional storage to maintain separate associated value tables for each letter position selected.

Table 2 summarises the relative utility for the four algorithms. Algorithm 1 produces spectacular utilities for keysets up to about 100 keys. When the sizes of the subsets produced by partitioning reach around 50 keys, however, these values decline rapidly. The utility of Algorithm 3 remains relatively constant for all test keysets.

5. APPLICATION OF PERFECT HASH FUNCTIONS TO NATURAL LANGUAGE LEXICON DESIGN

Retrieval methods usually assume equal likelihood of retrieval for each data item (Knuth[16]). Cichelli[6] pointed out the utility of perfect hash functions for use in compilers. It is well documented in the literature of lexicography (Carroll et al.[3], Dewey[10]) that this is not the case for the English language (or, presumably, for any natural language). We propose to make use of information about the frequency of occurrence of English words and judicious mix of common search and hash encoding techniques to provide an efficient organisational strategy for a natural language lexicon.

If the dictionary is formed by putting properties on LISP atoms (as is done in many natural language systems), the entire search is performed by a LISP system. Most implementations of LISP (Allen[1], pp. 275–277) use an "object list" to access atoms, usually implemented as hash buckets. A built-in general purpose hash function is provided which distributes the hash values of the complete set of keys in the dictionary (hopefully equally) among the hash buckets, each of which is searched sequentially. The access time is therefore dependent on the number of buckets and on bucket size. [The retrieval time is dependent on the actual distribution of the keys among the buckets. For any hash function, there exist some set of keys which will produce very uneven distributions. In the worst case, all keys will have the same hash value, so the average cost of a successful search would be $N/2$; for an unsuccessful search, the cost would be N (where N is the number of keys).]

In addition to this search for the atom name, the property list must be scanned for dictionary properties. If, for the majority of items in the lexicon, this is the only property on the property list, the time required for any lexical access is approximately equal to the hash encoding scheme time. Comparatively, the number of words with many properties remains insignificant and will not be considered.

Any desirable search technique can be imposed on an explicitly-stored dictionary. When we attempt to organise the lexicon in a way that minimises retrieval time, many factors affect our choices, such as the size of the lexicon and the need for secondary storage. Some design criteria, however, will improve the access time for any linear search algorithm of a natural language lexicon. One such design feature is to order the dictionary according to the relative frequency of the use of the letters in words (Cercone and Mercer[5]).

Table 2. Table of Relative Utility [$U = N \times LF/T$]

N	Algorithm 0	Algorithm 1	Algorithm 2	Algorithm 3
12	1333.33	2000.00	65.93	50.42
31	103.69	3100.00	16.71	70.62
33	N/A	2062.51	N/A	49.33
34	0.04	1789.47	7.00	59.96
36	61.22	2571.43	7.63	60.50
39	1.14	N/A	8.95	N/A
40	N/A	2857.14	N/A	56.02
42	N/A	1888.89	6.34	68.18
44	N/A	1466.67	N/A	53.04
64	N/A	344.09	2.33	59.73
76	N/A	2533.33	N/A	62.97
100	N/A	20.26	0.78	66.10
200	N/A	6.26	0.008	42.25
500	N/A	N/A	N/A	20.82

One proposal we will explore here is to divide the dictionary into two or more parts to form dictionary hierarchies. This feature is most interesting when one considers the very high frequency of use of a very small number of words, but it is also important when one needs to consider how to divide a dictionary over different storage media. For example, 732 items comprise 75% of the words used in representative text. A possible three-level hierarchy would be 64 items that account for 50% of the words in the text, 668 items that comprise another 25% and the remainder that provide the final 25%. A hash into the first level of 64 words followed by a binary search of the second level (which on the average would require about 9 accesses), followed by a trie search of the third level would provide a very efficient search.

Lexicon storage is as crucial an issue as the retrieval of lexical information. Common structure sharing and morphological analysis contribute towards efficient space utilisation; certain dialects of LISP use various techniques, such as CDR-encoding, to reduce the representational overhead. The dictionary represented as a trie, Knuth[16], requires less space because letters are not repeated unnecessarily in successive words. Some representational overhead is incurred, however, by the required pointers.

The previous discussion has considered how to minimise the space required by the lexicon. We now present a short synopsis of some typical lexicon designs. For the purposes of this discussion we will consider lexicons that contain large quantities of information in three representative sizes: (i) small—500 entries or less; (ii) medium—1000–5000 entries; and (iii) large—10,000 entries or more.

Typically, a small lexicon gains little from complex organisation schemes. Our interactive implementation of Algorithm 3, however, can compute almost-minimal hash functions for most lexicons of small size. One drawback its that we have to store $26 \times S$ associated values when S letter positions are selected, making this table's size the same order of magnitude as the dictionary itself. Of course, search time would be cut considerably, so the storage overhead might still be found acceptable.

Medium size lexicons need to be analysed differently; if the dictionary can fit in random access memory, a binary search would provide efficient access of items, supplemented by hash encoding into a mini-dictionary of the most common words. There is no space advantage using a trie structure because the overhead in associated pointers is high and there is little common spelling among so few words.

Another approach which utilises Algorithm 3 is illustrated in Listing 5.1. Satisfactory experimental results have shown that 500 words can be placed in a noncolliding hash table in under 20 seconds. Nevertheless the LF is only about 0.68 which we feel is unsatisfactory; increasing the LF results in a substantial increase in computation. When more than one hash function is used, an offset can be manipulated to start the next group of 500 words in the sparse part of the table occupied by the previous group of 500 words, typically resulting in a loss of about only 10% of storage space. In this example the medium sized lexicon is divided into group of 500 lexical items (more or less) and Algorithm 3 is applied successively, manipulating the OFFSET to interleave the 500-word pieces to effectively increase the LF to an acceptable level. Listing 5.1 illustrates this method using the 500 most frequently occurring English words divided into 5 groups of 100 words each (rather than the 2500 MFEW divided into 5 groups of 500 words due to space limitations). In Listing 5.1 the first 100 word chunk is fitted into a table of size 133; the first offset is set to 98 (because the first unused space is table location 100 and length is part of each hash function, thus 98 plus a length of 3 would place the next word in location 101), the index where the application of Algorithm 3 to the second 100 word lexical chunk begins to place items. This technique effectively makes use of unused spaces from previous applications of Algorithm 3. If the lexicon cannot fit into memory, it is appropriate to treat the medium size lexicon as a large lexicon.

Large lexicons typically require secondary storage, and the number of retrievals from secondary storage should be minimised. The favorable results from Algorithm 3 suggest including the 732 most frequent words in a single almost-minimal hash table, giving one-probe retrieval in 75% of the cases. The remaining 50,000 words could be mapped by a second hash function into 50 subsets of about 1000 words each and stored in secondary memory. In order to preserve the machine-independence of the algorithm, this second hash function could be based on the ordinal positions of letters in the alphabet rather than on the machine character code.

For each of these subsets, an almost-minimal perfect hash function could be computed, storing the associated values in the same secondary memory location as the lexical information itself. If the key sought is not in the table of most-frequent words, then a hash would be performed to select the proper second-level table from a secondary storage medium; this table would then be searched using its own perfect hash function. This organisation would allow retrieval of any key with three hash calculations and one probe of secondary memory.

6. CONCLUSIONS

Cichelli's algorithm provides a useful alternative to numerical approaches to the search for perfect hash functions. We have found methods of extending the application of this "simple" approach to larger problem sets.

We have considered improvements along the lines of (i) hash identifier choice; (ii) partitioning of the problem set; and (iii) improved search methods. In our empirical study of Algorithms 0, 1, 2 and 3 we conclude that the heuristics employed in Algorithm 3 appear the most promising for future research although both Algorithms 1 and 2 perform significantly better than Algorithm 0 (Cichelli's algorithm). The introduction of a limited backtrack in Algorithm 3 is an important contribution leading to almost minimal hash tables for large keysets (> 500 keys). Further analysis of the problem may reveal a better way of performing this limited backtracking.

Finally, we found three mathematical problems closely related to the search for perfect hash functions including: (i) harmonious labelling of graphs; (ii) graceful labelling of graphs; and (iii) additive bases. Krause[18] describes these problems.

Acknowledgements—We wish to thank Venkatakasi Kurnala and Paliath Narendran of Rensselaer Polytechnic Institute for their work on Algorithm 2. Thanks are also due Josie Backhouse for reading an earlier draft of this paper and to Carol Murchison for her extensive editing. This research was supported by the National Science and Engineering Research Council of Canada under Operating Grant no. A4309 and by the Office of the Academic Vice-President, Simon Fraser University.

REFERENCES

1. J. Allen, *The Anatomy of LISP*. McGraw–Hill, New York (1978).
2. B. Bloom, Space/time tradeoff in hash coding with allowable errors. *Commun. ACM* **13**, 422–436 (1970).
3. J. Carroll, P. Davies and B. Richman, *The American Heritage Word Frequency Book*, American Heritage Publishing, New York (1971).
4. N. Cercone, *Representing natural language in extended semantic networks*. Ph.D. Thesis, Technical Report TR75-11, Department of Computing Science, University of Alberta, Edmonton, Alberta (1975).
5. N. Cercone, and R. Mercer, Design of lexicons in some natural language systems. *ALLC J.* **1**, 37–51 (1980).
6. R. Cichelli, Minimal perfect hash functions made simple. *Commun. ACM* **23**, 17–19 (1980).
7. R. Cichelli, Author's response to technical correspondence. *Commun. ACM* **23**, 729 (1980).
8. R. Cichelli, On Peterson's spelling error corrector. *Commun. ACM* **24**, 322 (1981).
9. C. Cook and R. Oldehoeft, More on minimal perfect hash tables. *13th Southeastern Conference on Combinatorics, Graph Theory, and Computing* (1982).
10. G. Dewey, *Relative Frequency of English Speech Sounds*. Harvard University Press, Cambridge, Mass (1923).
11. R. Graham and N. Sloane, On additive bases and harmonious graphs. *SIAM J. Algebra and Discrete Methods* **1** (4), 382–404 (1980).
12. M. Greniewski and W. Turski, The external language KLIPA for the URAL-2 digital computer. *Commun. ACM*, **6**, 321–324 (1963).
13. Halberstam and Roth, *Sequences*, vol 1, Oxford University Press (1966).
14. G. Jaeschke and G. Osterburg, On Cichelli's minimal perfect hash function method. *Commun. ACM* **23**, 728–729 (1980).
15. G. Jaeschke Reciprocal hashing: A method for generating minimal perfect hashing functions. *Commun. ACM* **24**, 829–833 (1981).
16. D. Knuth, *The Art of Computer Programming*, Vol. 3. Addision Wesley, Reading, Mass. (1973).
17. D. Knuth, Estimating the efficiency of backtrack programs. *Math. Comput.* **29**, 121–136 (1975).
18. M. Krause, *Perfect hash function search*. M.Sc. Thesis, Department of Computing Science, Simon Fraser University, Burnaby, Canada (1982).
19. D. Moon, *MACLISP reference manual*, Project MAC, MIT, Cambridge, Mass. (1974).
20. R. Morris, Scatter storage techniques. *Commun. ACM* **11** 38–44 (1968).
21. R. Nix, Experience with a space efficient way to store a dictionary. *Commun. ACM* **24**, 297–298 (1981).
22. R. Schank, N. Goldman, C. Rieger and C. Riesbeck MARGIE: memory analysis, response generation and inference in English. *Proc. IJCAI3*, 255–261 (1973).
23. E. Schwartz, A dictionary for minimum redundancy encoding. *J. ACM* **10**, 413–439 (1963).
24. H. Simon and J. Kadane, Problems of computational complexity in artificial intelligence. in *Algorithms of Complexity* (Edited by J. Traul), 281–299 Academic Press (1976).
25. J. Slingerland, and M. Waugh, On Cichelli's algorithm for finding minimal perfect hash functions. *Commun. ACM*, **24**, 322 (1981).

26. R. Sprugnoli, Perfect hashing functions: a single probe retrieving method for static sets. *Commun. ACM* **20**, 841–850 (1978).
27. Y. Wilks, Preference semantics. Stanford AI Project, memo AIM-206, Stanford University Press, Stanford, California (1973).
28. T. Winograd, *Understanding natural language.* Academic Press, New York (1972).
29. W. Woods, R. Kaplan and B. Nash–Webber, *The Lunar Sciences Natural Language Information System*: *Final Report*, Bolt, Beranek & Newman, Inc., Cambridge, Mass (1972).

```
++++++++++ Listing 5.1. Interleaved Lexicon - 500 Most Frequently Used English Words. ++++++++++
# RUN XAPL  PAR=0
>   .v3.0  vsapl/aplfs
# EXECUTION BEGINS 09:58:37
>   clear ws
>   wssize is 46172
>  )LOAD  PERFECT  300000
>   saved 12:59:00  06/26/82
>   wssize is 300124
>
> HASH                                    ( preorders data for associated value calculation )
>   WORDS TO BE HASHED: c1               ( c1 is a variable containing the 1st 100 MFEW )
>   LETTERS TO BE USED: 1 2 3 4          ( for assignment of associated values )
>   IS BLANK TO BE A CHARACTER (Y/N): N  ( or use last letter of word if appropriate )
>   IS LENGTH TO BE PART OF FUNCTION (Y/N): Y
>   ORDER BY PRODUCT OR MINIMUM (P/M): P   ( product of letter frequencies or like Cichelli's )
>   CPU SECONDS USED IN HASH IS 2.258
>   THE DATA IN CORRECTED PREORDER FORM:
>
>     the then these when she we they there me he were her more be been them
>     than that what war was has some men man this their his time him made
>     say may for first shall would come can could must our one on i in an
>     any or are well will only but out into from who to so not no its it at
>     should before is as your you said had any my by how now of if us a over
>     upon with little do up all two have like such very about every great
>     other which people
>
> BIND 0                                 ( invoking the second ordering part - nonbacktracking )
>   BINDING STARTED AT  1982 7 20 14 4 36 19
>   TIME DURATION WAS 0 0 0 0 0 11 532
>   CPU SECONDS USED IN BASH IS  1.573
>   NUMBER OF TIMES THROUGH BASH MAIN LOOP IS  75
>
>   TERMINATION AFTER BACKTRACK 0
>   LETTERS USED 1 2 3 4
>   OFFSET USED 0
>
>   LETTER VALUES
>   'A'   4   6  14  54      'I'   2  12  21  24      'S'   4  43  12   0
>   'B'   9  28   0   0      'K'   0   0  34   0      'T'   0  41  19   2
>   'C'  18   0  25  72      'L'  43  41  26  13      'U'  20  17  15   0
>   'D'  21   0  16  39      'M'   5   0  14  12      'V'  79  57  76   0
>   'E'  30   4   0   0      'N'  22  26  14   0      'W'   2  29   0  62
>   'F'  19   0  33  41      'O'  14   2  59   0      'Y'  45  44  16   5
>   'G'   1   0   0   0      'P'   0   0   0  64
>   'H'   6   0  39  44      'R'   0  38   3   5
>
>   HASH TABLE
>      3  THE       4  THEN      5  THESE     6  WHEN      7  SHE      8  WE
>      9  THEY     10  THERE    11  ME       12  HE       13  WERE      . . .
>       . . .      94  SUCH     95  VERY     96  ABOUT    97  EVERY    98  GREAT
>     99  OTHER   100  WHICH   132  FROM    133  PEOPLE
>
> HASH
>   WORDS TO BE HASHED: c2                ( c2 is a variable containing the 2nd 100 MFEW )
>   LETTERS TO BE USED: 1 2 3 4
>   IS BLANK TO BE A CHARACTER (Y/N): N
>   IS LENGTH TO BE PART OF FUNCTION (Y/N): Y
>   ORDER BY PRODUCT OR MINIMUM (P/M): P
>   CPU SECONDS USED IN HASH IS 2.187
>   THE DATA IN CORRECTED PREORDER FORM:
>
>     money power most possible part case matter came home here best get per
>     government same far fact see yet does cannot down being going house
>     yours country found last less year years says days make take three
>     think things those through go too good food many day because where way
>     woman peace never between few new back work today world while nothing
>     himself give line since did without put much each place also always
>     another old once business away own ever even again against might am oh
>     half just know life long after don't right still under public present thought
```

```
++++++++++ Listing 5.1. (Continued...)
>
> BIND  98                        ( binding the next 100 MFEW into the hash table offset 98 places )
>    BINDING STARTED AT  1982 7 20 14 7 33 114
>    TIME DURATION WAS 0 0 0 0 22 926
>    CPU SECONDS USED IN BASH IS  1.48
>    NUMBER OF TIMES THROUGH BASH MAIN LOOP IS  77
>
>    TERMINATION AFTER BACKTRACK 0
>    LETTERS USED 1 2 3 4
>    OFFSET USED 98
>
>    LETTER VALUES
>    'A'  31   0   2  23        'I'   0  54   0   2        'S'  12   0   0   0
>    'B'   8   0  11   0        'K'  30   0   0   0        'T'   8  52   4   0
>    'C'   5   0  12  45        'L'  24  11   0  28        'U'  49  55  15  58
>    'D'  14   0  21  31        'M'   0   0   2  44        'V'   0  15   0   0
>    'E'  44   1   5   0        'N'  48  23   0  13        'W'  22  29   1  46
>    'F'   4  53   9  76        'O'  29   0   6  29        'Y'  14   0  20  43
>    'G'   7  43  17  64        'P'   0   0   0   0        ''''  0   0   0  75
>    'H'   6  23  30   0        'R'  20  89   3   9
>
>    HASH TABLE
>       3  THE        4  THEN       5  THESE      6  WHEN       7  SHE       . . . .
>       . . . .     100  WHICH    102  MOST      103  MONEY    104  POWER    105  PART
>       . . . .     131  MAKE     132  FROM      133  PEOPLE   134  SAYS     . . . .
>     199  PRESENT  200  THOUGHT  207  AWAY      214  SINCE    221  DID
>
> HASH
>    WORDS TO BE HASHED:  c3                    ( c3 is a variable containing the 3rd 100 MFEW )
>    LETTERS TO BE USED:  1  2  3  4
>    IS BLANK TO BE A CHARACTER (Y/N):  N
>    IS LENGTH TO BE PART OF FUNCTION (Y/N):  Y
>    ORDER BY PRODUCT OR MINIMUM (P/M):  P
>    CPU SECONDS USED IN HASH IS 2.258
>    THE DATA IN CORRECTED PREORDER FORM:
>
>        set let letter cent went want water battle general got something women
>        several gave done certain forty conditions given five find situation
>        both side wind morning soon seen means coal steel state statement stand
>        call either early tell name believe military nation small brought front
>        city fighting night doing whole though children thing taken gun full
>        during books took hand high amount among army dear end enough course
>        four large big until asked use used saw law why whose pay eyes left
>        next order interest ago off six it's known labor young almost myself
>        really capital purpose service necessary themselves
>
> BIND  195                       ( binding the next 100 MFEW into the hash table offset 195 places )
>    BINDING STARTED AT  1982 7 20 14 10 17 930
>    TIME DURATION WAS 0 0 0 0 5 327
>    CPU SECONDS USED IN BASH IS  1.492
>    NUMBER OF TIMES THROUGH BASH MAIN LOOP IS  79
>
>    TERMINATION AFTER BACKTRACK 0
>    LETTERS USED 1 2 3 4
>    OFFSET USED 195
>
>    LETTER VALUES
>    'A'  20   2  24   0        'I'  49  15  37   6        'S'   0  10  81  33
>    'B'   3   0  39   0        'K'   0   0  37  20        'T'   6  10   0   3
>    'C'   0   0  59   0        'L'   1  24  32   2        'U'  32  53  31   3
>    'D'   3   0   7   5        'M'   8  16   1  34        'V'   0   0   5  84
>    'E'  20   0  32   5        'N'  31  30   1   0        'W'   1   0   0  64
>    'F'   0   0  79   0        'O'  51   8  22  48        'X'   0   0  50  26
>    'G'   2   0  13  50        'P'  33   0  87   0        'Y'  64   0  17  31
>    'H'  50  24   0  15        'R'  69  22  12  33        ''''  0   0   0   0
>
>    HASH TABLE
>       3  THE        4  THEN       5  THESE      6  WHEN       7  SHE       . . . .
>       . . . .     100  WHICH    102  MOST      103  MONEY    104  POWER    105  PART
>       . . . .     131  MAKE     132  FROM      133  PEOPLE   134  SAYS     . . . .
>     199  PRESENT  200  THOUGHT  201  SET       202  LET      203  CENT     204  WENT
>     205  LETTER   206  WANT     207  AWAY      208  WATER    209  BATTLE   210  GENERAL
>     211  GOT      212  SEVERAL  213  GAVE      214  SINCE    215  WOMEN    216  DONE
>     217  CERTAIN . . . .        221  DID       222  SITUATION          . . . .
>       . . . .     300  PURPOSE  301  THEMSELVES 321  KNOWN   328  OFF
>
> HASH
>    WORDS TO BE HASHED:  c4                    ( c4 is a variable containing the 4TH 100 MFEW )
>    LETTERS TO BE USED:  1  2  3  4
```

```
++++++++++ Listing 5.1. (Continued...)
>    IS BLANK TO BE A CHARACTER (Y/N): N
>    IS LENGTH TO BE PART OF FUNCTION (Y/N): Y
>    ORDER BY PRODUCT OR MINIMUM (P/M): P
>    CPU SECONDS USED IN HASH IS 2.294
>    THE DATA IN CORRECTED PREORDER FORM:
>
>        feet sent send cents seems seemed need held soldiers hands told months
>        fell called land head help lost past party common committee complete
>        moment free save love truly true pounds miles lines times hear nor hour
>
>        hours keep kind face further turned perhaps point makes having making
>        saying cause real result value rather future building boys better view
>        knew knows wish wrong thousand show whether whom flour anything already
>        along become troops afternoon price special often open able hope look
>        wheat dinner office ask buy i'm girl idea above enemy quite action
>        itself number twenty subject beginning different yesterday impossible
>
> BIND  295                        ( binding the next 100 MFEW into the hash table offset 295 places )
>    BINDING STARTED AT  1982 7 20 14 12 42 107
>    TIME DURATION WAS 0 0 0 0 3 800
>    CPU SECONDS USED IN BASH IS  1.583
>    NUMBER OF TIMES THROUGH BASH MAIN LOOP IS  82
>
>    TERMINATION AFTER BACKTRACK 0
>    LETTERS USED 1 2 3 4
>    OFFSET USED 295
>
>    LETTER VALUES
>    'A'   8   5  13  18       'I'   0  25  11  15       'S'   0   0  10  43
>    'B'  34  60   0  48       'K'  26   0  31  69       'T'   2  81  16   3
>    'C'   1  52  33  32       'L'   6  51   6   9       'U'   0  25   0  11
>    'D'  24  70   0   4       'M'   7   0  15   6       'V'  30   0  24  18
>    'E'  53   0   0   1       'N'   5  30   1  29       'W'   2  63   0   2
>    'F'   0  36   9  36       'O'  20   0   2  31       'Y'  83   0  25   1
>    'G'  43   0  44   0       'P'   2  37  75  12       ''    0  65   0   0
>    'H'   0  59   0  27       'R'  52   0   0   0
>
>    HASH TABLE
>       3  THE       4  THEN      5  THESE    6  WHEN     7  SHE    . . . .
>       . . . .    100  WHICH   102  MOST    103  MONEY  104  POWER  105  PART
>       . . . .    131  MAKE    132  FROM    133  PEOPLE 134  SAYS   . . . .
>       . . . .    301  THEMSELVES 302  FEET 303  SENT   304  SEND   305  CENTS
>     306  SEEMS   307  SEEMED  308  NEED    309  HELD   310  HANDS  311  TOLD
>     312  MONTHS  313  SOLDIERS     . . . .
>       . . . .    327  TRUE    328  OFF     329  SAVE   330  LOVE   . . . .
>     401  BOYS    406  ASK     411  IMPOSSIBLE
>
>    HASH
>    WORDS TO BE HASHED: c5                    ( c5 is a variable containing the 5th 100 MFEW )
>    LETTERS TO BE USED: 1 2 3 4
>    IS BLANK TO BE A CHARACTER (Y/N): N
>    IS LENGTH TO BE PART OF FUNCTION (Y/N): Y
>      OFFICERS CONFLICTS WITH    OFFICIAL
>    WOULD YOU LIKE TO TRY A DIFFERENT ROUTE: N    ( we use the same hash function )
>    ORDER BY PRODUCT OR MINIMUM (P/M): P
>    CPU SECONDS USED IN HASH IS 2.278
>    THE DATA IN CORRECTED PREORDER FORM:
>
>        road read reason tea sea heard near hold needs heavy poor political
>        products position pretty that's cost charge thank change mean loan
>        coming remember comes together ten month clear plan truth court pound
>        third thirty child drive dollars following received glad proper company
>        trouble ground note modern alone around began family national hard
>        carried care wanted worth hundred guns built sure list million didn't
>        air force looking week street behind department second reports fight
>        electric eight others effort official offensive kept indeed yes cary
>        room can't opion except living school taking unless evening however
>        o'clock perfect question important knowledge
>
> BIND  395                        ( binding the next 100 MFEW into the hash table offset 395 places )
>    BINDING STARTED AT  1982 7 20 14 15 26 948
>    TIME DURATION WAS 0 0 0 0 3 472
>    CPU SECONDS USED IN BASH IS  1.508
>    NUMBER OF TIMES THROUGH BASH MAIN LOOP IS  80
>
>    TERMINATION AFTER BACKTRACK 0
>    LETTERS USED 1 2 3 4
>    OFFSET USED 395
>
```

```
++++++++++ Listing 5.1. (Continued...)
>     LETTER VALUES
>     'A'   8   5   0   6        'I'   0  32  20   3        'R'   0   2  43   7
>     'B'  21   0   0   0        'K'  42   0  82  44        'S'   2   0  11   2
>     'C'   3  13  33   0        'L'  13  20   8   6        'T'   0  10  40   9
>     'D'  24   0  30   3        'M'  11  31  19  77        'U'  34  32  22  33
>     'E'  40   1   6   5        'N'   2  44  19  12        'V'   0  34  40  12
>     'F'  23   0  49  51        'O'  19   0   8  38        'W'  20   0  88   3
>     'G'  21   0  21   0        'P'   0   9  27  33        'X'   0   8   0   0
>     'H'   0   9  36   0        'Q'  55   0   0   0        'Y'  70   0   0  33
>                                                          ''''  0  36   0  58
>
>
>     HASH TABLE
>      3  THE        4  THEN      5  THESE     6  WHEN      7  SHE      . . . .
>      . . . .     100  WHICH   102  MOST    103  MONEY   104  POWER   105  PART
>      . . . .     401  BOYS    402  ROAD    403  READ    404  REASON  405  TEA
>    406  ASK      407  SEA     408  HEARD   409  NEAR    410  HOLD    411  IMPOSSIBLE
>    412  NEEDS    413  HEAVY      . . . .
>      . . . .     501  KNOWLEDGE 528  EFFORT
>
>
>     TOTAL TIME IS:  5 HASHS - 11.275 SECONDS
>                     5 BINDS  -  7.636 SECONDS
>
>                     TOTAL    - 18.911 SECONDS
>
>
>     LOADING FACTOR IS:  500/528 = .947
>
>  )OFF
# EXECUTION TERMINATED 10:05:49


++++++++++ Listing 5.1. Interleaved Lexicon - 500 Most Frequently Used English Words. ++++++++++
```

Comp. & Maths. with Appls. Vol. 9, No. 1, pp. 233–244, 1983
Printed in Great Britain.

0097–4943/83/010233–12$03.00/0
Pergamon Press Ltd.

EXTENDED NATURAL LANGUAGE
DATA BASE INTERACTIONS

Bonnie Webber, Aravind Joshi, Eric Mays and Kathleen McKeown

Department of Computer and Information Science, University of Pennsylvania, Philadelphia, PA 19104,
U.S.A.

Abstract—An oft-heard argument for Natural Language interfaces is their promise of reducing the effort an infrequent user would have to exert in using a computer system. This viewpoint has led to a research concentration on removing "artificial" constraints on a user's freedom of expression, allowing it to move closer to everyday speech. This paper discusses two complementary directions for extending Natural Language interfaces to data bases, which can make them more useful systems. These extensions make Natural Language interfaces less simply "windows" through which data can be called into view, and more "articulate experts" on the data base system and what it represents. The two directions involve (1) broadening the range of *query types* that can be handled and (2) extending the range of *responses* that can be provided.

1. INTRODUCTION

If one considers the history of Natural Language interaction with computers, one is called to mind of the strongest reason given for wanting to use Natural Language: it promised to reduce the effort an infrequent user would have to exert in using a computer system. S/he would not have to learn and retain a host of different languages and protocols. S/he would be able to express his/her desires for information directly.

As Natural Language (NL) interfaces have been viewed in terms of this promise, their primary direction of development has been towards removing "artificial" constraints on a user's freedom of expression, allowing it to move closer to everyday speech. Developments along this line include:

● Enabling NL systems to interpret a user's query in light of his/her previous queries or of his/her perceived intentions. This permits the user to produce elliptic utterances and anaphoric expressions that will be understood by the system[1–3].

● Enabling NL systems to recognize the user's intended question, even though it might contain mispellings, simple grammatical errors, etc.[2, 4].

● Enabling users to set up "on line" whatever terminology they want to use in interacting with the system, for example by typing something like "By $\langle x \rangle$ I mean $\langle y \rangle$", where $\langle y \rangle$ is a form already interpretable by the system[2].

But just expanding the ways a query can be phrased and still understood does not in itself guarantee fruitful Natural Language interactions. What we shall discuss in this paper are two complementary directions for extending Natural Language interfaces to data bases, which can make them more useful systems. These extensions make Natural Language interfaces less simply "windows" through which data can be called into view, and more "articulate experts" on the data base system and what it represents. The two directions involve (1) broadening the range of *query types* that can be handled and (2) extending the range of *responses* that can be provided. More specifically, Section 2 describes a prototype system TEXT that is able to answer queries about the *structure* of a data base, and Section 3 discusses various ways a system may "take the initiative" and provide more than just a direct response to the user's query.

2. RESPONDING TO QUERIES ABOUT DATA BASE STRUCTURE

In asking a factual data base query, a user is seeking to establish either the existence or the identity of some restricted class of objects in the database. However, to ask such a question *and* have it make sense to the system, the user must already know what information is stored in the database and how it is structured. (Even if s/he does know what type of information is available, its structure in the database may not correspond to his or her conception of it and again, his or her questions may not be understood by the system.) The problem lies in acquiring such knowledge. Up to now, there has been no way for a user to request it from the system. The only recourse has been to the data base administrator or to documentation, which is usually either missing, out-of-date or incomprehensible.

In this regard, a number of interesting experiments have been conducted to find out just what kinds of abilities a data base system interface should ideally have [5, 6]. In these experiments, users were given a problem to solve and a data base system with which they could freely interact in Natural Language. (This was usually facilitated through another person hidden behind the scenes.) A user's goal was to acquire enough information from the data base to diagnose and solve the problem.

What is of interest is that factual questions about the contents of the data base were not the only kind asked. Before attempting the problem solving task, users commonly worked at familiarizing themselves with the data base system and what it could do for them. In addition, in the midst of problem solving, users frequently attempted to confirm their understanding of what they had learned. In both cases, interactions with the system included (as illustrated below) various types of questions about the *structure* of the data base as well as its contents: (1) requests for definitions, (2) questions about the kind of information available in the database, and (3) questions about the difference between entities existing in the database.†

(1) What do you know about unit cost?
(2) What kind of data do you have?
(3) What is the difference between material cost and production cost?

Providing "canned" (i.e. hand-coded) answers to such questions is not an ideal solution for many reasons, including the fact that for "difference" questions, one would have to can a response for each possible pair of concepts. More importantly, such canned responses can easily become out-of-date if the data base changes without their prompt re-adjustment as well.

In this section, we shall report briefly on a system, *TEXT* [7], that was developed and implemented to respond dynamically to the three classes of questions mentioned above. Responding to such questions requires more than a simple search of the data base, as it is rarely clear *a priori* just what information is sufficient to answer them. Moreover, such questions can rarely be answered in a single sentence. Thus a system must be able to determine not only what information is appropriate to include in the answer but also how to organize it effectively into a multi-sentential text.

TEXT uses general principles of discourse structure, discourse coherence and relevance in generating responses to queries. Its main features include (1) an ability to identify and select that information that is potentially relevant to the answer, (2) an ability to pair rhetorical techniques (such as analogy) with discourse purposes (such as providing definitions) and (3) the use of a focusing mechanism to both choose among the potentially relevant information and produce coherent texts.

The notion of *rhetorical technique* comes from linguistics [8], as a way of encoding aspects of discourse structure. Standard rhetorical techniques include *attributive* (i.e. association of properties with an entity or event), *analogy* (i.e. comparison with a familiar concept), and *constituency* (i.e. presentation of an entity's sub-parts or sub-classes). In TEXT these techniques are used to guide the selection of propositions from a *relevant knowledge pool*—the subset of its knowledge base which TEXT has identified as containing all information which can be included in the answer. TEXT's knowledge base is made up of taxonomic, functional and attributive information about the concepts in the data base. Currently, it is in part hand-coded and in part compiled automatically from the facts in the data base [9]. The *focusing mechanism* draws on work of Grosz [10] and Sidner [11] and is used to maintain discourse coherency, both

---

†Users asked other types of questions as well, including "why" questions, "can" questions both about the domain (e.g. "What courses can a freshman register for?") and about the system (e.g. "What functions can you compute?"), and confirmation questions (e.g. "Do you mean item cost and unit cost are the same?"). The research reported here does not cover system support for such queries directly.

by (1) constraining the selection of information to be talked about next to that which ties in appropriately with the previous discourse and by (2) influencing what sentence-level syntactic structures are chosen, preferring those which support the desired information flow. A propos the first function, what can be said next is limited via the application of an *ordered* set of legal focus moves developed especially for automatic text generation and embodied in TEXT.

The current TEXT system is implemented on a portion of a data base supplied by the Office of Naval Research (ONR), containing information about vehicles and weapons. Two examples of TEXT system responses to questions about this domain are shown below. The first is a response to a request for a definition of a ship, while the second constitutes TEXT's answer to a request to distinguish between an ocean escort and a cruiser. (TEXT assumes a parser capable of interpreting such Natural Language requests as "What is a ship?", "What is the difference between . . . ?" into the input formalism shown below. Such a parser is not part of TEXT itself.)

1) (definition SHIP)

;

; What is a ship?

;

A ship is a water-going vehicle that travels on the surface. Its surface-going capabilities are provided by the DB attributes DISPLACEMENT and DRAFT. Other DB attributes of the ship include MAXIMUM_SPEED, PROPULSION, FUEL (FUEL_CAPACITY and FUEL_TYPE), DIMENSIONS, SPEED_DEPENDENT_RANGE and OFFICIAL_NAME. The DOWNES, for example, has MAXIMUM_SPEED of 29, PROPULSION of STMTURGRD, FUEL of 810 (FUEL_CAPACITY) and BNKR (FUEL_TYPE), DIMENSIONS of 25 (DRAFT), 46 (BEAM), and 438 (LENGTH) and SPEED_DEPENDENT_RANGE of 4200 (ECONOMIC_RANGE) and 2200 (ENDURANCE_RANGE).

2) (difference OCEAN-ESCORT CRUISER)

;

; What is the difference between an ocean-escort and a cruiser?

;

The cruiser and the ocean-escort are surface ships. The ship's surface-going capabilities are provided by the DB attributes DISPLACEMENT and DRAFT. The ship has DB attributes MAXIMUM_SPEED, PROPULSION, FUEL (FUEL_CAPACITY, AND FUEL-TYPE), DIMENSIONS, SPEED_DEPENDENT_RANGE and OFFICIAL-NAME. Ocean escorts have a DISPLACEMENT between 3400 and 4100. All ocean escorts in the ONR data base have REMARKS of 0, FUEL_TYPE OF BNKR, FLAG of BLBL, MAST_HEIGHT of 85 and PROPULSION of STMTURGRD. Ocean escorts carry between 2 and 22 torpedoes, 16 missiles and between 1 and 2 guns. A ship is classified as an ocean escort if the characters 1 through 2 of its HULL_NO are DE. Cruisers have a PROPULSION of STMTURGRD and a LENGTH between 510 and 673. All cruisers in the ONR database have REMARKS of 0 and FUEL_TYPE of BNKR. Cruisers carry between 8 and 42 torpedoes, between 4 and 98 missiles and between 1 and 4 guns. A ship is classified as a cruiser if the characters 1 through 2 of its HULLNO are CL or the characters 1 through 2 of its HULLNO are CG. The ocean escort, therefore, has a smaller LENGTH and a smaller DISPLACEMENT than the cruiser.

The structure of these responses reflect communicative strategies that are widely used in conveying similar information[7]. For example, people frequently *identify* an object through some combination of: (1) identifying it as a member of some generic class, (2) describing its function, attributes, and constituency (either physical or class), (3) making an analogy to a more familiar object, and (4) giving examples of the object. People rarely use these techniques in random order, commonly identifying an item as a member of some generic class before providing examples, etc.

In TEXT rhetorical techniques such as these are encoded as schemas which guide the generation process. The schema used for the identification of an object is shown below. ("/" separates alternatives; "*" indicates 0 or more instances; "+" indicates 1 or more instances; and curly brackets indicate optionality.)

Identification (class & attribute/function)
{Analogy/Constituency/Attributive/Renaming}*
Particular-illustration/Evidence +
{Amplification/Analogy/Attributive}
{Particular illustration/Evidence}

In the first example above, a ship is *identified* as belonging to the *class* of water-going vehicles, *evidence* for its surface-going capabilities are provided, and additional data base *attributes* of the ship are noted. The example concludes by noting the Downes as a particular illustration of a ship.

In concluding this section, we want to emphasize that by giving the user the ability to get direct answers automatically to such questions as these, we have taken a good-size step towards more mutually-intelligible user-system interactions. The development of TEXT is continuing in several different directions, including (1) extending the range of structural questions it can handle (e.g. allowing it to answer both types of "can" questions noted above); (2) applying it to dynamic as well as static data base systems; (3) expanding the range of Natural Language constructions it is able to use[12]; and (4) giving it an ability to present its response in multi-paragraph texts instead of a single paragraph. All of these features will make a system such as TEXT a more useful addition to the facilities available in Natural Language interfaces.

3. TAKING THE INITIATIVE IN RESPONDING TO QUERIES

As noted earlier, in answering a factual query one can often provide more than just the answer explicitly requested. We have been looking at three ways in which a system could so "take the initiative" in constructing a response: (1) it can point out incorrect assumptions reflected in the user's query[13, 14]; (2) it can offer to monitor for information that it may later learn of[15–17]; and (3) it can provide grounds for its response[18]. The following responses illustrate "presupposition correction", "monitor offers" and "justification", respectively. ("U" refers to the user and "S" to the system.)

U: Did John take Physics 161 last term?
S1: No, John can't take any courses: he's not a student.
S2: No, shall I let you know if and when he does?
S3: No, he advance-placed Physics 161.

This section will discuss some of the problems involved in supporting such "initiative-taking" behavior and some techniques for dealing with them.

3(a) *Presupposition correction*

It has been widely noted that for conversants to interact intelligibly, each must have a good sense of the other's beliefs and viewpoint. Achieving this mutual understanding can come about in two different ways: (1) *after* the fact, after some remark can be seen to reflect an incorrect understanding of the other's beliefs or viewpoint, or (2) *before* the fact, in that the conversants already know or have taken steps to learn about each other's beliefs and viewpoint. In interacting with a computer system, a user can learn about these things beforehand by asking the kinds of structural questions that TEXT has been developed to handle. The "after the fact" situation is discussed here.

In certain cases, it is not difficult to identify those things a user would have to believe before sensibly asking a particular question. For example, in asking the question "Which French majors failed CIS531 last term?" a user would have to believe: (1) CIS531 was given last term, (2) there are French majors, and (3) there are French majors who took CIS531 last term. In asking the question "Which graduate students have taught CIS531?" a user would have to believe that graduate students can teach CIS531. Any direct answer to such a question would implicitly confirm these beliefs, including the answer "None". Thus if the system can recognize that any of these beliefs are wrong, it shouldn't just give a direct answer, but rather correct the misconceptions as well.

Computational work on this problem includes Kaplan's work on correcting beliefs which "fail extensionally"[13] by supposing there to be entities which satisfy a particular description when there are in fact none and Mays' work on correcting beliefs which "fail intensionally" by supposing that a relationship can hold between two objects or classes, when it in fact cannot[14]. The kind of interactions this work supports is illustrated below:

U: Which French majors failed CIS531 last term?
S1: I do not know of any French majors.
S2: I do not know of CIS531 being given last term.
U: Which graduate students have taught CIS531?
S: CIS531 is a graduate course. Only faculty can teach graduate courses.

The techniques supporting such interactions have been well-documented elsewhere. They rely on (1) the system's ability to keep tabs on the non-emptiness of set extensions while it is doing a data base retrieval and (2) its having an enriched data model which indicates whether subsets are mutually exclusive and/or exhaustive. Rather than describe these techniques in detail here, we shall mention one direction in which this work on correcting misconceptions can go.

In Kaplan and Mays' work, an object's features (e.g. properties, class membership, etc.) are assumed to be fixed. From this point of view, presupposition failures are similar to "type violations" in a programming language. But most data bases are subject to update, so an object's features *can* change. However, not all systems can access their knowledge of possible changes: they may only apply it mechanically as update constraints. Alternatively, a system can be aware of how it has changed and how it can change—of what was true in previous states of the data base, of what is true now, and what can and cannot become true in the future. Not only is the data base subject to updates, the data base system remembers previous items and values and can reason about future ones. We have termed this a "dynamic data base" system[15–17].

To return to users' misconceptions, one reason that a user may be mistaken is that s/he is unaware of some change. In this case, a dynamic data base system may be able to provide more information in correcting misconceptions than a static one can. For example, a static system can only determine that John is not now a student and can therefore only provide the following answer to the question "What courses is John registered for?"

S: John cannot register for any courses: he's not a student.

However, a dynamic data base system may be able to determine that while John is not currently a student, he once was. If so, it can make the more informative response:

S: John flunked out last year and is no longer a student. Thus he cannot register for any courses.

Joshi[19] uses this type of situation (i.e. where the discourse participants are not equally up-to-date on relevant aspects of their world) to illustrate a type of interaction he calls "squaring away" beliefs. He shows how one participant can sense the need for such an interaction based on knowledge of mutual beliefs and either the possibility for or an awareness of a misconception on the other participant's part.

To conclude, the search for such historical information may be motivated by trying to establish the reason for the user's mistaken impression, or it may be motivated by a desire to "take the initiative" in a way that we shall describe in the next section, i.e. offering to *monitor* for information.

3(b) *Monitor offers*

Dynamic data base systems, mentioned above in the context of presupposition correction, enable another significant type of initiative-taking behavior. That is, in addition to answering a user's question on the basis of the information the system *currently* contains, a dynamic system can offer to monitor for *additional* information which it will provide to the user if and when it learns of it. This enables the system to perform two useful functions: (1) to provide the user with additional information s/he has not explicitly requested, as in the first example below, or (2) to defer its response until it can give a better one, as in the second example.

U: Did John take CSE110 last term?
S: No. Do you want me to let you know if he does take it?
U: Did John pass CSE110?
S: No, the semester hasn't ended, so he hasn't received a grade yet. Shall I let you know then if he has passed CSE110?

To perform these useful services, a system must be able to recognize what events are really possible or what additional information it might really acquire. Otherwise, it might not distinguish between the following two situations, in which the same response is clearly not appropriate:

U: Is the JFK within 30 miles of L.A.?
S: No, but shall I let you know when it is?
U: Is Santa Cruz within 30 miles of L.A.?
S: No, but shall I let you know when it is?

In addition, a system must be able to identify when it is appropriate to perform such services: at a later time, the information may not be of *interest* to the user. In the following sections, we discuss both these issues.

(1) *Computing possible futures.* There are many things that will never be the case in the future because of what is true now or what was true in the past. If John is 30 now, he may turn 35 one day, but he can never become 20. If John received a grade in a course once, he can never register for that course again. In such cases, the system should not offer to inform the user if and when John turns 20 or registers for that course. In addition there are many things that are not true now and cannot become true unless some other event takes place. If John is not registered for a course, he cannot receive a grade for it until some time after he does register. In such cases, the system should not offer to inform the user if and when John receives a grade unless it first offers to inform the user if and when he registers for the course.

To compute whether an event can possibly occur or some state ever hold, a reasoning system is needed which can handle the notion of possible change. We are using a branching time temporal logic[20], which has the advantage over other temporal logics of being able to reason about contingent events, not just whether or not one event happened before/after another. In this logic, there are six composite temporal operators, made up of one operator on branches (E, for "some" branch, and A, for "all" branches) and one operator on times/states within a branch (X, for the next state after now on a branch; F, for now or some state after now on the branch; and G, for all states on the branch.) The composite operators have the following intuitive meanings:

$(EX)P$—holds iff P is true at some immediate future.
$(AX)P$—holds iff P is true at every immediate future.
$(EF)P$—holds iff P is true at some time of some future.
$(AF)P$—holds iff P is true at some time of every future.
$(EG)P$—holds iff P is true at every time of some future.
$(AG)P$—holds iff P is true at every time of every future.

To illustrate the use of these operators in specifying how the data base contents may or may not change, consider representing that portion of a university data base dealing with students passing courses and students registering for courses. Let the propositional variables P and R mean "student has passed course" and "student is registered for course", respectively .Then, among the axioms specifying the relationship of the current state of the data base to possible future states might be the following:

(1) $(AG)[P \rightarrow (AX)P]$—once a student has passed a course it remains the case that s/he has passed.

(2) $(AG)[(-P \ \& \ -R) \rightarrow (EX)R]$—if a student neither has passed a course nor is registered for it, then it is next possible that s/he is registered.

(3) $(AG)[R \rightarrow (EX)P]$—if a student is registered for a course then it is next possible that s/he has passed it.

(4) $(AG)[R \rightarrow (EX)[-P \ \& \ -R]]$—if a student is registered for a course then it is next possible that s/he neither has passed it nor is registered for it (i.e. s/he may drop it).

(5) $(AG)[P \rightarrow -R]$—if a student has passed a course, then s/he is not registered for it.

(6) $(AG)(R \rightarrow -P)$—if a student is registered for a course, then s/he has not passed it.

Suppose the question were posed "Is John registered for CSE110?". By virtue of the above axioms, there are three possibilities, depending on what facts are in the data base.

Possibility 1. John is not registered for CSE100 ($\tilde{\ }R$) but has passed it (P).

In this case, the direct answer would be "No, he is not registered for CSE110." If we now were to consider *monitoring* for the event "John registers for CSE110", we could rule it out on the basis that it is provable that there can be no future in which John is registered for CSE110. Specifically, from P and axioms 1 and 5, it is provable that $-(EF)R$. It would therefore be incompetent to offer to monitor for that condition.

Possibility 2. John neither has passed nor is registered for CSE110 ($-P \ \& \ -R$).

In this case, the direct answer is again "No". However, we could offer to monitor for John registering for CSE110, since $(EF)R$ is derivable from axiom 2, i.e. there is some future in which, at some point, John is registered for CSE110.

Possibility 3. John is registered for CSE110 (R).

In this case, the direct answer is "Yes". Moreover, we could competently offer to monitor for any of the following additional events:

(a) John no longer registered for CSE110; $(EF) - R$.
(b) John passed CSE110; $(EF)P$.
(c) John registered for CSE110 again; $(EF)[-R \ \& \ (EX)R]$.

This last case (3c) is interesting in that it can be viewed as a monitor for $-R$, whose action is to set a monitor for R (whose action is to inform the user of R).

Work in this area is still in an early stage. We are currently using a straight-forward Tableau Method theorem prover which is able to reason about possible events or states in this branching-time temporal logic. Improving its efficiency and extending its coverage are among our current areas of research.

(2) *Revelance.* The relevance of a monitor offer depends on whether or not the information, upon arrival, would still be of interest to the user. Because the information differs, we distinguish the discourse functions that monitor offers support: (1) that of deferring a response, when the system cannot answer the user's query immediately, and (2) that of providing additional information that the user has not explicitly requested.

In the first case, the system must determine whether the user would still be interested in getting the explicitly requested information from the system sometime later. This depends in part on why the system has to defer its response: that is, either the information about an actual event hasn't been registered in the system yet *or* the event itself hasn't yet happened. In the first case, the user might be able to get the information elsewhere, but not in the second. Therefore, the system must determine what role the information fills with respect to the user's goals—what problem s/he is trying to solve and what time constraints s/he is under in doing so. These form the aspects of a user model that are of significance here.

The second case is somewhat different and can be divided into two subcases, depending on what additional information the system offers to monitor for. If we look at a query as asking whether a given description once held, then one sort of additional information the system can offer is whether that same description will hold at some future time (whether or not it has already held in the past). For example,

U: Has John taken CIS531 yet?
S: No. Shall I let you know if he does?
U: Did John visit NSF last week?
S: Yes. Shall I let you know if he does so again?

Alternatively, the system can offer to monitor for whether some related description will hold at some future time. For example,

U: Did John check into the Statler Monday?
S1: Yes. Shall I let you know when he checks out?
   or
S2: Yes. Shall I let you know when the rest of the committee does?

Again, whether such information would be of interest to the user requires a model of the user's goals, but our feeling is that in this second case, it must be his/her more long-range, global informational goals. Moreover, we probably only want to concern ourselves with very sharply defined, strongly held goals, in order to restrict which "somehow related" descriptions would be considered.

Another type of monitor that may be of interest to the user, in a different way, is the complement of those so far discussed. That is, the user may be interested in learning that some earlier set monitor can no longer be satisfied, so that s/he does not continue to expect it to go off. For example, if the system has offered to inform the user if John registers for CSE110, then s/he should be informed if John receives advanced placement credit and can no longer register.

Finally, it may be the case that it is more appropriate to take some other type of initiative than offering to monitor (S1), perhaps justifying to the user what the system's *current* answer follows from (S2), as we shall discuss in the next section.

U: Did anyone fail CIS531?
S1: Yes, John and Martha. Shall I let you know if anyone else does?
S2: Yes, John received a C and Martha a D. Graduate courses require a B as a passing grade.

As noted before, work in this area is still at an early stage, especially with respect to a model of the user's informational goals, and we hope to have more specific results as we go along.

3(c) *Justification*

The third type of initiative-taking behavior to be discussed involves the system's *justifying* what its response follows from. We strongly believe that a user should not just have to accept the system's answer without comment. Rather, s/he is entitled to be given an *informed basis* for either accepting it or questioning the premises or reasoning involved in its derivation. In this regard, justification differs from *argument*, whose sole role is to *convince* a listener to do or believe something. Giving the user the means to make informed judgments is our motivating force behind this work.

There are at least three important issues involved in producing justifications:

(1) What justification does a query call for?
(2) What justification can the system give?
(3) What constitutes a clear and understandable justification?

(1) *What justification does a query call for?* This depends primarily on whether or not the user's perceived expectations have been fulfilled by the system's answer. For example, the use of "still" in a query indicates that the user expects that the potentially changing situation described in his/her query has not in fact changed. For example,

U: Does anyone still have an Incomplete in CSE110?
S1: Yes, John does.
S2: No. The last remaining Incomplete was made up on 1 December.

If the user's expectation is correct (i.e. not all Incompletes have been made up), then facts corroborating that expectation may constitute appropriate justification, as in S1. (A monitor offer may also be appropriate, as in the "yet" case noted earlier.) If it isn't correct (as in S2), then specifying the event that enabled/caused the change may constitute a more appropriate justification.

More often than not, the user's expectations will not be clearly identifiable. Again, a user model is called for, but here the significant aspects involve a characterization of what situation the user believes to hold and what s/he expects to learn from his or her queries. As noted earlier, this is the focal point of much research.

(2) *What justification can the system give?* In the case where the system knows no more than the particular facts in its data base, the only justification it can provide is those facts themselves (or some description of them). For example, suppose the system knows for each student-course pair only whether the student has passed or failed the course. Then only the following kind of justification is possible:

U: Did anyone fail CIS531?
S1: Yes, John and Martha.
S2: Yes, 50 seniors and 12 graduate students.

On the other hand, some reasoning may have been involved in deriving the answer, as in the case where the system knows (e.g. has an axiom to the effect) that "failing" a graduate course follows from a receiving a grade of C or worse. In this case, specifying the particular grade each failing student received could be used to justify the system's answer, i.e.

U: Did anyone fail CIS531?
S: Yes, John received a C and Martha, a D.

Or the system can also give some indication of its reasoning as well, as in

U: Did anyone fail CIS531?
S: Yes. With a graduate course, everyone fails who gets a C or below. In CIS531, John received a C and Martha, a D.

We believe that possible justifications are *related* but not *equivalent* to how the system comes to know an answer. The reason for this reservation has to do with the third issue mentioned earlier in justifying a direct answer, which we shall discuss next.

(3) *What constitutes a clear and understandable justification?* Answers to data base queries may be derived by straight look-up, by computation and/or by reasoning. Where reasoning is involved, producing clear and understandable justifications involves notions of (1) *succinct* justifications that do not say *more* than is necessary (lest they lose the user) and (2) conceptually *well-structured* justifications that the user can understand and evaluate.

There are many techniques for conveying information succinctly. The one we shall discuss here for illustration is a local technique for abbreviating proofs, that involves conveying part of one's reasoning by implication and has been called by Sadock[21] *modus brevis*. The notion of well-structured justifications we will discuss in terms of high-level strategies for reasoning. These highlight the strong similarity we see between reasoning and hierarchical planning.

(i) *Succinct justifications—modus brevis.* As a simple illustration of *modus brevis* and its use in making justifications *succinct*, consider a *modus ponens* deduction, possibly used in deriving an assertion and now to be used in justifying it. It has been observed that in presenting such reasoning one need not make explicit all three parts of the proof—the major premise $(A \rightarrow B)$, the minor premise (A), and the conclusion (B). Rather it is sufficient to state the conclusion, with either the major premise or the minor premise (but not both) as support. The listener is assumed able to infer the connection between the two—that is, they are steps in a proof that requires the missing premise to complete.

So suppose in response to the query "Did John fail physics?", the system makes the following *modus ponens* deduction:

Anyone who gets below a C fails physics. (* major premise *)
John got below a C. (* minor premise *)
John failed physics. (* conclusion *)

The system can then justify its "yes" answer in either of the following ways, relying on the user's ability to recognize the underlying deduction.

S: Yes. Everyone failed physics who got below a C.
S: Yes. He got below a C.

(Why the speaker chooses to give major premise over minor, or vice versa, is a matter yet to be investigated.)

Modus brevis can also be used in presenting other types of reasoning succinctly, both deductive and non-monotonic[22]—for example, "typicality" reasoning:

U: Is John taking Physics 281?
S1: I don't know, but probably. Students typically take Physics 281 after Physics 280. (* conclusion and major premise *)
S2: I don't know, but probably. He took Physics 280 last term. (* conclusion and minor premise *)

In any case, the speaker must be able to assume that the listener can, on the basis of what is essentially a *clue* to an argument, reconstruct that argument. Whether the listener is *convinced* by the argument s/he deduces, i.e. whether s/he *accepts* the inferred premise, is a separate issue: the listener can always attempt to confirm that s/he has inferred what the speaker has intended or to challenge it. For example,

U: Did John fail physics?
S: Yes. He got a B.
U: Is the failing grade really B or below?

(This goes beyond what has standardly been taken to be a "clarification dialogue" in Natural Language systems. The function of such a dialogue is usually seen as identifying terms and phrases which haven't been understood by the listener, or which are ambiguous, etc.[23].)

Since the successful use of *modus brevis* in justifications depends on the listener's ability to recognize the relevance of the additional material in the system's response as being part of some (implied) chain of reasoning, its primary use will be in place of very short reasoning chains, rather than in justifying an entire (complex) proof. Most of the techniques for producing succinct justifications will probably also have this local flavor.

(ii) *Well-structured justifications—hierarchical reasoning.* We believe there are appropriate schemas for presenting reasoning that are essentially independent of content. These schemas correspond to *valid* reasoning strategies (some of which are noted below), that everyday reasoning aspires to. That is, people usually explain themselves so as to give the impression that their reasoning is valid. Such explanations, while rarely adhering religiously to valid methods, are nevertheless understandable because (1) the strategies are accepted and (2) textual devices like "on the other hand", "suppose ⟨x⟩ were true", etc. make clear what strategies are being used.

Proofs using these reasoning strategies (and correspondingly, the justifications and explanations that follow them) bear a strong resemblance to structures found in hierarchical planning. This is not strange if one views reasoning as actions taken to support or deny a proposition. Just as hierarchical strategies for actions can be used in *forming* plans, *revising* plans, or *describing* them to another person[10, 24], so hierarchical reasoning strategies can be used in *constructing* a proof or *justifying* a result.

What reasoning strategies are we talking about? Many researchers have already observed that explanations have a tree-like structure, in which supported assertions correspond to non-terminal nodes with their support making up the sub-tree under them[25, 26]. Since a statement acting as a reason may in turn be supported by other statements/reasons, explanations have a recursive or hierarchical structure. This is *not* what we are talking about. The kinds of hierarchical reasoning strategies we have in mind are things like:

● *Simple case analysis*—to show that Q is true, find some proposition P from which Q from whose simultaneous satisfaction Q follows. For each Pi, show that it follows. Hence Q must be true.

● *Simple case analysis*—to show that Q is true, find some proposition P from which Q

follows, independent of P's truth value. Assume P and show that Q follows. Assume $\tilde{}P$ and show the same. Since either P or $\tilde{}P$ must be true, Q must be true. (Alternatively, to show Q is false, find some P from which $\tilde{}Q$ follows, independent of P's truth value. Assume P and show $\tilde{}Q$ follows. Do the same for $\tilde{}P$. Since P or $\tilde{}P$, $\tilde{}Q$ must be true—hence Q is false.)

● *General case analysis*—to show that Q is true, find some assertion P that is partitionable into $P1,\ldots Pk$. Assume each Pi in turn and show that Q follows from Pi. Since some Pi must be true given P is, Q must be true. (This has the obvious complementary strategy for showing Q false.)

● *Reduction* ad absurdum—to show that Q is false, find some proposition P whose both assertion and negation follow from Q. Assume Q and show that P follows. Show that $\tilde{}P$ follows. Since Q leads to both P and $\tilde{}P$, Q must be false.

(Other strategies are described in [18].)† These strategies are hierarchical or recursive in that wherever a strategy calls for showing "P follows" or "$\tilde{}P$ follows", there another strategy may be chosen and invoked in support. That such strategies can be used in reasoning is well-known. What is significant here is that where a justification is organized according to such strategies, it is that much easier to follow.

To illustrate this, consider the following tale, whose humor follows in part from the recursive use of *simple case analysis* in support of successive alternatives.

"WHAT IS THERE TO BE FRIGHTENED OF?"

War was on the horizon. Two students in the Yeshiva were discussing the situation.

"I hope I'm not called," said one. "I'm not the type for war. I have the courage of the spirit, but nevertheless I shrink from it."

"But what is there to be frightened about?" asked the other. "Let's analyze it. After all, there are two possibilities: either war will break out or it won't. If it doesn't, there's no cause for alarm. If it does, there are two possibilities: either they take you or they don't take you. If they don't, alarm is needless. And even if they do, there are two possibilities: either you're given combat duty, or non-combatant duty. If non-combatant, what is there to be worried about? And if combat duty, there are two possibilities: you'll be wounded, or you won't. Now if you're not wounded, you can forget your fears. But even if you are wounded, there are two possibilities: either you're wounded gravely or you're wounded slightly. If you're wounded slightly, your fear is nonsensical, and if you're wounded gravely, there are still two possibilities: either you succumb and die, or you don't succumb and you live. If you don't die, things are fine, and even if you do die, there are two possibilities: either you will be buried in a Jewish cemetery or you won't. Now if you're buried in a Jewish cemetery, what is there to worry about, and even if you are not... but why be afraid? There may not be any war at all!" [27].

In this example, "there's no call for worry" is the Q meant to be proven. The initial P being used to support Q independent of its truth value is "war will break out". Assuming $\tilde{}P$ (i.e. war won't break out), then Q follows because the derivable major premise $\tilde{}P \to Q$ is accepted as true. (This is an instance of *modus brevis*.) On the other hand, to show Q follows from assuming P, the speaker invokes a simple case analysis strategy again, this time finding P'—"they take you [into the army]"—meant to support Q independent of its truth value. Assuming $\tilde{}P'$ (i.e. they don't take you), then Q follows because the derivable major premise $\tilde{}P' \to Q$ is again accepted as true. On the other hand, to show Q follows from assuming P', the speaker invokes simple case analysis again, finding a P'', etc.

The point we want to make is that whereas the reasoning involved in finding a proof should be as computationally efficient as possible, that proof may not itself be structured in such a way as to map directly onto an understandable justification. Rather we want a justification that conforms to some "reasoning plan" using strategies such as those above, that is *faithful* to its derivation but not necessarily a mirror of it. The question is whether one could take a proof,

†"Follows from" is more than "implies": it represents the proof relation ($\mid$—), and not simply the implication connective ($\to$). While the above strategies refer to this proof relation, we believe there are comparable strategies for the more general notion of "gathering support" used in commonsense, probabilistic and other types of non-deductive reasoning.

recognize from it which of the above understandable reasoning strategies could be used in justifying the result, and then *construct* an appropriate valid justification in terms of those strategies. We discuss this issue in greater detail in [18], but research is still only in its early stages.

4. CONCLUSION

In this paper we have attempted to describe additional features that could usefully be incorporated into a Natural Language system for interfacing with data bases. Such extensions are not a luxury: they are necessary if today's data base question-answereing systems are to become tomorrow's decision support systems. We have argued elsewhere[28] that such systems, if they are to satisfy the legitimate needs of their users, must include communicative capabilities as sophisticated as those that are the subject of current Natural Language research. This paper has described several of those capabilities.

REFERENCES

1. W. Woods, R. Kaplan and B. Nash-Webber, The lunar sciences natural language information system: Final report. *Tech. Rep.* 2378. Bolt, Beranek & Newman, Cambridge, Mass. (1972).
2. G. Hendrix, E. Sacerdoti, D. Sagalowicz and J. Slocum, Developing a natural language interface to complex data. *ACM Trans. Database Systems* **3**(2), 105–147 (1978).
3. D. L. Waltz, An English language question answering system for a large relational database. *Commun. ACM* **21**(7) (1978).
4. S. Kwasny and N. Sondheimer, Relaxation techniques for parsing ill-formed input. *Am. J. Comp. Ling.* **7**(2), 99–108 (1981).
5. A. Malhotra, Design criteria for a knowledge-based English language system for management: an experimental analysis. *MAC TR*-146, MIT, Cambridge, Mass. (1975).
6. H. Tennant, Experience with the evaluation of natural language question answerers. Working paper #18, Univ. of Illinois, Urbana-Champaign, Ill. (1979).
7. K. McKeown, Generating natural language text in response to questions about database structures. *Tech. Rep.* CIS-82-5, Dept. of Computer and Information Science, University of Pennsylvania (May 1982).
8. J. E. Grimes, *The Thread of Discourse.* Mouton, The Hague (1975).
9. K. F. McCoy, Augmenting a database knowledge representation for natural language generation. *Proc. 20th Ann. Meeting Assoc. for Comp. Linguistics*, Toronto, Canada (June 1982).
10. B. Grosz, The representation and use of focus in dialogue understanding. *Tech. Rep.* 151, SRI International, Menlo Park, CA (1977).
11. C. L. Sidner, Towards a computational theory of definite anaphora comprehension in English discourse. Ph.D. dissertation, MIT, Cambridge, Mass. (1979).
12. S. Bossie, The tactical component for text generation: sentence generation using functional grammar. Forthcoming Masters thesis. University of Pennsylvania.
13. S. J. Kaplan, Cooperative responses from a portable natural language data base query system. Ph.D. thesis. Department of Computer and Information Science, University of Penn. (1978).
14. E. Mays, Correcting misconceptions about data base structure. *Proc. 3-CSCSI*, Victoria, B.C. (May 1980).
15. E. Mays, S. Lanka, A. K. Joshi and B. L. Webber, Natural language interaction with dynamic knowledge bases: Monitoring as response. *Proc. 8-IJCAI*, Vancouver, B.C. (August 1981).
16. E. Mays, A. K. Joshi and B. L. Webber, Taking the initiative in natural language data base interactions: monitoring as response. *Proc. 1982 European Conf. Artificial Intelligence*, Orsay, France (July 1982).
17. E. Mays, Monitors as Responses to questions: determining competence. *Proc. 1982 Natl Conf. Artificial Intelligence*, Pittsburgh, Penn. (August 1982).
18. B. Webber and A. Joshi, Taking the initiative in natural language data base interactions: justifying why. *Tech. Rep.* MS-CIS-82-1, Dept. of Computer and Information Science, University of Pennsylvania, April 1982. (A shorter version of this paper appears in *Proc. Coling-82*, Prague, Czechoslovakia, July 1982.)
19. A. K. Joshi, Mutual beliefs in question-answer system. In *Mutual Belief* (Edited by N. V. Smith). Academic Press, New York (1982).
20. M. Ben Ari, Z. Manna and A. Pneuli, The temporal logic of branching time. *8th Ann. ACM Symp. Principles of Programming Languages*, Williamsburg, Virginia, January 1981.
21. J. Sadock, Modus brevis: the truncated argument. Papers from the *13th Regional Meeting Chicago Linguistics Society*, Chicago, Ill, 1977.
22. *Artificial Intell. J.*, Special issue on Non-monotonic Logic **13**(1) (1980).
23. E. F. Codd, Seven steps to rendezvous with the casual user. In *Data Base Management* (Edited by J. W. Klimbie and K. Koffeman). North-Holland, Amsterdam (1977).
24. E. Sacerdoti, *A Structure for Plans and Behavior.* Elsevier, New York (1977).
25. J. Weiner, BLAH, a system which explains its reasoning. *Artificial Intell. J.* **15**, 19–48 (1980).
26. R. Cohen, Investigation of processing strategies for the structural analysis of arguments. *Proc. 19th Ann. Meeting of the Assoc. for Computational Linguistics*, Stanford, Calif., June 1981.
27. N. Ausubel (Ed.), *A Treasury of Jewish Folklore.* Crown, New York (1948). (Abridged edition published by Bantam, 1980.)
28. M. Pollack, J. Hirschberg and B. Webber, User participation in the reasoning processes of expert systems. *Proc. 1982 Natl Conf. Artificial Intelligence*, Pittsburgh, Penn., August 1982.

INDEX

Anaphoric expression 33
Automatic extraction 52-58
Automatic translation 45-47
Algorithm 59, 67-70, 79, 111, 122-127, 191-193, 215-231

Belief 71, 74-75, 99
Bottom-up 190
Backtracking 218-225

Case analysis 242-243
Composition 186-187
Concepts 1-7, 29-31, 77-79
Conceptual graphs 29-42
Content analysis 52-54, 83
Contextual reference 65-67
Control 62-64, 69, 111, 116-122

Data directed 116-117
Data structure 65-67
Database query type 233-236
Default reasoning 15-27
Default theories 15-27
Descriptions 111-120
Description directed 116-122
Discourse 71-81, 84-87, 97-102
Dialogue 97-102
Dictionary 215, 225-227
Domains 49-52

Extension 3-11, 15-16
Endorder languages 31

Frames 133
Fuzzy sets 154-170
Fuzzy logic 149-180

Generative grammar 41-42
Goal 71-81, 103-104
Goal hierarchy 201
Grammar 29-42, 87-90
Grammatical dependencies 124-127

Hash identifiers 215-231
Hierarchy 22-25, 29

Inference 59-70
Information retrieval 45, 47-49
Integrity 25-27
Inheritance 1-11
Intelligent garbage collection 211-212
Intended meaning 74-75
Intention 3-11, 15-16

Keys 215-231
Knowledge representation 185-194

Lexicon 215, 225-227, 228-231
Logic 1-11, 15-27

Matching 195-196
Meaning representation 170-180
Metaphor 138-146

Model 71-81
Modality 4-12
Monitor 237-238

Natural language 12, 149, 205-206, 233-245
Natural language generation 111-116
Natural language understanding 59-70, 71, 97-108, 131, 215, 225-227
Natural language interface 236
Networks 1-11, 22-25, 189
Network formalisms 1-11
Normalisation 55-56
Novel language 131

Organisation 201-212

Parsing 191-193
Perfect hash function 215-227
Phrase structure grammar 34-40, 191
Plans 71-81, 99, 133
Postorder languages 31
Presupposition correction 236-237
Production rules 35
Preorder languages 31
Property inheritance 150
Procedural models 190-191

Quantifiers 149-180
Quantifier extension principle 160-180, 182-184

Realisation 118-120
Recall task 201, 207-212
Recognition 185, 193-194
Relational database 56-58
Representation 15-27
Representation scheme 202-205
Responses 233-236

Scripts 133
Schema 133-138, 151
Schemata 185-194
Search 217-223
Semantics 1-12
Semantic interpretation 59
Semantic networks 1-12, 22-27, 29, 104, 215
Semantic processing 45-58
Semantic representation 29, 45, 86
Speaker meaning 72-74
Specialisation 186-187
Speech act 98
Sublanguages 45-58
Syntax 29-42

Test-score semantics 153, 170-180
Texts 45-58
Text processing 83-94
Top-down 189-190
Transcription 90-94
Transformational grammar 31, 42
Traversal 120-122

Universal grammar 87
Utterance path 30-34